CESARE PAVESE AND AMERICA

Life, Love, and Literature

――⦅⦆――

LAWRENCE G. SMITH

University of Massachusetts Press
AMHERST

Copyright © 2008 by Lawrence G. Smith
All rights reserved
Printed in the United States of America

LC 2008024531
ISBN 978-1-55849-673-6

Designed by Sally Nichols
Set in ITC Galliard
Printed and bound by Thomson-Shore, Inc.

Library of Congress Cataloging-in-Publication Data

Smith, Lawrence G., 1938–
Cesare Pavese and America : life, love, and literature / Lawrence G. Smith.
    p. cm.
Includes bibliographical references and index.
ISBN 978-1-55849-673-6 (cloth : alk. paper)
1. Pavese, Cesare—Knowledge—America. 2. Authors, Italian—20th century—
Biography. I. Title.
PQ4835.A846Z7746 2008
853'.912v—dc22
[B]
                                    2008024531

British Library Cataloguing in Publication data are available.

The following poems have been reprinted by permission of the publishers:

"Last blues, to be read some day" and "To C. from C."
from Cesare Pavese, Le poesie, ed. Mariarosa Masoero, intro.
Marziano Guglielminetti (Turin: Einaudi, 1998).

Translations of "Terra rossa terra nera," "Sei la terra e la morte,"
and "Verrà la morte e avrà i tuoi occhi" from Cesare Pavese,
Disaffections: Complete Poems, 1930–1950, trans. Geoffrey Brock
(Port Townsend, Wash.: Copper Canyon, 2002).

CESARE PAVESE
AND
AMERICA

For M.T.S.
Ripeness indeed is all.

Contents

Acknowledgments
ix

Abbreviations
xiii

"Introducing Cesare Pavese"
1

PART I

ONE
The End Game: Connie and Cesare
17

TWO
Family and Friends
35

THREE
Tina
57

FOUR
Einaudi, Fernanda, and World War II
86

FIVE
Liberation?
107

PART II

SIX
"Viva Walt Whitman"
135

SEVEN
"The peach of the world"
169

EIGHT
"Storia passata"
215

Notes
249

Suggested Reading
279

Illustration Source Credits
283

Index
285

Illustrations follow pages 132 and 214.

Acknowledgments

During my journey from the idea to the realization of this book, I have depended greatly on the kindness of friends as well as of strangers, many of whom have become friends. First among the former I must acknowledge Shaun O'Connell, whose bond of friendship did not prevent him from sharply critiquing the early drafts, much to my benefit. For different reasons, I want to thank Claudio Fasoli, who has helped me for decades in my efforts to understand better the subtleties of his native language. Two Smiths not related to me, Katherine and Sam, and two related, Flavia and Erik, gave me helpful comments on parts of this book, as did John A. Neary and Garfield Brown. Myriam de Bulhoẽs helped me obtain a copy of some particularly important material. Warren Myers answered my questions about Latin, Terence Murphy about German, and William Dambeck, Greek.

In Turin, Mariarosa Masoero, the director of the Centro Interuniversitario per gli Studi di Letteratura Italiana in Piemonte "Guido Gozzano-Cesare Pavese," provided advice as well as invaluable guidance to the rich store of Pavese documentation housed at the center. Silvia Savioli also helped me interpret what I was finding there. Tiziana Cerrato and Giorgio Brandone provided documentation from the Archivio Storico del Liceo Classico Massimo D'Azeglio that clarifies the number of years Pavese spent at that school. I thank Roberto Cerati, now president of Pavese's publisher, Guilio Einaudi editore s.p.a., and one of the few people remaining who worked there when Pavese and Vittorini did, for his reminiscences and comments. Also at Einaudi, Roberto Gilodi helped me during the very early stages of my research. I thank Riccardo Mazza and his colleague Alberto de Stefani at Riccardo Mazza Interactive Sound for providing digital copies of many of the illustrations in this book.

In Santo Stefano Belbo, Pavese's home town, Franco Vaccaneo, chairman of the Fondazione Cesare Pavese's advisory board, was generous with his time and books. I thank, too, Pierluigi Vaccaneo for his time and explanations.

I also want to acknowledge Pino di Branco, one of Italy's most active bibliophiles, for his input into this project.

In the United States I would like to thank: Richard Koffler, for lending me the original of his translation of Pavese's diary; Mark Pietralunga, for reading and commenting on my manuscript and for providing me with an advance copy of his edition of the Pavese–Chiuminatto correspondence; and Patrick Barron, for reading the manuscript and making useful suggestions.

In the course of my research I discovered that librarians and archivists are almost universally generous and courteous. Paola Novaria of L'Archivio storico dell'Università di Torino had waiting for me on my first visit there not only the original of Pavese's 1930 thesis, but all the records relating to his years at the university. Alessandra Fossati, at the Biblioteca Riccardo e Fernanda Pivano in Milan, assembled and made copies of photographs of Fernanda Pivano from the 1930s and 1940s. When I sent a request to the Harold B. Lee Library at Brigham Young University to have an out-of-print book by a faculty member photocopied, Linda Hutchings went to the trouble of contacting the author, Cinzia D. Noble, who in turn sent me one of her own copies of the book. I am also indebted to the personnel of the Ufficio Periodici of Turin's Biblioteca Civica Centrale and to many research librarians at the New York Public Library.

Without the support and competence of the staff of the University of Massachusetts Press, this book would not exist. I thank for their joint and several roles Bruce Wilcox, Carol Betsch, and Sally Nichols; also Ed Vesneske, Jr., and Mary Bellino for the sharpness and consistency of their editing, and Martin L. White for his experienced and comprehensive indexing.

My wife, Marguerite Tarrant Smith, worked as a professional journalist and newspaper editor before becoming the psychotherapist she is now. All of her skills came into play during my work on this book. Of what else she contributes to my life, I will not speak, for that is of another dimension.

Abbreviations and Pavese Editions Cited

Centro Gozzano-Pavese	Centro Interuniversitario per gli Studi di Letteratura Italiana in Piemonte "Guido Gozzano-Cesare Pavese"
Chiuminatto Correspondence	*Cesare Pavese and Anthony Chiuminatto: Their Correspondence*, ed. Mark Pietralunga (Toronto: University of Toronto Press, 2007)
Dialoghi	*Dialoghi con Leucò* (Turin: Einaudi, 1968), except for the one-page, untitled *avvertenza* (notice to readers) omitted in this edition; for that, the 1947 edition, reprinted with annotations (Turin: Einaudi 1965)
Einaudi	To avoid ambiguity I use Giulio Einaudi when referring to the person, and Einaudi alone when referring to the publishing house, Giulio Einaudi editore s.p.a.

Fuoco grande	Cesare Pavese e Bianca Garufi, *Fuoco grande*, ed. Mariarosa Masoero (Turin: Einaudi, 2003)
Il mestiere	*Il mestiere di vivere: Diario 1935–1950*, ed. Marziano Guglielminetti and Laura Nay (Turin: Einaudi, 2000)
Le poesie	*Le poesie*, ed. Mariarosa Masoero, intro. Marziano Guglielminetti (Turin: Einaudi, 1998)
Lett. am.	*La letteratura americana e altri saggi*, pref. Italo Calvino (Turin: Einaudi: 1962)
Lettere I	*Lettere 1924–1944*, ed. Lorenzo Mondo (Turin: Einaudi, 1966)
Lettere II	*Lettere 1945–1950*, ed. Italo Calvino (Turin: Einaudi, 1966)
Racconti	*Tutti i racconti*, ed. Mariarosa Masoero (Turin: Einaudi, 2002)
Romanzi	*Tutti i romanzi*, ed. Marziano Gugielminetti (Turin: Einaudi, 2000)
University Archives	Archivio storico dell'Università di Torino

All translations from the Italian are my own unless otherwise indicated.

CESARE PAVESE
AND
AMERICA

"Introducing Cesare Pavese"

That is the title Leslie Fiedler gave his 1954 essay on Pavese, an essay which in 2001 the Italian editors of a collection of pieces on Pavese translated and included because "Fiedler saw beyond all Italian criticism of the time; he succeeded . . . in digging deeply, writing truly illuminating pages well ahead of their time."[1] Fiedler described Pavese as "the best of recent Italian novelists," better than "Moravia, Vittorini, Berto or Pratolini . . . or Silone . . . Pavese is the most poetic of recent Italian fictionists." He wrote this four years after Pavese, at the height of his powers and fame, had killed himself. At the time, only three of Pavese's nine novels had been translated into English and none of his poetry, short stories, essays, diary, or letters. Now, over half a century later, virtually everything Pavese wrote has been translated into English, his poetry and last novel three different times, several of his other novels and diary twice. Yet, Cesare Pavese still needs to be introduced to most American readers, because what Fiedler said about the translations then available to him applies to all those since: "they have not succeeded in stimulating a general interest in or understanding of Pavese."[2]

Since Fiedler's essay, American academic critics have produced high-quality studies on various aspects of Pavese's works, including one book on a topic similar to my own.[3] Interest, however, has flagged; not one American book dealing with Pavese appeared between 1988 and 2007.[4] This relative indifference on the part of both the public and the academy contrasts sharply to what has happened in Italy. Pavese died in 1950 as one of Italy's most famous and respected writers. That reputation continues. His nine novels have never gone out of print, and all of them, as well as his short stories, poetry, essays, and diary, have appeared in many different editions, most of them well introduced and some annotated. Two of them, *La casa in collina* (*The House on the Hill*) and *La luna e i falò* (*The Moon and the Bonfires*), have secure places as classics of twentieth-century Italian literature. Furthermore, Italian scholars and critics, including a few Italian-Americans writing in Italian, have continued in recent years their production of Pavese-related works. For example, in the eleven years from 1996 to 2006, part of that longer period when no English-language books on Pavese appeared, I count twenty-five in Italian devoted solely to Pavese, including a new biography, plus a half-dozen others devoted mainly to him. Virtually all his papers—which are voluminous, for he was something of a packrat—have been collected at the Centro Gozzano-Pavese, which has become an engine of Pavese scholarship. The staff there, headed first by Pavese scholar Marziano Guglielminetti (1937–2006), and now by the equally eminent Mariarosa Masoero, has put all those papers in order, numbered every page, even those of Pavese's pocket notebooks, and created an index that can now be accessed on-site or online.[5]

That literate America knows Pavese only slightly despite his standing in Italy reflects the problems associated with literature in translation; few important foreign-language novelists transcend their own languages to make an impact in English. There are exceptions, of course, but they do not change the rule. Günter Grass, for example, has had great success in English, as have other earlier and towering twentieth-century writers in German such as Thomas Mann and Franz Kafka. But how many Americans outside the academy ever heard of Robert Musil before the 1995 full English translation of *The Man Without Qualities*? Or have read Heinrich Böll in translation or know that he won the Nobel Prize for Literature in 1972? Who, other than teachers of German literature, can name, beyond Grass, an important German-language novelist now writing? One could ask the same kinds of questions about literature in French. Among Spanish-language writers,

American readers tend to know Gabriel García Márquez and Jorge Luis Borges, but few others, if any. Italian literature follows the same pattern. For every international blockbuster like Umberto Eco's *The Name of the Rose*, hundreds of fine Italian novels go untranslated. For every Italian novelist who becomes well known in the English-speaking world, such as Italo Calvino, others, such as Leonardo Sciascia or Beppe Fenoglio, even when translated, barely register. Because Pavese's works have not yet resonated profoundly in English we must look to his place in Italian literature to understand his importance. In doing so we will see that America played a central role in his artistic formation and cultural vision. Examining that role shows us how this major foreign artist perceived America in the first half of the twentieth century; it also reminds Americans of the twenty-first century how much America has changed since then, and how very differently the world now perceives our country.

Pavese published two novels before World War II engulfed the Italian peninsula. The first, *Paesi tuoi* (*The Harvesters*), greatly overshadowed the second, *La spiaggia* (*The Beach*). Because Pavese was already known for his translations of and essays on American writers, and because *The Harvesters* involves lowlifes, common speech, incest, sex, and murder, critics immediately typed Pavese as an American-influenced neorealist. They correctly saw American influences but they went off the mark in considering Pavese a neorealist. After the war he published seven more novels and though he also wrote short stories, essays, and some important poetry, his artistic reputation rests mainly on the achievements of his novels. Writing in 1960, Italo Calvino said of them, "Pavese's nine short novels constitute the most concentrated, dramatic and homogeneous narrative of modern Italy. . . . They are above all texts of extraordinary density, in which one never ceases to find new levels, new meanings."[6]

Pavese's novels live because they draw the reader into the world he creates in each. He draws us in, not with plot—never something he emphasized—but with his taut, deceptively straightforward language and compelling dialogue, both of which make it easy to absorb the highly symbolic qualities of the novels and their moral coherence.

In 1950 Pavese boasted, only half jokingly, that he was one of the recognized masters of dialogue. Indeed he was, and few are the pages in a Pavese novel that contain none. He used dialogue both for characterization and movement. It can take the form of prolonged conversations among groups of characters, as in *The Beach*, *The Devil in the Hills*, or *Among Women Only*, or, more frequently, interchanges between pairs of characters, as between Eel and Nuto in *The Moon and the Bonfires*. A three-page-long conversation in *The House on the Hill* between the narrator, Corrado, and Cate, a woman with whom he has had an affair, exemplifies well Pavese's ability to combine brisk narration and effective dialogue. Just before this scene begins, Corrado learns for the first time that the real name of Cate's son, nicknamed Dino, is Corrado, and that the boy's age could make him the adult Corrado's son. First, Pavese uses dialogue with no comment, only an identifier:

> "Corrado," she said. "I was wrong to give Dino that name. But you see it doesn't matter. Nobody ever calls him that."
> "Then why did you do it?"
> "I was still in love with you. You don't know that I was in love with you?"

Then he shifts to a combination of quick declarative sentences and dialogue to move the scene along:

> I thought to myself that she would have said so long before if it were true. "If you love me," I said brusquely, pulling her arm, "whose son is Dino?"
> She freed herself. She was strong, stronger than I. "Don't worry," she said, "Have no fear. It wasn't you who did it."
> We looked at each other in the dark; I felt weak and sweaty. She had just a touch of sarcasm in her voice.

Later in the same scene, Pavese uses dialogue and brief narration to make clear how Cate has grown and changed; once meek and submissive to him, she now defines the relationship with Corrado, who has remained emotionally isolated. Cate speaks first:

> "You don't love anybody."
> "Do I have to kiss you, Cate?"
> "Fool!" She kept calm. "That's not what I meant. If I'd cared, you would have kissed me some time ago." She paused a moment. "You're like a boy, a conceited boy. One of those boys in whose lives something has gone wrong but they don't want anyone to know about it, to know they are suffering. That's why you bother me. When you talk to the others you are always resentful, malicious. You're afraid, Corrado."

The scene ends shortly after that with Cate clearly in control of the relationship:

> They were calling us from the courtyard, calling Cate.
> "Let's go back," Cate said, submissively. "Don't worry. No one will disturb your peace."
> She had taken me by the arm and I stopped her short. "Cate, if it is true about Dino, I want to marry you."
> She looked at me, not laughing or otherwise disturbed. "Dino is my son," she said quietly. "Let's go."[7]

Geno Pampaloni describes this kind of dialogue as "precise yet continually allusive" and considers it "one of the most splendid achievements of Pavese's prose."[8]

Roberto Gigliucci believes Pavese developed his "extreme narrative rapidity" as a result of his close reading of contemporary American writers such as James M. Cain, Sherwood Anderson, and Ernest Hemingway.[9] The opening paragraph of one of Pavese's prewar novels, *The Beach* (1941), shows he developed what he himself called his "rhythm of what happens"[10] early in his novelistic career:

> For some time my friend Doro and I had agreed that I would be his guest. I was very fond of Doro, and when he married and went to Genoa to live, I was half sick over it. When I wrote to refuse his invitation to the wedding, I got a dry and rather haughty note replying that if his money wasn't good enough for establishing himself in a city that pleased his wife, he didn't know what it was good for. Then, one fine day, as I was passing through Genoa, I stopped at his house and we made peace. I liked his wife very much, a tomboy type who graciously asked me to call her Clelia and left us alone as much as she should, and when she showed up again in the evening to go out with us, she had become a charming woman whose hand I would have kissed had I been anyone else but myself.[11]

While twentieth-century American writers—their styles, themes, situations, and settings—certainly influenced Pavese's own fiction, we do well to remember that he admired, above all other American novelists, Herman Melville (Pavese translated both *Moby-Dick* [1932] and "Benito Cereno" [1940]). I believe that the rich, almost baroque symbolism Pavese found in Melville combined with the flatter narrative techniques he found in, say, Sinclair Lewis or Sherwood Anderson (both of whom he also translated) to play a major role in the development of Pavese's mature style, a style most often described as "symbolic realism."[12] As he wrote in his diary after finishing his first published novel, "You need the richness of experience of realism and the complexity of meanings of symbolism."[13] William Arrowsmith described the style as "revelatory realism," Pampaloni as "lyric realism," "lyric intellectualism," and even "tragic lyricism." Fiedler characterized Pavese's prose as "at once absolutely lucid and completely incantatory." In a 1968 book review, John Simon declared Pavese's language to be "insinuating, haunting and lyrically pervasive." Simon quotes the narrator, toward the end of *The House on the Hill*: "I see I have lived a long isolation, a useless holiday, like a boy who creeps into a bush to hide, likes it there, looks at the sky from under the leaves and forgets to come out, ever." He comments, "There is something so straightforward about this, so brisk and limpid, that we do not notice that the piece of prose is all simile, metaphor, hyperbole . . . accomplished in intense compression. There is a superb decorum here."[14]

Early in his career, Pavese often introduced his symbols heavyhandedly, most notably the hill in *The Harvesters*, described more than once as being shaped like a woman's breast. In his maturity, however, he integrated symbols with the narrative line much more smoothly. As Arrowsmith puts it, "Pavese used symbols with extraordinary tact; they rise from his work naturally because they are a product of a lifetime's reflections."[15] For instance, when one finishes *Among Women Only* the realization comes that its opening—the narrator, Clelia, arriving in Turin during carnival time along with "street acrobats and candy sellers"—symbolizes everything to come. Carnival perfectly connotes the frivolous, decadent lives of the women who take her up, and she, the manager of a haute couture dress shop, becomes a high-class candy seller. Pavese's most extensive use of symbolism woven into narrative occurs in his last novel, *The Moon and the Bonfires*, which I will discuss at some length. Pavese imbued the realism of his work with symbols because he believed reality had meaning for people only as an unconscious continuum of personal symbols. Thus, as Pampaloni points out, Pavese's narrators "recognize under the facts the significance of a different, richer reality: this lyrical erosion of realism was for Pavese more than a search; it was a gift, a vocation."[16] Pavese believed that every person lives out a destiny foreordained by personal, mythic, childhood experiences, and he spelled out those beliefs in a series of essays on myth and symbolism. Those beliefs carried over into his novels. Pavese rarely judges his main characters harshly and his novels contain no memorable villains; he never blames his characters for their actions—or for their inaction—because he knows he created them destined to do what they did. He does not, for example, condemn Talino, the incestuous and murderous brother of *The Harvesters*; he does not moralize about Poli's drug addiction in *The Devil in the Hills* any more than he criticizes Santa in *The Moon and the Bonfires* for taking up with the Fascists and spying on the Partisans. That Pavese does not blame individual characters does not mean they live in an amoral fictional universe. Pavese's best novels, in fact, are highly moral, and he leaves little ambiguity in readers' minds about his judgments. We do not know, for example, what in Cate's personality gives her the ability to change herself after her affair with Corrado, but we certainly know Pavese admires her more than he does Corrado. Clelia, in *Among Women Only*, willingly becomes involved with the bored, sensation-seeking group of rich women she meets in Turin, but Pavese leaves no doubt that we are to value her more than the other women because she works for a living and keeps at least some perspective on what she is doing. In *The Devil in the Hills*, Oreste's two hardworking cousins are counterpoised rather obviously to Poli and his crowd of dissolute Milanese friends. In *The Moon and the Bonfires*, Pavese barely contains his moral indignation that the same powerful interests who before World War II kept the peasantry under heel remain in control after the war, thereby betraying the promise of the Resistance and the Liberation. Well-off landowners, the reactionary parish priest, the town doctor, the mayor, the municipal treasurer, and the local police commander manage to keep all social and business arrangements in the village just as they always had been. For the sharecropping peasantry, this means a continued penury that leads to the book's most senseless outbreak of violence. Pavese uses the character Nuto to express his own anger and resignation at the ongoing social obscenity; for example it is the carpenter Nuto who believes that "the world is badly made and needs to be redone."[17] Though he did not name it, Pavese set this novel in the town where he was born, Santo Stefano Belbo, located in the hills of the province of Cuneo. Because the lovingly described physical countryside plays such an important role in the book and because Pavese presented several of the characters so sympathetically, one can easily mistake the book for a paean to the life and rituals of rural Piedmont. It is nothing of the sort, as Nuto, speaking for Pavese, makes clear through his contempt for most of the residents of the town and their behavior.

While one can focus on his methods, we in the end return to Pavese's best novels for the same reason we return to all great narrative novels, for the story told in the particular way the author tells it. Pavese's novels rely not on intricate plotting but on specific, credible events described in accessible language. These events happen to specific, individual characters, but the events assume universal, or, as Pavese would say, mythic significance. *The House on the Hill* combines Pavese's language, realism, symbolism, and moral rigor better than any of his other works. Furthermore, as Anco Marzio Mutterle has pointed out, Pavese achieved in this 1948 novel something he had not in any of his previous works: "the effective" and, I would add, affective, "rendering of a collective historic drama through the eyes of a first-person narrator."[18] The drama was the Italian Resistance and civil war of 1943–45, which we see and feel through the consciousness of Corrado, the narrator. We do not always feel comfortable inside him; after all, he treated Cate with emotional indifference and he later opts out of joining the many available bands of Partisans in their guerilla war against the Fascist and German forces. He hides out under an assumed name in a Catholic boarding school and spends the last chapters of the novel making his way to the safety of his parents' home in a hillside village. Yet we never lose interest in him and come to see the interior coherence of his choices. In the next-to-last chapter of the book Corrado comes upon a group of dead Fascist soldiers, killed in a Partisan ambush. He sees beyond their uniforms to their humanity and is especially struck by one of the dead who "was on the grass where he had jumped from the road to defend himself by shooting; he was kneeling stiffly against the barbed wire as if alive, blood flowing from his mouth and eyes, a boy of wax crowned with thorns."[19] In the last chapter Corrado has arrived safely at his parents' home. The chapter begins, "Nothing has happened. I've been home for six months and the war still goes on."[20] Those two sentences encapsulate perfectly Corrado's—read Pavese's—dejection and resignation. Pavese does not posit a moral equivalency between the Fascists and the Partisans but he does remind us that the young Fascist, a boy, is just as dead as any Partisan hero, and through that death achieved a useless sanctity of his own. Almost unwillingly, we come to identify with Corrado's repulsion toward both the theatrics and reality of war-making. Corrado becomes, in fact, the reader and the reader Corrado, a symbolic symbiosis so smooth that it goes almost unnoticed. Regardless of our historical knowledge of Fascism, we just want the war, perhaps war itself, to end. Like Corrado, we become tired and suspicious of it because despite it, too often, "nothing happens." Pavese leads us to identify with Corrado's spiritual weariness, and with him we become an Everyman weary of war. He transforms Corrado's individual experiences into something universal; for an American, in particular, the ending of the book, with its lament for the dead and foreboding of endless war, brings to mind the chorus of one of the few songs sung by soldiers on both sides of our own Civil War: "Many are the hearts that are weary tonight, / Wishing for the war to cease."[21]

Pavese's war with himself ended with his 1950 suicide. At the time of his death Italy knew him not only as a novelist and poet but as what we would now call a public intellectual. He had just won Italy's most important literary prize; he was also the managing editor of Italy's most prestigious publishing house and contributed columns to the left-wing press. His death brought forth an enormous amount of published commentary, concentrated mainly on trying to explain why, at forty-one, in full possession of his artistic and intellectual powers, he killed himself. The speculation increased in 1952 with the first publication of his diary. Pavese became more interesting to many as an example of the suffering rather than the successful artist. (When the diary appeared in English translation a decade later, Susan Sontag, in the most influential English-language essay about Pavese after Fiedler's, continued in the same vein. In her first paragraphs she devoted cursory, mildly approbatory attention to Pavese's novels, before getting to the diary, her interpretation of which she had already indicated with the title of the essay, "The Artist as Exemplary Sufferer.")[22] It took Italo Calvino, writing on the tenth anniversary of Pavese's death, to remind everyone that

> Too much has been said about Pavese in the light of his extreme act and not enough in the light of his battle won day after day

against his own self-destructive drive. Pavese succeeded in making the morality of his classics—the morality of action [*la morale del fare*]—operative in his own life, in his own work, in his participation in the work of others. For those of us who knew him in the last five years of his life, Pavese remains the man of scrupulous industriousness, in his reading, his creative work, his work at the publishing house, the man for whom every gesture, every hour had its function and its fruit . . . whose few hours of relaxation and idleness were savored with the knowledge that they were those of one who knew how to work hard . . . He was the man who "made things" [*faceva*], the man who wrote books, and the books of his maturity carry the sign of this victory, even of happiness, though always a bitter happiness.[23]

Two years later, in his 1962 introduction to Pavese's collected essays, Calvino again stressed the importance of Pavese's works over the events of his life. The essays, said Calvino, provide "the richest and most explicit intellectual autobiography of Pavese, linked—as his life demands—to the practice of his trade, to his work. And it is this that truly counts in his life, as it does in anyone's."[24] The editors of the literary journal *Sigma* heeded Calvino's advice and confirmed the changed critical approach with their remarkable December 1964 double issue, in which twelve noted critics dealt with various aspects of Pavese's works with nary a speculation about the reason he killed himself.[25] Since the 1960s, Italian criticism has coalesced in general agreement with the approach Calvino urged, and, except for explicitly biographical books and articles, has concentrated on various qualities of Pavese's works. Pavese's two greatest books, *The House on the Hill* and *The Moon and the Bonfires*, though fiction, have entered into Italy's collective memory of World War II, especially the Resistance, and the immediate postwar years. *Among Women Only* and *The Devil in the Hills*, novels of less scope but no less skill, continue to reward readers, as does much of his poetry.

What becomes fascinating once one understands Pavese's place in Italian literature is to discover how important a role American literature played in his artistic formation. As Fiedler says, "Pavese's art, profoundly Italian as it is, is rooted in our literature and could not have existed without it,"[26] a judgment Patrizia Lorenzi-Davitti agrees with when she writes that Pavese's "political, human and literary ideals with their poetic consequences would be unthinkable without the formative experience of the American cultural world."[27] Building on those who have written before me, I try in this book to describe the special quality of the experience of American literature for Pavese and its lasting impact on him. I do so mainly through the written words he left behind, which include much more than what he published in his lifetime. Beginning in his adolescence, Pavese kept the drafts of most of his personal letters and the originals of most letters to him. He worked as a book editor, and the publishing house kept copies of his outgoing correspondence and the incoming originals. We have his evaluations of the books the house was considering; we know not only what American books he translated but also those he commissioned for translation. He dated the beginning and end of most of his manuscripts, so we know when he wrote virtually all that he wrote. He kept a diary for the last fifteen years of his life. Thus, in trying to understand Cesare Pavese, the task is not so much to discover but to interpret—in my case, to interpret the significant amount of documentation relating to his complicated and changing relationship with American literature. That documentation includes letters, diary entries, his university thesis, essays, and translations, as well as his fiction and poetry. Memoirs written by his friends are another important source. Concern with America formed one of the two grand enduring intellectual passions of his life (the other being myth), and it enthralled him for ten years, roughly from age sixteen to twenty-six. In those years Pavese passionately embraced American literature and culture as equal or superior to anything in Europe. Yet in his late thirties he began publicly to repudiate American culture as materialistic, with no value for contemporary Europe.

Why this change? I believe a specific answer to that question exists and can be found in the intertwining of defining personal events and his intellectual development. Pavese, born in 1908, came of age and lived most of life, one must always remember, in Italy's Fascist era. He had just turned fourteen when Mussolini took power in 1922; he died five years after Mussolini was executed by Italian Partisans. Indeed, without Fascism, the intellectual Pavese we know would not exist. Had Italy been a free and open society, the young Pavese might have heard there the kinds of bold and brave voices he found only in America; he might never have had the motivation to immerse himself in nineteenth- and twentieth-century American literature. But such voices did not exist in the Italy of his time, and it was his immersion in American culture that helped him form his own artistic voice and shape his literary persona. Pavese found in America not only what he considered great literature but models of ways to live in the world. He saw Walt Whitman not only as a great poet but as a compassionate, democratic, easygoing man who lived life fully both in body and mind. He admired Herman Melville's ability to combine scholarship with seamanship, that Melville could hunt a whale, swap stories in the fo'c'sle, and then go read Plato. These American artists came to represent personal ideals for Pavese. He saw them as balanced, healthy, courageous men who, in the American environment, had integrated life and art without sacrificing either. They valued freedom, comradeship, equality, frankness, courage, mercy, integrity—traits Pavese found mostly lacking in the Italy of the 1920s and 1930s. Beyond the enabling models of these authors' lives and works stood America itself, which he saw as vibrant, open, modern, adventurous, and democratic: everything Fascist Italy was not.

Italian writers who came to maturity after World War II have had the luxury of approaching America differently than did those of Pavese's generation. For example, both the extraordinarily well-known Umberto Eco (b. 1932) and the lesser-known Gianni Celati (b. 1937), both accomplished novelists and academics associated with the University of Bologna, have written extensively about American literature. For them, America is not an imagined country of the mind, not a counterpoint to a repressive Italy, but an accessible country whose rich literature and varied culture simply interest them. Further, America constitutes only one, and not the most important, among their varied interests; for neither does it give rise to the kind of intellectual fixation it did for Pavese during ten years of his life. Celati has translated American authors, including Melville, as Pavese did, and both Eco and Celati have taught in American universities. For them, America has become easily familiar, its culture something to be appreciated and analyzed but not idealized. Fascism would have made careers like theirs unimaginable.[28]

In circumstances radically different than those following World War II, Pavese, between 1930 and 1934, wrote a series of essays on American authors and translated four American novels, most importantly *Moby-Dick*. Though he was not alone in the field, he did more than anyone else in those five years to bring serious American literature into the Italian consciousness. Around 1934, Pavese's enthusiasm for American culture began to wane, but he never denied its importance for his youth. Nor did he deny the importance of the values he had internalized from his American encounter, even when he could not live up to them. I lay out, in the chapters that follow, a more detailed description of what Pavese found in American literature and why his change of mind about America occurred so abruptly when it did. I also follow him through World War II to the postwar period, when he joined the Italian Communist Party and wrote for the party newspaper overtly anti-American articles.

Because some knowledge of Pavese the man helps explain Pavese the *americanista,* I start this book with a brief biography that stresses the major turning points in his life. I go from there to discuss his first encounter with Walt Whitman, his university thesis on Whitman, his 1930–34 essays on American writers, and his translations of American novels. To put his writings on America and his translations of American fiction into context, I also deal at some length with the Italian cultural phenomenon of *americanismo* during the Fascist era. Nineteen thirty-four marks the transition year for Pavese as regards American culture, and I devote particular attention to the two essays he wrote that year and to important personal events. I end the book with a discussion of his turning away from America, which, though it began well before World War II, became public and politicized only afterwards. I also show how in the midst of the postwar period F. O. Matthiessen's *The American Renaissance* touched him deeply, reminding him of why he so loved American writers like Melville and Whitman.

As its title indicates, my book concentrates on Pavese's relationship with America; it does not survey everything he wrote. I deal at any length with only three of his nine novels, and those for specific reasons: two, *The Harvesters* and *The Moon and the Bonfires,* because of their American links, and *The House on the Hill,* which I believe to be his finest work, because of its importance as both literature and self-revelation.

I comment at some length on his relationships with four women, especially the five-year relationship with Tina Pizzardo and the much shorter one with Constance Dowling, a beautiful, minor American movie actress. She and Pavese had a brief affair in March 1950, a little over a week long, which he took much more seriously than she did. Pavese's misreading of Dowling and her return to America in April 1950 led directly to his suicide because her rejection of him triggered long-latent, self-destructive impulses.

In dealing with Pavese as *americanista* I try as much as possible to let his writings speak for him, an easy task since he wrote so extensively and well. I believe those writings show how America helped him form his own persona at the same time as he was using American literature as an implicit rebuke to the Fascist political system and the Italian literary establishment. I pay particular attention to his language because one sees there evident traces of American influence. In different ways, Pavese opened and closed his mature life with America: Whitman, intellectually, and Constance Dowling, physically and symbolically. In between, he formed his own lasting Italian literary identity. With Dowling he recognized, fearfully yet hopefully, the "ironic and sweet return" of America into his life.[29] When she left, Pavese's revived dream of fulfillment, symbolized by this American woman, disappeared. He never gave himself the chance to see if America might return again in any form: he killed himself four months after her departure.

PART
I

ONE
The End Game: Connie and Cesare

In his diary entry for January 14, 1950, Cesare Pavese, sitting in Turin, noted, "Thinking back on the Dowling sisters, I know I lost a great chance to fool around."[1] He was referring to Constance and Doris Dowling, two American actresses who had come to Rome to try their luck in the dynamically expanding postwar Italian movie industry. Constance, New York–born, twenty-nine when the forty-one-year-old Pavese met her, was an attractive sandy blond; Doris, twenty-six, a brunette. Doris had more success in Italy, as she had in the United States. In her best-known role before coming to Italy, Doris played Gloria, the good-hearted prostitute who, in the 1945 Academy Award–winning film *The Lost Weekend*, lends the Ray Milland character drinking money when no one else will. Her most important role came in Italy when the director Giuseppe De Santis cast her as the female lead in the Dino de Laurentis–produced 1949 film *Bitter Rice* (*Riso amaro*). That film, an enormous commercial success, included Silvana Mangano in her first feature role; Doris suffered in comparison. Bosley Crowther wrote in the *New York Times* that Mangano "is nothing short of a sensation on the international film scene . . . It is not too excessive to describe her as Anna Magnani minus fifteen years, Ingrid Bergman with a Latin disposition and Rita Hayworth plus twenty-five pounds! Alongside of her, Doris Dowling, an American actress here playing an Italian 'moll,' is pallid and physically unimpressive but fully adequate to the moral substance of her role."[2]

Pavese had possibly met Doris earlier, in Turin, but met Constance for the first time during a week-long trip to Rome over the New Year, 1949–50. Doris, however, did not accompany Constance in early March 1950 when "Connie," as Pavese called her, came to Turin to spend time with a couple Pavese knew, Giovanni Francesco Rubino and his wife, Alda Grimaldi. Even if her movie credits of the period do not indicate an overly taxing workload, Constance came purportedly because she was nearing exhaustion from overwork and needed a break. Alda Grimaldi asked Pavese to accompany the three of them to dinner as Constance's escort because Pavese spoke English well and had already met Constance.[3] The Rubinos also intended to take Dowling to the mountains for a few days as part of their recreation plan for her; Constance asked Pavese to come along. Pavese, who openly detested the mountains, agreed, and in the middle of winter went with them to Cervinia, a fashionable ski resort on the Italian side of the Matterhorn.

A trip Pavese made to a different mountain resort with a woman sixteen years earlier resulted in a humiliating disaster. Cervinia turned into a triumph for him, a true ecstasy of sexual and emotional release. Even knowing what happened later, one wants to cheer for him up there in the mountains: the not very good-looking, complicated, sexually inadequate Italian intellectual gets the dazzling blond American movie actress in bed and they both have a wonderful time. It took a few days. They were close to sex on Monday, March 6, but "Connie was sweet and submissive but at the same time detached and firm." Pavese's diary entries show that Pavese worried about his performance and that Constance understood his anxiety: "Beating, trembling, sighing without end. Is it possible at my age? It was no different when I was twenty-five. Yet, I have a sense of hope, of (incredible) serene hope. She is so good, so calm, so patient. So made for me. After all, it was she who sought me out. But why did I not try Monday? Fear? Fear of 'Friday the thirteenth'; fear of my impotence? It is a terrorful step."[4]

While still in Cervinia, he wrote Constance a poem, in English, the first poem he had written in four years. It shows the emotional afterglow of their sexual encounter and the beginning of Pavese's idealization of her. He entitled it "To C. from C." and gave her the original:

> *You,*
> *dappled smile*
> *on frozen snows—*
> *wind of March,*
> *ballet of boughs*
> *sprung on the snow,*
> *moaning and glowing*
> *your little "ohs"—*
> *white-limbed doe,*
> *gracious,*
> *would I could know*
> *yet*
> *the gliding grace*
> *of all your days,*
> *the foam-like lace*
> *of all your ways—*
> *to-morrow is frozen*
> *down in the plain—*
> *you dappled smile*
> *you glowing laughter.*[5]

A week later, after putting Constance on the train back to Rome, he noted, "The step was indeed terrorful and yet it is taken. Her incredible sweetness, words of hope. Darling [in English in original]. A smile, the long repeated pleasure of staying with me. The nights in Cervinia, the nights in Turin. She is a girl, a normal girl. And yet she is—terrorful. From the depth of my heart I say: I did not deserve so much."[6]

Pavese found himself in a daze. In his youth he had idealized Walt Whitman and other American writers, indeed America in general. By 1950, he had long since lost interest in America and worried that maybe he was deluding himself; he asked himself in a hopeful tone, "This America, that returns ironically and sweetly, it does arrive as a human value, no?"[7] Could it really be that after several women had rejected him he had finally found *his* woman, and she was an American, an actress, and beautiful? He knew the painful depression that rejection by a woman could cause him; he debated with himself, but only briefly. He let himself fall helplessly and, as it turned out, hopelessly in love with Constance Dowling. Walt Whitman had been for Pavese the first incarnation of America, Dowling the last, and she an incarnation in both the physical and symbolic sense. She resurrected in him a hope in the future that he had not felt since he discovered Whitman as a teenager.

Constance apparently understood Italian well, because the day after she left for Rome Pavese wrote her a long letter in Italian:

> Dear Connie,
>
> I wanted to play the strong man and not write you immediately, but what sense would that make? It would only be a pose.
>
> Did I ever tell you that when I was a boy I had a superstition of "good behavior"? When I had any risks in front of me, for example, an exam to take, I was always careful to do nothing bad, to offend no one, not to raise my voice, not to think any bad thoughts. All this was so as not to alienate destiny. Well, I have now became like a boy again and since I have in front of me a great risk, since I have a terrorful examination to pass, I do not dare to be bad, to offend people, to think evil thoughts. The thought of you is something that cannot go together with anything unworthy or ugly. I love you.

It is worth noting that in this declaration of love, Pavese did not use the Italian *ti voglio bene*, which can mean either "I love you" or something less, "I care greatly for you"; he used *ti amo*, which leaves no doubt. He went on, "Dear Connie, I know all the weight of this word—its horror and its wonder—and yet I say it to you almost calmly. I have used it so little and so badly in my life that it is like new for me." After telling her that the Rubinos missed her he ended the letter:

> Love, the thought that when you read this letter you will be back in Rome—with all the discomfort and messiness of the trip over—that you will see your smile in your mirror and will be back living your normal life and sleeping like a good girl, moves me as though you were my sister. But you are not my sister, you are something sweeter and more terrorful and to think of it makes my wrists shake.
>
> Dear. I am working for you. Till soon.[8]

By "working for you," he meant ideas for movie scripts. He sent her the first two days later, "The Two Sisters." He said it was only an idea, but "as to the dialogue I am one of the recognized masters of the genre (!)." He admitted that he knew nothing about "the syntax of the cinema," but that for her he could learn: "I have already learned in life how to be a translator, a poet, a critic, a fiction writer, a copy editor, an editorial adviser, a teacher—all things that I did not know how to do when I was twenty." He ended the letter with English phrases from the poem he had given her, "You, dappled smile, you wind of March."[9] Either before or just after returning to Rome, Constance traveled to Monte Carlo, as did her sister. They sent him a picture postcard ("Le casino et les Terrasses") on which Constance jotted, half in Italian, half in French, "Non ho trovato ancora il principe! Mon coeur reste encore à toi." (I have not found the prince yet. My heart remains with you.) It might have meant more to Pavese had not Doris continued the conceit with "Les jours sont longs mais mon coeur aussi reste à toi."[10] Still, Connie's sentence in French pleased him, even if, he admitted to himself, it was "the phrase of a superior said benevolently to someone below her."[11]

In a complete reversal and with truly stunning rapidity, the day after receiving the postcard Pavese began a downward emotional spiral that ended with his suicide five months later. On March 9, they had slept together in Cervinia; they slept together again in Cervinia and in Turin before she left on March 16 for Rome. On March 17, Pavese declared, "I love you"; on March 20, he noted having received the postcard. But on March 22, only thirteen days after their first sexual encounter and five days after Dowling's departure for Rome, he wrote, "Nothing. She writes nothing. She could be dead. I will have to get used to living as though this were normal." He adds in the same diary entry, "How many things I never told her. In the end the terror of losing her now is not the anxiety of 'the possessed' but the fear of never being able to say these things again. What these things are now, I don't know. But they would come out like a torrent when I was with her. It is a state of creation. Oh God, let me get her back."[12]

The most important woman in Pavese's earlier life, Tina Pizzardo—the first to reject him—considered Pavese an "eternal adolescent." His most important teacher, Augusto Monti, wrote that he was "an adolescent for whom it was impossible to become a man."[13] Pavese's close friend, the writer Natalia Ginzburg, and others often used the word "adolescent" to describe the adult Pavese and much of his behavior. They are all correct if one defines an adolescent male in the melodramatic sense as someone who considers himself misunderstood, alone, and alienated; a not fully mature person whose thoughts run to death and unrequited love; a man who falls quickly in love with an idealized woman, and then, with equal passion, throws himself into despair when the woman rejects him, finding suicide the only appropriately dramatic response. In these senses Pavese truly was an adolescent and that part of him tragically took hold in March 1950. He was forty-one, at a peak of artistic accomplishment and literary power, yet he let his growing fear of rejection by Constance Dowling override all that, and turn him into a woeful adolescent.

On the same day that Pavese implored God to help him get her back, he composed for Constance one of the greatest adolescent poems ever written by an adult, the poem that has become his most famous, "Death Will Come and Will Have Your Eyes." Geoffrey Brock's translation:

> *Death will come and will have your eyes—*
> *this death that accompanies us*
> *from morning till evening, unsleeping,*
> *deaf, like an old remorse*
> *or an absurd vice. Your eyes*
> *will be a useless word,*
> *a suppressed cry, a silence.*
> *That's what you'll see each morning*
> *when alone with yourself you lean*
> *toward the mirror. O precious hope,*
> *that day we too will know*
> *that you are life and you are nothingness.*
>
> *Death has a look for everyone.*
> *Death will come and will have your eyes.*
> *It will be like renouncing a vice,*
> *like seeing a dead face*
> *reappear in the mirror,*
> *like listening to a lip that's shut.*
> *We'll go down into the maelstrom mute.*[14]

Three days later, Pavese linked death and women more generally: "One does not kill himself for love of *a* woman. One kills himself because love, any love, reveals us in our nakedness, misery, defenselessness, nothingness."[15] From that point on, Pavese made only twenty-one more diary entries; they all involve "Connie," or suicide, or both. A sampling:

> Nothing. I have charcoal burning in my body, embers under the ashes. Oh, Connie, why, why? (March 27)
>
> The cadence of suffering has begun. Every evening, at nightfall, my heart constricts—until night. (May 8)
>
> Now the pain comes even in the morning. (May 16)
>
> All this complaining is not stoic. And therefore? (May 30)
>
> Stoicism is suicide. (July 14)
>
> Suicides are timid murderers. Masochism instead of sadism. (August 17)
>
> A little courage is all it takes. (August 18)[16]

The American scholar and critic F. O. Matthiessen committed suicide on April 1, 1950, when Pavese had already entered into this downward spiral. As someone who knew Pavese at the time wrote, "Pavese was profoundly affected."[17] Because of Matthiessen's special significance for Pavese (see chapter 8), his death added to Pavese's growing depression.

In the midst of all this inner torment, Einaudi published, in April, his last novel, *La luna e i falò* (*The Moon and the Bonfires*). Its dedication page reads, in English, "For C. / Ripeness is all." Pavese sent Constance her copy with a melodramatically sad little cover note in English: "I have seen the days when to have written a book like this would have meant something. / Here's to you, darling."[18] He sent the book to an American address she had given him. She had left for America earlier in April, supposedly to make a film.[19] Before she left he went to Rome; he wanted their relationship defined before her departure. As unsatisfactory as it was, he got that definition. Afterward, while still in a Rome hotel, he wrote for her, in English, the last poem he ever wrote. He called it "Last Blues, to Be Read Some Day."

> *'Twas only a flirt*
> *you sure did know*
> *some one was hurt*
> *long time ago.*
>
> *All is the same*

year has gone by—
some day you came
some day you'll die.

Some one has died
long time ago—
some one who tried
but didn't know.[20]

He sent her the poem when he returned to Turin, enclosed with a letter, also in English. He told her he wrote the poem in Rome and was now "no more in the mood to write poems. They came with you and go with you." Referring to "To C. from C.," he explained, "You see, I began with an English poem and end with another. In them is the whole range of what I experienced in this month—*l'orrore e la meraviglia* of it." The rest of this goodbye letter shows no adolescent bravura but rather adolescent self-pity, a judgment tempered, as we read, by the knowledge that Pavese really was feeling what he was reporting:

> Dearest, don't be cross, if I am always speaking of feelings you cannot share. At least, you can understand them. I want you to know that I thank you with all my heart. The few days of wonder I snatched from your life were almost too much for me—well, they are past, now horror begins, bare horror and I'm ready for it. The prison door has banged again.
>
> Dearest, you'll never come back to me, even if you will set foot again in Italy. We both have something to do in life that makes for us improbable to meet again, let alone to be married, as I desperately hoped. But happiness is a thing called Joe, Harry or Johnny—not Cesare.
>
> Will you believe—now that you can no more suspect that I'm "acting" in order to entrap you someway—that last night I wept like a child thinking on my lot, and also on yours, poor strong clever desperate woman fighting for your life?
>
> If I've ever said or done anything you could not approve of, forgive me, dearest, I forgive you all this pain gnawing at my heart, yes, I welcome it. It's the true horror and wonder of you.
>
> *Viso di primavera*, good-bye. I wish you a big luck in all your days and a happy marriage, yes . . .
>
> *Viso di primavera*, I used to love all of you, not only your beauty, which is easy enough, but also your ugliness, your bad moments, your *tache noire*, your *viso chiuso* and I pity you too. *Non dimenticarlo.*[21]

On May 15, Constance wrote Pavese a short note from New York:

Dear Cesare,
    Hello, how are you, what's new?
    The picture is going along slowly, and not so surely.
    Am still in N.Y. It's wonderful to be back but I miss Italy very much. Please forgive me if I don't write often but I feel that I shall be back very soon.
                    Affectionately,
                    Connie[22]

Pavese knew enough about English intonation to understand the implications. He ended his slightly longer return letter, "Remember me in old N.Y. I loved it with all my heart already, when I didn't know you were a little girl in it. Can I send you my love? Ces."[23] They exchanged no more letters, which makes this a good point to look a little closer at Constance Dowling and ask ourselves if Pavese needed to pity the "poor strong clever desperate woman" fighting for her life.[24]

She was born July 24, 1920, in New York City. She was living in an apartment with her mother in 1937, ushering at the Belasco Theatre, when Elia Kazan, playing there in Clifford Odets's *Golden Boy*, noticed her. They began an affair (Kazan was married) in a burst of sexual frenzy; they were, in Kazan's words,

> like animals in season or two criminals closely pursued, consorting everywhere—on cold nights up against the radiator that warmed the lobby of her apartment house; on the first miracle-warm day of spring, on the roof, back of the chimney stacks. Walking the dark city streets, we might suddenly turn into a narrow alley between tall buildings. Or, when the impulse insisted, we'd meet in a box in the Belasco Theatre before the audience had entered, our sounds muffled by the heavy weight of the drapes. Even during the performance (I wasn't in the first act of *Golden Boy*), we'd do it up against the rail at the back of the orchestra—just for the hell of it—or quickly in the lounge below. Afternoons we had more time and met in rooms borrowed from agreeable friends—I had a list—or, when I had money to spare, in an air-shaft single of a cheap hotel just off Eighth Avenue at Forty-sixth Street, sixteen dollars well spent. More than careless, I'd become reckless. Did it matter that the cabdriver was watching us in his rearview mirror? Was I trying to smash my well-ordered life so it couldn't be put back together?[25]

When they met, Kazan thought she was nineteen; she was seventeen. Kazan felt guilty about his relationship with Dowling because his wife, Molly, had recently given birth to their daughter. He says he broke it off when *Golden Boy* went to London in 1938, but found staying away from Dowling difficult because for him she was "literally the girl of my dreams." He felt jealous when he learned she was having an affair with the photographer Robert Capa. Kazan decided he would "live in conflict and confusion"; he contacted Dowling when he returned to the United States, and the affair, with one more intermission, lasted until 1945.

In 1942 he agreed to direct the Irish playwright Paul Vincent Carroll's *The Strings, My Lord, Are False*. One of the reasons he did so "was that it had a part for Constance, the best part she was ever to play in the theatre." "It is customary in our world," he went on, "that when a man of some power in the performing arts attaches a young woman to himself, he will see to it that his darling is, in good time, offered certain professional benefits. Which is what I did. I gave her a part in the play, the play that my wife was still working on with the producer and the author. I was doing the play for Molly; I was doing it for Constance."[26]

Kazan's description of her and their lovemaking in the early 1940s explains why Pavese went crazy for her in 1950. An entry from Kazan's diary even presages in a less poetic way Dowling's little "ohs": "She's so hungry for it! Always ready. I can see her standing in front of me still, her full little breasts, her perfect legs, her belly protruding sensually like the paintings of Italian Renaissance women we used to study in the art class at Williams. And her secret, fragrant bush. I love her eyes when she's being fucked. My pleasure is to see her pleasure. When she comes, she calls out, 'Oh, darling!' then she'd say, 'Oh, my God!' rather sadly and then, 'Don't stop. Don't stop,' her face a mixture of joy and pain. When I think of those moments, I never want to die."[27]

During the affair with Kazan, Dowling repeatedly saw other men. Capa proposed marriage. She stood Kazan up once to go off for a weekend in the country with John Houseman, who at that time was best known as the co-founder with Orson Welles of the Mercury Theatre company. Kazan should not have been surprised; Houseman had directed the 1941 musical *Liberty Jones*, and as a "professional benefit" had found Constance a part in that. She told Kazan about an unnamed man in the back of a Pontiac and he once spied her coming home with a man when he neared her apartment building in Hollywood on an unannounced visit, a man he assumed to be an "intellectual," a species he deemed dangerous.[28] She had a short affair with Charles Boyer. Within days after the final breakup with Kazan in 1945 she was sleeping with Helmut Dantine, the handsome, Austrian-born actor who had a starring role in the 1943 *Edge of Darkness* but has been seen millions of times more in *Casablanca* (1942), as the young Bulgarian refugee whom Humphrey Bogart lets win at roulette so his wife won't have to sleep with police captain Claude Rains.

The show in which Constance had "the best part she was ever to have in the theatre" closed after fifteen performances and led to nothing more in New York. Samuel Goldwyn, however, either saw her in it or met her some other way, because soon after the show closed he asked her to come to Hollywood. He wanted her to audition for a movie he was planning as Danny Kaye's feature film debut (*Up in Arms*, 1944). She went and for one shining season it looked as though she would become a bona fide movie star.

It did not happen. Kazan, no mean judge in such matters, thought "she had little acting talent."[29] Bosley Crowther agreed; in his review of the film for the *New York Times* he wrote, "A new girl named Constance Dowling doesn't act but she improves the atmosphere."[30] Before that movie came out Goldwyn lent Dowling to United Artists to play opposite Nelson Eddy in the film version of the Kurt Weill–Maxwell Anderson musical, *Knickerbocker Holiday*, a vehicle most remembered now for one number, "September Song," sung hauntingly by Walter Huston on stage and laughably by Charles Coburn in the film. *Up in Arms* did not have the success Goldwyn hoped for it and *Knickerbocker Holiday* flopped. Dowling performed adequately but somewhat woodenly in both. It was not her fault that Nelson Eddy could sing but not act; Danny Kaye, however, could do both. It was her failure to measure up to him that convinced Goldwyn he had made a mistake. MGM did not pick up the option on her contract. Goldwyn placed Virginia Mayo, whose part in *Up in Arms* is barely noticeable, opposite Kaye in his next movie (*Wonder Man*, 1945), and she made of her debut in a starring role everything Dowling had hoped to do with hers. Before leaving California, Dowling found roles in three 1946 B movies, including the female lead in *Blind Spot* and a supporting role in *Boston Blackie and the Law*, the twelfth of fourteen films in the "Boston Blackie" series. She moved to Italy in 1947; she made seven movies there, none significant.

At one point in his book, Kazan calls Dowling a "hoyden."[31] That little-used, sexually tinged word, meaning "a boisterous, bold, and carefree girl"—and more—describes Dowling well. It could also be used to describe several other women who had rejected Pavese. As Tim Parks says of Pavese, "He was invariably attracted to glamorous and brashly erotic women whom he also found frightening."[32] Constance Dowling enjoyed sex and used her sexual gifts to advance her career, as did her sister (Doris was sleeping with Billy Wilder when he gave her the part in *Lost Weekend*). Constance made her way in a man's world by using men and being used by them. She was not using Pavese in March 1950, however, she was just having fun. So far as we can tell, she had no self-interest in sleeping with Pavese, and certainly her expertise made the sex enjoyable for both of them. She was in a mountain resort with a man; in such a situation she slept with the man, whether it was John Houseman, Elia Kazan, Robert Capa, or Cesare Pavese. Neither she nor Pavese was married; neither was betraying anyone. She personally had nothing to do with Pavese's history and bears no blame for the symbolic importance Pavese attached to her. She could not know that after she left for America he wrote in his diary, "Surely in her there is not only her, but all *my* past life, the unknowing preparation—America, aesthetic discipline, my craft. She *is* poetry in the most literal sense."[33] America, which had once filled him with such hope, now symbolically betrayed him, and that betrayal put into question his belief in the value of his own life.

It also triggered a self-destructive mania that took the form of a preoccupation with suicide interrupted by the occasional hopeful thought. He stopped writing fiction and poetry. After the last poem for Constance Dowling he composed just two short essays, which appeared after his death. He did send Doris Dowling several ideas for films that would star the two sisters, none of which amounted to anything, and he did continue his editing work. Ironically enough, in the midst of his suicidal depression he also had to rouse himself to receive on June 24 Italy's most prestigious literary prize, Il Premio Strega, named for the yellow Italian liqueur whose owners established it. The jury awarded Pavese the prize not for *The Moon and the Bonfires*, as is sometimes stated, but for his 1949 literary triptych, *The Beautiful Summer*.[34] Doris Dowling accompanied Pavese to the award ceremony in Rome, an event of social as well as literary cachet. Photographs show an uncharacteristically beaming Pavese and a glamorous Doris Dowling together at the bar and mingling with the crowd. He even bought a new suit for the ceremony. He expressed his real feelings about the award, however, in a letter he wrote Doris (in English) after returning to Turin; he thanked for her for coming with him to the ceremony but added, "The trouble about these things is that they always come when one is already through with them and running after strange, different gods." Doris did not know him that well and would not have known what Pavese meant by that last phrase. She also may not have caught the implication of something else he said in the same letter, "Well, Doris, from Saturday to Monday, eighth–tenth, I'll pay a visit (a last one) to my country. Don't telephone me in those days."[35]

North Korean troops crossed the thirty-eighth parallel into South Korea on June 25, 1950. The United Nations passed a joint resolution condemning the action the same day; by July 5 the first American troops had arrived on the Korean peninsula and engaged in combat. Though it did not involve him directly, the war depressed further an already disheartened Pavese. He mixed thoughts of Rome, Doris, and Constance with those of the war when he wrote in mid-July:

> Back from Rome for a time now. In Rome, apotheosis. And so?
> Here we are. Everything is falling apart. I had the last sweetness from D[oris] not from her.
> Stoicism is suicide. Besides people have started dying again on the fronts. If there ever should be a peaceful, happy world, what will they think of these things? Perhaps what we think of cannibals, of Aztec sacrifices, of witch trials.[36]

The war seemed one more piece of evidence for Pavese that all life repeated itself, not just his own personal "horror" but also the horror of war. At about the same time a tall, elegant, eighteen-year-old woman, Romilda Bollati di Saint Pierre, arrived in Turin to spend time with her brother, Giulio Bollati, who had recently joined the Einaudi publishing house where Pavese worked. She fascinated Pavese and he immediately asked her out for walks along the Po and in the hills. He called her "Pierina," a play on her extended last name. He knew he was heading toward suicide, which was supposed to be about fate and Constance, and here he was captivated by someone else. He disliked himself for it: "One cannot finish in style. Now it's the temptation of her."[37]

Severely depressed, he left Turin in early August for the beach town of Varigotti, where he normally spent two weeks every summer as the guest of his friends Alfredo and Eugenia Ruatta. This year he cut his visit short after only a few days. He did not return directly to Turin but traveled to Bocca di Magra, another beach town where Giulio Einaudi and others associated with the firm spent part of every August vacation. Among them this year was Romilda Bollati, which is probably why Pavese went. On August 16, back in Turin, he addressed her in the privacy of a diary entry, "Dear, perhaps you are the best—the real one. But I no longer have time to tell you, to let you know—and then, even if I could, there would remain the test, the test, the failure."[38]

The remainder of this entry marks a division in the period that began with the composition of "Death Will Come and Will Have Your Eyes" and ended with Pavese's actual death. Before August 16 he had been contemplating the idea of suicide. From this point it becomes clear he had made up his mind. "Why die? I have never been more alive than now, never more *adolescent*." Probably referring in his mind to the four women who had rejected him, he added, "A nail drives out a nail. But four nails make a cross." He ended this entry with two sentences: "I have finished my public role. I have worked, I have given art to men, I have shared the pain of many." Part of the second, *ho dato poesia agli uomini,* is carved into the marble slab that covers his grave.

The next day, writing in a Turin hotel room, he gave even clearer evidence of his intention. The "tormented restless one" (*l'inquieta angosciosa*) he mentions is Pavese's symbolization of the women who had wounded him (all echoes of the sea goddess Aphrodite, about whom Pavese used that exact phrase in one of his books, *Dialogues with Leucò*):[39]

> It is the first time that I sum up a year before it is finished.
> In my profession, then, I am king,
> In ten years I have done everything. If I think of my hesitations of then.

In my private life I am more desperate and lost than then. What in the end have I accomplished? Nothing. For some years I ignored my basic faults; I lived as though they did not exist. I was stoic. Was it heroism? No, it didn't take any effort. And then, at the first attack of "the tormented restless one" I fell back into the quicksand. Since March I have been arguing with myself. The names are not important . . . It remains that I now know what is my greatest triumph—and this triumph lacks flesh, lacks blood, lacks life.

I have nothing more to wish for on this earth except that which fifteen years of failure already rule out.

This is the summary of the unfinished year, which will not finish.[40]

The next day, August 18, 1950, his full entry reads:

That which is most secretly feared always happens.
I write: oh You, have pity. And then?[41]

All you need is a little courage.

The more pain is defined and precise, the more the instinct for life fights and the idea of suicide weakens.

It seemed easy thinking about it. And yet piddling women do it. You want humility, not pride.

All this disgusts me.
Not words. An act. I will write no more.[42]

He wrote no more in his diary but he did write another ten letters. One, to "Pierina," still at the sea, indicates that even though he was drowning, he would probably have accepted the right kind of life buoy: "Pierina—if you have not buried me under the waters of the Magra [River]—I am living in the Roma hotel in Piazza Carlo Felice. If you have buried me, may you live happily and know that I will remember always those days. / Pav."[43]

He wrote his sister, who had gone to the country—it was mid-August, *Ferragosto*, the height of the summer vacation season—to tell her he had checked into a hotel and that everything was fine at the apartment where he lived with her and her family. He closed by saying, "I hope you are all well. I'm fine, like a fish on ice."[44] Most of his friends had gone out of town but a few remained, or had returned early from their vacations. He ran into Bona Alterocca, later one of his biographers. They ate dinner together on Friday, August 18, at a restaurant in the hills and then went to a bar on the banks of the Po. Alterocca remembers that at one point, sitting by the river, Pavese looked at its dark water and said that he would not like drowning himself; poison was better.[45] Davide Lajolo, Pavese's first biographer, says that Pavese went to Rome on the weekend of Saturday–Sunday, August 19–20, to see Doris Dowling. No confirmation exists for this trip but it is possible. A lacuna exists in Pavese's letters between Thursday, August 17, and Monday, August 21. It seems perfectly possible that, in his feverish state, after writing "an act" on Friday, August 18, he got on an overnight train to Rome. If he did, it was because, as he allegedly told his old friend Pinolo Scaglione, "Constance's sister will give me the answer. She expects a telephone call from America. If the answer is positive, I will marry Constance."[46]

Whether he went to Rome or not, he was in Turin when, on Monday, August 21, his sister, either in response to his letter or because of previous plans, returned to the city with her two daughters; Pavese moved back home. He spent several days in his room, putting his papers in neat files and, as his sister remembers, burning letters and photographs. Alterocca had sent him a playful note to try to shake him out of the morbidity she felt in him. He responded brusquely on Wednesday, August 23, and, sensing something was out of sorts, she phoned a mutual friend, Adele Vaudagna, wife of one of Pavese's oldest friends, Giuseppe Vaudagna. She phoned Pavese and he was as brusque with her on the phone as he had been in writing with Alterocca. Pavese, who almost always felt guilty after acting discourteously with a friend, wrote Giuseppe a note, postmarked August 25:

> What are all these hysterics? I'm sorry if I used a black tone speaking with Adele but it is simply that my soul is scraped raw for reasons of my own. I am in pieces and have no desire to see anyone and I would pay in gold for an assassin to knife me in my sleep. I guess she heard all this in my voice.
>
> I am not looking for comfort. I have neither the desire nor the will. I am pulling forward under my own steam, hoping that it will all soon be over.
>
> For you and your fraternal concerns, I am grateful and thankful.
>
> Don't worry about anything else. Ciao. Pavese[47]

By that time, he had left home again. His sister did not think it odd that he had asked her toward the end of the week to pack him a weekend bag. She always did his packing and he often went on weekend visits to various of his friends. This time, however, he just took the tram to the Central Station stop and checked back into the Hotel Roma. He was given room 43 on the third floor, a narrow single, without bath, but with one window and, as he requested, a telephone. Though Einaudi's offices were virtually deserted for the August vacation, they were open and Pavese went there on Friday, August 25, to write a few business letters, including an ill-tempered message to the woman who had translated James Joyce's *Dubliners* for Einaudi, telling her not only not to complain if Einaudi paid slowly, but also that her own poetry, which she had submitted for publication, disgusted him.[48] His last recorded letter, dated Saturday, August 26, to Mario Motta in Rome, suggests that Motta had written Pavese something about the possible return to Italy of Constance Dowling. Pavese responded, "Who 'has returned'? The American? I've got other things to think about. / Ciao. / Pavese"[49] After that, he truly wrote no more.

The summer of 1950 was one of Turin's hottest to that point. Saturday, August 26, passed sticky and quiet. Those who could afford it had gone weeks ago on vacation, and most of the rest had left for the weekend, the last of the summer. Like any well-designed city, Turin seems especially sad when empty. The hazy Piedmont sky hovers closer than usual, lowering the horizon and turning the hills into constraining barriers. Many stores are closed during the August holiday. Shutters remain down all day. The few pedestrians under the arcades seem awkward, as though they had by accident stumbled in on the rehearsal of a pageant. Pavese walked through the city that day for the last time. He went up to his room just before noon. At some time in the afternoon or evening, he peeled open twenty-some packets of powdered barbiturates, then available without prescription for sleep disorders, dissolved them in water, drank them down, stretched out face up on the bed, shoeless and without jacket, and waited for what would happen. He was, as he no doubt intended, unconscious when his pupils dilated, his breathing became shallow, his heart rate slowed, and he died.

The police found remains of burnt paper on the windowsill in the room. Perhaps he had meant to leave something more specific, but the only suicide note found consisted of three short sentences he had written on the frontispiece of a copy of the book he loved best among all he had written, *Dialogues with Leucò*: "I forgive everyone and I ask everyone to forgive me. Okay? Don't gossip too much." (Perdono tutti e a tutti chiedo perdono. Va bene? Non fate troppi pettegolezzi.)

His body was discovered late the next day, Sunday, August 27, with his left arm across his chest and the right hanging down over the edge of the narrow bed. The maid assigned to the third floor became concerned when, by the end of her shift, his door remained locked from the inside. She went downstairs and asked the owner of the hotel, Teodoro Cernuschi, to come check the room with her. Cernuschi, his daughter recounts, was on the short side and bald. When he used his house key to open room 43 and saw the nearly six-foot Pavese dead on the bed, he exclaimed in Piedmontese dialect, "Folaton, con cola bela testa d'cavej!"[50]—in English, "Oh, you poor fool, and with that gorgeous head of hair!" Pavese would have approved of Cernuschi's use of the Piedmontese dialect for the first words said over his dead body, even if the reference to his hair would have puzzled him. In his life, he never seemed to realize that his dark, thick hair was one of his defining physical characteristics, just as pulling at a front lock of it was one of his defining tics.

In many ways Pavese had been building up to suicide since his teens. Pavese's friend and schoolmate Elico Baraldi committed suicide soon after they both finished high school. Pavese considered it a brave and romantic act. His dairy is full of thoughts of suicide. He talked about it so often to his friends that they were surprised when he actually did it.[51] Their reaction is instructive. While Pavese believed differently, fate did not foreordain that he kill himself. He had a life full of choices. Let us look at that life and see how the choices he made, and his reactions to choices made by others, led to the point that he could attribute to an American woman he scarcely knew so much symbolic weight that her departure would fatally crush him.

TWO
Family and Friends

To chart the beginning of Pavese's life we must move from the center of Turin, where he ended it, about sixty miles southeast to a region of undulating hills called Le Langhe, in the midst of which lies the nine-square-mile municipality of Santo Stefano Belbo. An unremarkable agricultural town of about four thousand inhabitants at the edge of the province of Cuneo, Santo Stefano typifies the whole Langhe area. Low-growing grape vines, planted with almost military regularity, march in straight lines and closed ranks up the easy sloping hills. Corn covers large areas and in some of the vineyards a row of corn appears between each several rows of vines. Hazel and fruit trees punctuate the open areas where neither corn nor grapes are growing and some wheat is also planted. Thus, the hills above the town, lightly treed as they are, seem covered with alternating spotted patches of golden brown, dark blue, and faded yellow.

Autumn sees the Langhe in their fullest glory. The corn has grown tall and the grapes are full and sweet. The light blue sky and hazy atmosphere prelude the inevitable and seemingly endless winter fog that settles over the whole lower Piedmont in late October and stays until April. On September 9, 1908, just north of the town center, on Provincial Road 592 that leads to Canelli, the larger town that will figure prominently in his first published poem and last novel, a boy was born in a large, L-shaped farm villa at six in the morning.

Five days later his father carried the baby to the town hall where the mayor registered the child's birth with the name Cesare Camillo Luigi Quinto Pavese.[1]

Pavese's birth was, geographically speaking, an accident. He was born in Santo Stefano only because the end of his mother's pregnancy coincided with the end of the summer, which the family usually spent there. His parents made their home in Turin, where his father, Eugenio Pavese, served as a Clerk of the Civil Court. The family did, however, have close links with Santo Stefano and the Langhe. Eugenio Pavese was born in Santo Stefano of land-owning, land-working people, and his wife, Consolina Mesturini, came from a successful commercial family of Casale Monferrato, a larger town forty-five miles north of Santo Stefano. At the time of Cesare's birth the immediate family consisted of his parents and Maria, a sister six years his elder. Two other boys died in their infancy and a girl died at six.

Presumably because of his mother's delicate health, he was put out to a wet nurse in a neighboring village and, according to one biographer, was cared for in his own home more by a young woman from Santo Stefano, Vittoria Scaglione, than by his own mother.[2] Vittoria's younger brother, Pinolo, early became one of Pavese's dearest friends, a friendship that lasted Pavese's entire life.

Eugenio Pavese, sick most of the years of Cesare's life, died an agonizing death of brain cancer on January 2, 1914, at age forty-seven, about four months after his son turned five. Other than that, we know virtually nothing about him. Much, though, has been written about Pavese's mother. Davide Lajolo described her as "one of those courageous, austere, strong women. A Piedmontese who had learned not to waste words but to work seriously, to keep her self-esteem and to ride short rein on her children. Her affection could only show itself in her working for them. Her method of bringing up children was more like that of a harsh and dry father than that of a solicitous mother in that it made them feel more the weight of her authority than the warmth of tenderness."[3] Bona Alterocca describes Consolina as "austere, not attractive and with fragile nerves," a woman whose self-esteem was weakened by her husband's long and rather public affair with another woman.[4] The most recent biography of Pavese, by Lorenzo Mondo (2006), describes the mother only obliquely by quoting a presumably autobiographical passage from an unfinished short story Pavese wrote in 1942:

> My father died when I was six years old and I reached twenty without knowing how a man should behave at home. Even as an eighteen-year-old I continued to escape to the fields, convinced that without a run and at least one prank the day was wasted. My mother brought me up severely as would a man and as a result there were no kisses between us or superfluous words and I had no idea what a family might be like. So long as I was weak and depended on her I was mostly afraid of her—a fear, however, that did not exclude running away and returning—and when I became a man I treated her with impatience and tolerated her as you would a grandmother."[5]

She died at age sixty-three on November 4, 1930. The day after, Pavese's ex-teacher, then friend and mentor, Augusto Monti, wrote him a rather gruff but personal letter of condolence:

> Dear Pavese,
>
> Courage. What can you do? This is the way the world is. And in any case three more months of life would have been another three months of agony; and more than old, one never gets. Now will come the visits to you, the condolences, the grimaces of the indifferent who want to show "they share your pain." Then, unfortunately, everything returns to the way it was. And the person who is gone lives on in us in her sayings, her smiles, in her way of moving. "The earth is low; it's hard to work it; you've got to put your back into it." I remember her saying that at [the house in] Reaglie with her delicate smile, that smile that our people have [*un sorriso fine, nostrano*]. Ah, well. Sooner or later we all face this kind of pain. It will be difficult for me to make the funeral but not for any lack of "sharing your pain." Remember me at this time to your sister. And when you can, come visit me. We'll talk of other things. Ciao.
>
> Your A. Monti[6]

Unlike Pavese's biographers, Monti knew Pavese's mother personally, and his letter supports the idea of a serious woman who exuded little warmth. So far as we can tell, Pavese never wrote her any letters or if he did they have not survived. In his diary, begun when he was twenty-seven, he never mentions his mother or father and only one entry touches on his upbringing:

FAMILY AND FRIENDS · 37

Certain banal or indifferent things I do that could help me when I feel uneasy—such as covering up the bed when I stay home in the morning; spending a lot to entertain someone who expects it; washing myself with a great deal of soap—fill me with an instinctive horror and to do them—when I think of them—I have to make a great effort. This is the mark of a severe upbringing inflicted on an extremely sensitive and shy personality. It is the remnant of the terrors of much of my childhood. And to think that my parents were not wicked or exaggerated. But then, how do those who are truly mistreated turn out?[7]

The combination of an absent father and a stern mother who demonstrated little affection can leave a young boy starved for emotional nurturance. Such a boy, when grown, might well look to women for personal affirmation, which the adult Pavese did. If such a boy turned into a writer, he might well treat his subject matter at an emotional distance, which the adult Pavese also did.

His sister, Maria, the only direct family member remaining after his mother's death, was devoted to him—she named her first child Cesarina—but Pavese's emotional link to her seems somewhat tenuous. Most of his letters to her sound compressed and he was more a boarder than a brother during the twenty years he lived with her, her husband, and their two daughters. Lajolo calls Maria a "loving shadow" in Pavese's life.[8] His good friend Natalia Ginzburg writes, "He lived with a married sister who loved him and whom he loved, but when he was with his family he behaved in his usual uncouth way and his manners were those of a boy or a stranger."[9]

With father, mother, and sister, the young Cesare returned to Turin not long after his birth. The family returned to Santo Stefano each summer and so for Pavese's first five years summer meant Le Langhe, the rest of the year Turin. They returned again in the summer of 1914 after the father's death and this time stayed on in the fall because Maria developed a communicable disease, typhus apparently, and the mother decided to keep the children in Santo Stefano. Pavese had been scheduled to begin school that fall in Turin but began his education in Santo Stefano before completing the remainder in Turin. At the time, the Italian educational system divided the twelve years of school a student had to attend before university into four components: four years of *scuola elementare*, three of *ginnasio inferiore*, two of *ginnasio superiore*, and three of *liceo*.[10] He finished elementare at the Istituto Privato Trombetta, a small secular elementary school run by ladies of the same name. The ginnasio inferiore he attended, the Istituto Sociale, was (and remains) a considerably grander institution. One of the few Jesuit-run schools in Italy, it provided a rigorous education from the first grade through the last year of liceo for those who could afford it. Many of Pavese's classmates at Sociale came from the comfortable middle class, as he did, but many also from the rich and noble families of Turin. (Italy remained a kingdom until 1946.)

His years there prepared him well enough to pass the entrance examination for the ginnasio superiore of the Ginnasio Liceo Massimo D'Azeglio, one of Turin's most prestigious public secondary schools. The school had two sections, "modern" and "classic," with the main difference being that in the classic section the students studied Greek. Pavese enrolled in the modern section but later made up for his lack of Greek instruction by teaching it to himself. In his first year there he met Mario Sturani; the two became fast friends and remained so. Sturani left Turin in 1924 to study art in Monza (near Milan) and went on to study in Paris. He did the cover art for several of Pavese's translations, including his most important, Moby-Dick. In the beginning of Pavese's second year at D'Azeglio, Benito Mussolini and his Fascist cohorts "marched" on Rome. The king installed him as prime minister; Mussolini soon officially added the title, "Il Duce." The Fascist era had begun.

After these last two ginnasio years, Pavese continued at Massimo D'Azeglio, for what turned into the three most important years of his life in terms of cultural formation, intellectual direction, and personal friendships. The school, though founded earlier, has occupied the same three-story building in Turin since 1857. Its high-ceilinged classrooms are now better lighted than when Pavese attended, and the principal no longer greets students each morning with the Fascist salute, but one senses the same energy among the student body that characterized Pavese's years. During the time he attended it, Pavese had no more than a five-minute walk to school from the apartment building on the Via Ponza into which his mother moved the family in 1915. When, now fifteen years old, Pavese walked there on October 23, 1923, for the first day of liceo classes, Augusto Monti, a career secondary-school teacher, was preparing to greet his first class at D'Azeglio. The administration had assigned him to teach Italian and Latin language and literature to Section B, one of the two sections of the incoming class. Pavese was assigned to Section B, and since both Italian and Latin were three-year subjects, and a teacher stayed with a given class for its three liceo years, Monti and Pavese interacted on virtually a daily basis for three academic years.

Getting to D'Azeglio had been harder for Monti than for Pavese. Then, as now, Italian schools beyond the elementary level were administered on a national basis and teachers assigned school postings on the basis of credentials, competitive examinations, publications, and seniority. Thus it was nothing out of the ordinary that Monti, a Piedmont native, had taught in Sardinia, Calabria, and Lombardy before gaining, at age forty-two and after some twenty years of teaching, the desirable post in Italian and Latin at a prestigious metropolitan liceo in his own region. Monti had a passion for teaching and his effect on the bulk of his students, including Cesare Pavese, would be hard to overestimate. Using Latin and Italian literature as vehicles, he forcefully brought home to his charges fervently believed ideas about morality, integrity, individual responsibility, the proper relationship of art to life, and the dangers of not living up to one's abilities. A published writer on educational matters even before Pavese's class met him, Monti, who went on to write several novels, disliked unnecessary ornamental additions to style; he considered "art for art's sake" a sham motto.[11] He saw literature, especially the classics, as healthy and popular, and ideally available to anyone willing to approach it openly. In terms of creating literature, an aspiring writer had first to "dive" into life and bring his experiences back to his art. For Monti, a person detached from life could contribute nothing vitalizing to literature. Every person with literary ambition should have another job or profession (*mestiere*), for only through absorbing the real, if commonplace, experiences of daily life could the writer make any kind of meaningful cultural contribution. Monti particularly disliked the fake kind of *letterati* (men of letters) he considered poseurs, the kind who contended that art justified itself through the enjoyment it gave the limited number of connoisseurs truly able to appreciate it.[12] His war against this type of letterati was, as he said himself, always one of my fixations. Hammering and hammering again on this nail I tried to say in short: he who wants to contribute to literature—poetry, prose, epics or novels, lyrics or short stories—must first have another trade [*mestiere*], a serious job, must work at a profession from dawn and for years and then on vacations or holidays write poetry, start stories, in short write as long as he wants or likes to, with the clear understanding that only on these terms will his literature, his poetry, his art succeed as something vital and worthy. This has been one of my fixations, I repeat, an idea that guided and animated all my teaching.[13]

Monti was teaching literature, however, not conducting writing seminars, and he affected his students most by the way he taught the Italian classics. Looking back at age eighty on his years at D'Azeglio, Monti remembered that he consciously taught the Italian canon in such a way as to make political statements without bringing politics directly into the discussion. He did so by enlarging on Benedetto Croce's idea of history as the story of liberty to include literature as part of the documentation of that history. He wanted to teach his students to read the entire canon, from Dante to Manzoni, "as classics of freedom. That is, as classics of anti-Fascism, that is as classics of RESISTANCE."[14]

Norberto Bobbio, one year younger than Pavese, followed him at D'Azeglio. Late in his life (he lived to 95) this distinguished political scientist and philosopher of law wrote:

> When I read Monti, it is as though I can still hear him speaking. Every word contains his lively character whose voice captivated us. He was austere and tolerant but never easygoing. He could appear melancholic, yet he also knew how to be cheerful. He liked to tell stories about everyday things in a light-hearted almost jaunty manner, while at the same time imparting a lesson without appearing to do so. That lesson was always meaningful, and concerned respect for oneself through respect for others, a question of resoluteness and dignity.
>
> When asked what Monti's secret was, Carlo Mussa Ivaldi, one of his pupils who was never to forget him, replied that it was the ability to translate literary values into inner qualities and civic virtues.[15]

Monti emphasized Dante in his Italian classes and developed a certain fame for the way he read selections, not so much reading lines as acting them out dramatically, energetically. Monti believed that his students could find in the classics, especially Dante, everything they needed to know about literature, morality, human nature, and how to live the good life. Monti gave a little farewell speech to each of his classes at D'Azeglio at the end of their three years together, and, as he remembered later, it went like this: "In Dante, as in all the masterpieces of human genius, *there is everything*: each of you can see there—search and find—all that you wish. For myself, in bringing to an end this course I want to emphasize and urge on you this example, this lesson—never start something you cannot finish. And in the name of Dante I wish this for you: that you never author *anything incomplete*, that you are never failures."[16]

That valedictory peroration captures well both his inspiring belief in the classics and his moralizing faith in work. One might think graduating teenagers would feel anxious about their ability to finish every task they start or about never failing in life, but not Pavese and his classmates. Pavese wrote for himself and his classmates the following inscription on the back of the class photograph presented to Monti as the traditional class memento: "Without quotes and without fine words, for you have taught us that becoming letterati is the lowest priority in life. We will show you our gratitude with our works."[17]

Monti had the build and quickness of a bantamweight boxer. Beyond his intelligence and deep culture, he exuded energy, physical and mental health; he had an intellectual and psychological wholesomeness that Pavese admired but never achieved for himself. The students who have written about him all remember a strict but engaging, exceptional, truly inspiring teacher. While none of them speak of a particularly warm personality, Monti did treat some, the more talented, of his ex-students as equals and friends. Monti developed a particular fondness for Pavese, which the young man fully reciprocated. "He was the first of my students," Monti wrote, "who, having graduated, wanted to become my friend, and therefore chronologically the first of those students truly mine."[18] Their relationship lasted the rest of Pavese's life. Pavese's mother had sold the family property in Santo Stefano soon after her husband died and with the proceeds bought, as a second home, a villa in the hills of Reaglie right across the Po from Turin. From that villa Pavese wrote his first letter to Monti in the summer after graduation, a long missive in which Pavese described how he was spending the vacation—reading, writing, wandering the hills near the villa—and reported, "I have also begun to visit those places which Cato recommended and, I am not saying this just to say it, the struggle was hard. I overcame it and a completely new aspect of the world was revealed to me. This is just meant to show that I actually do not live just for books and by books." That an Italian teenager in 1926 should write his ex-professor of Latin and Italian a 1,300-word letter is unusual in itself, but that he should describe his first brothel experiences is extraordinary. Pavese justified his adolescent frankness by reminding Monti that, "If my way of saying things seems too pointed to you, console yourself that these are my real feelings and, therefore, it would be against our principles to dress them up in a more beautiful but less sincere style."[19]

By the end of that summer the eighteen-year-old and the forty-five-year-old were dealing with each other as intellectual equals, although their letters make clear that the personal relationship remained at that time one between an uncertain adolescent and a mature, self-confident, and confidence-inspiring teacher. Two years later Pavese was already rebelling against Monti's "healthy" ideas about the way to create literature. "Dear Professor," he wrote Monti,

> I am a man who is slow to connect different ideas and I reason with much difficulty and generally in a foggy way, while you are precise and limpid and full of vital experience, so much so that I listen to you with the same sureness with which I abandon myself to nature; nonetheless as regards the matter of the creation of art, I now think just the opposite of you.
>
> You say that to create great art it is enough to live as intensely and deeply as possible any real life whatsoever and that if our spirit has in itself the qualities for a masterpiece, the work will come out almost by itself, naturally, wholesomely [sanamente], as happens with all living phenomena.
>
> You, in short, see art as a natural product, a normal activity of the spirit that has, as its essential characteristic, healthiness [sanità].
>
> Well, I disagree with the most part of the significance given these things, and especially the last.
>
> No, as I see it, art requires of the spirit long struggles and mortification and such an unending Calvary of efforts, most of which will fail before any masterwork is created, that we should rather classify art as among the most anti-natural activities of men.

Pavese went on to say that while a true work of art was healthy because organic and full of life, that did not mean it sprang naturally from the mind of a balanced artist. For his part he intended to keep slaving away at his craft, because only through what he called "anti-human" efforts and after "long torments and failed experiments" could the spirit create "those miraculous new creatures that live in this world like other living beings." The one-sentence paragraph that immediately follows reads at first glance like the kind of posing both Monti and Pavese disdained, but it in fact expresses something which Pavese, then only nineteen, deeply believed and acted on the rest of his life: "Because of this, art is the highest of human activities and brings man closer than anything to divinity: it permits him to create living beings."[20] He expressed himself more grandly in this letter than he would later in life, but the ideas remained constant, especially that of art as a willed and perfectible profession.

Monti and Pavese came to disagree on many other things, including the value of several of Pavese's published books; they once came close to a rupture but neither let the friendship die. The friendship meant as much to Monti as it did to Pavese. Monti loved the young scholar and in his memoirs Monti acknowledges that Pavese did pay him back with his works, just as the student promised on the back of the class photograph: "You Pavese—have given me everything—you have even given me your pardon [a reference to Pavese's suicide note]. And you have given me more with your commitments, your work, your sacrifice, you have even given me what little reputation I enjoy in the cultural world . . . Because of you, Pavese, only because of you even last August on the anniversary of your death people came from far off to visit me on the hill outside Turin, *our* hill, people who said they knew of me only because they knew you."[21]

Monti's impact on Pavese went deep. The professor's insistence on the value of clear, immediate writing, his dislike of rhetoric, of poseurs, his love of the provinces, his moral and political integrity, all found lasting resonance in Pavese. Monti first made Pavese aware that style has a moral as well as a literary dimension, that literature must serve social as well as personal needs, and that art by definition implies community. No teacher ever had as much importance for Pavese as did Augusto Monti. Someone else, however, did—a dead American poet he discovered at this time, Walt Whitman.

Pavese's first recorded reference to Whitman occurs in a note he passed in class to his good friend Tullio Pinelli during their last year at the liceo; Pavese was seventeen.

A moment does not negate the past. He says that the past has already happened, it has already had its moment and now the present must have its. "What is the present if not the son of the past?" he says. He says that the entire past is reassumed in the present and that the living must work on life and give it the imprint of the present. It is not a philosophy that negates everything, but one that places itself above all life; it does not love this or that action, but action for action. And it exalts above everything the great forces of the modern world, *love of liberty, human love, justice, energy, enthusiasm.*

He does not have a systematic philosophy, a moral line. He has overcome the line of moral conduct with modern thought. He exalts the forces which I mentioned because *he likes them.* For no other reason (Viva Walt Whitman). He rejects grace, weakness, sentimentality—why? Because "I prefer force." And with these forces he contributes to "his union."

And anyhow, he is a thinker who bounces back and forth; he exalts democracy, the Union of the States, and he exalts the individual which is the opposite.

He is a poet in whom all modern life resounds, who has put religions in a museum. He has no moral line, he only has *preferences.*[22]

One can see evident here influences of Futurism and early Fascism—both stressed action for the sake of action, force, and modernity—but they do not explain Pavese's highly charged, personal enthusiasm for Whitman. Whitman did not just interest him, Whitman excited him because Pavese saw him as a liberating ideal, an ideal most definitely not sanctioned by official Fascist culture, and therefore even more alluring. The following August, in the summer between liceo and university, in the same letter in which he recounted his first sexual experiences to Monti, Pavese described, somewhat boastfully, what he called "my work": "I study Greek so as one day to understand Homeric civilization, Pericles' century, and the Hellenic world. I read alternately Horace and Ovid and thereby discover all of imperial Rome. I study German via *Faust*, the first modern poem. I devour Shakespeare, I read, alternately, [Matteo Maria] Boiardo and Boccaccio, all the Italian Renaissance, and finally the *Légende des Siècles* [Victor Hugo] and the *Leaves of Grass* of Walt Whitman—this is the greatest."[23]

That same August he wrote to Pinelli, "In these woods I exult in Walt Whitman."[24] In September, before the new school year began, he wrote again to Pinelli, "I don't know if it is the influence of Walt Whitman but I would give 27 countrysides for one city like Turin... life, the real modern life that I dream of and am afraid of, is a great city, full of noise, of factories, of enormous buildings, of crowds and beautiful women."[25] He also wrote to Pinelli a month later, just before matriculating at the university.

> I fumble about, caught between darkness and light. I don't know what I want. Or better, I do know but do not know how to reach it.
> I need character, a strong soul that would impose itself on my internal anarchy... I fear I am good for nothing, that I'm just pretending to have the qualities of a precocious and powerful adult with heroic poses à la Byron, à la Leopardi, à la De Musset, à la Ibsen (am I or am I not literary?). And the really funny thing is that I model myself on Walt Whitman who does nothing but thunder against these weaknesses.[26]

Pavese was already writing poetry at this time, but his love of Whitman had more to do with psyche than with poetry. Pavese was one of those teenagers "whose transforming passion for reading provided a means of establishing identity and transcending the given of childhood."[27] His self-identifying idealization of Whitman and his poetry reminds an American of the way generations of book-reading teenage girls have identified with *Little Women*, or boys with Ernest Hemingway or J. D. Salinger. At the beginning, Pavese identified more strongly with Whitman's ideas and persona than he resonated to Whitman's poetry. None of his early written references even mentions Whitman's poetics or quotes a line of Whitman's poetry. Later, Pavese would analyze that poetry at length, but Whitman first entered his life as a symbol of manhood and freedom. Pavese wanted to be like Whitman and live in a country like Whitman's. For instance, Pavese could say in the summer after his first university year that "I feel nature with my brain like Darwin and with my heart, the heart of poets like Walt Whitman."[28] At about the same time, Pavese had a character in one of his (posthumously published) short stories, a discontented young teacher who feels he lets himself be too influenced by his reading, wish that "he had sufficient internal spiritual strength not to be influenced by any mound of journals, as, for example, was the case for the great American, Whitman, a ferocious cultural iconoclast, and yet suffused with culture, and a genius of almost incommensurable originality."[29] No better description exists of the identity the teenage Pavese wished for himself.

Pavese began to see the world partially through Whitman's eyes; this shows up in his letters and also in fragmented short stories he was writing at this time, all published after his death. The Turin in which Pavese set these stories, *Lotte di giovani* (Struggles of Youths), is the city that Pavese, under Whitman's sway, desired, "full of noise, of factories, of enormous buildings, of crowds and beautiful women." As Mariarosa Masoero noted of Pavese in her introduction to the first publication of these stories, "Whitman had entered powerfully into his life and his writings and with him progress, crowds, 'urban modernity.'"[30] Whitman possessed in Pavese's view something he did not: sanità, that is, wholeness, saneness, healthfulness, balance. Whitman seemed to the young Pavese a wholly integrated artist and man, someone at peace with himself in the fullness of his powers. Pavese saw himself, rather, as someone racked by doubts, who still needed to overcome weakness and sentimentality. Further, Whitman lived in a country where you could express yourself freely and, unlike Fascist Italy, where authors could be published and judged great even if they offended the political and literary establishments. It was in these liceo years that Pavese began to see America as the model land of the imagination, and Walt Whitman as its ideal citizen.

It was also at the liceo and in the years just afterwards that Pavese cemented friendships that lasted his entire life. Many of these friends went on, as Pavese did, to make major contributions to Italy's cultural life, especially Leone Ginzburg, Massimo Mila, Norberto Bobbio, Giulio Einaudi, and Tullio Pinelli. The group, which named itself the "confraternity," shared an attraction to literature and other arts, explicable in part by the cultured background from which they came. With few exceptions, Pavese's friends came from well-educated, wealthy, and even noble Piedmont families. Bobbio's father was a famous surgeon; Einaudi's father, Luigi Einaudi, was already a well-known economist, university professor, and senator of the realm (and later served as the first president of the Italian Republic); Pinelli's father was a count; and Pavese's own family, though his father had been only a mid-rank civil servant, had both an apartment in Turin and a villa in Reaglie. These families took culture seriously; in their homes one might of a winter's evening hear a piano recital or listen to a Dante scholar read and comment on *The Divine Comedy*. Some knowledge of the arts, like good manners, was assumed. Something else characterized this group of friends—precocious political involvement. Political beliefs varied more among the group than did the love of the arts, but one can characterize the overall tone as liberally anti-Fascist.

Mussolini consolidated the dictatorial nature of his regime in early 1925 after the Matteotti crisis.[31] The Duce signed the Lateran Pacts with the Vatican in 1929; they ended the standoff between the Catholic Church and the Kingdom of Italy that had gone on since 1870. In the late 1920s Mussolini, despite his growing authoritarianism, enjoyed great prestige within and outside Italy. It was only the 1930s that brought the invasion of Ethiopia (1935) and the "pact of steel" with Hitler (1938). In the late 1920s, to be anti-Fascist meant to be so out of political or moral principle, not as a reaction to the ruin that Mussolini later brought on the country.

The most politically oriented members of the group, Ginzburg, Bobbio, and Mila, for example, shared the liberal ideas that motivated Monti—who considered many of these boys as much his friends as he did Pavese. For liberals like these, Communism carried as great a charge of evil as Fascism because both subordinated the individual citizen to the abstract idea of a canonized state. They looked for political orientation mostly to the thinking of Piero Gobetti, the brilliant young founder of *La rivoluzione liberale*, both a review and a movement. Gobetti, a Turin native, graduated from the University of Turin in 1922 with a degree in law. Fascist thugs savagely attacked him in late 1925 and he never recovered from the beating; he died in Paris five months later at age twenty-four. Gobetti believed that classic Italian liberalism had failed, as Mussolini and Fascism made evident, and he wanted to infuse liberalism with new energy and new ideas, to make it possible for all classes to take part in the renovation of society he thought so necessary.[32] Gobetti also founded a cultural-literary journal, *Il Baretti*, to which Benedetto Croce and Eugenio Montale contributed, and established a short-lived publishing house whose main achievement was the publication of Montale's first, and perhaps most important, group of poems, *Ossi di seppia*.

Pavese, then and afterwards, had little interest in politics. But in Turin, during Fascism's ascendancy, in the midst of this group of friends, one could not ignore politics. Pavese may not have cared much for politics, but those whom he admired, and whose respect he wanted, did. For these friends, as for Monti, to ignore politics was unthinkable because immoral, so Pavese found himself in a sense forced to consider politics despite himself. Leslie Fiedler put it well when he observed that Pavese "was political out of the instinct of self-preservation."[33]

Pavese loved being part of this intelligent, interesting, comfortable group of teenage boys, eager to write, to read, to be read; willing to challenge and anxious to contribute to Italian culture. The confraternity brought him out of himself; furthermore, the group helped him find outlets for his adolescent energies—parties, mountain climbing, rambles in the hills, and especially boating and swimming in the Po River. (If they also went in small groups to the kind of houses Cato recommended, they never recorded the visits.) They were friends in need, also: they comforted Pavese when his crushes on a classmate or a local dancer proved disastrous, and they stayed close to him through adulthood. If, later, Pavese felt alone, it was not because he lacked friends. As Monti said when thinking back on Pavese's life, "The truth is Pavese knew very well that he had many friends; one by one he got them by himself. In fact, that boy passed his whole life making everyone who came near him love him."[34] For Pavese, these friends signified a constant in his life—people he often took for granted, usually giving priority to his own feelings and problems. He wished them well, indeed loved them, but in the last analysis he expected more from them than he was willing to give. Since the terms of friendship are never openly stated, neither Pavese nor his friends found anything unsatisfactory in this arrangement.

Because of Pavese's later fame, the confraternity has generally been viewed as *his* group of friends, but the real intellectual, or, as Italians would say, moral center was Leone Ginzburg, who by all accounts was a prodigy and a remarkable human being. Born in Odessa, Russia, on April 4, 1909, and thus seven months younger than Pavese, Ginzburg, though he never knew it, was the natural son of an Italian, Renzo Segre, with whom his mother had a brief affair in Viareggio during the summer of 1908. His mother's husband, Fedor Nikolaevic Ginzburg, recognized him as his son, however, and Leone was raised as a full brother of his two siblings in an extraordinarily warm, intelligent, lively, and loving family.[35] The family left Russia in 1913 and established itself in Turin, where Leone's older brother, Nicola, had already entered the university-level Polytechnic. The father's commercial activities led the family to Berlin between 1921 and 1923, after which all except the father returned to permanent residence in Turin. Ginzburg's father spent more time in Germany than Italy from then on, until his 1930 death in Berlin. The father's letters to Leone show extraordinary affection, especially considering that Fedor knew Leone was not his biological son.[36] One year after returning from Berlin, Leone, who at fifteen spoke fluent Russian, Italian, German, and French, entered the Liceo Massimo D'Azeglio in the class of 1927, one year behind Pavese.

Ginzburg began his literary career while still in the liceo. Before graduation he had translated into Italian Gogol's novella *Taras Bulba*, and was well into *Anna Karenina*. His first published article, on *Anna Karenina*, appeared as he was entering the University of Turin in the Faculty of Law. He met Benedetto Croce in 1928 and, perhaps because of the philosopher's influence, switched later that year to the Faculty of Letters and Philosophy. He became an Italian citizen in 1931, the same year he graduated from the university. Ginzburg played an active role in the Turin section of Giustizia e Libertà (GL), an anti-Fascist political movement founded in the late 1920s by Italian exiles in France. Its founder, Carlo Roselli, based many of his ideas on those to be found in Gobetti's *La rivoluzione liberale*, but GL put a higher stress on action. The movement organized cells in Italy—Turin's was among the most active—to oppose Fascism and work toward an eventual democracy based on social justice. Under an assumed name, Ginzburg wrote articles for the movement's illegal newspaper and took part in other clandestine activities. In March 1934 the police arrested him and about sixty others in a roundup aimed at the Turin GL group. He was sentenced to four years in prison; the regime eventually suspended two of those and he spent exactly two years in jail.

His moral compass always pointed to true north. He held himself and others to high standards but did not criticize his friends; he did not need to, because his personal example so struck them. Norberto Bobbio, his classmate at the liceo and the university, recalls that

> among our group, Ginzburg stood out not only culturally but also morally. Our wonder, mixed sometimes with affectionate

parody, for the variety of his cultural interests and the immensity of his knowledge, took second place to our unconditional admiration for the strength of his convictions. By eighteen, his personality was fully formed. Leone was above all a man of character; he knew what he wanted. He had no hesitations about questions of principle, and no enticement could move him from a decision already made. In ethics he was rigorous; he conceded nothing for practical reasons. Among the morality of the law, of justice, or of equity he definitely chose the first, only the law that he observed was an interior law, deeply believed and experienced, and of which he himself had been, with painful effort but lucid mind, the legislator.[37]

This moral seriousness had its first negative consequences two years before his arrest. In 1932 he qualified as a *libero docente* at the University of Turin—an untenured position similar to that of instructor in an American university—and planned to teach a course on Pushkin, which would have put him on the first step of an academic career ladder. The government, however, had recently changed the required loyalty oath to include fidelity to the Fascist regime, in addition to the monarchy; Ginzburg refused to sign it and therefore became ineligible to teach at the university (or any public school, for that matter).

Leone Ginzburg's writings, including his letters, show not only his wide range of interests but also his editorial sharpness—he effectively co-founded with Giulio Einaudi the Einaudi publishing house—and an intellectual vitality that never waned, not even during his two years of jail and, later, three of *confino* (internal exile). In his essays and reviews he wrote in a clear, though somewhat formal, Italian that gives no evidence he learned it as a second language.[38] This cultured, sociable, kind, caring, severe, and courageous man eventually died in February 1944 after being tortured by Nazis in the section they controlled of the main Roman prison. So strongly did Ginzburg influence the people who knew him that Bobbio, writing twenty years after Ginzburg's death and thirty-five after the confraternity period, could say, "His convictions became in my mature years a yardstick for measuring good and evil, the voice of conscience. 'What would Leone have said?' 'What would Leone have done?'"[39] Thus, while Ginzburg measured himself by his own standards, many of his friends measured themselves by him.

I believe that in many ways Pavese did just that—and thereby turned his friendship with Ginzburg into one of the continuing misfortunes of his life. Ginzburg represented ideas and a way of living that attracted, indeed convinced, Pavese, but which he could not emulate. Ginzburg always knew what was right; Pavese struggled for moral and intellectual certainty. Ginzburg was self-confident and directed; Pavese insecure and often adrift. Pavese set Ginzburg up as a moral standard and thereby doomed himself to failure, for in many situations Pavese was simply incapable of saying what Leone would have said, or doing what Leone would have done. Especially after his death, Ginzburg came to represent for Pavese an examination he had failed, an ideal he had not lived up to, a friend he had morally betrayed. Those kinds of feelings generate guilt, and certainly Ginzburg's death contributed to the free-floating guilt that characterized Pavese's interior life in the six years he lived after Ginzburg.

At the time they met in the liceo years, though, all that lay in the future. Pavese did well in almost all his classes at the liceo, which, given his intelligence and work habits, surprised no one. In October 1926 he passed the nationally mandated Esame di Maturità Classica, with the maximum grade of eight in six of the eight subjects; his lowest grades, a six, came in mathematics and physics.[40] Passing that examination allowed Pavese by right to enroll in any of the faculties of any of Italy's twenty-one universities. He chose the Faculty of Letters and Philosophy at the University of Turin.

Pavese left behind virtually nothing that describes his university experience, which went from October 1926 to June 1930. He continued to live at home with his mother, which now meant that getting to class required a fifteen-minute tram ride rather than a five-minute walk; he continued to spend time with the same friends and continued to study the same kinds of subjects he had in the liceo. His letters of the period mention nothing about his university experiences, except a few references in the last year to his degree thesis. In one important sense, though, the university years meant more intellectually than just a continuation of his liceo experience: it was a time of increased attraction to American literature and American culture. Chapters 6 and 7 of this book discuss at length Pavese's ten-year love affair with America; it is enough to note here that America, which, in the persona of Walt Whitman, had begun to interest him at the liceo, became as early as his second year at the university his most important intellectual and artistic concern.

It is also a good time to introduce Anthony Chiuminatto, who met Pavese in the winter of 1926–27, Pavese's first at the university. Chiuminatto, an Italian-born American citizen four years older than Pavese, had not enrolled in the university, however, but in Turin's conservatory, where he was studying violin and from which he graduated in 1929. He returned to America that year; he pursued graduate studies in music in the United States, performed professionally, and spent most of his career teaching at St. Thomas College in St. Paul, Minnesota, where he chaired the music department from 1946 until his death in 1973. In Turin he met through a mutual friend both Pavese and Massimo Mila and for two years the three of them met frequently, with Chiuminatto teaching them English in return for lessons in colloquial Italian and Piedmontese dialect, the latter of which interested him because his family came from, and he was born in, Rivarolo Canavese, a small town in the province of Turin. Pavese had a special fascination with American slang, and the topic comes up frequently in the letters they exchanged between November 1929 and March 1933. These letters, in English on both sides, make fascinating and enjoyable reading. For one thing, they constitute a great part of everything that Pavese wrote in English and show his fearlessness in trying to express himself in this foreign language, as when he exclaimed, "Look me over! I wonder if ever there was in U.S.A. such a snappy eater of American language,"[41] or closed a letter with, "Now pardon me my long silence and have a friendly wallop on the shoulder by your / Cesare."[42] Also, as Mark Pietralunga puts it, the correspondence "is one of the most interesting and fertile sources from [Pavese's] younger years, fundamental as a witness to the joy of his discovery of America, and it provides an insight to the beginnings of his activity as translator and writer."[43] Chiuminatto willingly served as Pavese's personal slang dictionary and went to considerable trouble to send Pavese the American books he wanted but could not find in Italy.[44] In his letters to Chiuminatto we find some of Pavese's earliest comments about American writers and the first evidence of Pavese's conviction that America had created a new language, "the American vulgate." Chiuminatto asked little of Pavese in return, just a couple of Italian books over three years, and Valerio Ferme is probably right when he says, "I think that one can say without belittling Pavese that right from the beginning he understood that Chiuminatto could become a rich source of help while requiring on his own part a minimum dispersion of energy and money."[45]

Pavese compiled a good record at the university. He received the equivalent of American A or B grades for every examination he took except one: in his third year he failed the written examination involving the translation into Latin of Italian texts (*Versione dall'italiano in latino*), receiving twelve points. (Italian university examinations are graded on the basis of thirty points maximum, with eighteen the minimum to pass.) He took the examination again the following year and passed with a grade of twenty-six. He graduated in June 1930. Each graduating student is also given a comprehensive grade for the entire university career based on a maximum of 110; Pavese received 108, which in context meant good but not excellent. The obligatory degree thesis he submitted in the spring of 1930, "Interpretation of the Poetry of Walt Whitman," marked the culmination of his university experience and represented his first major work on American literature.

In the months leading up to his graduation Pavese began the process of applying for a graduate teaching fellowship at Columbia University in New York City. He received a general information packet from Columbia in June and wrote back to the secretary (later provost) of the university, Frank D. Fackenthal, asking in an English that is really Italian in English words for more details "about the precise conditions which are likely to be granted to me. I should pray you, if something is not yet on mail, to send me a kind notice of yours about."[46] In July he wrote a letter in highly formal Italian to Giuseppe Prezzolini, who had just begun his long career at Columbia as professor of Italian and director of the university's Italian cultural institute, Casa Italiana, also asking for more details of the teaching assignment, especially the financial terms of the fellowship.[47] Prezzolini responded five months later, on December 18, 1930: "Esteemed Mr. Pavese: I am sorry not to have seen immediately the letter that you sent me or that of His Excellency Farinelli. Unfortunately it is too late for a scholarship but I hope to have a couple available for the coming year and I ask that you remind me of your interest in April. It would be good if you could send me a few copies of your articles on American literature."[48]

In April 1931, Pavese did respond, but only to tell Prezzolini "with deep regret" that he had not been able to gain an exemption from his obligatory military service, which would go from July 1931 to June 1932. He asked Prezzolini if he might count on a scholarship for the academic year 1932–33. Prezzolini responded in May: "At the moment there is no possibility of awarding you a scholarship but you can be sure I will keep your name in mind."[49] In telling Chiuminatto that he would not be coming to America after all, Pavese commented, in the kind of slang he often used in this correspondence, "Surely Daddy above is a funny guy, you bet."[50] Pavese never applied again.

In his correspondence with Prezzolini, Pavese stressed his thesis on Whitman and his competence in American literature. That competence led to the start of his literary career and helped him support himself in the years after graduation. Three months after he graduated, his mother died, and he moved into a room in the large apartment of his sister and brother-in-law in the Crocetta neighborhood, a tony zone of Turin about a half-mile south of Via Ponza. The Einaudis lived on the same street his sister's family did, and Croce's daughter moved there when she settled in Turin. Maria's husband, Guglielmo Sini, held a good enough management position at a large cement company, l'Unione Italiana Cimenti, to afford the neighborhood. Pavese lived at Via Lamarmora, 35 for the rest of his life, as a plaque now attached to the building's facade attests:

>CESARE PAVESE
>1908–1950
>LIVED IN THIS BUILDING
>FROM 1930 TO 1950
>THE FRUITFUL YEARS
>OF HIS CIVIC LIFE
>AND LITERARY EXERTION

The first phase of those exertions began with an essay on Sinclair Lewis in 1930 and ended with a second, shorter essay on the same author in 1934. In between he published eight essays, five full-length translations (including, most importantly, that of *Moby-Dick* in 1932), four book reviews, prefaces for two translated books, and a "notice to readers" (*Avvertenza*) for another. All of these works—with one exception, the translation of James Joyce's *Portrait of the Artist as a Young Man*—involved American books, American authors, American culture. Apart from the essays and translations of these years, Pavese was composing poetry of surprising maturity and lasting value, but he supported himself with the modest fees paid for the book translations and articles in literary journals. He also tutored individual students and worked as a substitute teacher at several schools, including, briefly, D'Azeglio. Despite the affluence of many of his friends, money and economic status never appeared as driving forces in Pavese's life. That he never owned or rented his own apartment, nor had a car or any significant savings, did not seem to bother him. As an adult—his mother would not have permitted it in her lifetime—Pavese was known for the knockabout quality of his clothes and his indifference to what Italians call *bella figura*. Finances did worry him enough, however, to lead him to join the National Fascist Party in 1933. Given his preparation and mentality, teaching represented a logical, though not necessarily a first, choice for him as a permanent job, and by 1933 regulations required party membership for a position in any public school. For Pavese, joining the party was an apolitical act of expediency, and that it caused no friction between him and his friends, not even with Leone Ginzburg, shows they accepted it as such. In fact, his party membership proved useful to Giulio Einaudi; he asked Pavese in 1934 to assume the editorship of the journal *La Cultura*, which Einaudi had just taken over, because, as a party member, Pavese would attract less attention than anyone else in their circle of collaborators.

In the middle of this fruitful period Pavese met a Turin-born woman five years his elder named Battistina Pizzardo. No one had a greater impact on the remaining eighteen years of his life.

THREE
Tina

Battistina Pizzardo was first introduced to the literary world as a series of editorial asterisks in Pavese's published letters and the early editions of his diary; then as "the woman with the hoarse voice" to readers of the earliest biography of Pavese.[1] Pavese and all her other friends called her Tina.[2] Like Pavese, she came from a middle-class family, hers strongly Catholic. Her mother died when Tina was nine and her father, employed in the Turin office of one of Italy's large insurance companies, placed her in a strict, all-girls Catholic boarding school, which she attended for eight years. Then, after a year of private tutoring and preparatory courses, she matriculated at the University of Turin in 1920. Her father's support for her university education was, at the time, as Giovanni De Luna comments, "unusual given their social position."[3] So was her choice to study mathematics and physics; it meant, among other things, that she went from a religious secondary school with only female teachers and students to a secular university department overwhelmingly male in both categories. She coped well, loved her years at the university, and remembered them as a time of cultural and social exploration, learning, and, above all, friendships formed. Also at the university she made her first contact with communists. She received her *laurea* in 1925 and in March 1926 went to Rome to take the written parts of two competitive examinations for public school teaching positions.

While there, she made contact with the local communist students' cell and met one of its members, Altiero Spinelli, four years younger but already much more committed and politically active than Pizzardo. They began to spend time together. She found him interesting but notes in her memoirs that she was for him more an ideal than a love and claims she never truly fell in love with him. Nonetheless, in April 1927, while on a short break from her first teaching job, she spent two days with him in Milan, where they had, as she puts it, their "first intimacy." It turned out to be their last because Spinelli was arrested on June 3, 1927, in Milan and not long afterward sentenced by the Fascist Tribunale Speciale to sixteen years and eight months in jail. He ended up spending ten years in various Italian prisons and then six years in confino.[4] For Pizzardo, however, he figured for many years mostly as an obligation. She says that they eventually would have broken up because of their incompatible personalities, but with his imprisonment, and his refusal to petition for a pardon, she thought it her duty to maintain the fiction of their relationship. Spinelli's mother managed to convince the authorities that her son and Pizzardo were officially engaged and thus Pizzardo was able to visit him from time to time and they could write each other, though knowing full well all their letters were being censored.

For her first teaching job the Ministry of Education posted her to a liceo in Grosseto, a medium-sized city in southwest Tuscany, where she taught mathematics. She also became the secretary of the city's small communist cell—five members in all—and weekly met with a messenger from the regional center in Ancona, across the Apennines on the Adriatic coast. As happened to virtually all inscribed communists in Fascist Italy, she was put under surveillance and eventually arrested. In the summer of 1928 she was sentenced to a year in jail, three years of special surveillance, and barred for life from any public position, which included teaching in public schools. Because she had already served over ten months in jail awaiting trial, she was set free a month and a half later and returned to Turin in September 1928. Pavese at this time was entering his third year at the university. In the five years before they met, while Pavese was writing his Whitman thesis and his first essays and doing his first translations, Pizzardo was trying to figure out how to make a living. She found temporary work in various offices and tutored privately before the influential mother of a friend from boarding school found her a permanent job in Igea Marina, a seaside town on the Adriatic seven miles north of Rimini. There, from 1929 to 1932, she managed the year-round juvenile educational and recreational facility sponsored by the Fascist Women's Auxiliary of Milan (Colonia permanente della delegazione dei fasci femminili di Milano).

During these three years Tina realized she was beginning to lose both faith in communism and interest in Spinelli. When she returned to Turin in May 1932, in need of a new job, one of her schemes was to find a post teaching in Republican Spain. Nothing came of it, but during the search she met several Giustizia e Libertà (GL) members and, as Pizzardo puts it, "The invitations followed and dinner by dinner I came to know all the intellectual anti-Fascists of Turin."[5] One of them was Cesare Pavese. In 1932 Pizzardo had read "in a rapture" his translation of *Moby-Dick*. The two were introduced in the winter of 1932–33 at a social gathering in the house of one of her new GL friends, Barbara Allason, but they conversed only briefly and did not see each other again until July 31, 1933. On this Monday afternoon she went in a rowboat on the Po with a friend to whom she mentioned that she wanted to learn how to manage a punt. As it happened, when they returned to the dock they found Pavese about to set out in a punt. Thirty years later Pizzardo wrote, "I can still see him—tall, with a suntanned adolescent's body, bathing trunks and a felt cap pushed down right to his eyeglasses. (On the Po, only Pavese and the sand dredgers wore a hat with bathing trunks.)" She asked if he would take her out. "His face screwed up and you could see that he would have liked to say no, but didn't dare. 'Come on, quick, jump in.' And I right away jumped, and if I had fallen in, it would have pleased him greatly."[6]

Pizzardo and Pavese went punting on the Po five times that summer, three times with Pavese's good friend, Mario Sturani, twice alone. Just after their first outing, Pizzardo met Henek Rieser, a Polish citizen resident in Turin and a member of the Communist Party, as she, technically, still was. She would eventually marry Rieser, but at this point she was much more interested in Pavese than in the young comrade, and certainly more than she was in Altiero Spinelli, still in prison: "For the first time since Altiero I had met a man who had all the qualities: intelligence, education, character, physical presence, and he was a poet, while Altiero reproached me always for being more interested in art than philosophy. Not that I compared the two of them or projected anything into the future; but I did think of Pavese with wonder because a poet, an artist, was for me a kind of superman that I had never thought I would meet."[7]

After each of the first four outings Pavese asked her, "And so, when can you make it again?"—but not after the fifth, which occurred on August 18. When they climbed down from the tram in front of Turin's central station Pavese did not fix a time for another meeting. Pizzardo wished he had but says she was reluctant to take the initiative herself. Writing in 1962, she mused about her hesitation: "How many times have I since thought that that moment of hesitation decided our lives. If we had continued to see each other I would not have sought out comrade Henek and our lives might have taken who knows what turn."[8] But Pavese dropped out of sight; she continued to see Henek during that autumn and winter while also continuing to write Spinelli in prison. She was growing disillusioned with the Communist Party of which Henek was a faithful and, as she found out, intelligent member. He was, in Pizzardo's words, "a comrade who did not follow blindly the order of the day, but who analyzed and complained. Perhaps I had found the ideal friend! But, I am ashamed to confess (and I always feel stupid in remembering this), the thought came to me: why is he not falling in love with me?"[9]

That was not a problem she had with Pavese. Pavese and Pizzardo met again on January 25, 1934, and, somewhat to her surprise, Pizzardo found Pavese lively and happy to see her. He suggested that they get together so he could teach her English, and two days later they started to see each other virtually every day. Not only did they read together *A Farewell to Arms* and *Spoon River Anthology*, but they talked about themselves—and Pizzardo found, again somewhat to her surprise, that Pavese treated her as an equal and said he liked her because of her easygoing, unconventional ways.

By March she realized she enjoyed Pavese's company a great deal, but more as a friend than as a potential husband or lover. She was still seeing Henek, who seemed to have no romantic interest in her. Pavese, on the other hand, was falling deeply and rather dramatically in love. She tried to put him off, saying that he had to accept her as a friend or not see her at all; he agreed and she called the arrangement their "friendship pact." The pact did not last; in April 1934 they made love for the first time. Pizzardo remembers the event as not changing her essential feelings about Pavese, that she still wanted him as a friend, not a lover. She also remembers that his infatuation with her consoled her for Henek's seeming indifference. Their first sex signified much more for Pavese, as Pizzardo's own account (the only one we have) makes clear: "It was an evening at his place. Lights out, window open to the sky. Kisses that broke our pact of friendship (and avenged me on the other). And then a moment of clear folly, of abandonment. And then I came back to my senses and while I was happy to realize that nothing important had happened, he is already on his knees and says that *now* we have to get married and we will be ever so happy."[10]

She goes on to describe this second phase of their relationship, the one that lasted from early 1934 until Pavese's (and her less consequential) arrest in May 1935:

> If our friends-only pacts had to be renewed (and they were, more than once), it was because of my fear that Pavese would do something drastic; that, and to distance myself from the other [Rieser], led me to break them.
>
> Useless to continue; it's an old story: a heart can sincerely divide itself between a love that causes only sadness, even if it is the only one that counts, and a love that makes you feel young and matchless, and provides, too, the absolving sense of being set free.
>
> Indeed, the usual story, with one small difference: the discovery that the love that gives you the sense of being set free, etc., is hopelessly . . . well, let's say elusive.
>
> My elusive love called me "Tina," "Treasure," "honey" [all English in original], and I called him "Cesarino" and [my friend] Ebe marveled that the diminutive did not offend him.[11]
>
> Cesarino: He was at that time a tall, good-looking youth, thin, with hair that curled up in a pompadour on his low forehead, a smooth face, rose-tinted light brown skin, perfect teeth. I liked his in-love eyes, his poetry, his conversation so intelligent that I became intelligent in turn; I liked the sense of fraternity that coming from the same kind of people gave us, as did our having both spent our infancy in towns in the Langhe, and I liked other similar things, too.
>
> But how could you take him seriously when he talked of marriage and then cried when I said no; or when he tried to act like a tough guy and would get excited and curse, only, like

a bad actor, getting everything wrong; or when he would try to get me to break our friends-only pact by threatening to kill himself?

He had put himself blindly in my hands and I did not want to hurt him. I kept stubbornly trying to make him a friend only, with no success, but, I thought, who knows, after one broken friendship pact after another, maybe I could finally convince him.

And then, the hours that we two spent together, in a café, in a boat on the Po, or at my house with Carlottina, with Ebe, sometimes Estella, were the only happy hours of my harried and hopeless life. Those who knew him later remember him as dour, full of himself, disparaging; they cannot imagine how easy and enchanting it was to be with him when he was young.

I remember so often the delight of our conversations that I ask myself, what on earth did we talk about?

A point, any point whatsoever might set us off; something like, "What a lovely day," or "You've got a new hat," could lead to a conversation interwoven with imagination, with memories, with discoveries. And because we were young each of us found real interest, and wonder, and admiration for what passed through the other's mind.

I had as my mantra that summer: All's fair in love. I repeated to myself that I did not have to answer to anyone. I felt—not remorse, only a sense of fastidiousness, a certain unease, and that only every now and then.

I remember that above all I regretted that I could not meet Altiero face to face so I could explain to him what to me seemed so clear, logical, correct.[12]

The spring of 1934 turned into summer, a summer which Pizzardo remembered fondly.

And then came "the beautiful summer" [*La bella estate*—the title of the 1949 trilogy that won Pavese the Strega Prize in 1950]. His memory of it seems to me to pervade some of his works and I too remember it as a happy summer.

From the middle of July to the end of the August holidays I had few lessons to give, and I enjoyed the sense of vacation in Turin in the summer, when in the heat and haze the city seems to stop working and only the hills and the rivers—the Po, Stura, Dora, Sangone—have any life.

Entire days in a punt. Go up the Po as far as Moncalieri. Overcome the small rapids and come on to the Sangone. Midday stops and, when the sun was low, playful games on the wooded banks. The two of us reading together under the ancient trees of the Parco Michelotti in the morning, or at my place in the afternoon with the Venetian blinds down and the currents of air that puffed out the curtains.

We were sometimes at home with friends, but more often there was just Carlottina, she too on vacation after school at Valtournanche. She seemed almost a young boy and she did not intimidate Pavese, and when she was there he was at his best and became again what I had believed him to be before the tears and the histrionic tirades.

It was the time when he was revising, reordering, and choosing those of his poems to be printed [in what would be the Solaria edition of *Lavorare stanca*, his first published book]. I was flattered and very embarrassed when he would ask me my opinion. I was supposed to decide if a poem would or would not be included in the collection (painful decisions: from that time on my interest in poetry, which had been lively, fell away). I had to decide between two adjectives or a word's place in a line, and because he accepted my choices without questions I felt responsible toward the future readers. I did not understand that he put his faith in me only when either of the choices would have worked just as well and he could have decided by tossing a coin.

Happy hours, because it was enough to turn the conversation to the beauty of his poetry, or to his "genius," or his future glory to make him forget his impossible love for me. He was very vain, Cesarino; my girlfriends and I laughed a little about him and said to ourselves that maybe all artists are like that.

I felt so good with Pavese and his poetry that summer and I was always so unhappy with the other [Henek] that, at times, in a rebellious fit, I'd say to Carlottina, "I'll marry Cesarino and that'll be that." (I never said that to him, however.) Adored by him on his knees in the beginning, then, when he got over that, a life from hell. This is what waited for me and almost explained again why I found this elusive love so repellent.

After the August holidays I began again with my many private lessons, and during them Carlottina and Pavese would be in the other room, she sewing something for me or reading while he would be mulling over a poem, fussing with his front curl and folding and refolding into thin strips the paper he was writing on.[13]

The beautiful summer, regardless of how much Pavese and Pizzardo both enjoyed it, turned into a rather different winter and spring. Pizzardo tells a most unflattering story about Pavese involving a trip to the mountains for the year-end holidays of 1934. Tina and a group of friends were going to Cheneil, a mountain resort in the Valle d'Aosta. Pavese actively disliked the mountains and skiing, but he asked to join the group because, says Pizzardo, he did not want to spend so many days apart from her.[14]

> I would have preferred to leave him in Turin because I knew that in a large group he liked to make himself unpleasant. But he wanted to come no matter what and we had to work to equip him. Perhaps it was the too-tight shoes (an old pair that I had around the house) that made Pavese unbearable to everyone that week, not to mention ridiculous.
> At Cheneil we were staying in rooms of five-six beds and only the women's room was heated by a small stove, and badly at that. That it was often colder in the cabin than outside was for most of us, eager to explore the nearby mountains, something to laugh about.
> Wrapped up in a scarf with only his long, red, cold nose showing, his hat pulled down to his eyeglasses, and the most woeful of tragic expressions on his face, Pavese stayed fixed outside the door of the women's room, his back to the wall, so when we opened from inside the door would almost hit him in the face. With tearful eyes he would cry from time to time, "Tina!" An abandoned dog whining, that's what he seemed.
> With a whine he saw us leave in the morning, and with the same whine he greeted us on returning. In an entire week, never a word, never a smile. Thinking about it, I am amazed that no one in our group, or in the other groups there, paid any attention to him. Coming and going, there were those who bumped into him, those who stepped on his feet, all without thinking about it. It could have been because the astute Bastiani, the father of two young boys, had suggested that if we ignore him it would pass.
> To me it seemed that once he adopted the role of the beaten-down dog he did it with too much gusto to be pretending.
> When we returned to Turin, he returned to normal, but we saw each other less frequently because I was so taken up with my work. (But he was nonetheless capable of getting himself up at five to see me off on the six o'clock train for Ivrea [where she taught in a private teachers' college].) I was able to enforce the friends-only rule for longer periods now, perhaps because I remembered that whining in Cheneil.[15]

On May 15, 1935, Pavese, who professed no interest in politics, and Pizzardo, who always had such an interest, were both arrested along with over a hundred others in a long-planned police roundup of virtually everyone the police thought was involved with Giustizia e Libertà in Turin. From a police point of view it made perfect sense to include Pavese in this grand roundup. They had every reason to suspect that a pupil and friend of Monti (also arrested), a close friend of Mila (also arrested), Ginzburg (already in jail), and other known GL agitators, the managing editor of *La Cultura*, a journal known for its anti-regime tone, and the lover of Pizzardo, a convicted communist, might be actively involved in anti-Fascist activities. Their discovery of letters in Pavese's home addressed to Pizzardo from Bruno Maffi, a known GL conspirator in Milan, provided more evidence to produce at his various interrogations and then at his appearance before a special court in Rome.

On May 15 both Pavese and Pizzardo ended up in the Turin jail. Pizzardo had entered there the first time seven years ago, and this time, too, as the grand-niece of two of their oldest and most beloved colleagues, she was treated well by the nuns in charge of the women's section. She convinced two different officials who interrogated her that she had nothing to do with the GL movement, a task made easier by her communist past. After six weeks of jail, she was set free, with the relatively light sentence of two years of "admonition," a mildly onerous type of "special surveillance" which included a personal curfew. Pavese, however, did not get off so lightly. He was transferred from Turin to the Rome prison and in July 1935 he was interrogated to determine where his case should be heard. He learned soon afterwards that he was going to be tried before the Rome Commissione provinciale per l'assegnazione a confino (Provincial Commission for Assignment to Internal Exile), which as the title indicates was a provincial entity, separate from the national special tribunal the Fascists had established to judge anti-regime crimes, the Tribunale speciale per la difesa dello stato (Special Tribunal for the Defense of the State). The distinction relieved Pavese because it meant the worst he could expect was five years of confino, the maximum sentence the commission could then impose. The special tribunal, on the other hand, could impose any sentence, even death. The commission found him "a danger to national order for having undertaken in Turin and Milan political activities designed to cause damage to the national interests" and sentenced him to three years of confino.[16] While the Milan connection—Maffi's letters to Tina—probably added to the number of years of his sentence, Pavese nonetheless got off lightly compared to some of his friends arrested the same day as he: Mila and Monti were sent before the Tribunale speciale, which sentenced Mila to seven and Monti to five years in prison.

Many countries have used internal exile as punishment for political crimes, but in the twentieth century no country other than the Soviet Union used it as actively as Italy did during the Fascist years. The laws sanctioning confino originated in nineteenth-century pre-Fascist liberal Italy; *domicilio coatto* goes back to legislation approved in 1865.[17] The Fascists introduced new legislation in 1926 and used the mechanism more than any administration before or after. Between 1926 and 1943, when Mussolini fell, the various provincial commissions sent 12,330 prisoners to confino.[18] Pavese became one of them on July 15, 1935. Using the laconic language of telegrams, two days later he informed his sister, "Assigned three years confino don't know where."[19] The where turned out to be the small town of Brancaleone Calabro. After an overnight stop in the Naples jail, he arrived there on the afternoon of August 4, 1935, accompanied by two policemen who led the handcuffed Pavese past the many Sunday strollers to the local police station in the town hall.

Brancaleone, physically, has certain similarities to Santo Stefano Belbo. They have roughly the same number of inhabitants, both lie on state highways, and for each the highway is the town's main street. In both, men (never women) sit outside the town's main bar and watch the cars and people go by. Both towns sit at the base of hills and in both the main street parallels the water, with the bulk of the houses in each town on the side away from the water. In each the railroad tracks are near the water and the two stations look alike. The most significant difference is that the water that runs through Santo Stefano is the modest Belbo River while Brancaleone lies directly on the Ionian Sea, which separates Italy from Greece. Figuratively speaking, Brancaleone is situated just around and under the toe of the boot of Italy, six miles north of the southernmost point on the Italian mainland. Pavese found himself as far from Turin as he could imagine both geographically and psychologically. The prospect of thirty-six months among strangers in an alien part of Italy discouraged him deeply, as did the fear of losing Tina.

Pavese started taking care of himself as best he could, something he had not had to do before thanks to his mother and then his sister. He was not joking when he wrote to Maria that "I fix my own meals, which means that I eat cold stuff. It's a terrible thing to set up as a family without a family."[20] On his fourth day there he requested in writing the five lire per day subsidy the law gave the Ministry of the Interior discretion to award. The ministry eventually granted that plus fifty lire a month for rent, which covered the forty-five he was paying. The subsidy meant he no longer had to depend totally on his sister for money while at Brancaleone. He soon established a routine that lasted until the cold weather came:

> I get up early each morning when they deliver the milk. I boil my quarter-liter on the alcohol stove because if I wait till noon it curdles. Then I go to the [hotel/café] Roma for a coffee. I stay there till ten trying to read or write poetry but it is so hot and the ambience so different that I get little done. I take a look at the *Gazzetta del Popolo* [a Turin newspaper] to see if there have been any disasters in the mountains.[21]
>
> Then I go for a swim. The salt water gives me a kind of neuralgia in one ear and so I can't go underwater anymore. So I've lost one more of my pleasures. When I come back I do my shopping, bread and fruit. At noon I drink the milk I boiled and either the bread and fruit or an egg fried in oil. Then I try to sleep, but I cannot so I try to read a bit till four. I go out then and at five present myself at the town hall, and then I go to the town center and try to write poetry or to chat but it bores me. If I haven't already spent too much that day, I go for a beer. I come home at seven and fix my supper, the same as my lunch. I wash the dishes. I loaf around in or near the house till eight, trying to write poetry, and then I come back and fall into bed, but not without taking first a quinine pill (which the marshal [the police chief] tells me is a good precaution).
>
> From seven in the evening on, the cockroaches take over my kitchen and little pantry area. You can't do anything about them. Insecticides fatten them and they piss on roach killer. They love to lick the saucepan where I boil the milk and the frying pan as well. They are as big as your thumb. They disappear with the dawn light. Since I live on the ground floor I got a chicken to come into my pantry and closed her in there so that she would devour the roaches. Instead, she upended my alcohol stove and ate a bunch of grapes I had been saving.
>
> Once or twice a week I have lunch at the Roma to put some meat back on my bones. And yet, it is incredible how much I spend even living this kind of life. The first couple of days it was always twenty or thirty lire a day (rent, a few necessary things, deposits, stamps, etc.) and now I cannot get by on less than five lire a day. I keep a daily register of my spending, but the

money goes anyway. In the evening I do okay because between the smell of the alcohol stove, the smell and crackling of the cockroaches, and the heat, I don't have much appetite anyway and so I save a considerable amount.[22]

Pavese had to request permission to write or receive correspondence from anyone other than Maria, and gradually the list expanded. Knowing he would never receive approval, he never asked for permission to send Tina letters, but he did write her postcards, one on the twenty-fifth of each month to commemorate the day of the month they first kissed and he declared his love for her. He managed to get one letter to her via a student in Brancaleone who was going to Turin. It was a short letter, a love letter, in which he told her that May 13 (the last time they saw each other before being arrested) was his "last human memory" and that his sentence was not "the official one, it is you." He ended it, "I thank you for all the thoughts you have had for me. For you, I have only one and it will never end."[23] Lorenzo Mondo, who edited the first volume of Pavese's letters, worked in this case from a draft of that letter Pavese left behind. Pizzardo confirms having received the letter from the student and says it did not surprise her that Pavese had kept a draft, because "he was the kind of man who keeps a diary, who notes everything he spends no matter how small, and besides he was obsessive about dates, about memories."[24]

A few weeks after writing that letter, Pavese made the first entry in the diary that after his death would be published using the title he gave it, *Il mestiere di vivere*, a work that forms an important part of his corpus as literature and as self-reflection.[25] Indeed, Sergio Pautasso contends that it is "the central text of Pavese's work."[26] *Mestiere* is one of those Italian words that often vex English-language translators because, like its French equivalent *métier*, its meaning depends on context and shading. It can mean simply "job," and the book's two English-language translators have used that or a variation. Richard M. Koffler entitled his annotated translation *The Job of Living*, and Alma Murch her virtually noteless version *This Business of Living*, which, however, her U.S. publisher changed to *The Burning Brand*.[27] *Mestiere*, however, can also mean a skilled craft that one learns through apprenticeship and practice, the way, for example, Pavese's good friend Pinolo Scaglione learned carpentry. "The Craft of Living" implies something different from job or business, though it overlaps with both. I believe Pavese intended something close to "craft" and that the book records his efforts, generally unsuccessful in his view, to learn the craft of living.

Most of the entries he made in Brancaleone involve ruminations on literature and his own poetry. They give no indication of the kind of life he was leading there, nor, with a few exceptions, do they mention Tina, and then only indirectly. We learn much more from his letters, from "Terra d'esilio" ("Land of Exile"), the short story he wrote four months after returning to Turin, and from the novel he began in 1938, *Il carcere* (literally, "The Jail"; translated into English as *The Political Prisoner*).[28] Using a writer's fiction or poetry as a biographical source can be problematic, but it is often justified with Pavese. As Ettore De Giorgis put it in his influential 1980 retrospective essay on Pavese, "with few writers indeed is there such a close connection between life and works as there is with him."[29]

The people in Brancaleone treated Pavese well; he found them much warmer and more welcoming than he expected. The marshal in charge of the local office of the national police (*carabinieri*), Pavese's official supervisor, treated him leniently. Within the limits of the town Pavese could go wherever he pleased, including up to the small hamlet of Brancaleone Superiore. He earned a little money tutoring some students, including the marshal's son. He had enough money to rent adequate quarters and to pay for having his laundry done. Still, it was a miserable time for him, physically and emotionally. In November the weather turned chilly but remained just as damp as rains set in. Pavese's chronic asthma worsened and to judge from his letters he rarely got a full night's sleep. To his old friend Sturani he wrote, "the winter has already begun in the form of rain, torrential winds, and nighttime humidity, which are like pepper for my asthma."[30] To Monti, "Keep in mind that I wake up some six times every night and every night I begin a fight for my breath."[31] The pipe was Pavese's preferred method of smoking and, despite the asthma, he continued to smoke heavily at Brancaleone. It was one of his few pleasures there and he noted in his diary in December, "Life without smoking is like smoke without a roast" [La vita senza fumo è come il fumo senza l'arrosto].[32] Stefano, the protagonist in *Il carcere*, forms a sexual liaison with the woman who cleans his room, Elena, but in reality, in a Calabrian town as small as Brancaleone, that would have been well-nigh impossible for Pavese.

Reading proved a major consolation. Pavese's letters are full of requests for books and thanks for having received them; in his seven months of confino he records reading dozens of books. He also wrote about four hundred lines of poetry. He read much more than he wrote because for him writing poetry or fiction meant resolving psychic tension, while studying meant forgetting that such tension existed. As he noted at the end of December 1935, "Of the two things, writing poetry and studying, I find greater and more constant comfort in the second. I do not forget, however, that I like studying with an eye toward writing poetry. But in the end, poetry is always an open wound through which the life blood flows out."[33] He also corrected the proofs for a small volume of his poetry (forty-five poems in a book measuring roughly 6 by 9 inches [15 x 23 cm]) that the Florentine publisher Solaria published in 1936 under the title *Lavorare stanca*. (The title means, literally, to work tires. The collection has been translated into English three times, separately as *Hard Labor*, as *Work's Tiring* in a collection of his complete poems, and without translation of the title in a selection of his poetry.)[34]

As the winter wore on Pavese became more discouraged, especially after he learned on February 3, 1936, that the ministry had denied a pardon he had requested. A letter he wrote to his sister about a month after the pardon was denied catches well his melancholy:

> Dear Maria,
>
> Ugly thing, memory.
> I look out at night and see Orion, beautiful, limpid, and it reminds me of a book read in other times.
> From my window I breathe in the smell of sap and I remember when I went to give lessons to Corradino at the end of Via Nizza two years ago.
> A train passes and it comes to mind that tomorrow morning at four another one will be going through the pines of Viaraggio [the train route to Turin].
> I look at the mountain in the distance and I shiver with cold thinking back to the Christmas at Cheneil (three days then—now three years).
> I get undressed for bed and I cry for my naked body, so youthfully lovely and so alone.

I go out in the morning as early as I am allowed and I remember when I used to go to a café at dawn, smoking my pipe and waiting [for Tina].

I read in "Gazzetta del Popolo" what's playing at the various theaters and I imagine that I'm watching a film at the Statuto, the Alpi, the Ideal . . .

I touch the mole on my cheek to make sure I am really me.

I sing to myself "Carogna carogna" [an Italian jingle].

I look back on the times when I was translating Moby-Dick and everything was still to come.

I remember when I would not let myself sleep at night because of a little jealousy—I dared give it that name—and I did not know that absence feels like the bite of a shark, like starving, like cancer.

I remember how angry I got when anyone wanted to come with me when I went boating on the Po and I regret my past unhappiness.

I find myself incredibly stupid to have believed in the past, even for a second, that individual isolation was happiness.

I spend all day reciting these litanies and others without end.[35]

Pavese had felt nervous about requesting the pardon because he feared Tina would think badly of him for doing so, a fear he expressed in a letter to a mutual friend that he knew would reach Tina.[36] Also, through a letter that has not survived or through some other mechanism, Pavese got his sister to ask Tina directly what she would think if he requested a pardon. It would not bother her at all, she told Maria; every person has to make his own political decisions and she knew each person had a different situation.[37] Pavese not only worried about Tina's opinion of him, he worried about her in general. While still in Rome awaiting his hearing he wrote his sister, with conscious irony, "Tell the young lady that I think of her always, indeed, in the situation I'm in, it would be hard not to think of her."[38] Beginning in February 1936 his anxiety reached a crescendo amply documented in a series of letters and telegrams he sent Maria. On February 23 he wrote, "I don't give a fig for anything any more. I only want news of the young lady."[39] The next day he sent Maria a telegram: "How is Tina? Telegraph urgently."[40] Five days later he wrote Maria, anticipating some of the language of his longer letter quoted above: "I continue to receive nothing. You and the Almighty Father are working together: he sends me asthma and you heartsickness. If she knew that absence feels like the bite of a shark, like starving, like cancer, Tina would write me. I had sent her on

January 24 a copy of my book [*Lavorare stanca*]. I ask her for nothing more than a postcard with her signature. February 25 was her birthday."[41] Pavese was here sending a coded message to Tina via Maria; February 25 was not her birthday, it was the day in 1934 that Pavese first kissed Tina and declared his love for her and he wanted to make sure Tina knew he remembered it. On March 3, Pavese wrote Maria: "You ask me (February 23) for more news and seem to be offended. But you don't even think about relieving the torture I feel every moment by a note in Tina's hand. That she thought my poetry beautiful was the last thing on my mind when I sent it to her. I would not have believed a man could suffer so much without going mad."[42]

Maria had apparently answered his telegram of February 24 because on March 5 he wrote, "Dear Maria, I did receive your telegram of February 25 and as I have already told you, I would like something more specific. I have heard nothing from Tina for a long time and I don't know if she is angry with me. I continue to wait."[43] His letter of March 12 shows his increasing frustration:

> You are a real pain in the ass. I couldn't care less about Frasinelli, about that prick Franco, and whether or not I eat at the hotel.
> When are you going to finish pretending not to receive my requests for news, news, news, and a postcard signed by Tina?
> And you still have the nerve to write asking if I need anything. For a month I've not asked for anything else.
> Confino is nothing. It's relatives that make one tear his hair out.
> I wish a cancer on all of you.[44]

One day later, March 13, he telegraphed Maria: "Telegram 25 not satisfactory. Telegraph urgently real news Tina."[45] He did not have to send any more letters or telegrams because within days he saw Tina again himself. On March 15 he received the totally unexpected news that he had been pardoned; on March 19 he arrived back in Turin.

He had never received any real news from Tina because while he was away she had made up her mind to marry Henek Rieser. Before she could marry Rieser she felt she had to tell Spinelli, but not Pavese, because she "worried about Altiero, not Pavese, to whom I had never given any hopes."[46] She also says she informed Pavese that she would never marry him via his sister Maria, though Maria did not pass the message on to Pavese.[47]

Pavese learned about Pizzardo's coming wedding from either friends or Maria, not from Tina, because when he came to see her soon after his return he already knew about it.

> He was sad but strangely passive. Supplications, yes, some truly touching, but never any of the outbursts you'd expect from someone who felt betrayed. In fact, I thought, he knows he has no right. I was always (within the limits of decency) frank with him and I never gave him any hopes.
> It seemed that he had accepted the proper role of friend. As always, it was easy to confide in him. No, I was not a trembling and happy bride; I was rather sad instead because I knew that I was only "cared about" [*voluta bene*] and not loved [*amata*].[48]

As she remembers, they met three or four times in the month between his return home and her wedding on April ninth.[49] During that period, "I well remember his expression of suffering and of tenderness, and his tone of slow and deep sincerity. It was as though we had been separated ten years, not ten months, and now we found each other, me older and wiser, he still young and in love with me as he was before but aware of the barrier that life had placed between us."[50]

She says also that Pavese confided in her about his eight months in Brancaleone, "completely and sincerely." He could not, she believes, ever lie to her. And thus she can lay to rest certain "legends" that portray an unfaithful Pavese:

> He loved no other women in those months nor even had any desire for them. He saw the girl, who according to legend gave her love to him, only from a distance and never spoke with her. The legend was started by those who understand little about his books and nothing about him if they could believe that with his heart first full of hope and love, and then anxiety, and then desperation for *her*, Pavese could have given in to the desire for another. It's been accepted by those who do not know how intensely a poet can experience feelings created from memory and fantasy.
> I say this for love of the truth because I always preferred to believe, and still today prefer to believe, in love for another. I wanted him to fall in love with someone else and understand that we two were made to be friends.[51]

Pizzardo ends the chapter in her memoirs dealing with the pre-wedding month with another unflattering story about Pavese. This one involves her girlfriends making sure to stay with Pavese at all times so he would not do something desperate, i.e., kill himself. "One picked him up in the morning and a few hours later passed him off to another, and then to another, till late in the evening when he was returned to his sister. To be precise, they were not there to follow him but to make sure he was never left alone." One of those friends, Pizzardo adds, still remembers "with irritation" that "having accompanied Pavese, who wanted to get drunk, to a tavern and having some wine with him, she had also to help him afterwards while he vomited forth wine and threats."[52]

Natalia Ginzburg also remembered Pavese as sad and resigned in the spring of 1936. Her future husband, Leone, had just returned from jail and his continuing special surveillance involved a personal curfew that kept him at home with his mother and sister from dusk to dawn. He could receive visitors, however, and both Pavese and Natalia came frequently. He was "very melancholy," she writes, "having suffered a disappointment in love." Pavese was visiting Leone not to cheer Ginzburg up, but because "otherwise he would not have known how to pass the evenings and he could not bear to spend evenings alone." Sometimes on these evenings Pavese would barely talk and "smoked his pipe, all evening, silently," while "other times curling his hair with his finger he would talk about himself." Around midnight Pavese would leave and walk down the broad avenue in front of Ginzburg's building, "tall, pale, his coat collar up, the unlit pipe between his healthy white teeth, with his long, rapid gait and sullen shoulders."[53]

Pizzardo believes that while he was still violently in love with her, Pavese had in fact begun to accept the reality of her marriage, and, despite the histrionics and thrown-up wine, would have gotten over her if not for her own later behavior. As she put it, "If later—but still much too soon—I had not sought him out, I would have left no trace in Pavese's life other than one poem dedicated to me and a couple of lines in his diary and perhaps in his memory. I would have remained the first and the kindest of his unhappy loves."[54] Pavese's April 1936 diary entries, particularly that of the day after her wedding, make it doubtful that even if they had never seen each other again he would have considered her kind. She is right, however, that what happened afterwards affected him profoundly and colored forever his memory of her.

When Tina married Rieser she says her life became calmer but she still found Henek to be more caring than loving. She felt she loved him more than he did her and she felt as often depressed as happy. In July 1937, fifteen months into the marriage, she was alone in Turin because Rieser had gone to Poland due to his father's death; Rieser had not written and Tina feared he might have taken up with an old girlfriend. She felt alone and anxious in their "empty home." She writes:

> Sunday, July 4th, late afternoon, I start telephoning to find someone to go out with, to chat with. Useless because no one's in Turin.
> I dial Pavese's number.
> Did I think about it, hesitate and then with beating heart decide to do it? No, I remember nothing like that. I believe I just did it—without thinking twice about it. This expression that I use so often in evoking the past is revealing: to obey in a snap a sudden impulse without worrying about the consequences is in my nature, even though at other times I can be reflective and rational. And, despite all the bad things that had happened to me, I still had the taste for action, adventure, life.
> I dialed that number and was ready to hang up without a word if the sister answered or if Pavese on hearing my voice took offense or whined. Instead, he hit just the right note "Oh, Tina! It's you. What a pleasure. How come . . ." I remember the words, I remember the tone, which was what I wanted, that of friendship.[55]

Pavese was more laconic in his diary: "On July 4 Tina returned."[56]

Tina thought that they had parted friends and she found it natural that "after fifteen months without seeing each other and more than two years since the last violation of the friends-only rule" he would be friendly again, that he would be "the only true friend that fate had given me."

> We met that evening after dinner and walked the streets near my house talking with renewed abandon, very gay, bantering. I remember that we sat in a field among new houses (now the Piazza Risorgimento), and it seemed to me the field was immense, that the houses had moved farther out to give us space to talk under the stars. Alone, just the two of us, gaily confiding in each other just like the days of my first English lessons.
> The next two days we chatted by phone; on the seventh we took an early morning walk in the hills. We had dinner together on the eighth and ninth. He was scheduled to leave on the tenth for Ancona for a month's vacation at his friend Monferrini's house, but now he did not want to go.

> He wanted me to divorce Henek and marry him.
>
> I had thought of divorce often in those first months of marriage but then and always I knew I did not want to marry Pavese. To live unloved with a man I love, or live free and alone, these were the alternatives.
>
> He left on the tenth; on the eleventh I receive a telegram, on the thirteenth a long letter by special delivery, on the fourteenth a telephone call.
>
> Henek returned the fifteenth and I told him that I had seen Pavese again and had spent a lot of time with him.[57]

To her annoyance, Rieser did not create a scene or even raise his voice. He said he wasn't hurt, just annoyed, and that was all. Tina thought his reaction so mild that maybe he really was still involved with the old girlfriend back in Poland. Then Pavese cut short his vacation and returned to Turin on the eighteenth. On the nineteenth they met in a café and the old pattern began to reassert itself.

> We go well together, we care about each other, we always have thousands of things to say to each other, we understand each other instantly, we admire each other—from which he concludes, let's get married, and I, let's remain friends.
>
> Not even then did I have the courage to tell him, "Do you not know or are you pretending not to know that love, do you understand what I mean, love is out of the question? We have everything needed to be happy together, and have for some time now, so long as you leave out—you know what. Why do you pretend not to understand? And besides, it's a great deal that you want from me."
>
> Is it only because of this that I don't want him? For this in itself and also because of the way it reflects on his character. And is it not true that I am in love with Henek? I am in love with Henek, but it's a love that humiliates me and makes me suffer and from which I don't know how to pull myself away. If Pavese had been a normal man, a man and not an eternal adolescent, I would have in desperation trusted him to tear the other man from my heart, from my mind, from my life.[58]

During this phase, on August 3, 1937, to be precise, Pavese entered remarks in his diary which, while Giovanni De Luna considers them "stunning in their banality," are certainly understandable in view of what was going on between him and Pizzardo.[59] "A woman who is not stupid sooner or later meets a wreck of a man whom she tries to save. Sometimes she succeeds. But a woman who is not stupid sooner or later meets a healthy man and reduces him to a wreck. She always succeeds."[60] While Pizzardo is silent on the subject, her renewed relationship with Pavese also involved sex, at least until August thirteenth. On that day, Pizzardo decided to break with him for good.

> Finally, on the thirteenth of August of '37 (at a table in a café in Porta Palazzo), to put an end to his unending insistence, I find the courage to tell him what for compassion I had kept silent about, that which he knew and pretended not to know, that which he never wanted to hear.
> "It's the end of everything," he says.
> I respond, "any day that you want to, we can again be friends, and only that." And we parted.[61]

Piecing Pizzardo's enigmatic remarks together with several of Pavese's diary entries from 1937 and 1938, it becomes clear that what she had kept silent about "for compassion" and what Pavese "never wanted to hear" was that Pavese had never satisfied her sexually. August 13—a Friday in 1937—became a negative talismanic date for him, signifying sexual failure and failure in general. At the end of 1937, for example, he wrote, "My long and secret shame was forced into the open this year. In this new 1934 there is in addition August 13. And yet I am still alive. A miracle, no?"[62] And on the very next day, "your August 13 will come also in art."[63] And on March 27, 1938, "And don't forget August 13. Think about all the nights that she *came* with him. This happened, and happened, and they told you and it will happen again."[64]

Pavese's sexual dysfunction, *ejaculatio praecox*, premature ejaculation, seems to have had a mental, not physical origin. Bona Alterocca, a generally reliable source, reports that after his death, Pavese's friend and doctor, Francesco Rubino, told her that "Pavese was perfectly normal, in all ways."[65] She thought it one of Pavese's greatest misfortunes that he did not understand the nature of his problem and that Pizzardo did not care to help him.

> Pavese was a perfectly normal man. Not a great lover—romantic, emotion caused him to hurry, sometimes to malfunction. He confided this to his friends, and women who knew him intimately were aware of it.[66] There were those who understood and those who did not. There were women who even though they understood did not want to know about it and broke off, leaving him, looking for another whom naturally they found.

> That he encountered one of those kinds of women when he was young was Pavese's doom. He became convinced that *all* women were like her and that he was worthless, destined never to form a lasting relationship with *any* woman.
> Every once in a while he let it go, believing that he had learned what to do, and he smiled again. Then, at the first difficulty, he fell back again into pessimism and he masochistically took pleasure in what he had convinced himself was an irreparable deficiency. An experienced man, as many thought he was, would have easily adapted to the situation. Not him; he had lived little and badly in the real world; he did not understand.[67]

In October 1937 Pavese wrote Pizzardo, she says, a "declaration of implacable hatred (letter destroyed)."[68] It was also in October that Pavese wrote in his diary, "That in love one nail drives out another may be true for women for whom the particular problem is to find another nail to put in their hole, but for men, who have only one nail, it is less true."[69] Despite the hate letter and these musings, Pavese phoned Pizzardo on November 5 and "with a calm tone" asked to see her. Pizzardo says she thought she had finally won the battle.

> If he wants to see me now, after everything cruel I had said to him two months ago, it means he does not want to lose the bond of affection and confidence that, beyond love, unites us. That's what I want to believe.
> The first meeting takes place at a café on November eighth. "Better friends than nothing" he says again as before and then as before he wants more. We keep meeting now because I feel sorry for him, because I really do enjoy myself with him, because his stubborn love consoles me, because this way I can get back at Henek for his silences.[70]

Five days after that meeting, Pavese wrote to himself, "A man does not cry for the love that betrayed him, but for the humiliation of not having merited confidence."[71] And so it went for another eight months, eleven months in total after it was supposed to be "the end of everything." The only difference in their relationship before August 13 and after November 8 was the lack of sex. Breaking the "friends-only" pact now meant only that Pavese started imploring her again to marry him: "Periods of meeting and pleasant hours alternated with ruptures that I, with relief, thought definite. If after every rupture I ceded again to his request to see me it was because he threatened me, 'If you don't come, I'll kill myself,' or 'I'll kill him.' I have a saying that words kill no one, but sometimes, still now, I get a little afraid."[72]

During these months Pavese filled his diary with entries that revealed his torment, bitterness, and occasional hope. Some examples:

> November 25, 1937: I write: T., have mercy. And then?
>
> November 28, 1937: The only thing that counts is to have the woman in bed and at home. All the rest is crap, simply crap.
>
> December 4, 1937: After so much foolishness on your part she has returned and has embraced you. Shouldn't you get down on your knees and thank the God you don't believe in?
>
> December 23, 1937: Does not the boy who passed days and evenings among men and women, knowing vaguely but not believing that it was reality, suffering, in sum, because sex existed, presage the man who passes among men and women, knowing, believing that it is the only reality, suffering cruelly because of his mutilation? This sense that takes and breaks my heart, this vertigo that rips and crushes my chest is something that not even the distress of April caused me . . .
>
> Neither disappointment nor jealousy ever gave me this *vertigo of the blood*. [Emphasis in original.] For that you need impotence, the conviction that no woman enjoys fucking with me and never will (we are what we are) and thus this agony. Well, at least I can suffer without being ashamed—it's no longer love that causes my pain. But this is truly a pain that kills all energy. If one is not a man, if he does not possess power in that organ, if he must pass among women without being able to demand anything, how can he go on, how can he bear up? Was ever suicide more justified? . . .
>
> And she thinks herself demeaned because—to amuse herself—she does some little pleasant thing. And she tells me this after August 13. And she doesn't cry. And "she cares for me!" Give me a break!
>
> December 25, 1937: If fucking was not the most important thing in life, Genesis would not begin with it.
>
> Naturally everyone says, "It doesn't matter. That's not the only thing in life. Life is full of variety. A man counts for more than that." But no one, not even men, look at you twice if you do not have that power that radiates out. And women say to you, "What does it matter? etc." But they marry someone else. And to marry means to make a life. And you will never make one. This means you've been a baby for too long, that's what it means.
>
> If it's gone badly with her who was all you dreamed for, with whom can it go well?
>
> Remember how all your dreams . . . all your poetry of the first year were annihilated for ever by April 9?[73]

The repeating pattern of definitive breaks "for always" followed by an imploring call from Pavese and Pizzardo's agreeing to another meeting continued through late 1937 and into 1938. She says that after his "desperate" phone calls she would acquiesce "always more reluctantly," but acquiesce she did, until what she thought would be the definitive break in May 1938.

> "I'm expecting a child," I tell him, "now it truly is finished; you can't expect me to come rushing to you with a baby in my arms."
> He receives the news with indifference. "A trick to get rid of me?"
> On June 13 he insists that this is a definite goodbye. He swears he is going to get a life, a family, and that then we can see each other alone, or with others; he swears he will send me a copy of every book he writes. But on July 4, the anniversary of my ill-omened telephone call, he manages to induce me into another final goodbye. This third and truly final goodbye takes place on the sixth of July near the Michelotti Canal. Here, after solemnly renewing the pledges of the previous two goodbyes, he offers me, as a symbol of the end of the romance, the diary that he began writing in Brancaleone and that off and on he had me read . . .
> I refused the diary because of my foolish generosity that I have so often come to regret. I had read it, I knew it was his only copy and I knew that he attached a great deal of importance to everything he wrote. (I am not so sure now that it was the only copy; I have the "only copy" of several poems and stories he later published.) He would have come to regret sacrificing so many pages for me. Maybe I hoped that in rereading his diary he would see himself, me, clearly. Who knows?[74]

Either she or Pavese got the date wrong by one day because he recorded that long conversation by the river as taking place on July 7. His entry for the ending of this second phase of his relationship with Pizzardo rivals for brevity that which recorded its beginning; his entire entry for July 7, 1938, reads, "The conversation by the Po."[75] Pavese lived twelve years after their final-final goodbye, and during those years Pizzardo and he ran across each other several times in Turin, but, according to Pizzardo, never exchanged a word. She was vacationing in the mountains when Pavese killed himself; she did not go to his funeral.

The five-year relationship between Pizzardo and Pavese began in

June 1933 when he let her jump into his punt on the Po and it ended in July 1938 by the Po when they said their truly last goodbye. It had two distinct phases, the first going from their outing on the Po till her marriage to Rieser in April 1936, and the second from July 4, 1937, when she phoned Pavese, till the end. The second phase is much more troubling than the first. Pizzardo's throwing Pavese over in 1936 devastated him, as his diary entry of April 10, 1936, makes abundantly clear. Yet, however unwillingly, he accepted the situation as final. His *not* contacting Pizzardo after her wedding and his 1936 and early 1937 diary entries demonstrate that. Thus, while they were both consenting adults in July 1937 when she called him, I do believe that Pizzardo's behavior in the following twelve months can be properly described as destructive. She was thirty-four, married, and sexually experienced, he twenty-eight, single, and struggling emotionally and financially. She was bored in her marriage and unfortunately she decided to toy with Pavese for relief. She may phrase it—and believe— that she was just searching for a friend to pass time with, but that rings false. One gets the feeling in reading her telling of this tale that she enjoyed Pavese's inability to stay away from her even after their conversation of August 13, 1937. Maybe he made her feel desired, and she certainly was, but maybe it made her feel just plain powerful; Pavese gave her total control of the relationship, something her husband did not. From this distance one cannot determine what psychological needs Pavese and Pizzardo were satisfying during these months of clearly neurotic behavior, and in the end it does not much matter. They did what they did together but came out of it differently, Pizzardo annoyed and disappointed that Pavese would not accept the role of friend, Pavese scarred for life.

Until Pizzardo's memoirs saw light we did not realize that it was not their entire relationship that made Pavese so bitter about her, but rather the second phase. His 1936 diary entries after her marriage show him discouraged and defeated and still emotionally involved, but not obsessed by her. They show more resignation than anger. On April 25, 1936, the first twenty-fifth of a month after her wedding, he made a three-word entry in his diary: "This twenty-fifth, nothing."[76] The tone of his entries concerning Pizzardo changes dramatically after August 1937, especially after August 13; then the bitterness and railing begin, never really to end. Seven years after their last meeting

Pavese could still write in his dairy, "The low blow that Tina gave you, you still have in your blood. You did everything to get it out of your system, you even forgot it, but it's useless."[77] Not so subtle traces of his bitterness also show up in the fiction he composed during the summer of 1937.

After finishing in 1932 the last of the stories published after his death as *Ciau Masino*, Pavese turned his creative attention to poetry and did not write another short story until July 1936.[78] In early June 1937 Pavese started composing the most violent and misogynistic story he ever wrote, "Temporale d'estate" ("Summer Storm"). He revised the short work throughout the summer and that revised version appears in the definitive edition of his short stories as "La draga" ("The Dredge").[79] Both versions still jolt the reader with their casual cruelty and violence. Violence often occurs in Pavese's stories and novels, and often to women: one thinks of Talino stabbing his sister to death with a pitchfork in *Paesi tuoi*, Pavese's first published novel, or the machine-gunning of Santa in *La luna e i falò*, his last. Pavese generally integrated the violent acts symbolically and seamlessly into his fiction; in "La draga," however, a story of rape and murder told from the point of view of the criminal, the violence has no symbolic value. The plot is simple: two men, Aurelio and Moro, an ex-convict recently released from jail, and two women, Bianca, who swims well and loves the river, and Clara, who has come along to keep Bianca company, happen to go boating separately the same day on the Po. A thunderstorm develops and while Bianca is swimming Clara falls from the boat and is swept away by the river's strong current. Bianca swims to the boat, hauls herself into it, and after searching the river desperately but unsuccessfully for Clara ties up to a sand dredge moored in mid-river, the same dredge where the two men have taken refuge from the storm. Bianca pleads with them to help her search for her friend. Instead, after making fun of her and her friend for not knowing the river, Moro throws Bianca on some sacks in the dredge's small cabin and rapes her while Aurelio waits his turn. When Moro finishes and is getting up to yield to Aurelio, Bianca manages to scramble up and jump into the river to escape. The men watch as she fights against the current, gradually weakens, and is swept under and away to the same death Clara met earlier. Aurelio is disappointed that he did not get his turn with Bianca, but Moro consoles him, saying that it is just as well that she fled into the river: "women like her talk." The story ends with Moro saying to Aurelio, "Have a cigarette. You can go first next time."[80]

This violent story has no saving grace and it is hard not to read into it Pavese's disillusion with Tina and with women in general, especially since he revised the first version shortly after Tina reactivated her relationship with him and finished it after August 13.[81] Tina prided herself on how well she swam, how well she could handle a boat in heavy currents, and she loved going on the Po. It does not require much of an imaginative stretch to see Pavese getting back at her by letting Clara, representing all women, be drowned, and Bianca, representing Tina, be raped and drowned.

Pizzardo wrote the chapters in her memoirs concerning Pavese in the 1960s, soon after the appearance of Davide Lajolo's biography of Pavese.[82] It was not until the 1990s, however, that anyone took serious notice of them. When Giovanni De Luna became aware of their existence, Tina's son, the same one who caused her to stop seeing Pavese, granted access to them and eventually prepared them for publication. In doing so, Vittorio Rieser has contributed significantly to Pavese scholarship. Knowing what was going on between Pavese and Pizzardo after July 4, 1937, puts into context many of Pavese's diary entries from the second half of that year and 1938. His many comments about women during that period did not result from a free-floating misogyny, as previously thought, but rather refer specifically to what was happening contemporaneously between Pizzardo and him. Indeed, his diary from summer 1937 to the summer of 1938 makes little sense unless one knows what was going on between them at the time. Also, Pizzardo's memoirs explain the significance in the diary of Pavese's repeated references to certain dates, especially the twenty-fifth of a month, April 9, and August 13.

In general, Pizzardo comes across in her book as an extraordinarily vivacious, sexually active, strong-minded, independent woman. Alterocca characterized her as "sports-loving, decisive, and concrete."[83] Her memoirs, though, which tell much, do not tell all. They proceed, as one Pavese scholar wrote in a personal message, "with winks and nods." She lets it be known that she slept with Spinelli and with Pavese, but tells us nothing about her sexual experiences before Spinelli. Still, one senses that when she slept with Spinelli in 1927 she was already, at twenty-four, much more experienced than he, and when, at thirty, she met Pavese, she was even more so. She never admits cheating on Rieser after she sought out Pavese in July 1937, but Pavese implies that he and she had sex at least once between July 4 and August 13, 1937. She clearly enjoyed flirting and makes no secret of that. She claims that after Pavese exited her life in 1938 she enjoyed a long, loving, and happy marriage with Rieser, and we have no reason to doubt that. (The last sentence of her memoirs reads, "With Pavese gone from my life it was no longer chance that dictated my way, but only love for Henek and our son.")[84] But up until 1938, by her own recounting, she *always* had at least two men on the string at the same time, often three, as during the first years with Pavese. I think it fair to say that Pavese was simply overmatched with Tina. He might have come out of the five-year relationship with her less damaged had she treated him more caringly after her marriage, but that is not what happened. When they finally broke off, two months shy of his thirtieth birthday, a shattered Pavese finally and painfully accepted that he had lost Tina for good, and with that loss he lost much more.

Above all, he lost the belief in his capacity to connect meaningfully with other people. He came to believe that his failure to satisfy one woman meant that he could never satisfy any woman, and that his sexual failure indicated malignant and incurable defects in his own personality. For Pavese, a man who could not satisfy a woman could not call himself a complete man, and an incomplete man was an incomplete human being. Incomplete human beings, his interior reasoning went, cannot participate fully in life; they can never form truly complete relationships; they will always remain outside the circles of happiness they see around them. Furthermore, they can do nothing about their condition, and, knowing this, feel sentenced to lives of deserved emotional deprivation. A letter Pavese wrote in January 1938 to his old friend Enzo Monferrini exemplifies this line of thinking and shows some of the impact that the previous August 13 had on him. Pavese is referring in the letter to his vacation trip to Ancona the previous summer, the one he cut short before August 13 to return to Turin to spend time with Tina.

> The time I spent with you in Ancona seems more remote than the Garden of Eden. I had some small hopes then and the

example of your home moved me and seemed something I might try to replicate. No longer, and I think enviously that, if a man's misdeeds indeed arise from his ignorance and incapacity, how can someone by nature ignorant and incapable of all prudence escape his ordained destiny?

Because it's not a moral sense that's involved—I don't believe, as you know, in the mystical immanence of a categorical imperative; we're dealing here with the ability to understand, to think ahead, to get by—this is the art of life—and I am convinced that you have these attributes by eighteen or you'll never have them. But, like me, some people are born crippled . . .[85]

Pavese coupled this nascent conviction of his inadequacy with a growing sense of fatalism, an unfocused belief that forces beyond control are propelling us toward fates already decided. Later in life he would clarify that belief and write extensively about fate, but one finds examples of it beginning in April 1936 when he returned to Turin from confino and Tina confirmed her plans to marry Rieser. One finds it, for instance, in one of his first poems after returning:

> *We will go out one morning . . .*
> *we will tremble to be alone. But we'll want to stay alone.*
> *We will look at those passing by with the dead smile*
> *of one who has been beaten, but does not hate or scream*
> *because he knows that from remote times fate*
> *—all that has happened or will happen—is in the blood,*
> *in the indistinct whispering of the blood.*[86]

The day after Tina married, Pavese noted in his diary, "What has she done! Maybe she doesn't know, or knows and doesn't care. And that is proper because she is she and has her own past that traces out her future."[87] Long before he developed the idea intellectually, Pavese had already begun to feel that he did not control most of the forces that controlled his life.

The end of the relationship with Tina, even more than confino, marked the major dividing line in Pavese's personal life. It also signaled a turning point in his artistic life.

FOUR
Einaudi, Fernanda, and World War II

Between 1930 and 1936 the major part of Pavese's creative energies went into translations, critical essays, and poetry, while beginning with 1936 his efforts went mainly into short stories, novels, and editing. He did continue to translate to support himself. He translated four books in 1937, all of which were published in 1938: John Dos Passos's *The Big Money*, John Steinbeck's *Of Mice and Men*, Daniel Defoe's *Moll Flanders*, and Gertrude Stein's *The Autobiography of Alice B. Toklas*. Teaching would have been a natural choice for more income, but his expulsion from the Fascist party and his confino barred him now from both state and private schools. In terms of teaching, personal tutoring remained the only possibility, and at that he had some success.[1] Nonetheless, he still could not get by without his sister. When the telephone company informed him in 1937 of a rate change—from the residential to the more expensive professional category—he wrote them, "In my capacity as Doctor of Letters, ex-political confinee, not a member of the National Fascist Party, nor, therefore, inscribed in the professional registry, I cannot undertake, even privately, the type of work I should. Presently I am a *lettarato* [emphasis in original], which means I more or less live off the sister with whom I reside, who pays her telephone bill and mine."[2]

Between his return to Turin in March 1936 and the end of 1937, Pavese wrote thirteen short stories, none of which he submitted for publication in his lifetime. Yet one sees in them, even in a travesty like "La draga," signs of his mature, compactly efficient style. Pavese wrote no poetry in 1937 until after August thirteenth. Given the traumatic August conversation with Pizzaro and his consequent feelings about himself, it is not surprising that the nine poems he wrote in the remainder of the year, all short, bitter, and resigned, center on situations past and now remembered: old men recall their women who have run off ("Gelosia"), young men remember last summer's affair ("Estate"), and broken country prostitutes remember the lovely feel of the sun when they were young ("La puttana contadina").[3]

In 1938 he regularized his work situation. He had worked as a paid consultant for Einaudi since Giulio Einaudi founded the house in 1933. By 1938 Giulio Einaudi finally felt the firm had become secure enough financially to take Pavese on as a salaried employee. It was Pavese's first and, as it turned out, only full-time job of his life. Giulio Einaudi's April 27, 1938, letter contained the terms of Pavese's employment and shows why Augusto Monti would later call him the "workhorse" of the firm.[4] "Dear Pavese," wrote Giulio:

> I am happy you will be working full-time for the Einaudi publishing firm as of May 1 of this year.
>
> Your responsibilities will be the following:
>
> A) Translation from English of about 2,000 pages per year. (Naturally this figure represents a maximum and it is most unlikely that I will ask you to reach it.)
> B) Editing of manuscripts and proofs of English translations done by others.
> C) Examination of works, including unpublished works, both Italian and foreign, for which it is felt your opinion would be useful, with your opinions expressed in writing when appropriate.
> D) Miscellaneous necessary drafting and editing of English correspondence, for which you will be required to come into the office during mutually convenient hours once or twice a week.[5]

For all this, he was to be paid one thousand lire a month. This annual salary of twelve thousand lire represented a considerable improvement over his 1937 earnings, which we can estimate at between seven and nine thousand lire.[6] Leone Ginzburg played a more important role in the earliest years of Einaudi, but Ginzburg (who had returned from jail at about the same time Pavese returned from confino) was, as a convicted criminal and a Jew, sent to confino in 1940 when Italy entered World War II. The years 1936–40 saw Einaudi beginning to create its distinctive character and profile; it was growing in influence and prestige, if not in profitability.[7] Ginzburg's forced departure in 1940 increased Pavese's workload, but, despite his grumblings, Pavese loved his job. He was also well qualified for it. His formal education plus his enormously varied reading had made him what the Italians call a man of great culture. His innate sensibility and his own writing gave him a feel for language and structure. To those attributes he added another: his own disposition; he was by nature hardworking, thorough, and stubborn. As Natalia Ginzburg put it, when he joined "that small publishing house he became a dedicated and meticulous employee, criticizing the other two [Ginzburg and Giulio Einaudi] if they came late in the morning and then maybe went to lunch at three."[8]

Pavese never considered editing just a day job to support his own writing; he loved creating books and spent much more time throughout his adult life on other people's books than on his own. Especially in the post–World War II years, he virtually lived at the Einaudi offices, sometimes in Rome or Milan but mostly in Turin. Colleagues remember a desk always piled with manuscripts or proofs, and Pavese looking up at them, a little surprised, behind his large glasses. Giulio Einaudi meant it as high praise when in the 1990s he described Italo Calvino, who joined the house in the late 1940s, as "a hard worker, of the school of Pavese."[9] Pavese loved everything about what he called "making books." He developed, for instance, the form of the file that accompanied each manuscript. It was something rather like a hospital chart that collected in one place all information deemed relevant, such as who proposed the book, what others in-house had said about it, the final decision, and the contractual terms, and then tracked the stages of the book's production. He decided on typefaces and style rules down to the point of determining which words would take acute accents and which grave.[10] After World War II, Einaudi worked with three co-equal offices—Turin, Rome, and Milan. Pavese felt that the arrangement caused unnecessary duplication, especially in regard to choosing and accepting foreign books. A memo he circulated in 1945 neatly demonstrates the level of precision he thought proper in a publishing house: "Until we have a central office that dictatorially decides things, we will have these uncertainties and small conflicts, that seem nothing, but which can cause trouble for our contacts with authors and publishers. To sum up: extreme clarity in our communications. Make clear if a book has been suggested, if it has been requested, if we have it in hand, if it is accepted, if it is assigned, if the rights have been requested, if they have been agreed. Seven Points."[11]

During his tenure at Einaudi he worked concurrently as an acquisition editor, series editor, project editor, copy editor, and, well before he died, chief editor, second in the organization only to Giulio Einaudi. Italo Calvino worked as an editor under him, as did several others who, though not writers like Calvino, would make their marks in Italian publishing, especially Giulio Bollati and Paolo Boringhieri. His influence on the house lasted long after his death. Ernesto Ferrero joined Einaudi in 1960 and remembers that "Cesare Pavese had been dead for more than ten years and yet his presence was still palpable." For some years Ferrero worked in Pavese's former office, and, he says, "I felt his severe gaze over my shoulder."[12] The job with Einaudi brought Pavese a steady if modest income, but more importantly, it provided a contractual meaning to his life. With Tina only nine months behind him he needed something other than failure with women to define himself. Writing did that, but editing did it in a way that involved other people; it provided a way into the real world that he felt his writing, for all its worth, did not.

After starting his diary Pavese summed up his feelings about most years in an entry just before or after year-end. The entry for 1937, written seven months before the final break with Tina, showed a calmness that by the end of 1938 he realized had been illusory. Going into 1939, he cautioned himself not to feel too sure about what he considered a generally successful year, among whose accomplishments was his new job:

> Finished a year of much reflection, of freeing myself from bondage (half *in*, half *out*) ["in," "out": English in original], of scant creation, but of great straining to free myself and to understand. *We begin now.*
>
> Now that I have steady work, my active suffering must have emerged from chaos by now. A life of wise separation will now follow; all energy concentrated on *creating.*

> But remember that the calmness of 30 December 1937 was illusory and that we continued the mania for another six months. Remember.[13]

In fact, Pavese was never to fully escape the "bondage" that Tina represented, but by the beginning of 1939 he had healed himself as well as he could. As his diary entry indicates, he began the year full of hope. He had already begun his first novel and he felt he would be able to pace himself so that in addition to his work for Einaudi he could also concentrate on "creating." And create he did: the next two years mark the peak of his first period of mature creativity, both as translator and editor, for which he was paid, and as a writer of fiction, for which, so far, he was not. In November 1938 Pavese began *Il carcere*, his first novel, and finished it on April 16, 1939. His handwritten manuscript—Pavese wrote almost all his work with a fountain pen— takes up 121 pages, and in the 2000 edition of his collected novels 84 pages.[14] He also wrote in 1939 a second novel, *Paesi tuoi*. These are the first examples of his preferred format, the short novel. (He would write nine in all, with an average length in collection of 93 pages. The shortest, at 56 pages, is *La spiaggia*; the longest, with 133, is *Il compagno*.[15] His two finest works are of almost identical length: 117 pages for *La casa in collina*, and 116 for *La luna e i falò*.)[16] He published neither of the two novels composed in 1939 immediately. *Paesi tuoi* had to wait two years, and *Il carcere* ten.

Still, well before any of his novels were published, Pavese's year-end entry for 1939 shows a growing sense of pride and inner calm. He had put in another year of steady work at Einaudi, done several translations, and written his first two novels.

> I close out '39 full of aspiration, by now confident in myself, tense as a cat lying in wait for prey. Intellectually I have the same agility and contained energy as a cat.
> I am no longer manic. I have lived to create, and this I have done. On the other hand, I have come to fear death greatly and am terrified that my body may betray me.
> It was the first year of my life that I lived with dignity because I have applied myself to a definite plan.[17]

In 1940 he wrote two more novels, *La bella estate* and *La spiaggia*, published in 1949 and 1942, respectively.[18] He also wrote three short stories and six poems. When he finished this group of poems,

Pavese essentially abandoned poetry as a means of aesthetic expression. After 1940, poetry served Pavese as an outlet for sexual tension only—*all* his poems after that year were written for or about women with whom he could not establish a satisfactory relationship. While *Paesi tuoi*, published in 1941, became and has remained the most famous of the novels he wrote in this period, all four of them have in common the already recognizable Pavese rhythm, tension, and deceptive evenness. *La spiaggia*, the last of the four, represented what Gianni Venturi calls the end of "the preparatory decade of Pavese's activity. Having consumed in the novels, the poetry, and the translations whatever remained of a personality in search of itself, Pavese could now confront the highest moment of his art."[19]

As it turned out, the highest moment of his art had to wait quite some time: after he finished *La spiaggia*, five and a half years passed before he began his next novel. Despite the considerable achievements of 1940, he noted, in his first diary entry for 1941, "If you did not do an examination of conscience for last year it is because you needed it more than ever—you were in a state of transition and you lacked inner clarity."[20] Pavese's "state of transition" lasted almost exactly as long as did Italy's state of war, that is, until the summer of 1945. A beautiful young Turinese student, Fernanda Pivano, provided the main thread of personal continuity during these years.

They first came into contact in 1934 at D'Azeglio, when Pavese walked into her classroom one morning as the substitute teacher of Italian. He was twenty-five, she sixteen. Pavese, involved at the time with Tina, did not particularly notice her. She certainly noticed him; she particularly remembers from that first time his voice. "He opened a book and started to read from it, and there came forth the miracle of his mesmerizing voice."[21] "It was like hearing the voice of an angel, because he had a fantastic voice. One of the most fascinating things about Pavese was surely his voice."[22] They had no contact outside of class until well after Pavese returned from confino and she was in her last year at the university. They met again in the spring of 1940 at a Turin swimming pool. According to Pivano, when she told him she was going to do a thesis in English literature, Pavese asked her, "Why not American?" She said, "What's the difference"? That night she found at the porter's desk in her apartment building four books, *Spoon River Anthology, A Farewell to Arms*, Sherwood Anderson's *A*

Story Teller's Story, and *Leaves of Grass*. She would end up translating the first three into Italian, but in the meantime switched her topic to American literature and in 1941 received her laurea with a thesis on *Moby-Dick*. She received another laurea two years later in philosophy, and, before either, a diploma in piano performance from the Turin conservatory.

Pivano first appears in Pavese's diary in the one-word entry of July 26, 1940: *Gôgnin*, the Piedmontese nickname Pavese gave her, meaning both "little pretty-face" and "kid," in the slang sense of "here's looking at you, kid."[23] He had asked her that day to marry him. Pivano refused to take Pavese's offer seriously; her refusal did not seem to affect their relationship, as they continued to see each other regularly. It may be because of pleasant times spent with her in the next few days—or possibly because of her refusal—that on July 28 he wrote a one-sentence entry that has become so well-known as to be made into refrigerator magnets and rubber stamps: "We do not remember days, we remember moments."[24]

Pivano, in Pavese's eyes, had little in common with the brash, athletic, activist, adventurous Tina. He described Fernanda at various times as "likeable and intelligent . . . with a young face . . . large eyes . . . always smiling . . . fresh . . . a virgin . . . with deep and honest feminine understanding . . . with delicious and irresistible feminine qualities . . . cordial, crystalline."[25] In poems dedicated to her he spoke of a face "*without memories . . . with a shadow humid and sweet like sand.*" She was "*like a cloud seen through branches . . . like a sweet white cloud entangled one night in ancient branches.*"[26]

The summer of 1940 continued with bicycle rides in the surroundings of Turin, walks along the Po, many confidences exchanged. Pavese tried to adopt a light tone in a burlesque of a school assignment he sent her, "How I spent my summer vacation."[27] He described bicycle trips and outings with his friend, "Nando"; his changing her gender probably indicates that he sensed he would never have sex with her, and that making her a boy reduced the pain of that refusal. He attached a darker cover note to the "assignment": "Nando's friend is an idiot. For five days for the second time in his life he finds himself thrown in prison."[28] About a month later, their relationship came to some kind of crisis the nature of which we can only guess at. As a rule, very short diary entries, aside from aphorisms, indicate serious events in Pavese's life, the most notable being that of July 4, 1937, when he noted Tina's telephone call in an entry of six words. His entire entry for September 25, 1940, reads, "letter," and the next entry, four days later, "*pf!!!!*"[29] *Pf* translates well to its English phonetic equivalent, "pfft," which, as *Webster's Unabridged* indicates, is "used to express or indicate a dying or fizzling out." The Italian editors of the unexpurgated version of the diary offer no explanation for "letter." Richard Koffler suggests in his annotation of Pavese's entry of September 25, 1940, that it was "probably from Pivano to Pavese."[30] He is surely correct, for in that note he cross-references Pavese's diary entry of November 27, 1945, in which Pavese lists three dates representing crushing blows from women: August 13, 1937, September 25, 1940, and November 26, 1945.[31] Almost certainly, Pivano wrote Pavese a letter that not only rejected him but did so in terms that reminded him of Tina. Pavese's remarks at the time, and Pivano's later, make it seem overwhelmingly probable she was a virgin at this time, so while not impossible, it seems unlikely they had attempted sex. A good guess is that Pivano, who, according to Pavese, had a great fear of being raped, panicked when Pavese gave her "a certain violent kiss that *perhaps* was for her the first."[32] Whatever the content of Pivano's letter, it was serious enough for him to note, the day after the "pfft," "My behavior with Gôgnin (assuming it is finished . . .) has been a condensed version of '34–38."[33] Indeed it was, and would be. Just as he once tersely noted that Tina had returned, he now made a five-word entry on October 5: "No, it is not over."[34] The same on-again, off-again pattern of the Pizzardo-Pavese relationship now began to repeat, so much so that a few weeks later Pavese could write, "The most appalling lesson of this latest blow is that you have in no way changed, in no way *improved*, despite two years of meditation. That takes from you even the comfort that you might climb out of this hole, with meditation."[35] Pivano's rejection of him, coming after Tina's, reinforced his belief that he would *never* succeed with a woman: "In order to console the young man to whom a misadventure happens, we tell him: 'Be strong, take it like a man; you'll be all the tougher for the future. It happens once to everyone, etc.' No one thinks of telling that man what instead is true: this same misadventure will happen to you twice, four times, ten times—will happen to you always, because if you are so made that you've shown her your weak side now, the same will *have* to happen to you in the future."[36]

Just as happened with Tina, Pavese's relationship with Pivano would go on several years after the first and second temporary ruptures, and Pivano would end up marrying someone else. Pivano, however, never generated in Pavese the kind of impotent rage that Pizzardo had. He continued to entertain hopes for her during the war and wrote her many letters. As Lorenzo Mondo correctly says, his courting of her was "perhaps, above all, written."[37] He also assisted greatly in the launching of her literary career by encouraging her to translate Masters's *Spoon River Anthology*, which he edited and, as we will see, also warmly reviewed after its publication.[38] He proposed marriage once again after the war and once again she gently turned him down. Pavese may have realized from the beginning that this tall, beautiful woman represented another of those unreachable goals he set in front of himself as part of his obscure ritual of nonfulfillment. Certainly, many of his references to her indicate a private awareness of impossible attainment. She was, in his words, "a closed chestnut."[39] For all their touching affection, even his letters to her show an inward reserve, indicated outwardly by his use of the formal third person (*lei*) rather than the familiar second person (*tu*). Only someone with Pavese's peculiar personality could propose marriage twice to a woman without ever using the familiar form of address.

Their relationship eventually ended in 1946 on a friendly, and partly professional, level. In February of that year he wrote what turned out to be his last letter to her, a short and cordial note, both professional and personal, that shows he had by then distanced himself emotionally. Einaudi had entrusted her with the translation of Sherwood Anderson's *A Story Teller's Story*, which Pavese was to edit. Pavese had already reviewed the text of the translation when he received Pivano's preface. He wrote:

> The umbilical cord is truly cut. The preface is lovely and "has style" and I'm not the only one who thinks so. The teacher has nothing more to teach.
> Wait for the manuscript with the text to give it a last look for copy errors. Then, good luck on the seas of life. Pavese[40]

The day after Tina Pizzardo was married in 1936 Pavese wrote in his diary a long, bitter self-critique. The day in the fall of 1946 when Pivano married an American officer stationed in Italy, Pavese wrote, "I'm working on the novel. Pivano was married this morning. I've got a cold. There it is."[41]

Pivano became in the second half of the twentieth century as important a translator of American authors into Italian as Pavese had been in the first. She translated most of Hemingway's and all of Fitzgerald's important works, along with some Faulkner. She made herself into a literary celebrity with the Beats: she not only translated Ginsberg and other Beats, she went to America, traveled with them, became friends with them, but, according to her, never slept with any of them. Of Kerouac she said, "With Jack, nothing. He was always too drunk."[42] She has her own web site, and the pictures she has included there, though taken later in life, indicate that Aldo Cazzullo is certainly accurate when he remarks that when Pavese first met her she was a young woman of a "bellezza non banale."[43]

Pizzardo was five years older than Pavese, Pivano nine years younger. One studied mathematics, the other literature, music, and philosophy. Pizzardo's father was a clerk, Pivano's a banker who had a personal library of nine thousand volumes. The two women shared intelligence, education, and a desire to follow their own bents—Pizzardo's political, Pivano's literary. Pivano was the more conventionally beautiful, Pizzardo the more athletically graceful. They both liked to swim, as did Pavese. Tina and Cesare had sex, Nando and Cesare, no. Pizzardo left Pavese crushed and he hated her for it. Pivano managed to disentangle herself without causing major damage. In emotional terms, Pavese lamented her break with him mainly because it confirmed the deep doubts the Pizzardo debacle had generated. How to achieve a mature, loving, sexual relationship with a woman remained a mystery to him.

The summer of 1940, when Pavese reconnected with Fernanda Pivano, coincided with Italy's entrance into World War II. When the war started, Pavese was a few months shy of his thirty-second birthday. Because of his age and his asthma he was in no immediate danger of being drafted and certainly had no intentions of volunteering. World War II for Italy divides into three periods. The first lasted from the June 1940 declaration of war until June 25, 1943, when the king and a rump group of Fascist hierarchs, convinced that the successful Allied invasion of Sicily that began on July 10 signaled the certain defeat of Italy, unseated Mussolini and sent him to a form of military confino. The second phase lasted forty-five days, from Mussolini's arrest until September 8, 1943, when Italy signed an armistice with the Allied powers. The third, and most brutal, lasted from then until April 25, 1945, officially "Liberation Day," when various combinations of Partisans, urban workers, and Allied troops took control of all major northern Italian cities. In the third phase not only did the Germans fight the Allies, as the latter advanced so agonizingly slowly northward up the Italian peninsula, but Italians also fought Italians in a pitiless civil war that took place in all German-occupied areas. Pavese's war began only with the third of these phases.

The first phase of Italy's war affected Pavese's translating career but not his editorial work or his own writing. In 1940, in addition to writing *La bella estate* and *La spiaggia*, he translated three American works, Melville's "Benito Cereno," Gertrude Stein's *Three Lives*, and Christopher Morley's slight, satiric comedy, *The Trojan Horse*. In 1941 he translated Faulkner's *The Hamlet*; with this book, his translation career essentially ended.[44] As he wrote to a publisher in Rome who had queried him about possibilities, "As to translations, I only know English and I don't believe it's considered hygienic at the moment. In fact, I've begun concentrating on my own writing because I've just about had to give up translating."[45]

In this period, in addition to the novels he composed in 1939 and 1940, that writing included three short stories written in 1940, nineteen in 1941, and ten in 1942. While doing his own writing and translations, he continuing working full-time at Einaudi; now, with Ginzburg gone, he was even more important to Giulio Einaudi. The listing of his works shows his productivity during these years, and his letters and diary entries show him working in an unusually calm state of mind, despite the catastrophic events taking place in Europe and Asia. Particularly striking in those letters and diaries is the lack of that kind of destructive self-doubt that had so crippled him before, and which would later return so destructively. Despite Pivano's rejection of him in 1940, he remained mildly hopeful about her, and his many letters to her show no bitterness, much humor, and great affection; without realizing it he had become her Augusto Monti. His office correspondence gives us the picture of an active editor, opining on books, accepting some, rejecting others, suggesting new series, proofing copy, coordinating with the firm's Rome office. As a writer he was discussed and as an editor he was accepted. He even found himself throwing over a married woman who had fallen in love with him.[46] In February

1942 he spent some time in the firm's Rome office, and in early 1943, when Giulio Einaudi transferred the firm's head office to Rome for safety reasons—neither the Allies nor the Germans bombed the center of Rome—Pavese moved there on a semipermanent basis. In late February he was drafted, or, as the Italians say, "called to arms," as part of the third call-up of men born in 1908. He was told to report to the medical hospital in Rivoli, a town outside Turin, for his medical examination. He did, and the medical examiners rejected him, probably because of his asthma. He was told to report back for reexamination in six months, in mid-September 1943. After the medical appointment he spent a few weeks in Turin and then returned to Rome. In the third week of July, Giulio Einaudi and he agreed that Pavese should return to Turin, and thus by happenstance he was traveling back on July 25 when Mussolini fell. When he arrived in Turin on July 26 he expressed in a letter to Pivano the feelings of most Italians when they learned that the twenty-one years of Fascist rule had ended: "The world is totally changed."[47]

When the king removed Mussolini from office—the Duce was officially only the prime minister—he installed Field Marshall Pietro Badoglio as head of government. Badoglio's first moves were meant to assure the Germans that Italy remained an ally and had no intention of withdrawing from the war. The Germans did not believe this for a moment and began immediately increasing their already significant forces in Italy, readying themselves to disarm the Italian army as soon as the inevitable armistice with the Allies came. They were wise to do so, because Badoglio's representatives had begun negotiating with the Allies as soon as he took office, and an armistice was signed on September 3, 1943, the same day the Allies crossed from Sicily to mainland Italy. The armistice was announced on September 8, a day before the major Allied landings at Salerno. The King and the Italian government fled to the sliver of south Italy so recently gained by the Allies, and the Germans pounced on Rome, Milan, Turin, Naples, and all other significant urban centers and put them under military government. The Germans also managed to free Mussolini in a raid in which German commandos arrived at his mountaintop containment area in gliders. He was flown to Germany for a quick meeting with Hitler and then returned to Italy, where he established the puppet state officially know as the Repubblica Sociale Italiana (Italian Social

Republic), or RSI, but often called the Republic of Salò, for the small town on the western bank of Lake Garda that served as its capital. Its sovereignty supposedly extended over most of northern Italy. This ersatz state managed, during its twenty-month life, mostly through coercion and fear, to put about a half-million men under arms for various periods of time, including a black-shirted militia whose members were called, by the Partisans, *i repubblichini* (little republicans). Once the RSI was established, the Italian resistance movement (la Resistenza) then had three targets: German soldiers, regular Republican army units, and the repubblichini. Clashes between the last of these and the Partisans were usually savage, and left the most scars in the Italian psyche after the war.

The armistice of September 8, 1943, brought to a close the phase of Pavese's life that began in 1939 as he began to recover from the relationship with Tina. It was a period of creativity and productivity during which, despite the Pivano rejection, he showed more mental balance than at any time since 1934. He had become a noted writer and a respected editor. Only in retrospect do these years appear as a temporary calm between extended crises. At the time, Pavese felt he was finally moving forward with his life. Between his July 1943 arrival in Turin and the armistice of September, Pavese wrote no poetry or fiction. He worked at Einaudi's Turin office as best he could. Turin, a major industrial city, constituted a prime target for Allied, mostly British, bombers. The explosive and incendiary bombs fell not only on industrial targets, but, deliberately at times, on all parts of the city, including the historic center.[48] A raid during the night of July 12–13, 1943, set on fire the building that housed Einaudi's offices; the staff recovered what material they could and Giulio Einaudi found them space in another building. That one, where Pavese worked, was also bombed, during the night of August 7–8, and the firm moved again. Throughout, Pavese continued to review manuscripts and deal with printers and authors and correspond with and occasionally see Pivano, whose family had taken refuge in a small town in the Langhe.

Pavese, too, would leave Turin soon after the September 8 announcement of the armistice. His last letter from Turin, to Pivano, carries the date September 10; by September 11 he had arrived in Serralunga di Crea, a village forty miles east of Turin where his sister had taken refuge with her husband's family. He made no diary entries during his summer stay in Turin. He made the last in Rome on July 10; between that and the entry of September 11, Pavese wrote:

> Turin and
> armistice—
> > then
> > > Serralunga[49]

He decided to get out of Turin before the Germans established the mechanisms for their occupation government. Pavese's record of arrest and confino made it likely he would either be interned again, conscripted into the army of the Republic of Salò, or, worse yet—and quite possible, given his history of asthma—rejected for service in that army and shipped off to Germany in a labor brigade. He had four choices in this situation: wait openly to see what would happen, go underground in the city, join one of the Partisan units forming in the hills and mountains, or hide out somewhere in the countryside. He chose the last alternative. He did so out of a complex mixture of disinterest, stubbornness, and plain physical fear. (Even a communist apologist like Lajolo had to admit that "Pavese's physical courage was never as great as his moral courage. Explosions, guns, blood terrified him.")[50] Pavese was not a pacifist, but neither did he see participation in the war as a moral imperative. He had not refused to respond to his draft notice earlier in the year, and if he had not failed his medical examination he would have found himself in an Italian army uniform at the time of the armistice. But he was a civilian on September 8, 1943, and he made a choice that hundreds of thousands of Italian men of military age made: he headed home and opted out of the war. He made his "separate peace" without joining the army, just as Hemingway's fictional Lieutenant Henry made his after joining the Italian army. Although it is not known how many Italians chose not to participate in this last stage of the war, they probably outnumbered the men and women who joined the active resistance against the Germans and Mussolini's puppet regime; the most generous estimates put the latter at around three hundred thousand. These Partisans have justly received recognition, honor, and glory. The approximately five hundred thousand men who, voluntarily or under threat, joined the armed forces and irregulars of Mussolini's Italian Social Republic have generally been vilified. Those who made Pavese's choice have mostly been ignored.[51]

The choice profoundly affected the remaining seven years of his life. It led to great guilt, and also—directly to one, indirectly to the other—to his two finest novels. In addition, the twenty months between September 1943 and April 1945 provided him time to tease out, through reading, conversation, and meditation, the implications of ideas on myth, childhood, and the sacred that had begun to interest him in 1933 and eventually replaced America as preoccupying intellectual themes.

At some point when the bombings became dangerous, Pavese's sister, Maria, left Turin with her two daughters for Serralunga di Crea, and stayed until liberation at her husband's home there. Guglielmo was in the Italian army but managed to visit from time to time. The household consisted of Maria, her daughters (of whom Pavese was quite fond), and Maria's sister-in-law. About two months after he arrived there Pavese found work in Casale Monferrato, the small city twelve miles from Serralunga where his mother had been born. It was work that suited him, tutoring the resident ginnasio and liceo students at the Collegio Trevisio, a Catholic boarding school located in one of the landmark buildings of Casale. The Palazzo Trevisio dates back to the fifteen hundreds and, under one authority or another, has always housed a school. The Somaschin Fathers, a small Italian order, were in charge of the school when Pavese worked there. The Fathers gave him a room in the school and he split his time between there and Serralunga. The move to Serralunga and Casale represented, at first, an enormously disorienting change for Pavese. For the last few years he had been both writing and actively involved with his Einaudi editing in the large cities of Turin and Rome. Now he found himself in the geographical orbit of a village of about eleven hundred and a city of about thirty-seven thousand inhabitants. In fact, he was more closed in than that: the rector of the collegio, the fifty-two-year-old Father Luigi Frumento, had put Pavese on the rolls as "Professor Carlo Deambrogio," and Pavese had to stay out of sight as much as possible because he had no identity papers with that name.

The winter of 1943–44 saw the front line between the Allies and the Germans stabilize, still south of Rome. Partisan bands had begun to harass smaller German units in the north and the larger Republic of Salò formations. Pavese's old friend, Massimo Mila, was with one of those bands. Leone Ginzburg, upon the fall of Mussolini, had left confino and sped to Rome; he remained there when the Germans entered after the armistice, going underground and concentrating on producing and circulating clandestine newspapers. Giaime Pintor, an officer of the Italian army as well as a more recent colleague at Einaudi and a dear friend to Pavese, crossed the lines south of Rome to offer his services alongside the Allies. Pavese, cocooned in the safety of the collegio, turned his thoughts inward, to religion, myth, and his own self. It was as though he were trying to shut out the war by building a thick wall from the outside in.

Father Giovanni Baravalle, seven years younger than Pavese and at that time a priest for two years, served as the school's chaplain. Pavese struck up a friendship with him that led to the younger man's becoming his spiritual adviser during Pavese's time in Casale. Pavese, a not particularly observant Catholic, asked Baravalle on February 1, 1944, to hear his confession, after which Pavese received communion. Two days before that he wrote in his diary, "We humble ourselves in asking for an act of grace, and discover the secret sweetness of the Kingdom of God. We almost forget what we are asking for: we would wish only to enjoy forever that outpouring of divinity. This without doubt is my road to arrive at belief, my way of being a believer, a renunciation of everything, a submersion in a sea of love, a fainting in the glimmer of this possibility. Perhaps it's all here: in this trembling of 'if it were true.' If it really were true . . ."[52]

Fr. Baravalle confirms that Pavese approached him that day with "a shyness I was unacquainted with in him, and asked me to help him as a priest."[53] On February 1, after receiving communion, Pavese wrote, "We feel the outpouring of divinity when grief has brought us to our knees, At the point when the first hint of grief gives us an impulse of joy, of gratitude, of expectation . . . We go so far as to hope for grief. The rich and symbolic reality behind which stands another reality, true and sublime, is it other than Christianity? To accept it means literally to enter the world of the supernatural."[54]

Pavese's thoughts and musings during 1944 remained centered on God and the mythic. At the end of the year he wrote, "A strange, rich year that began and ended with God, with much deep thought on the primitive and the savage, and which has seen some notable creative work. It could be the most important year of your life so far. If you persevere with God it certainly will be. (It must not be forgotten that *God* means also a technical cataclysm—symbolism built up through years of following the gleam.)"[55]

Pavese's short and apparently calm description of the "strange rich year" of 1944 belies the interior strain the outside world caused him, no matter how much he sought refuge in God. Leone Ginzburg died in Rome on February 5, 1944, after being tortured by the Nazis. On March 3, Pavese wrote, "I learned of it March 1. Do others exist for us? I wish it were not true, so as not to suffer. I live as in a fog, thinking about it but always vaguely. It ends up that in this state you develop the habit of always putting off the *true pain* until tomorrow, and that way you forget and have *not* suffered."[56] And five days later: "The secluded wait in front of the hills. It returns again for the second time."[57] The "it" that returned (in Italian, the verb *torna* without a subject) was Pavese's old sense of dread and insufficiency in front of life—the overall emotional state which characterized the years 1936–39 and which later he called his "horror." Most likely he had learned earlier of Giaime Pintor's death, which took place two months before Ginzburg's, and Leone's death brought it on a second time. Nineteen forty-four, in fact, saw many swings take place inside Pavese. He wrote to his friend Giuseppe Vaudagna in December, "I am in the country with my relatives. I work a bit in the town nearby but as in certain novels it is not the outside facts that count. What counts is the interior tension; and release counts, and the way they follow one another and fight each other."[58]

Pavese's diary entries in Casale and Serralunga document an enormous amount of reading, much of it religious, much of it classical, much of it Shakespeare, and much of it whatever he could find in the school library. His diary also shows that he was searching for something inside himself during this enforced stay in the hilly and evocative Monferrato countryside. To say he was looking for the meaning to life might sound grandiose but would be correct. He certainly was trying to work out some intellectual coherence for his own life, and in a sense he did. He developed ideas about myth-driven destiny and symbols that he applied to the rest of his life and writings. While he remained in the hills, those ideas continued to mix with his recent personal experience of God: "The very suggestion that the subconscious may be God, that God lives and speaks in our subconscious mind, has exalted you. If, with this idea of God, you review all the thoughts of your subconscious scattered here and there—don't you see—you are changing your whole past and discovering many things. Above all, your labored search for the symbol is illumined by its infinite significance."[59]

This comment comes from his diary, published only after his death. He also wrote about his labored search, however, in essays composed in Casale and Serralunga, some of which were published in 1945. In them he detached symbol and myth from the Christian God and located each person's personal destiny, his included, in the events of childhood—which, Pavese believed, take place outside of time, and therefore outside the child's consciousness. The child first experiences reality without realizing he is doing so, and does so through symbols, without realizing they are symbols. "No child is aware of living in a mythic world. And more, no child knows anything of the 'infantile paradise' which, later, the adult becomes aware that he lived through. The reason is that in the mythic years the child had much better things to do than to give a name to his state. It is his time to live this state and to know the world. Now, as a child, one learns to know the world not—as it would seem—with immediate and original contact with things, but through the signs of these: words, illustrations."[60]

Because the child is not aware of his original contacts with the world through symbols, this awareness in a sense takes place outside of time. The discoveries are not, however, forgotten; they come back to the adult as rediscoveries. "If we think back on any one moment of ecstatic emotion in the face of anything in the world, we find that we are moved because we had been moved before; and we were moved before because one day something appeared to us as transfigured, separated from the rest by a word, a fable, a fantasy that spoke it and contained it. For the child this sign becomes a symbol, because naturally at that time fantasy reaches him as reality, as objective consciousness and not as an invention. (That infancy is poetic is only a fantasy of adulthood.)" Or, as he put it in 1946, "there's no such thing as an empty landscape: wherever a boy has lived, wherever he has rested his eyes, something is created that persists in time."[61]

The symbols the child absorbs become absolute for him, without him realizing it at the time, and that leads to Pavese's formulation that nothing is seen for the first time: "This is the nature of infantile mythmaking and we find the confirmation of this in that we discover things, we baptize them only through the memories we have of them. Because, absolutely, there does not exist a 'a first time to see things: what counts is always the second."

Pavese's, though not a theory of original sin, is one of predestination, because those absolute symbols the child has absorbed, and will later see for a "second time," determine the outlines of his life. "The mythic concept of infancy is in sum a reach into the sphere of unique events and absolute successive revelations of things, through which these things live in the consciousness as normative patterns of the affective imagination. Thus, everyone has a personal mythology (a faint echo of the other) that gives value, an absolute value, to his most remote world and envelops little things of the past with an ambiguous and seductive light in which they seem, as in a symbol, to sum up the sense of all his life."

If we all have a set of personal myths that give value to our lives, it follows for Pavese that we each by definition also have a personal destiny determined by those myths. We do well as adults, then, to try to understand our destiny, to follow rather than fight it. "We must accept the symbols—everyone's own mystery—with the calm conviction with which we accept natural things."[62] Destiny is sacred, as "in Greek tragedy everything is sacred—that is, predestined, willed by God."[63] One year after leaving Casale he would note in his diary, "the one who blunders is the one who does not yet understand his destiny. That is, he does not understand that which is the result of his entire past—that which points toward the future. But whether he understands it or not, it marks it out for him just the same. Every life is that which it had to be."[64]

The last component of the Pavesian concept of childhood-symbol-myth-destiny involves repetition. Just as religious rituals repeat some event that happened outside of time, so we in our own lives repeat over and over patterns that we absorbed symbolically as children without realizing we were doing so. In the impersonal sense, "Myth is that which happens infinite times in the real world and yet is unique, outside of time, just as a recurring festival rite plays out every time as though it were the first time, in a time that is the time of the festival, of the nontemporal, of the myth."[65] Personal myths, personal rituals, work the same way, and generally destructively: "That which has been, will be. There is no forgiveness."[66]

While his ideas on myth and symbol enriched his later fiction, they had depressing implications for his own life. A sequential summary of Pavese's ideas hints why: (1) a child first encounters reality through symbols in a time outside of time; (2) these symbols become his personal myths; (3) when he discovers them later, thinking them new discoveries, he is always in fact discovering them for the second time; and (4) in doing so he is constrained to live out their implications in ritual repetition. A loop back from (4) to (1) makes it clear that in essence Pavese is saying, symbolically or not, that a child's first experiences determine the repetitive patterns of his whole life. Pavese's concept goes beyond the aphorism that the boy is father to the man to make the man little more than a boy in grown-up clothing. As Pavese has a beggar tell Oedipus in one of the dialogues he wrote after World War II, "We all have a mountain which is part of our childhood. And however far away we wander we always find ourselves walking its paths again. There we were made what we are."[67] Pavese felt when he left Casale and Serralunga that he understood better what made him what he was. His ideas, however, also preconditioned him to expect defeat—crucially, personal, not artistic defeat—because he believed he had already experienced it from the beginning of his life and was therefore destined to repeat it.

In addition to his contemplation of myth, symbol, and religion, Pavese also commented to himself from time to time on events happening outside his private world. In 1990, Lorenzo Mondo published in the Turin newspaper *La Stampa* an article that ran three full pages under the headline, "Pavese, The Secret Notebook."[68] It caused an enormous stir because in these previously unpublished notes Pavese appears to comment favorably on Nazi Germany and the then newly created Republic of Salò. He also complains that some anti-Fascists annoy him because they talk as if they know everything:

> One thing enrages me. The *antiF[ascists]* know everything, surpass everything, but when they debate things all they do is argue . . . and this clearly shows that the *virtu latina* lacks nothing except discipline . . . F[ascism] is this discipline. The Italians moan about it but in the end it's good for them . . .
>
> We never realize how sweet home is except in these terrorized escapes from the bombed city. And those who cannot flee? And the soldiers and the workers? One understands the deep motive behind the [Russian] revolution of 1917: *the soldiers and*

> *the workers* are the entire society. If only F[ascism] truly could abolish its excesses and free itself from the profiteers, why not follow it? Certainly this war teaches us many things . . .
> Stupid like an antiF[ascist]. Who was it who said that?[69]

Those don't seem like the comments of a man who two years later will join the Italian Communist Party and write for the party newspaper. In retrospect it is clear that the notes represent mostly transient musings; unlike his thoughts on myth, symbol, and destiny, he developed none of the ideas contained in the notebook and carried none of them away with him. They do, however, in their unwillingness to glorify the Italian Resistance, dimly foreshadow the central scene of *La casa in collina*, the semi-autobiographical novel based on *his* war, in which he makes clear that the Fascist dead have no less intrinsic value than the Partisan dead.

The Allies broke through the last German defensive line, between Florence and Bologna, in the late winter of 1944–45 and in April advanced rapidly northward. In late April the coordinating command of the Partisan units called for a general insurrection in all major northern cities, and the combination of the advancing Allies, Partisan attacks, and civil insurrection led to the collapse of German resistance in Italy. On April 25, Partisans openly marched into the cities, including Turin. By May 4, Pavese had gone back to Turin, and, even before Giulio Einaudi's return, was working to reorganize the publishing house. While he brought back with him his ideas of myth and destiny, he did not carry back his embrace of Catholic sacraments and rituals. Perhaps he knew he would not: on the day after receiving communion in February 1944, he wrote, "A certain pattern of daily life (with fixed hours, confined spaces, always the same people, religious rites and places) induces thoughts of the supernatural. Break away from that pattern and those thoughts vanish. We are wholly creatures of habit."[70] Though they kept in touch until Pavese's death, he no longer viewed Fr. Baravalle as a spiritual adviser; he did, however, always remember the kindness that Baravalle and the Father Rector showed him, and portrayed both of them realistically and favorably in *La casa in collina*.

FIVE
Liberation?

For many Italians, particularly those on the political left, the immediate postwar days and months carried great hope. They felt that the blood shed in the civil war *surely* would lead not only to peace, but to a renewal and reordering of Italian society. Intellectuals were to play a leading role in bringing about a more just and equitable society, a public role. Both because he wanted to believe in that role and because he needed to atone for his nonparticipation in the civil war, Pavese joined the Italian Communist Party in 1945 and began writing for the party newspaper, *l'Unità*. His first article appeared on May 20, 1945, about two weeks after his return to Turin. It is, as Lorenzo Mondo notes, "significant not only for the sincere passion that animates it but also for its confessional tone, something between sorrowful and stubborn."[1] It is indeed as much confession as profession, a public confession that corresponds to the private one he asked Fr. Baravalle to hear in 1944. It also shows his deeply felt desire to connect with other people, and contains obvious references to his months in the Monferrato hills.

Italian journalists, when writing commentary as opposed to news, conventionally use the first person plural. Pavese, too, but in writing this piece every "we" also signified himself. If, in reading it, one substitutes "I" for "we" and "me" for "us," that equivalence becomes affectingly evident. Entitled "The Return to Man," it starts with his commenting that, because of the vacuousness of Italian culture during the Mussolini era, he and others sought authenticity in the vitality of various foreign cultures. Things are different now:

> We now know in what direction we must work. The scattered signs that we received during the dark years from a friend's voice, from something we read, from a little joy and much pain, are now synthesized in a clear discourse and a certain promise. The discourse is this: we are not moving toward the people because we are already the people, and all the rest is nothing. If anything, we are moving toward man because this is the obstacle, the crust to break, the loneliness of man, our own and that of others. The new legend, the new style is all here, and with it our happiness.
>
> To propose to move toward the people is to confess in principle a guilty conscience. Right now we feel guilty about many things, but at least we never forgot of what flesh we are made. We know that in the social stratum that one usually calls the people laughter is more open, suffering more alive, words more sincere, and we take all this into account. But what else does all this signify except that, in the people, loneliness has already been overcome, or is on the road to being overcome? . . .
>
> These years of blood and agony have taught us that blood and agony are not the end of everything. One thing was saved in all the horror and that is the opening of man toward man. We are certain of this because man has never been less lonely than in these times of fearful loneliness. There were days when a look or sign from a stranger was enough to surprise us and to keep us away from the precipice. We knew and we know that everywhere, in the most unlikely or glaring eyes, there lies hidden a tenderness and innocence that we must share. Many barriers, many stupid walls crumbled in those days. Even for us, who for some time already heeded the unconscious petition of every human presence, it was a shock to feel ourselves struck with, submerged in so much richness. Truly, man, in the sense that he is more alive, has awakened and is now waiting for us, whose job it is to learn, to understand, and to speak.
>
> To speak. Words are our profession. We say this without the slightest shyness or irony. Words are tender things, inviolate and alive, but made for man and not man for them. We all feel that we are living in a period in which we must carry words back to the solid and naked clearness of the time when man first created them for his own use.[2]

Pavese was far from the only creative writer to become engagé immediately after the war. Natalia Ginzburg remembers that "it was, in the years right after the war, a fairly widespread opinion that writers ought to break out of their restricted circles and through the left-wing parties immerse themselves more in real life."[3] Pavese's own language shows that he had mixed results in trying to do so. Much of what he wrote in "The Return to Man" resonates as authentically his voice. "We know that in the social stratum that one usually calls the people laughter is more open, suffering more alive, words more sincere" does not. A letter he wrote the next month indicates even more of an effort to try to express what he believed he ought to feel. In 1943 Einaudi had accepted a novel submitted by Silvio Micheli. Wartime events interrupted its publication, and, with the war ended, Micheli wrote to inquire about its fate. Pavese responded, "Your letter was a great pleasure for me. I appreciate and am grateful for everything you wrote us. It is in fact our intention, that of Einaudi himself and of us on the staff, to work together toward the construction of a new socioeconomic order, toward that collective well-being, the fruit of collective work. We, too, hate false and bourgeois literature, and your novel has interested us since 1943 because we feel in it a fraternal spirit and energy."[4] From his first essays to his last, Pavese wrote sharply, personally, and concretely when dealing with issues that truly involved him. In his business letters, too, he wrote briskly and specifically. The kind of cliché-ridden language in the letter to Micheli—bereft of any "tender" or "inviolate" words—indicates that no matter how much Pavese might have wished otherwise, he had not internalized the left-wing ideology he was espousing.

During the rest of 1945 Pavese gave second priority to writing of any kind; his energy went to rebuilding Einaudi. Ginzburg's and Pintor's deaths, beyond their personal effect on Pavese, represented incalculable losses for the house. At least in the early 1940s, when Pavese's importance was already growing, Ginzburg could participate in decisions by mail. With him dead, Pavese had to become the new Ginzburg—not the sole driving force behind the house, but certainly the most important person after Giulio Einaudi. He located manuscripts, solicited new ones, put works into the production schedule, and rounded up the firm's old translators (foreign works in translation have always represented roughly two-thirds of Einaudi's catalog). After Giulio Einaudi returned to Turin, Pavese left for Rome in July—one day after proposing marriage to Pivano for the second and last time—

to reestablish the Rome office which he had helped close down in 1943. This time, however, Rome was not to function just as a satellite, but as one unit in the tripartite organization that Giulio thought best fitted the times: three coequal offices, in Turin, Milan, and Rome. That kind of organization almost invariably generates duplication and bureaucratic friction; the house of Einaudi proved no exception. Pavese's correspondence that summer is filled with objections to practices that he considered a waste of time: "A few days ago," he wrote to Giulio Einaudi, then in Milan, "we received from Milan a directive that imposes on us a bureaucratic system of weekly reports from the various offices. We are totally against this. Here [in Rome] we already spend too much time creating reports, lists, memoranda. After all, we have all come together to create books, not office literature."[5]

One book he created that year was *Feria d'agosto*, a collection of twenty-four of his own short stories and five short essays on myth. Its ironically sweet dedication page acknowledged his acceptance of the end of his relationship with Fernanda Pivano:

Feria d'agosto
In memoriam
†
26 July '40–10 July '45

Those were of course the dates of his two marriage proposals and her two refusals.

When he went to Rome in 1945, now thirty-seven and over the relationship with Pivano, Pavese found as the office's administrative manager (*segreteria generale*) a twenty-seven-year-old Sicilian woman named Bianca Garufi. Bona Alterocca calls her "a beautiful and intelligent woman"; Mondo, "a brunette with striking, strong features, endowed with a vivid intelligence."[6] Pavese described her as "made of energy" and capable of engendering "pure joy."[7] She shared Pavese's interest in myth (she was undergoing a Jungian analysis at the time); she found him interesting and they began seeing each other. By November he had proposed marriage. On November 24 they argued and she apparently turned down his proposal. He left for Turin and the next day wrote her a long and revealing letter. He sensed he was losing her but did not want her to become another Tina, another Fernanda:

I understand what my sickness is. It is called pride and one can overcome it. I am not overly sensual, I am not stingy, I am not anything but proud. You share some responsibility in my latest outbursts of pride because you have never humiliated me in the past. In fact, you have always exalted me, my intelligence, my importance.

Only yesterday evening, things being the way they are, did you act as my friend. You told me that I was twisted, that I was trying to trap you, that nothing between us was worth saving. Bianca, I have kept this phrase in my heart all night . . . and it has finally forced me to write. I have tried to understand if this phrase is so terrible for me because it offends my pride. Indeed, it is partly this, but above all I believe it is intolerable because it is not true, because it hurts more than it needs to. Leave aside all my troubles, but do not forget that you, too, are part of this "between us" and with you, values that go beyond just passion. No one knows as well as I do how sterile and vain passion can be (for this reason I told you yesterday to read my diary, and when you refused, I have to confess, I felt a bit of author's pain), but passion has been, so far, my instinctive way of attaching myself to a person and to her things, just as one who is drowning grabs another person by the neck . . .

I sometimes told you in jest that I am Catholic—well, this is Catholic (or Christian, if you will): to believe in the souls of others and respect them. I have violated, murdered, and attacked other souls but I always knew I was doing wrong. I propose to do it no longer.

I propose to stop my melodramatic drinking exhibitions and to stop beating my own head. In this sense yesterday was already a victory. I did not want to tell you that I was leaving for Turin. I wanted to disappear in order to impress you. Instead, I told you. Today I tell you that when I arrived in Turin I wanted to tell Giulio that I quit—to impress you. And instead, I will not.

If we count the (too) sweet days of our friendship—the idyll—yesterday was in a certain sense the first day of the real "between us." Think! What really happened? It happened that I spoke to you without pride. I began with the half intention of being hard and sharp—and instead? Instead you forced me to face my soul. How could we have fooled ourselves that something could exist between us before every single one of our shames was discovered? . . .

One day I said to you, "I will never do anything cowardly in front of you," and I believe that today it would be cowardly if I broke away from you just out of fear of burning myself or making you suffer. I will not burn myself and you will not suffer anymore because of me, whether I leave the Rome office or not.

Bianca, I will now confess to you the rest of my shame:
I still hope to marry you—

> When I acted desperate with you, it was to impress you—
> The most delirious pleasure I know is to be compassionate—
> I have to force myself to "feel" politics—
> With everyone, I give myself the air of not giving myself airs—
> When I told you, "everyone has his own pathology," I thought that would impress you more than some other phrase—
> There was a whore in the middle of the famous five years of chastity I boasted about—
> I pretend to be ordinary—
> I think about money—
> I am ashamed of my cousin who runs a tobacco shop—
> I used to masturbate a lot.
> Bianca, do you not love me even a little? . . . Do you want the blood of humiliation that from now on I will search for like a monk? To overcome my pride I will close myself in a monastery where I will especially control my thoughts. I will retain only one shred of pride, the hope of overcoming it. Maybe you are right to say that I will never find flesh and blood, but you are wrong when you say that I do not know how to become what you want me to be. I must become that because *I do not want* our story to resemble the others that I destroyed.
> Tell me what to do. I will follow you as a monk follows his rule, no matter what it costs me.[8]

Once again, he had turned over control of a relationship to the woman involved. He returned to Rome almost immediately to find out what she would tell him. On November 27 he recorded one of the saddest diary entries of his life.

> That day has come again for the third time. It is dawn, a dawn of soft mist, a purple freshness. The Tiber has the same color. A lingering melancholy, ready to be dissolved by the sun. Houses and trees, everything sleeps.
> I saw dawn, that's not much, from her windows in the wall nearby. It was the mist, it was the building, it was life, it was human warmth.
> Astarte-Aphrodite-Mèlita is sleeping. She will be sullen when she awakes. For the third time my day has come. The most atrocious part of the pain is to know that the pain will pass. Now it is easy to humiliate myself. And then?
>
>   Aug. 13, '37 Sept. 25, '40 Nov. 26, '45
>   (afternoon) (evening) (night)[9]

The dates, of course, refer to rejections of various kinds by Tina, Fernanda, and now Bianca. Alterocca suggests that Pavese and Garufi had sex that night and that he performed poorly, adding to the humiliation of his rejection.[10] Whether they did or not, his linking Garufi's name to Pizzardo, with whom he had had sex, and to Pivano, with whom he had not, indicates that what hurt most was the rejection itself, not the motive. On December 7, he noted in his diary what the three women had said about his poetry, and added thoughts, one of which has already been partially quoted (see page 104): "That's twice in these days that you have put side by side T., F., and B. It is a reflection of the mythic return. That which has been, will be. There is no forgiveness. You were thirty-seven and all the conditions were favorable. You *look for* defeat."[11]

Indeed, patterns are clearly visible, though not the same for all three. As they were heading toward breakup, he wanted two of them, Pizzardo and Garufi, to read his diary, perhaps in the hope it would make them understand his inadequacies. He wrote poems about two of them, Pivano and Garufi, during or right after breakup, and with all three maintained a nonsexual relationship after the breakup. Italo Calvino noted in his 1962 edition of Pavese's poetry that "From [1940] onward Pavese's need to write poetry returned during episodes of his love life; the poems were always for a woman and presuppose an interlocutor . . . as opposed to his earlier poetry, which, even when love poetry dedicated to a woman, did not assume a dialogue (real or imagined) with the interlocutor but rather only expressed an emotional situation in epic-lyric form."[12] Two of the poems Pavese composed for Garufi in imagined direct address reveal the rapid trajectory of their affair. He wrote the first in mid-October; many of the images refer to Sicily, where Garufi was born and brought up.

> *Red earth black earth*
> *you come from the sea,*
> *from the arid green,*
> *place of ancient words*
> *bloodred weariness*
> *and geraniums among stones—*
> *you bear more than you know*
> *of sea and words and toil,*
> *you, rich as a memory,*
> *as the barren countryside,*

> *you, hard and honeyed*
> *word, old as the blood*
> *gathered in your eyes;*
> *and young, like a fruit*
> *that is memory and season—*
> *your breath rests*
> *beneath the August sky,*
> *the olives of your gaze*
> *calm the sea, you live*
> *and live again*
> *as expected, certain*
> *as the earth, dark*
> *as the earth, grinder*
> *of seasons and dreams*
> *that moonlight reveals*
> *to be ancient, like*
> *the hands of your mother,*
> *the hollow of the brazier.*[13]

One senses some hope in Pavese. Garufi, though she carries antiquity with her, is earth, which can blossom; she is fruit; she can grind dreams but she can also calm the sea. But a week after she rejected him, she had become not earth and sea but earth and death:

> *You are earth and death.*
> *Your season is darkness*
> *and silence. Nothing alive*
> *is more distant than you*
> *from the dawn.*
>
> *When you seem to wake*
> *you are nothing but grief,*
> *it's in your eyes, your blood,*
> *but you do not feel it.*
> *You live like a stone lives,*
> *like the enduring earth.*
> *And you are dressed in*
> *dreams gestures agonies*

> *that you ignore. Grief*
> *like the water of a lake*
> *trembles and encircles you.*
> *There are rings on the water.*
> *You allow them to vanish.*
> *You are earth and death.*[14]

Pavese's relationship with Garufi lasted into 1946, and, as he did with Pivano, he adopted toward her a stance of mentor-encourager. He had urged Pivano to "translate, translate, translate"; he encouraged Garufi to try fiction, and with her composed in alternate chapters the beginning of a novel, published after his death as *Fuoco grande* (*A Great Fire*).[15] She eventually left publishing and became a Jungian analyst with a successful practice in Rome.

Ten days after Pavese wrote his last poem for Garufi in December 1945, he began a work partially influenced by their discussions about myth and indirectly dedicated to her, *Dialoghi con Leucò* (*Dialogues with Leucò*). (Leucò is Pavese's shorthand for Leukothea, a sea goddess in Greek mythology, literally "the white goddess," and is a play on Garufi's first name, Bianca.) He felt that with these short (usually four-page) dialogues between different mythological figures he was developing a new means of expressing the ideas he had been forming for so long. Neither poetry nor the short story form seemed adequate, and the essay appeared too didactic. The dialogue form suited best the exploratory mood in which he approached his own thoughts at this time. It took him longer than usual to compose this book; he did not have it ready until 1947. Most readers found it baffling. Augusto Monti disliked it intensely as an attempted recasting of Greek mythology ("a total reduction of mythology to poetry . . . in trying to redo mythology you have undone it . . . the problem of destiny is reduced to the issue of the man for whom death is fate, but he does not know when or how this death will come so he gets on as best he can"), but placated Pavese by adding that he had succeeded in "a manipulation of *poetry*."[16] Yet, of all his books, this one remained Pavese's favorite; he defended it the rest of his life and chose to write his suicide note on its frontispiece.

Soon after writing the first of these dialogues, he entered into his diary his annual "examination of conscience" for 1945:

> This, too, is finished. The [Monferrato] hills, Turin, Rome. I put four women behind me, published a book, wrote some beautiful poetry, discovered a new form that integrates many strands. Are you happy? Yes, you are happy. You have the strength, you have the genius, you have things to do. You are alone.
>
> You toyed with suicide twice this year. Everyone admires you, compliments you, dances around you. And so?
>
> You never fought, remember that. You will never fight. Do you mean anything to anyone?[17]

Pavese's "remember that" is, in Italian, *ricordalo*, and in sense and rhythm brings to mind the Italian words of the Ash Wednesday penitential rite, *Ricordati, o uomo, che sei polvere* (Remember, man, that thou are dust). He never shook off the feeling of guilt that arose from sitting out the war comfortably while others, particularly Ginzburg and Pintor, died. That he mentioned suicide at this particular time also has special significance. He had not "toyed" with self-destruction since the black period of the late 1930s after Tina's rejection had sent him into depression. From this point onward, however, that is, after Pivano and Garufi had both definitely rejected him, Pavese played with the idea of suicide with depressing regularity. The idea fascinated him. That it was a broken love affair that touched off these thoughts again only confirms the existence in his mind of a strong connection between failure in love and death. Success, or at least the hope of success in love, meant life; failure in love, death. The woman he hoped would love him was the moon seen through branches; the woman who rejected him, earth and death.

During 1946 the rhythm of Pavese's production increased. In addition to his ongoing, heavy editorial responsibilities, he completed in January alone five dialogues, his next-to-last short story, one book review, and one long essay. In the spring he began a relationship with another woman in Rome, Teresa Motta, the wife of Mario Motta, a Turinese friend of Pavese living in Rome: "Ter is the usual *aftermath* of your passions. The others, tall, she short; they tough, she sweet and cheerful; they difficult and complicated, she open and friendly; they enemies, she the good comrade. She abandons naturally a passion that has left her exhausted and *wistful*. Just like all her precursors. Will she finish like them?"[18]

She did not; she left no further identifiable trace in Pavese's diary and, unlike most of his other relationships, this one, whether consummated or not, caused no emotional fireworks. He did, though, write two short poems for her.[19] During the summer of 1946, Pavese, now working out of Einaudi's Milan office, concentrated, in terms of his own work, on the dialogues. All the dialogues showed the same concern with the irreversibility of destiny, but Pavese worked into some of the later ones bits of his self-willed political commitment. The father and son in "The Bonfires" talk more like politicized Italian *contadini* than ancient Greek peasants:

> *Father:* Look, the gods are our masters, They're like the landowners—they're our masters, too. You think they'd let one of their own kind burn? Not them. They help each other out. But with us it's different. Nobody helps us. Rain or shine, what do the gods care? We're lighting the bonfires tonight. Brings on rain, they say. But do the landowners care? Ever see one of them come down to the fields?
>
> *Son:* No, never.
>
> *Father:* Figure it out for yourself. Let's suppose a bonfire can make it rain, and burning some useless loafer can save the harvest. Well, how many owners' houses would you have to burn, how many owners would you have to kill in the streets to bring some justice back to the world and make us our own masters again? . . .
>
> *Son:* The gods aren't just. Why do they have to burn people alive?
>
> *Father:* They wouldn't be gods if they didn't. They don't have to work—how else do you expect them to spend their time? In the days before there were landowners and there was still some justice in the world, somebody had to be killed every once in a while to keep the gods happy.[20]

The political overtones of some of these later dialogues turned into a dominant chord in the novel Pavese began in October 1946 when he returned permanently to Einaudi's Turin office. When it appeared in 1947, *Il compagno* (*The Comrade*) led to a new public image for Pavese: he was no longer the American-influenced neorealist of *Paesi tuoi* but a certified left-wing, politically committed writer. *Il compagno* certainly represented Pavese's highest expression of intentional political commitment, but in many respects politics intruded on the work's real inner development and caused the bifurcation so evident in reading it. He divided the book into two halves, the first set in Turin, the second in Rome. During the late 1930s, in Fascism's high period, Pablo, the first-person narrator and protagonist, becomes involved in Turin with Linda, the girlfriend of his best friend, Amelio, after a motorcycle accident cripples Amelio and confines him to bed for life. The first half of the book describes a delicate dance of seduction and guilt—and of Pablo's actions in the face of his uncertainty over how much Amelio knows. Pablo moves to Rome in the second half, where he becomes involved with an activist woman and gradually begins to take part in anti-Fascist provocations. The second half of the book, while not forced in the way some of Pavese's political prose was at this time, has none of the emotional complexity of the first. The plot becomes programmatic and the tone flat in comparison with Pablo's earlier relationship with Amelio and Linda. Pavese tries to make Pablo's progress toward class consciousness the main point of the book, but he does not succeed. The book has no main point; it has, rather, two separate halves that do not make one full book. Pavese never defended this book the way he did the *Dialoghi*, but he did love its prose. Two years after composing it he opened it to a random page, and reported that he'd felt "the effect of touching a live wire. There is a tension superior to the normal, mad, coming from the rhythmic cadence of the phrasing. A drive forward continually braked. A gasp."[21] When Pavese started *Il compagno* in the fall of 1946 he wanted to write a political book with class consciousness as a theme; paradoxically, his real Resistance novel, *La casa in collina*, begun nine months later, portrays not a youth developing class consciousness but a man running away from the Italian civil war.

The two years between the fall of 1947 and that of 1949 constitute the most fruitful and creative period of Pavese's artistic life. He went from strength to strength as editor, and even more so as a writer, for it was in these years that he wrote the books that have given him his place in the modern Italian canon. On September 11, 1947, he began *La casa in collina*, and on November 9, 1949, he finished *La luna e i falò*, his last novel. In between he wrote *Il diavolo sulle colline* and *Tra donne sole*. Further, he had no doubts about his creative work; while he always doubted his capability of satisfying or even connecting with women, he never as an adult questioned his vocation as a writer or his ability to write well.

His work at Einaudi in 1947 gave him particular pleasure because Giulio Einaudi approved his plan for a series of works to be called the Collezione di studi religiosi, etnologici e psicologici (the Library of Religious, Ethnological, and Psychological Studies), often referred to as the *collana viola* (violet series) because of the color used for their covers.[22] Philosopher and anthropologist Ernesto de Martino collaborated with Pavese at the beginning of the series (and directed it after Pavese's death), but Pavese generated the idea and drove it forward. He took pride in the series—his main editorial focus from 1947 to the end of his life—and enjoyed working on it as much as anything else he ever did at Einaudi.

Two of Pavese's books appeared in 1947, *Il compagno* and the *Dialoghi*. He wrote several essays for *l'Unità* and had fully come into his own as an editor. Yet, despite the progress he was making as a writer and editor, and despite his growing public recognition, the disquieting undertones of his personal unhappiness remained. His diary recorded no tenebrific musings on self-destruction, but several passages belie the overall calm tone of most of the 1947 entries. "You are alone and you know it," he wrote on April 12, "but you are not enough by yourself, and you know it."[23] A week before that: "In the clandestine period everything was hopeful; now everything is a prospect of disaster."[24] Loneliness continues as one of the main themes of the diary, and he had mixed feelings on the subject. In one sense he dreaded loneliness, but he could also write, "No matter how strong the joy of being with friends, with someone, the joy of leaving afterwards alone is greater. Life and Death."[25] When, in November 1947, Einaudi published the second of his books to appear that year, he noted in a positive tone, "*Compagno* and *Leucò* published. Works of 1946—you were thirty-eight. You want to write now more than ever. Thank heaven for that."[26]

Pavese ended 1947 in the middle of writing *La casa in collina*, a book that Lorenzo Mondo notes "occupies a position of absolute centrality" among Pavese's works.[27] He started 1948 in a highly optimistic mood, despite a coming third operation for nasal turbinate dysfunction:

> Like a Rome morning today with sun on the earth and water, sparkling, flavored, alive. A New Year's Day never seen before. Will an incredible year follow?

I'll do the third operation; that will give me peace again. In 1947 I did not write anything (a few dialogues and the beginning of a novel). I did not *do* anything. The two books came out. I spent time in Rome, at the sea, but always in a hurry, always in a rush. Fear or just an itch?

But what a day today! It doesn't seem Turin. It is a stranger winter than that of 1943–44.[28]

In personal terms, 1948 proved more calm than incredible. His diary entries that year create a notably even impression. There are reflections on death, but without the fascinated personal insistence that characterized many earlier periods. These 1948 entries carry obvious personal overtones for him but basically reflect Pavese's semi-objective interest in death as part of his investigation of myth, history, and religion, the same concerns that occupied him as the editor of the *collana viola*. Yet the year did turn out to be "incredible" for him in one important sense, the completion and publication of *La casa in collina* and its appearance with his first novel, written nine years earlier, *Il carcere*, in one volume entitled *Primo che il gallo canti* (Before the Cock Crows).

Pavese based both books on personal experience, *Il carcere* on his seven months in Brancaleone, *La casa in collina* on his experiences during the civil war years. Both have a thematic importance in relation to his work as a whole, but one cannot compare them artistically; he had grown enormously as a writer since 1938, and with *Casa*, as he generally referred to it, he produced an incomparably finer novel. *Il carcere* tells the story of a Turinese engineer, Stefano, sentenced to confino in a Calabrian coastal village. Using abstract language uncharacteristic of his later work, Pavese creates a brooding mood and through various devices conveys his main points: life is a prison, people are isolated, and walls are everywhere, even when one border of a town is the sea. He told the story, such as it is, slowly, and did not manage to convey the uncertainty and tension that in fact he himself felt in Brancaleone.

In *Casa*, tension and uncertainty underlie everything: the characters, the plot, the environment, and the ending. The dialogue is crisp and Pavese moves the plot from scene to scene with smooth efficiency. Many of the characters and places are clearly identifiable; Pavese never pretended otherwise. The first-person narrator, Corrado, is Pavese; Father Felice is Baravalle; the unnamed rector, Father Frumento; Cate, the woman Corrado had an affair with before the novel begins, is Tina Pizzardo, although more loosely characterized than the others. Dino, Cate's daughter, possibly by Corrado—one of the novel's uncertainties—might have been based on the student "Corradino" Pavese mentioned in a 1936 letter to Maria (see page 70). The bar/inn Le Fontane in the hills just outside Turin is the Fontana Dei Francesi, a place where Pavese and the entire Einaudi group ate often. The town of Chieri is Casale Monferatto, and the village where Corrado ends the novel is Santo Stefano. A reader need know none of that to appreciate the mastery of the work.

The plot: Turin, the summer of 1943. Because of the allied bombing, Corrado, an apolitical liceo teacher, has rented a room in the hills above the city. At a nearby inn, Le Fontane, he comes across his old girlfriend, Cate, who is part of a lively but serious group of young, presumably communist, anti-Fascists. He begins to spend time there. It hits him that the name of her son, Dino, is also a common nickname for Corrado. He wonders if the child is his son. The boy's age makes it possible but Cate never confirms it. The police raid Le Fontane at a time when Corrado is not there. Dino manages to run off but the police carry off all the adults, Cate included, and they never appear or are heard from for the rest of the book. When Corrado finds out that the police are making inquiries about him at the liceo he decides he has to leave. Elvira, the older woman from whom he rents his room, gets the parish priest to provide an introductory letter to the rector of a collegio in Chieri. Corrado goes there, is welcomed, and finds temporary peace. Father Felice helps in this process. Elvira eventually brings Dino to the collegio and the priests accept him as a student. During Corrado's temporary absence because of a possible roundup, Dino runs off to join the Partisans—his exit from the novel. Later, a German army contingent decides to billet soldiers in the collegio and the commanding officer requests a list of all the teachers and students. Corrado leaves immediately through a back way. He makes his way on foot across the Piedmont countryside, heading toward his home village. At a village near his, he encounters Giorgi, an old friend from Turin, now a Partisan group leader. Corrado and Giorgi smoke a cigarette and talk, then Giorgi leaves by car with his men. Heading again toward his own village, Corrado hears explosions and gunfire. He rounds a bend in the road and comes upon the aftermath of the action Giorgi drove off for: the ambush of a truck carrying Fascist soldiers. He observes it, talks with a priest who is administering last rites, and continues homeward. After a further short interval of hiding out in a farmyard he reaches his village. The novel ends with Corrado—home six months, the war not yet over—thinking about all that has happened.

In the twenty-three short chapters of this episodic novel Pavese artfully examines the moral underpinnings of the Italian civil war. He presents Cate and her friends as brave and sympathetic, but, tellingly, sets up no cowardly or vile Fascists as moral counterparts. Pavese neither explains nor defends Corrado's choices nor seems overtly preachy, even though by the book's end he has reminded us through Corrado that men of good faith died on all sides. Pavese questions *any* triumphalist view of the war—quite effectively so in the scene where Corrado and Giorgi meet.

> Then I risked the question. I said the last time I saw him he was talking of war, but the Fascist war. He had put on a certain uniform and had it in for certain people. Had he possibly been touched by grace?
> "Disgrace, you mean," he said. "It was my disgrace that I took an oath."
> "But the Fascist war was different. Who are the subversives now?"
> "Everybody," he said. "There's not an Italian left who isn't subversive." He smiled dryly, abruptly. "You don't think we're fighting for those damned fool friends of yours?"
> "What fools?"
> "Those who sing 'The Red Flag.'" He threw his butt away in disgust. "Our work with the blackshirts is finished, now we begin with the redshirts."
> "I thought you sympathized," I said.
> We were silent and looked at the valley.
> "Tomorrow I hope to reach home," I broke in, getting up from the wall.[29]

In the next chapter, Pavese sharply contrasts Giorgi's cynical tone in speaking of the violence of the civil war with the brutal and mythic results of the violence itself. Giorgi has gone on ahead; Corrado has heard the gunfire and explosions. After a safe interval he rounds the bend in the road:

> I saw the big troop truck. It was stopped, empty, across the road. A trickle of gas was darkening the road, but it was not only gas. Alongside the wheels and in front of the truck, bodies were lying and the gas grew redder as I approached. Some women and a priest were running around.
> One soldier—gray-green streaked uniform—had fallen on his face with his feet still on the truck. Blood and brains spilled from beneath his cheek. A little man, his hands on his stomach, was looking up, yellow, bloodstained. Then more contorted bodies, sprawled facedown, of a dirty livid color. Some of them were short men, looking like bundles of rags. One was off on the grass where he had jumped from the road to defend himself by shooting; he was kneeling stiffly against the barbed wire as if alive, blood flowing from his mouth and eyes, a boy of wax crowned with thorns.
> I asked the priest if the dead all came from the truck. This sweating, energetic man looked at me wildly and said that the houses farther up were also full of wounded. "Who attacked?"
> Partisans from above, he told me. They had been waiting for days.
> "The Fascists had hung four of them," screamed an old woman, weeping and fingering a rosary.
> "And this is the fruit," the priest said. "Now we'll have savage reprisals. It will be one bonfire from here to the high valley of the Belbo.[30]

Barbed wire as a crown of thorns, reprisals as a ritual bonfire: Pavese deftly moves the realistically described scene of the ambush toward a different plane.

The next chapter, the book's last and one of his best, brings together in the terms of this story themes that had preoccupied Pavese for years, and would continue to. He conflates Corrado and himself in a way that rings true, autobiographically, without violating the character of the narrator. Corrado is speaking six months after arriving home:

> Now that the countryside is bare, I go back to my walking; I go up and down the hill, reflecting on the long illusion that gave me the impulse to write this book . . . Obsessed by the chance encounters of this year, I keep asking myself: "What is there in common between me and the man who fled the bombs, fled the Germans, fled from remorse and pain?" . . . I see now that throughout this year and earlier too, even during the season of my meager follies, of Anna Maria, Gallo, Cate, when we were

still young and the war a distant cloud—I see that I have lived a long isolation, a useless holiday, like a boy who creeps into a bush to hide, likes it there, looks at the sky from under the leaves and forgets to come out, ever.[31]

Corrado's musing on the fates of his captured friends and the dead Fascists leads to what may be Pavese's most quoted paragraph (given here in R. W. Flint's translation, unfortunately a little stiff in this important passage):

> I don't know if Cate, Fonso, Dino, and all the others will return. Sometimes I hope so, and it scares me. But I have seen the unknown dead, those little men of the Republic. It was they who woke me up. If a stranger, an enemy, becomes a thing like that when he dies, if one stops short and is afraid to walk over him, it means that even beaten our enemy is someone, that after having shed his blood, one must placate it, give this blood a voice, justify the man who shed it. Looking at certain dead is humiliating. They are no longer other people's affairs: one doesn't seem to have happened there by chance. One has the impression that the same fate that threw these bodies to the ground holds us nailed to the spot to see them, to fill our eyes with the sight. It's not fear, not our usual cowardice. One feels humiliated because one understands—touching it with one's eyes—that we might be in their place ourselves: there would be no difference, and if we live we owe it to this dirtied corpse. That is why every war is a civil war; every fallen man resembles one who remains and calls him to account.[32]

The biblical allusion of the title under which *Casa* appeared, *Prima che il gallo canti*, meaning "before the cock crows," implies that the two novels in the volume will deal with the theme of cowardly betrayal, and *Casa* on the surface seems to. After all, it tells the story of a man who sat out the war in the comfort of a boarding school and his parents' home, who had plenty of chances to join the Partisans and did not. With that title Pavese accomplished something quite sophisticated: he led the public to assume that he now acknowledged his betrayal of the anti-Fascist cause, while writing a book that in fact did no such thing. Rather, by refusing to demonize the *repubblichini* or canonize the Partisans he put in question the whole idea of one-sided betrayal in a civil war. Pavese may have meant the book as a justification for his own behavior—after all, if both sides are morally defective, there's no guilt in not choosing sides—but even if he did, he created, against a realistic background, a symbolically coherent moral drama in which his themes play out to their quiet crescendo with enduring effect.

The book solidified his reputation; he was no longer seen as a new, young writer but as an established figure in the Italian literary world. He gave interviews and refused requests for articles. He had also become a prime moving force in one of Italy's most important cultural institutions, for Einaudi had by 1948 established itself as the country's most prestigious literary and nonfiction publisher. It is the Pavese of this period that Natalia Ginzburg remembers when she writes:

> The small publishing house had become large and important. Now many people worked there. Because the building where the original offices were was hit by bombs in the war, the firm had new offices, in Corso Re Umberto. Pavese now had his own office and on its door was a little sign that read, "Editorial Director." Pavese sat at his desk, with his pipe, and corrected proofs with amazing speed. In his down time, he read the *Iliad* in the original, loudly chanting in a sad sing-song. Or he wrote his novels, rapidly and violently crossing things out. He had become a famous writer.[33]

Natalia Ginzburg, Leone's widow and herself a gifted writer, worked in those postwar years as an assistant editor at Einaudi, under Pavese. Neither she nor Pavese mentions their most embarrassing misjudgment during those years: in 1947 she took less than a week to reject, with Pavese's concurrence, the manuscript of Primo Levi's holocaust masterwork, *Se questo è un uomo* (literally, "if this is a man"; published in English as *Survival in Auschwitz*). Levi had submitted it first to Einaudi specifically because of Ginzburg's presence there. Yet she and Pavese believed that Italians did not want to read a bleak memoir about Nazi death camps, and simply missed its literary value. In the end, after five other houses turned it down, the small De Silva firm published it, ironically enough as the third volume in a series called Biblioteca Leone Ginzburg.[34]

The busy, hardworking, successful Pavese recognized how far he had come. He had found an outlet for his talent and had become famous while doing in art and work what he wanted to. His year-end examination of conscience for 1948 reads:

> An extremely conscientious year of definite and sure work, of technical and material acquisition. Two novels. Another in gestation. Editorial dictator. Recognized by all as a great and good man. By all? I don't know.
> It will be hard for you to go any further. Don't be too impressed by what you've done. You did not hope for it and it amazes you. You arrived here simply by trying to work hard and well. Keep going, ready to accept the idea that tomorrow the result might be ashes. You should not let it bother you. Only in this way will you make amends for your good luck and show yourself deserving of it.[35]

Pavese was referring to *La casa in collina* as the first of the two novels mentioned; the second was not *Il carcere*, a work from 1938–39, but *Il diavolo sulle colline*. He composed this book in three and a half months running from the summer of 1948 into October and published it in 1949. It does not take place in the time of war, but Pavese based one of its memorable characters, Poli, on another real person he met while at Casale Monferatto, Count Carlo Grillo, a flamboyant, complicated, drug-addicted cosmopolite. Pavese met him through Father Baravalle and carried the name of Grillo's estate, Il Greppo, into the novel without changing it.

He began to bring forth the novel "in gestation," *Tra donne sole*, in March 1949; he finished it in exactly ten weeks. During this intense period of composition (he finished the last chapters at a rate of one per day) he maintained, as always, the dense rhythm of his editorial work. The realization came to him again that he had entered his full maturity. On April 10 he noted, "Your solid position and the regard people have for you has come to you just as you imagined it would when you were a child. This is amazing—that maturity is just as you thought it would be when you knew nothing about it. Could it be you have forgotten the wild dreams of those times and little by little changed into that which you think you then wanted? Nonetheless, you made no mistake about one thing, and that was to believe that you would now feel satisfied with your beginning and your hoping."[36]

Pavese had read in 1946 F. O. Matthiessen's *American Renaissance* and it had impressed him enormously. Now, in 1949, Pavese began describing his own maturity in terms of the line from *King Lear* that Matthiessen reported Melville had underlined in reading Shakespeare: "Ripeness is all." In June 1949, with *Tra donne sole* finished, he noted, "This is probably your most intense season and you are beginning to spoil—you are even aware of it yourself. What new things will we discover—that is, what new thing will we live and afterwards discover, when it has begun to reek? The end will surely come. And then?"[37]

Maturity, the balance point of growth and decay, remained much on his mind during 1949. At times he felt that he had begun the descent to decay. On a Friday evening in July he went to dinner in the hills with Giulio Einaudi, Natalia Ginzburg, and others. He records that at that dinner he "felt for the first time—objectively—physical decline, the inability to make an effort, a jump, an *exploit*. Felt bad and out of sorts all evening. To make up for it I hated the world, man, the company."[38] He reflected more philosophically in an essay composed in August that demonstrated even more clearly how much he had taken to heart the Shakespearean concept of maturity. After attacking the romantic image of the rebellious youth as culture hero, Pavese countered:

> This century has forgotten that the beginning is only a point of departure, that we are born to live and to age, and that between birth and death there is a stage of proper maturity, a perfect and courageous balance for the love of which, as the father of all of us has already said,
>
> > man must endure
> > his going hence e'en as his coming hither.
> > Ripeness is all.
>
> These rebels in short pants are essentially incapable of accepting nature—that maturity follows adolescence, and that maturity balances itself tragically for a brief, brave instant that contains in itself an entire culture.[39]

In the fullness of his own maturity Pavese had recently finished *Tra donne sole*, a dense novel of social interplay, much richer than *La spiaggia*, which had dealt with some of the same themes. He now began *La luna e i falò*, the novel that contends with *La casa in collina* for lasting primacy among his works. During its composition he noted, "You have no hesitation, no fear, no existential confusion."[40] After finishing it in fifty-three days he observed, "Almost a chapter a day. It is certainly your strongest *exploit* so far."[41] It is certainly the novel that brought him the most fame abroad. It has been translated into twenty-three different languages, including Japanese, Hebrew, and Turkish, twice into Spanish, and three times into English.

When he finished the novel in November 1949 he felt convinced that he had also finished a cycle in his artistic life, which in turn reflected the times through which he had lived. "You have concluded the historical cycle of your times: *Carcere* (anti-Fascism in confino), *Compagno* (underground anti-Fascism), *Casa in collina* (the Resistance), *Luna e i falò* (post-Resistance)."[42] A week later he listed all his works in chronological order, characterizing each. *Lavorare stanca* was "word and sensations." The four novels written before the war were "naturalism." The short stories written between 1941 and 1944 represented "poetry in prose and the awareness of myth." He saw the *Dialogues* and *Il compagno* as "the extremes: naturalism and detached symbols." Finally, he categorized his last four novels, from *Casa in collina* to *La luna e i falò*, as "symbolic reality."[43] He had fallen into a stock-taking mood in late 1949, looking backward more than forward. Einaudi published three of his novels, *La bella estate*, *Il diavolo sulle colline*, and *Tra donne sole*, in one volume that carried the same title as the first of it three components. It represented another sign of his established position and reminded him of his maturity: "Respectful party by my colleagues. Gave advice from the heights of age to the young Calvino."[44] A few weeks later he admitted to himself, "The fact is that you have become that strange beast, the successful man, an authoritative name, a *big* [English in original]."[45] Still, in the midst of all this success he remembered the peacefulness of his times at the collegio in Casale, using the English word "snug" to describe how he felt then, and wondering, "will that return again?"[46]

Pavese finished 1949 proud and satisfied, as well he should have, but also wistful, with vague premonitions of failing powers. The first reviews of *La bella estate* appeared in December and were uniformly favorable. He knew that chances were his public reputation would grow even more in 1950, since he had in reserve *La luna e i falò*, which he considered as good as anything he had yet published. He had indeed become a "big," but he also knew that to be big means to be mature, and that maturity means decay can soon begin. He also felt what he had earlier called "the ambiguous sadness, the idleness of *après l'oeuvre finie*."[47] He had scheduled for over New Year's a weeklong pleasure trip (the Italians call it a *gita*) to Rome with his friends, the Rubinos. Because he had not been to Rome in a while he was looking forward to the trip; he wondered if he would find it as it was when he worked there right after the war. In the last diary entry before leaving, he wrote, "I am genuinely agitated (tomorrow we go to Rome). Will it be like July 1945?"[48] As it turned out, there was one important similarity: both times he met a woman who fascinated him; in 1945 Bianca Garufi; this time, Constance Dowling. Eight months later he killed himself.

Through the spring of 1935, when he was twenty-six, Pavese had been happy more often than not. In the ginnasio, the liceo, and at the university he led a lively, extroverted life, and was part, and sometimes the center, of an interesting, concerned group of friends. After university he engaged himself with real enthusiasm in his translations, essays, and poetry, leading the almost full life of a promising provincial intellectual. Later, his failure with women would torment him, but in his early adult years he had as much success with them as did most of his friends. Before confino and Tina Pizzardo's marriage to Henek Rieser, Pavese was open to the world and to the future.

However, confino, Pizzardo's marriage, and her toying with him in 1937 and 1938 changed everything. In particular, her informing him on Friday, August 13, 1937, of "that which he never wanted to hear" (his sexual inadequacy), traumatized him. It marked the turning point of his personal life, throwing him into a depression that lasted intermittently until 1939. Still, despite Fernanda Pivano's rejection of him, the years from 1939 to 1943 saw Pavese notably happy, with his work going well in terms of both fiction and editing. The twenty months of the civil war period spent in Serralunga and Casale formed a parenthesis, during which he matured his ideas on myth and from which he emerged richer intellectually, but scarred emotionally, due to the death of Leone Ginzburg, Giaime Pintor, and others.

Engagé journalism, communist party membership, and the deliberately political novel *Il compagno* helped assuage his guilt. His competence as an editor and his mastery as a writer led to the years "of grace," 1948 and 1949. When he finished *La luna e i falò* at the end of 1949 he felt written-out, that he had nothing more to say. He had gone through fallow periods before, though, and, with time, new ideas had always found the way to "gestate." In March 1950, Constance Dowling interrupted that process. Pavese's depression after her departure made it somehow impossible for him to think about writing—indeed, about anything else other than her and his own inadequacy.

Pavese's "act," his suicide, was the last scene of his own tragedy. It took place on a stage of his choosing, against the backdrop of an oppressively hot, dispiriting Turin. His always-present suicidal urge had formed the leitmotif of this drama; the emotional vacuum caused by a temporary creative barrenness and despair over Constance Dowling set up the final scene. Pavese's interpretation of Dowling's departure as an irrevocable confirmation of his personal inadequacy—repeated, always to be repeated—determined that the play would end in self-destruction.

Pavese in the end saw killing himself as neither cowardly nor heroic, but as an act of resigned acceptance. There was simply no reason to go on living. He had proved—had he not?—that he was *always* going to fail with women. He had, he thought, nothing more to write; everything was already down on paper. If there was nothing to live for, no one to live for, if life meant only more failure, one should accept the logical consequences and kill oneself—quietly, undemonstratively; not at home but in a hotel room, thereby not inconveniencing one's loving sister.

Natalia Ginzburg, who knew him well, believed that

> In the end he did not have any real reason for killing himself. But he gathered together a group of reasons and added them up, with a striking precision, and then he added them up again, and again saw, approving with his malicious little smile, that the results were identical and therefore exact. He also looked beyond his life into our future time; he saw how people would react to his books and his memory. He looked beyond life as do those who love life and don't know how to tear themselves away from it, and who, though thinking of death, imagine not death but life. And yet he did not love life, and his looking beyond his own death was not love for life but a rough calculation of probabilities, so that nothing, not even after death, would take him by surprise.[49]

More than anything else, the death of hope led Pavese to kill himself that August weekend. At forty-one he found it much harder to rebuild hope than he had at twenty-eight. In the summer of 1950, everything appeared final; he could not find the way out of his last prison. The long rest of death became, in his eyes, the only repose he could hope for.

His suicide immediately became a major news event. Newspapers across the country reported it with front-page headlines beginning with the evening editions of Monday, August 28. The *Corriere della Sera* story recounted that experts had determined he took twenty-eight packets of sleeping powder.[50] If the number is correct, it could be read as one last indication of Pavese's obsession with dates and anniversaries: it was at twenty-eight, in August 1937, that his life began to fall apart.

His sister most likely arranged, for the early morning of Tuesday, August 29, some kind of private religious rite, at least a blessing, for her brother. A public Catholic funeral was out of the question for a well-known card-carrying communist who had committed suicide. Instead, his body was brought later that morning to the largest room available on the ground floor of the Einaudi offices on Corso Re Umberto. Colleagues, family, and friends gathered there around his closed coffin. Meanwhile, telegrams poured in, including one from the president of the Republic and his wife—Giulio Einaudi's parents. Others gathered outside, and a funeral procession followed, photographs of which indicate a crowd of several hundred people drawn at short notice. Pavese was taken to Turin's grand municipal cemetery, where he was interred in plot C-31.

In 2002, Pavese's two nieces acceded to requests from various officials and cultural figures that his remains be transported to Santo Stefano Belbo. Pavese would certainly have agreed with the move, having written, "A town means not being alone, knowing that in the people, the trees, the soil, there is something of yourself, that even when you're not there it stays and waits for you."[51] His grave has become, as the local authorities hoped, one of the town's main tourist draws.

1. Pavese's father, Eugenio Pavese, who died at forty-seven when Pavese was five.

2. Pavese's mother, Consolina Mesturini, came from a well-off commercial family of Casale Monferrato.

3. Santo Stefano Belbo, where Pavese was born in 1908.
Photograph by Paolo Smaniotto.

4. Typical Langhe landscape.

5. Pavese in his first communion outfit, c. 1915–16.

6. Pavese with his mother, sister, niece, and brother-in law, c. 1926–28. His mother was approximately fifty-eight at the time.

7. Pavese, on the right, playing chess with an unidentified friend, c. 1923–26.

8. Pavese in the yard of the family villa in Reaglie, with friends Pippo Traglio and Mario Sturani, c. 1926–28.

9. Pavese, far left second row, in secondary school class picture, c. 1924. Friends Remo Giacchero and Tullio Pinelli are indicated in handwriting on the original. Third from right in the first row is Carlo Predella, whose suicide in 1929 left a lasting impression on Pavese.

10. Augusto Monti, Pavese's most influential teacher.

11. Pavese, Monti, and members of the "confraternity," c. 1928–30. From left to right: Carlo Pinelli, Tullio Pinelli, Dan Carli, Remo Giacchero (in aviator-style helmet), Pavese, Giuseppe Vaudagna, Monti, Enzo Monferini, Mario Sturani.

12. Natalia Ginzburg.

13. Massimo Mila.

14. Norberto Bobbio.

15. Giulio Einaudi.

16. Pavese of the Po.

17. Pavese with friend Enzo Monferini. It was in a punt like this that Pavese's relationship with Tina Pizzardo began in July 1933.

18. Breakwater on the Po, just downstream from the bridge that connects the center of town with the church of the Gran Madre di Dio.

19. Summertime on the Po, Turin, 1930s.

20. Center city Turin, 1920s. This street, looking south to the main railroad station, Porta Nuova, was completely rebuilt in the 1930s as the monumental Via Roma.

21. Stazione Porta Nuova, constructed in the late 1860s and still in use.

22–24. In its center, Turin is a city of arcades and porticos.

25. Pavese, Leone Ginzburg, Franco Antonicelli, Carlo Frassinelli during an excursion to the Langhe, 1932. Antonicelli edited and Frassinelli published that same year Pavese's translation of *Moby-Dick*.

26. Between 1931 and 1935 Pavese worked as a supplemental teacher in several private and state schools as well as night schools. Here, an all-female class surrounds him.

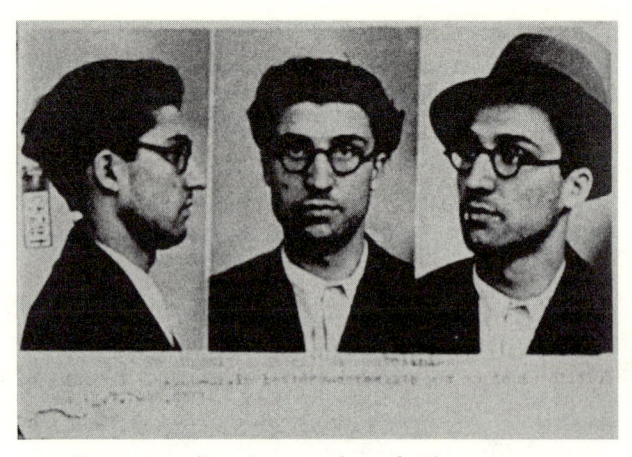

27. Pavese in police pictures taken after his arrest in 1935.

28. Pavese during his seven months of *confino* in Brancaleone Calabro. The kindness of the townspeople surprised him.

PART II

SIX
"Viva Walt Whitman"

Cesare Pavese never lived in or visited America; indeed, though he grew up seventy miles from Switzerland and fifty miles from the French border he never set foot outside Italy. The Italian liceo curriculum in the 1920s included neither English as a foreign language nor American literature in translation. Yet before he graduated from D'Azeglio in 1926 he read English well and preferred Walt Whitman above all other English-language writers.

By the end of his third year of university Pavese had already chosen Whitman as the subject of his degree thesis (*tesi di laurea*). Just before his fourth and last year began he started gathering in earnest what Whitman materials he could find, a difficult problem in the Italy of 1929.[1] In addition to secondary materials, Pavese prepared himself for the thesis by reading every poem in *Leaves of Grass* and making notes on each—oddly enough, on the kind of journal paper used by accountants for double-entry bookkeeping, 12 inches high by 7.8 inches wide (30.5 x 20 cm).[2] These capsule summaries make fascinating reading in themselves and contain *in nuce* some of the final thesis's most important points. We do not know how systematically, but we do know Pavese had been reading Whitman since liceo days, and some of his marginal notes remain in the liceo's library copy of Luigi Gamberale's Italian translation of *Leaves of Grass*.[3] Thus, while the reading notes he made in preparation for the thesis do not record his first impressions of Whitman, they do show what he thought about each poem, read in English with a purposefully critical eye in preparation for drafting. He finished his research during the academic year 1929–30 and wrote the thesis that winter, finishing it in the late spring of 1930.

The thesis, his first extended piece of criticism, documents engagingly the intersection of Pavese's enthusiasm for Whitman with then-current Italian critical theory as well as the interaction of his growing appreciation of America with the political reality of Italian Fascism. The work excited Pavese; he felt he was exploring new ground, especially in the context of Italian scholarship. In November 1929, even before he started drafting, Pavese wrote Chiuminatto, in English, "I succeeded barely in finding something I wanted for my degree's thesis about Walt Whitman. (You don't know, I'll be the first Italian to speak at some extent and critically of him. Look me over, I'll almost reveal him to Italy.)"[4] By February 1930 he was drafting and had apparently presented Whitman formally as his thesis topic, for he wrote Chiuminatto—again in English as were all his letters to this friend—"As you know I'll get my degree this fall and I have just choiced to present an essay about an American literature topic—the poetry of Walt Whitman which I've long been perusing and out of modesty I think I know better now than anyone else in Italy. I've hunted since two years all what is attainable here about him. Now I'm writing my essay and am quite satisfied the way the work goes on."[5] During the same week he wrote one of his Italian friends that "the thesis keeps progressing and it is continually more impressive."[6]

This sense of exploration, of revelation, together with his affection for Whitman, formed the background of Pavese's thesis. He was writing about a poet he loved, though one who was barely read in Italy. Pavese saw himself not just as a literature student writing a mandatory piece of criticism with the hope of obtaining professorial approval but also as a teacher himself, pointing out to the rest of the Italian intellectual community the real worth of a truly great but not sufficiently appreciated poet. Pavese worked from the conviction that others did not understand Whitman but that he did and that he had to share this understanding. As he said in the thesis, "I am trying to separate as much as possible the true nature of Whitman's poetic creation from its own inherent dross and to make it visible despite the fog created by others."[7]

This youthful excitement and missionary zeal explains many of the virtues of the thesis as well as most of its faults. It combines a coherent theoretical approach, deep insight, energy, and several wonderful close readings of Whitman's poems with loose prose, sophomoric posing, unnecessary repetition, and an arrogant, unwarranted dismissal of earlier criticism. The original of the still commercially unpublished thesis rests in the university archives on the Via Po, in the same building where Pavese defended it.[8] With all its dozens of overstrikes and even more manual corrections it comprises, including notes and bibliography, about 51,000 words on 305 double-spaced typewritten pages, measuring 20 cm (7.8 inches) wide by 27.5 cm (10.8 inches) tall. It contains seven chapters of text, seventeen pages of notes (placed at the end of each chapter), a three-page bibliographic essay, and a bibliography of five pages. The title page, as interesting for what it omits as for what it includes, reads:

Interpretation
of the
Poetry of Walt Whitman
Degree Thesis
Cesare Pavese
1930–VIII

While the obligatory Roman numeral identifying the year of the Fascist era does appear, the name of Pavese's thesis adviser, which was also obligatory, does not, an absence that has given rise to much unresolved speculation. All graduating university students in Italy must choose—and be accepted by—a *relatore*, a professor who approves the topic of the student's proposed thesis, guides the research, and afterward acts as its first reader. This professor also chairs the committee for the oral examination that immediately precedes the actual awarding of the *laurea*. The relatore's name must be mentioned on the title page of the thesis and in the minutes of the oral examination. In Pavese's case it appears in neither. The most logical candidate for relatore would have been Federico Olivero, then an untenured assistant professor, the only teacher of English literature on the faculty. Olivero was a competent scholar of both English and American literature. In 1912 he translated for Laterza the poetry of Edgar Allan Poe and during his long subsequent career he published monographs on Poe and Francis Thompson, a three-volume compilation, with commentary, of English religious poetry, a collection of essays on English literature, and even an introduction to an Italian translation of *Beowulf*.[9] Pavese had taken two courses with him, one required and one an elective; the professor had given him high marks in both—the maximum possible, thirty *con lode*, for the obligatory course and a straight thirty out of thirty for the elective. Almost certainly Pavese presented Whitman as his thesis topic to Olivero, probably, as the letter to Chiuminatto indicates, in February 1930. Pavese was the only one of the university's twenty-six spring 1930 candidates for the laurea in Letters and Philosophy who had concentrated, that is, chosen a thesis topic, in English literature. Thus, it also seems odd that not only does Professor Olivero not appear as relatore on the thesis, he neither chaired nor even sat on Pavese's examining committee. Complicated reasons may have caused him to absent himself, but his absence the June day of Pavese's laurea could just as easily have been caused by illness or a last-minute appointment. The faculty's administrative committee scheduled three other laurea exams for the same afternoon as Pavese's and placed Olivero on all four committees. He attended none of the four examinations.[10]

Neither Olivero, who died in 1955, nor Pavese left any account of the actual academic journey of the thesis. For Olivero, of course, Pavese's submission was only one of hundreds in the professor's extended career. While we have no direct testimony from the principals, the combined reminiscences of Pavese's friends indicate that Olivero did indeed approve Pavese's thesis topic, but in the end turned down the thesis itself. Why he rejected it is a matter of speculation. The reasons generally proposed are either that Olivero, a conservative though not extreme Fascist, disliked the political implications of Pavese's finished thesis, or that since Olivero specialized in English Romantic writers he felt he had nothing to say about a long essay on Walt Whitman.[11] One knowledgeable scholar of the era believes that Olivero rejected Pavese's thesis because of the student's too enthusiastic acceptance of Crocean aesthetic theory, a conjecture Augusto Monti's memory supports.[12] Most likely Olivero did deliberately sidestep the thesis, and probably because of the Croce link. In June 1929 Croce had spoken out in the Senate against the ratification of the Lateran Pacts, causing Mussolini famously to characterize Croce as "a shirker from history" (*imboscato della storia*). Soon after,

Croce's works were proscribed from course readings in Italian universities and liceos. In mid-1930, an untenured professor might well have thought twice about appearing as the relatore on a thesis that, as we will see, used Croce's aesthetic criteria so abundantly.

Thus, Davide Lajolo's dramatic and political retelling of the incident (as usual, with no citation of sources), which casts Olivero as a Fascist-leaning intransigent and Pavese as a heroically intellectual resistance fighter, probably has a kernel of truth: "That courageous work [Pavese's thesis] caused him his first bitter difficulties. The thesis was rejected. The professor attributed a political interpretation to the Crocean influence and Pavese was given the alternative of revising his dissertation or changing the topic. He did not give in and peremptorily refused to do either."[13] Lajolo goes on to say, again with no evidence cited, that Leone Ginzburg came to Pavese's rescue by convincing the tenured full professor of French, Ferdinando Neri, to approve the thesis and chair Pavese's examining committee. This scenario seems realistic because the faculty treated Ginzburg as virtually an equal. It is, however, just as possible that Pavese himself approached Neri, who had given Pavese the good grade of 29 out of 30 in French literature and was known for his openness to comparative literature studies.[14] In any case, Pavese's thesis was accepted and Neri did chair Pavese's thesis examination committee and signed off on Pavese's final grade. Since Olivero had rejected the thesis, he could not permit his name to appear as the relatore on the copy deposited with the university, and since Neri replaced Olivero officially only as the chair of the examining committee, neither could Neri's name appear on the thesis. Thus, no name appeared, a compromise that seems to have satisfied everyone and permitted Pavese to get his laurea.

The second date on the title page, "VIII," though unnecessary for the examiners, reminds us that Pavese finished his thesis in the eighth year of Benito Mussolini's Fascist regime. By 1930, the year after he concluded the Lateran Pacts with Pope Pius XI, Mussolini had consolidated his position and attained a level of prestige and power that would not significantly diminish until the second year of World War II. His Fascist party and the Italian government had become virtually indistinguishable. The government had established formal censorship offices and permitted no overt, public, especially political, criticism of the regime. The effects of Fascism's inflated rhetoric and pressured conformism were felt everywhere. The reality of the political and intellectual environment of the time perforce meant that a thesis on the most democratic of a foreign democracy's great poets, submitted for a degree at an Italian state university funded entirely by the Fascist Ministry of Education, had political overtones. As H. Stuart Hughes, making a broader point, put it, "In the 1930s an interest in the United States was itself an act of political protest, a token of admiration for a free and dynamic society."[15]

Pavese's choosing to write on Whitman did in fact constitute an act of calculated critical subversion, and its political subtext represented an oblique rebuke to Italy's sanctioned culture. In praising Whitman's and America's vitality, Pavese was intentionally making an unspoken comparison to what he saw as Italy's lack of creative vitality under a stifling, conformist political system. With censorship a reality and imprisonment or internal exile (confino) always possible, as Pavese personally learned five years later, only a free society could produce or even permit a poet to utter, in Whitman's phrase, a "barbaric yawp over the roofs of the world."

The thesis contains nothing explicitly hostile to the regime; Pavese knew that no adviser or examining panel could accept a work with openly political criticism. So Pavese, like all like-minded writers of the period, had to make literary criticism sometimes do double duty as political commentary. For example, in his analysis of "Song of the Broad-Axe," he wrote, "The poem's great defect is already expressed in its title. I refer to the axe, the symbol of conquest, methodical labor, destruction, and various other things."[16] For any Italian in 1930, among the "various other things" the axe would have symbolized was the Fascist regime, whose emblem, harking back to ancient Rome, was the fasces: a bundle of rods surrounding an axe with blade protruding. Thus, while Pavese's enthusiasm for Whitman gave the thesis its driving force, Fascism set limits beyond which it could not go. Pavese's principal passion, however, unlike that of some of his close friends (Leone Ginzburg and Norberto Bobbio, for example), was literary, not political; his thesis is primarily a work of literary appreciation and a document of cultural history. To read it solely with political eyeglasses would be to read it with blinders.

Its index page lists the thesis's chapter titles.[17] They suggest, as the text bears out, that Pavese by and large organized his long essay as a running, aesthetic-poetic, sometimes political, commentary on *Leaves of Grass*, prefaced by an introduction and interrupted with references to Whitman's prose. The work is literally an extended thesis, that is, a proposition advanced and defended: early on, Pavese states his position, and then he proceeds to point out how each important poem supports or constitutes a logical extension of that position. Such an approach makes perfect sense as a way of buttressing an argument, but it also runs the risk of turning into a species of literary lawyering that uses poetry more as evidence than art.

Pavese's core contention, the proposition he advanced and defended, concerned what he called Whitman's "myth of discovery," or, equivalently, "the poetry of making poetry." In his view, Whitman did not so much create poetry about a newly discovered world as create poetry out of the act of discovery itself. Whitman did not discover a new kind of poetry but wrote good poetry about his effort to create a new poetry. Countless times, Pavese came back to a similar interpretation as the key to Whitman: not the poetry of an emotion, act, or incident but the poetry of discovering and writing about the emotion, act, or incident. In sum, he approached Whitman's poetry as a self-reflexive act of self-creation, a lesson Pavese would remember. He stated his proposition for the first time in chapter 1 when, after describing what he considered Whitman's declared aims, he wrote:

> He did not write the primitive poem he dreamt of, but rather the poem of this dream. He did not in fact create a book qualitatively different from "European" books. He did not create a book that was not a book, but like every "European" poet worthy of the name he created his own book in which his dream resolved itself in the poetry of the dreaming, the lyric of the world seen through this dream.
>
> Walt Whitman did not achieve the absurd goal of creating a poetry adapted to the democratic world and newly discovered land, because poetry is always only poetry. But by devoting his life to the repetition of this design in various ways, he made poetry of the design, the poetry of discovering a new world and singing it. Did it not seem a mere pun I would say that Walt Whitman made poetry of making poetry. It is this, in another form, that I call in him the myth of discovery.[18]

This "myth of discovery" had as its corollary the figure of the pioneer, the one who did the discovering and who, more importantly, sang the act of discovery. Early in his second chapter, after using the first to emphasize the crucial nature of the "myth of discovery," Pavese stated that "to say Walt Whitman sang the pioneer is of course not to say much at all. Many have said it, thereby supporting Whitman himself . . . We need, therefore, to examine the different attributes of this pioneer in different poems, to describe this myth of the pioneer and thereby, at a minimum, distinguish it, for example, from that other picture-card figure of a pioneer, the young hero of Longfellow's *Excelsior*."[19] Pavese draws the distinction a few pages later:

> Walt Whitman's pioneer is not the rough and elemental man one would expect. Nor is he someone who just gets on with the realities of his life and who, because of the way he proceeds, cannot bother with reflection. Walt Whitman's pioneer knows he is a pioneer and this makes an enormous difference. It means that instead of the more or less conventional figure of a pioneer, we have here the poetry of being a pioneer . . . The pioneer, while retaining his traditional appearance (pistol, axe, leather trousers, etc.) becomes the "minstrel latent in the prairies," the poet of the States, he who proclaims a new life.[20]

Throughout his discussion of Whitman, Pavese insisted on this kind of second-level interpretation: not the pioneer discovering, but the pioneer aware of being a pioneer and singing not a discovery but the act of discovery. This distinction between the poetry of discovering something and the poetry of the act of discovery links Pavese to, and yet sets him off from, such critics as Richard Chase, who said, "Whitman was always *discovering* nature as if for the first time, and this enhanced that sense of novelty, the sense that there *are* new things under the sun, which is one of Whitman's strong points."[21] Pavese would have agreed with Chase about the prime importance of discovery and nature in Whitman's poetry but would have added that the act of discovering nature deserves more attention than the nature discovered.

"The myth of discovery" ("the poetry of making poetry") and the "pioneer" constitute perfectly valid entry points for an interpretation of Whitman—and Pavese held to them, and virtually them alone, for 275 pages that comment on 240 of the some 400 poems that make up *Leaves of Grass*. For him, only these two ideas yielded a true grasp of Whitman. Of the poetry of making poetry he wrote, "I am ever more convinced that this is Walt Whitman's true world, the critical formula that best explains him," and "We thus see Whitman repeat himself with infinite variety and bring to life the same myth: the man who discovers and proclaims the meanings of life in a world seen with virgin eyes. He sings the enchantment of this discovery and proclamation . . . [with] the pleased satisfaction of the man who describes it and prides himself on being new and different." As for the figure of the pioneer, it establishes "a poetic unity for *Leaves of Grass* which, resolving its contradictions, defines its significance."[22]

His two themes, pioneer and discovery, merged at times. The pioneer who made the discoveries also proclaimed or sang the act of discovery:

> I have stated before in this study, indeed by now it must seem a cliché, that through his intention to proclaim a new gospel, Whitman above all created the poetry of this intention, the figure, that is, of the proclaimer who is also a poet and a good comrade on the road. This poetry does not arise from just two or three songs particularly dedicated to this . . . Rather, we hear the consciousness of the mission reecho and express itself many different ways in every page of the book: in the description of a march, in the joy of friendship, in the praise of a piece of music.[23]

"The pioneer," "the proclaimer," "the good comrade on the road" are all embodiments of Whitman, the radical, democratic individual who, by implication, had freed himself of all conformity. In the context of Fascist Italy, Pavese's literary approach constituted both thinly-disguised self-empowerment and indirect political commentary.

Pavese repeated his two points so frequently that he began his last chapter by saying he did not need to repeat them again—and proceeded to do so:

> Since this chapter will be the last I hope it will also be the most convincing. I will offer definitive proof and clear theoretical demonstrations of everything I have so far affirmed.
>
> I believe I have already put forward my thoughts about the persona of Walt Whitman as pioneer, a persona that possesses those characteristics analyzed throughout my study. I see no need, therefore, to polish up material that I have presented clearly and at length elsewhere. To conclude and present the last proofs of the absolute preponderance of this persona in *Leaves of Grass*,

> I propose now to demonstrate that even death, the passage to the beyond, and what lies beyond the self—all, in sum, which in a hasty phrase is called Whitman's mysticism—is for him yet one more myth of discovery, a pioneer's conquest, the continuation of the earthly march expressed with the same figures.[24]

Because he believed that one formula best contained Whitman, Pavese fell into the trap of interpreting virtually every poem in *Leaves of Grass* in ways that would support his argument, and he roundly attacked and denigrated those critics who had not seen what he had. Pavese's effort calls to mind Edwin Miller's comment on William James's reading of Whitman: "Geniuses, like lesser men, read into a book what they want to find there, and too often because they are intent upon generalizations they neglect the all too contradictory nature of their subject matter."[25] Whether genius or lesser man, Pavese certainly did neglect the varied and contradictory nature of *Leaves of Grass* in order to muster support for his two basic generalizations. As a result, and despite a lively appreciation of Whitman's art, Pavese denied himself a more complete vision. In attempting to reveal the "true" Whitman, Pavese in fact added one more stone to what Willard Thorp has called "the cairn of criticism and commentary—Whitman as Hegelian, Whitman as Transcendentalist, Whitman as the Prophet of Personalism or Democracy or World Government, Whitman as the most Genuinely American of our Poets, Whitman as the Christ of our Age."[26] Pavese's stone could be described as Whitman as the Poet of Making Poetry.

In his thesis Pavese adopted a disparaging and almost arrogant attitude toward most earlier Whitman criticism, both foreign and Italian, an attitude that does him little credit—especially since he had in fact overlooked much of the best English-language criticism published before he began drafting, and let himself be convinced that what he had read fairly represented all Whitman criticism. He defended his choices by writing, in his bibliographic essay, that it was "virtually impossible to generate a satisfactory bibliography of Whitman in Italy because the materials for American studies are so scarce. Added to this general situation is the particular difficulty that my author presents because of his having been, as I have noted, the subject of too few truly critical monographs and of too many articles and essays dispersed among the newspapers and journals of the world."[27] Yet that difficulty does not excuse his overlooking *all* of the following works (listed in reverse chronological order): T. S. Eliot's 1928 and 1926 remarks on Whitman; D. H. Lawrence's important essay in *Studies in Classic American Literature* (1923); Stuart Sherman's 1922 piece in his book *Americans*; Paul More's 1906 essay; the lecture of William James printed in *The Varieties of Religious Experience* (1902), which had been translated into Italian and published in 1904; Barrett Wendell's chapter in *A Literary History of America* (1900); and the criticism of William Dean Howells (1889) and John Jay Chapman (1898).[28] Of all these pieces, only those by Eliot and Howells were "dispersed among the newspapers and journals of the world"; all the rest had been published in book form well before Pavese began drafting. Certainly some were not easily available in Italian libraries, but had Pavese asked, Chiuminatto, who returned to America in September 1929, could have supplied them, just as he did other books in 1929 and the following few years.

Also, Pavese's contention that he is "revealing" Whitman to Italy unfairly belittles the Italian scholarship that preceded his. As early as 1879, Enrico Nencioni had written his first article on Whitman, which brought immediate and enthusiastic responses from artists of the level of Giosuè Carducci and Gabriele D'Annunzio.[29] In 1887 Luigi Gamberale translated a selection of forty-eight of Whitman's poems and in 1898 Pasquale Jannaccone published his study of Whitman.[30] In 1907 Gamberale completed a full translation of *Leaves of Grass*.[31] Critical pieces on Whitman appeared in Italian periodicals throughout the first three decades of the twentieth century. All in all, one can fairly say that Italy had produced a respectable though not abundant body of Whitman criticism before Pavese began his research.[32] But even if the prior commentary on Whitman in Italy had been more copious, Pavese's stance would have remained the same. He did not want to offer mere critical observations, but rather to drive home what he considered *the* truth about Whitman. Pavese did not mean that Italy needed *a* revelation; he meant *his* revelation. He had found his poetic master and he felt obliged to spread the truth about him. In 1930, at least, Pavese used the word "reveal" in regard to Whitman in an evangelical, missionary sense.

Thus, Pavese stood on dangerous ground when he so roundly dismissed earlier Whitman criticism as mostly useless. In his first chapter, Pavese laid out that dismissal at some length:

As I hope I have made clear, Walt Whitman was also and above all else the poet of the desire to be such a poet. That which I have just highlighted in de Selincourt constitutes the high point that criticism has so far reached in trying to delineate an aesthetic figure for Whitman. Indeed, all the other scholars, including those who wrote after de Selincourt, not only came to no conclusions in this regard but did not even try.

All of them, including the best of this century such as Perry, Noyes, Bailey and Michaud, have operated for the last twenty years within the same framework. Each presents a summary and even criticism, often excellent criticism, of Walt Whitman as a man and thinker. They generally also include rhetorical or abstract resolutions of various technical issues in his work. But not a word as to how Whitman expressed—that is, created— the poetic world for which it seems he has become so famous. The comments in this regard that one does find tend always to draw conclusions one could reduce to de Selincourt's already-mentioned formula: *"Walt Whitman is the poet of the principle of life, etc."* They lack any singularity and all merge into the same foggy generality. Even Bailey, who in 1926 advanced so far as to say that Whitman's merit was to have created a new human figure out of his own experience, then goes astray and describes a biographical rather than poetic figure.

But I do not want to review all Whitman's critics here. I do not want to write, as one might say, a critique of criticism. That is not my goal; nor is it my goal to deal with, for example, the historical issues of Whitman's sources and influences. It would be too easy to attack these critics in the name of a principle they did not even consider and that I did not personally discover. It is only natural that if one looks at Whitman from a point of view no one else has used, one will have something to say no one else has said.[33]

What no one had said, of course, was that Whitman is the poet of making poetry. After one of his many affirmations of that point, Pavese added, "Here lies the deep heart of Walt Whitman and the failure to grasp this point leads to innumerable errors of judgment, as the body of Whitman criticism shows and I have already sufficiently demonstrated."[34]

The use Pavese made of the critics, particularly of two now mostly forgotten writers, weakens the thesis as a scholarly work. All totaled (that is, including in text, endnotes, and bibliography), Pavese mentioned thirty-nine different critics/scholars. In the text, however, he actually cited or referred to more than once only nineteen. A numerical analysis confirms the impression one receives in reading the text: Pavese concerned himself primarily with two critics, John Bailey (1864–1931) and Basil de Selincourt (1876–1966). Excluding Whitman titles or quotes, Pavese included roughly 150 citations or references in his text, and over one-third of them involved Bailey or de Selincourt.

Each of these prolific critics wrote a full-length study of Whitman: de Selincourt's *Walt Whitman: A Critical Study* appeared in 1914 and Bailey's *Walt Whitman* in 1926.[35] Given the stance he adopted, Pavese had to demonstrate that he had more insight than either, and he lost few opportunities to do so. In the thesis's second chapter Pavese stated that de Selincourt "loses himself in absurdities" and "devises strange theories." He later described "de Selincourt's habitual failing: he speaks too abstractly and does not deal with specifics, which explains why reading him is so often like driving in a fog."[36] Yet, Pavese had a certain respect for this critic whom at one point he called "my de Selincourt."[37] Of all the critics he dealt with, de Selincourt came closest to Pavese's own views on Whitman, especially as regarded the structure of *Leaves of Grass*, Whitman's use of catalogs, and Whitman's aesthetic stance.[38]

Pavese felt less ambivalent about Bailey. He did include him among the "best" critics of the (then twenty-nine-year-old) twentieth century and found a few good things to say about him, for example, that Bailey occasionally "arrived at subtle conclusions."[39] But as a rule Pavese characterized Bailey as representing the worst in Whitman criticism. The young student disliked the old critic for unclear reasons stated with exceptional clarity. Bailey's opinions just seemed to annoy Pavese in principle and led to several sophomoric tirades. Bailey, for example, did not much care for Whitman's use of foreign words. Pavese did. He analyzed the poem "Song of the Open Road," quoted a line that includes "Allons!" and continued thus:

> At this point, Whitman suddenly truncates the praise of embraces and the "fresh and sweet" contact amidst nature and with section 9 raises a shout, a call, an incitement to action, aimed, after the manly rapture of the "idler," at the pioneer who acts: "Allons! whoever you are . . ." This entire second movement is densely spangled with these inciting "*Allons!*" and I regret that they raise another instance in which Bailey must be challenged.

> On page 92 of his cited work he states that Whitman's use from time to time of foreign words (*Libertad*, *Omnes*, *Accouchez*, etc.) is a grave defect and an indication of an even more serious general decay in his poetry. Whether Whitman uses these foreign phrases to show off or for some other reason is not terribly important. What is essential is that they help in better expressing an idea. And, allowing for my modest knowledge of English, I believe in this case that nothing could better serve to distinguish the particular fervor of the incitement from all the rest than this almost international "*Allons!*" uncompromising and impressive in its positioning and repetition. What would Bailey prefer? A feeble "come on!" or a prattling "get up!" or a "forward" or "let's go!"? Or maybe a picturesque and "slangy" "shake a leg!"?[40]

Despite the unnecessarily flip remarks at the end designed to show just how familiar he was with colloquial American English, Pavese's point here has merit. The same holds true elsewhere in the thesis, and it seems a pity that he so often deflected attention from valid observations with strident ad hominem arguments, as he did, for example, in another attack on Bailey over the question of Whitman's catalogs. In the middle of the excerpt below, Pavese quotes Bailey (identified elsewhere as the source) and interjects his own comments within parentheses before going on to call Bailey a "malcontent":

> I want to demonstrate how Walt Whitman, by simply returning to the old attitude of one who goes wandering among landscapes and things, enjoying revelation and evocative richness, succeeded in writing two works which, if they are not considered among his best, the fault lies solely with the critics: "Our Old Feuillage" and "O Magnet-South."
> I believe I have said elsewhere of the former that in the heat of the anti-catalog campaign it has been defined as "little more than a catalogue, which contains, however (Thank God) items that only the most curious (!) eye would have noticed." What do I have to do? Explain all over again my entire theory of style? I have already done that too often. I can, however, state that if someone were to complain that we have here a list of vignettes inserted carelessly and without order among casual protestations of love for and faith in America, concluded with a gesture that is not a conclusion, that would be sufficient evidence to doubt if the malcontent ever understood anything about Walt Whitman.[41]

In a similar vein, Pavese, in his discussion of "Song of the Broad-Axe," managed to attack both Bailey and de Selincourt at the same time:

> For Bailey, this song was "perhaps chiefly remarkable" because it begins with "six rhymed lines." For all I know, the distinguished American scholar was here amusing himself with a bit of irony, and if that is the case I bow to him, because in my opinion nothing is more agreeable than a critic who knows how to drop the rigid mask of his profession. Though I hope not, it is possible that Bailey, in here noting the anomaly of the six rhymes, truly believes that they are the most interesting thing about the poem because of his principle that the more willingly Whitman accepts rhyme schemes, the better he succeeds. If this is the case, then I will drop my mask, and remembering de Selincourt's remarks already cited in relation to "Native Moments," comfort myself with the knowledge that no matter how badly my study of Whitman may turn out, some one else has said something more ridiculous about him.[42]

This kind of remark does not increase one's confidence in Pavese's judgments, and not just because Bailey was English, not American.[43]

Pavese attacked other critics besides Bailey and de Selincourt in the same tone, and sometimes lashed out at "Whitman criticism" in general. He complained most often that earlier critics, no matter how well they talked about Whitman's ideas and occasionally his technique, understood little about Whitman's aesthetics, how he created poetry. Every chapter in the thesis contains examples of this attitude, from a short remark about "Crossing Brooklyn Ferry" ("a song about which much has been written but nothing said") to a long tirade that ends, "all those scholars who have compiled long chapters on the 'grey poet' would have done much better to cut short their marveling about this miracle of human compassion since they can say nothing that Whitman did not say better in his own recollections. But let's move on."[44] One hears in this kind of overreaching rhetoric echoes of Whitman's bravura prose; Pavese may well have been deliberately attempting to adopt a Whitmanian tone to attack Whitman critics.

In the end, Pavese's attitude toward Whitman criticism, both generally and specifically, detracted from the value of the thesis. While this is only speculation, it does seem possible that these clear attacks on accredited literary scholarship figured among the reasons that

Professor Olivero rejected the thesis. Indeed, an objective reader has to make some effort to drain off Pavese's own "inherent dross" to get at the hard core of his work.

Pavese's prose does not help in this process: he chose a tone so intentionally relaxed as to be distracting. Pavese had read enormously in several languages by the time he started drafting this thesis, he knew about levels of formality in prose—and yet he chose one so inappropriate for the one formal academic presentation required of all Italian degree candidates that it might well have provided another of Olivero's reasons for rejection. A few examples from Pavese's original Italian text show the conversational tone he established:

> Page 40: "I critici se la son sempre cavata." (The critics have always gotten by.) *Cavarsela*, the idiomatic construction used here in the present perfect tense, is based on the reflexive infinitive *cavarsi* and means to get out of a difficulty, to manage, to get by. While Pavese's use of the phrase is straightforward in its context, its tone is not that of the usual academic paper.
>
> Page 88: "Qualche volta troviamo, va bene, accenni alle generazioni future." (Sometimes we find, okay, allusions to future generations.) *Va bene*, one of the most common spoken Italian idioms, means literally, "it goes well." Italians use it in the sense of "okay" or "all right." "Va bene" sounds as out of place here as "okay" would in an American PhD dissertation.
>
> Page 92: "È veramente una gran cosa questa poesiola e ci vuole un bel coraggio a discuterla" (This little poem is truly something wonderful and it takes nerve to argue about it.) Here, dropping the two final letters ("–de") from *grande* and the use of the colloquial *ci vuole un bel coraggio* continue the idiomatic, spoken tone Pavese has established.
>
> Page 140: "Ora, le poesie elegiache, o tragiche, di W.W. sono solidamente gran belle poesie non mica per la tenebrosa ragione che più toccano 'il fondo di tristezza che è la finale rivelazione di ogni profondo squardo all'esistenza' come diceva non so più chi . . ." (Now, W.W.'s elegiac, or tragic, poems are assuredly great and beautiful, but not at all for the gloomy reason that many of them touch "the depth of sadness that is the final revelation of every profound look at existence," as I forget who said.) Here Pavese aggravated the effect of using initials instead of Whitman's name—something he did frequently throughout the thesis—by using the (highly colloquial) negative adverbial emphasizer *mica*, and by concluding with the malapert "I forget who." A professor could reasonably suggest that a student leave

out a quotation if he does not know the source, and spell out the name of his thesis's subject.

Pavese apparently wanted to make the thesis a conversation between him and the reader, and so adopted an appropriately lively conversational tone. In his own way, he wanted anyone who touched the work to feel the man behind it, just as Whitman said so grandly about himself in "So Long!"[45] Such a tone, however, lacks the formality expected in an academic presentation. Pavese, by twenty-one already a literary sophisticate, knew what he was doing. He chose the tone deliberately, as a second act of cultural subversion, the first being his choice of topic. His prose implied that informality and freshness take precedence over formal and formalistic Italian. His style has a certain goliardic élan, even if in the context of the work at hand it actually represents a lapse of taste and creates the impression of intellectual carelessness—not an impression a candidate wants to give to the professors reading his thesis. Apparently, those readers noted the same issues, because the day after defending his thesis Pavese wrote to Chiuminatto, "Gosh all fish-hooks! It's my lot to-day to be lectured by all. I've been lectured by the Board of Teachers of the University about the fondness of slang I showed in my degree thesis (which I got safely, I'm a PhD. Now, ah!)"[46]

Regardless of the prose style he used, Pavese did not write his thesis in a critical vacuum. Educated Italians would have recognized immediately the influence in the thesis of Benedetto Croce, even though Pavese never cites him and his name does not appear in the bibliography. Living in the twenty-first century, it is easy to forget the enormous literary and intellectual influence that Croce, born in the nineteenth, had in and on Italy during the twentieth century, especially its first half. As H. Stuart Hughes has said, Croce was a figure "whose influence in his own country, over which for a half-century he exercised a kind of literary and philosophical dictatorship, was without parallel in our time . . . Not since Goethe had any single individual dominated so completely the culture of a major European country."[47]

Croce, born in 1866, began publishing his historical, literary, philosophical, and political works before 1900. By 1910 his reputation had already grown so solid that the Italian government appointed him "Senator for Life." He served as minister of education in 1920–21, but resigned from the cabinet and never served under Mussolini.

A firm anti-Fascist, though less and less outspoken as Fascism consolidated its power, Croce's extraordinary prestige within and outside Italy prevented Mussolini from taking any but verbal action against him. By the mid-1920s he had become not only Italy's intellectual arbiter but also the living symbol of serious intellectual resistance to the regime.

His influence was felt in Turin as much as anywhere else in the country, perhaps even more so because of personal links. Though born in the province of L'Aquila northeast of Rome and identified forever with Naples, which he made home his whole adult life, he married a woman from Turin, Adele Rossi, and for many years spent summers with her and their growing family in a resort town in the Piedmont mountains. They also frequently visited their daughter Elena, who settled in Turin. His Turinese in-laws and many Turin intellectuals knew Croce personally through these connections. For example, Luigi Einaudi, then a professor of economics, shared Croce's love of books and antique furniture. Einaudi's son Giulio, writing his memoirs in 1988, still remembered Croce's Turin visits, where he was respectfully addressed as "Don Benedetto."[48] Leone Ginzburg's sister Marussia in her maturity recalled Croce's talking with Leone and friends in the Ginzburgs' Turin apartment.[49]

Augusto Monti referred to Croce as "our master," and recounted in his memoirs how, despite the necessity of following the Fascist-imposed curriculum, he taught all the books required by the syllabus in the 1920s just as Croce would have done.[50] Norberto Bobbio, Italy's most noted political philosopher of the second half of the twentieth century, and a member of the confraternity, wrote that for this circle of friends Croce was in the 1920s "not just a philosopher but a spiritual guide," "the grandmaster of freedom," "the royal road of anti-fascism."[51] Aesthetically, "Croceanism was a secure criterion of delineation between those who had entered into the possession of the truth and those who . . . were still groping in the shadows."[52] A reading of Pavese's thesis with Croce in mind makes it abundantly clear that by 1930 its young author felt he "had entered into the possession of the truth."

Croce, as a philosopher usually classified as neo-idealist, developed what he called the "philosophy of the spirit."[53] Croce saw all of history as a playing out of the human spirit into a multitude of individual acts, all driving toward an ever-increasing sense of freedom. He believed that this human spirit, universal yet individual, spilled over into art in specific ways, ways that he described with equal specificity in his philosophy of aesthetics and his countless articles of literary criticism.

Croce first presented his ideas on aesthetics in book-length form in 1902 when he published *Estetica come scienza dell'espressione e linguistica generale* (*Aesthetic as Science of Expression and General Linguistic*).[54] He followed up with many articles in the review that he founded, *La Critica*, and with other books. His 1928 essay, "Aesthetica in nuce" ("Aesthetics in a Nutshell," written in Italian despite the Latin title), became, as translated by the English philosopher R. G. Collingwood, the entry "Aesthetics" in the fourteenth edition (1929) of the *Encyclopaedia Britannica*.[55] This twelve-thousand-word essay, peremptorily and almost belligerently prescriptive, remains the single most forceful statement of Croce's philosophy of aesthetics. (Only in 1974 would the editors of the *Britannica* replace it with a much broader and descriptive entry by English philosopher Stephen C. Pepper and American art historian Thomas Munro, with the publication of the fifteenth edition. Thus, for forty-five years, readers of the *Britannica* mistook Croce's description of his own theory for an explanation of aesthetics in general.)[56]

For Croce, all art, literature included, was "neither feeling nor image, nor yet the sum of the two, but 'contemplation of feeling' or 'lyrical intuition' or (which is the same thing) 'pure intuition'—pure, that is, of all historical and critical reference to the reality or unreality of the images of which it is woven, and apprehending the pure throb of life in its ideality."[57] Crucially, if a work does not contain the fused conjoining of both image and feeling that constitutes "lyrical intuition," it does not succeed as a work of art, indeed is *not* a work of art. To make it perfectly clear that *only* works that successfully deliver "lyrical intuition" deserve to be called art, Croce famously listed seven strictures of what art is *not*. Among those that eventually had relevance for Pavese's thesis were "Art is not philosophy," "Art is not history," "Art is not the play of fancy," and most importantly for someone dealing with Whitman, "Art is not instruction or oratory."

Croce believed that each successful work of art was its own individually happy fusion of image and feeling into "lyrical intuition."

Thus, categories such as "tragic, comic, lyrical, heroic, erotic, idyllic, romantic, and so on" were useful only after the fact, for mundane tasks, such as "to distribute an artist's work, for purposes of publication." He also rejected any concept of a work of art as a social or historical document; a work of art might *also* illuminate some characteristics of the time in which it was created, but that was not what made it a work of art. As Croce put it, "Dante is not simply a document of the middle ages, nor Shakespeare of the English Renaissance; as such they have many equals or superiors among bad poets and non-poets."

Since for him all art—poetry, fiction, music, architecture, painting, sculpture, etc.—came into being only when successfully infused by the artist with "contemplation of feeling" or "lyrical intuition," and because art resists categorization, Croce believed that at the moment of creation all art is one. He put this unitary idea simply: "art is one and cannot be divided into arts."

Croce's assertion of the unity of art, despite the individuality of different works of art, meant that all criticism of art could and indeed *should* proceed along similar lines. The reader/viewer/listener needed to use his trained discernment to determine if the personality of the artist infused the individual work with "lyrical intuition." If it did, the critic should proclaim the work "successful," that is, as art; if it did not, the work, whatever its other merits, must be declared unsuccessful, that is, as not art. While not an issue when he developed the theory, Croce's concern with a work of art only as a work of art had by 1930 taken on political overtones. As Antonio Catalfamo puts it, "Croce's concept, according to which poetry is 'lyric intuition,' that is, the expression of the poet's immediate emotion and nothing more, challenged the Fascist regime's concept of literature, which saw literature as an instrument of political propaganda, aimed at the exaltation of the nation and its conquests."[58]

Because Pavese's thesis remains commercially unpublished, there exists little critical commentary directed specifically to it. Still, those who have read it have noted the work's obvious Crocean foundation. Gian-Paolo Biasin defines the work as "an application of Crocean criticism to Walt Whitman."[59] Literary critic Michele Tondo, who read in 1969 a marked-up copy provided by Pavese's sister, wrote, "The school of Augusto Monti, in which Croceanism was enriched with a lively ethical-political dimension, found in Cesare Pavese the ideal student, capable of standing on his own and advancing the lessons of the master."[60] Monti described Pavese's thesis as "a Crocean thing."[61] Pavese's first biographer said the thesis showed that "the Crocean aesthetic had been completely assimilated by Pavese."[62] The one scholar who disagrees with this Crocean interpretation, Valerio Ferme, does so only to the extent that he considers the Pavese of 1930 an imperfect Crocean who in the thesis was trying to escape the master's "ivory-tower" idealism.[63] Art as one, art as "lyrical intuition," the importance of individual personality, criticism as the discernment of what is successful and what is not (and therefore is or is not art), judgment of each work of art on its own, definite things that art is not (especially not history, instruction, or oratory)—all these aspects of Croce's aesthetics had evident impact on Pavese when he was writing his thesis on Whitman. Pavese fashioned for himself the concepts of "the poetry of making poetry" and the figure of the "pioneer" who discovered and sang the act of discovery. As his preparatory notes make clear, he filtered Whitman first though his own sensibility. Yet, in the finished thesis, he adopted a thoroughly Crocean critical vocabulary.

For example, Pavese used such words as "lyric" and "poetry"—as in "the lyric of the world seen through this dream," "because poetry is always only poetry," and "did it not seem a mere pun I would say that Walt Whitman made poetry of making poetry," to quote from one passage—as interchangeable words in a precise Crocean sense.[64] In short, poetry equals lyric equals the contemplation of feeling equals lyric intuition equals art. Indeed, the last use of the word "poetry" in the almost disavowed pun makes the point clear. It is this Crocean use of the words "poetry" and "lyric" as shorthand for "art" that allows Pavese elsewhere in the thesis to say that Whitman's prose pieces "occasionally rise to the level of poetry" or to describe a certain strain of Whitman criticism as an "a-esthetic approach that does not deal with the poetry as poetry."[65]

Also, the seemingly tautological statement that "poetry is always only poetry" is not casual comment, but Crocean credo. It restates in Pavese's words Croce's dictum that "art is one and cannot be divided into arts." Pavese took his aesthetic stand with that statement early in the thesis; later, in the midst of his analyses of the poems, he restated it in even more obviously Crocean terms: "for us the issue is clear: Art is one unity and there are no higher levels of subject matter nor a dramatic mode that is better than a lyric mode."[66]

Pavese's persistent summary judgments of Whitman's poems and his assigning of almost all of them to one of two categories—success or failure—can be puzzling, if not downright annoying, but they do make sense in a Crocean context. This binary system of classification is in fact a Crocean imperative, for Croce insisted that the critic's first obligation is to judge a work and explicitly declare if it is art or not. Croce delineated his concept of "criticism as judgment," as one of his translators called it[67] as early as 1911 when he wrote: "Criticism gives only the knowledge that what stands before us is, or is not, a product of art. Its problem is formulated in these terms: 'A is art; or A is not art'; or 'A is art in parts a, b, c; it is not art in parts d, e, f.' In other words, criticism enunciates: 'There is a fact, A, which is a work of art'; or 'it is mistakenly believed that there is a fact A, which is a work of art.'"[68] As outlined above, the critic fulfills this first obligation, of establishing whether the work is art or not art, by determining the presence or absence of lyric intuition.

Pavese accepted this obligation to make such judgments. Of only the second poem he dealt with, for example, he said that "A moment's reflection is enough to make one realize that even 'Song of Myself,' the tremendous 'Song of Myself,' cannot be anything except lyricism, a poem. (Whether it succeeds or fails is our job to investigate.)" Elsewhere, in the same vein, he writes, "Whitman does or does not succeed depending on whether he does or does not fashion the material according to a unifying image, usually the vision of America or the figure of the pioneer, and give the material at least a dynamic form."[69] For Pavese, the presence or absence of feeling-infused images, life-giving images, or, as one critic put it describing the core of Croce's aesthetic, "emotions translated into images," made the difference, as it had to for any Crocean, between art and not art.[70] Pavese declared that the "the tremendous 'Song of Myself'" did "succeed," as did, among many others, "By Blue Ontario's Shore," "Myself and Mine," "Crossing Brooklyn Ferry," "Passage to India," "L. of G's Purport," "Sail Out for Good, Eidólon Yacht," and "Good-Bye My Fancy." These poems were "lyrics" or "art." Many of Whitman's poems failed the test, however, and Pavese judged them in whole or part to be "failures." Those that did not pass the test included

"Scented Herbage of My Breast," "Fast Anchor'd Eternal O love!" "Song of the Broad-Axe," "Song of the Exposition," "Song of the Answerer," "Faces," and "Chanting the Square Deific."

While Pavese frequently used a Crocean vocabulary, he approached each poem first on its own terms. He may have written his thesis carelessly but he read Whitman carefully. Indeed, Pavese's close readings of Whitman's poetry give the thesis its enduring critical value, making it more than just a marker in the early intellectual development of Cesare Pavese. His readings of several of the longer poems in *Leaves of Grass* show Pavese at his best—not least because he takes the time with these to develop his arguments, as opposed to the often rather cursory treatment forced by his decision to treat so many of Whitman's poems in the thesis.

Consider, for example, his five-page commentary on "When Lilacs Last in the Dooryard Bloom'd." While using "the great elegy" to bolster one of the subsidiary contentions of his thesis, he also examined the way Whitman put the poem together, what means the poet used to make it so extraordinarily effective and affective. Because of its importance, I quote here the entire passage. All quotes from Whitman are in English in the original and I have emphasized any other words also originally in English.

> I want to demonstrate that this elegy is not only a hymn to immortality, a rather vague word, but also a distinct reprise of the themes of the comrade and of America's prosperity, developed together even in the song of the thrush, which forms a synthesis of serene and passionate joy. The poem is constructed almost thematically and were it not for the extraordinary fullness of each theme one might consider their interweaving artificial. But this would be "*hair-splitting*" and besides the themes have a definite common source that, just beneath the lines, develops into a harmonious crescendo.
>
> There are four themes: nature, the star, the thrush, and the funeral. The backdrop of greenery that opens the song (sections 1–3) is the same as that of the journey in "Calamus": lilac, perfume, flowers, "heart-shaped" leaves, the shady nook surrounded by green, the ineffable suggestions of friendship in solitude. This merges into the western star (section 2), which, in that first unexpected sunset, is less a symbol than a dear departed person, a comrade (he will say of the star in section 8, "as we wander'd together," and in 9, "The star my departing comrade . . .").

Then, in section 4, the first chord of the "hermit's" song comes to life like an outpouring of surrounding nature, "Death's outlet song of life." This is the type of musical *"utterance"* that, as I have said before, seems to Whitman to echo the fullness of nature. And finally, the two sections (5–6) of the funeral procession bring to an end the first ideal movement of the symphony, reprising the tender infinity of nature, creating in their panoramic view of an entire America in mourning an intimation of the figure of Lincoln, a diffuse presence made up of pensive sadness and love. Lincoln the man is never clearly delineated, not here nor later in the poem; Whitman will refer only to the "grave of him I love." But all the portrayals of the countryside, of America, and of the "thrush's" hideaway will be such as to give continuity to the presence I have described, the ideal figure, the "dear comrade."

The themes already identified return in the refrain of the second movement: nature (section 7), the star (section 8), and the singer (section 9). Whitman now makes more specific what was first an identification with all of nature: "Now I know what you must have meant . . . O singer bashful and tender, now I understand you." What is meant is the knowledge of death. The tone now becomes almost exultant, an affection and passion that find an outlet in the last gesture of love: "Blossoms and branches green . . . fresh as the morning . . . bouquets of roses . . . O death . . . early roses and lilies . . ." And the funeral (sections 10–11–12) is a fullness of love; the sea-winds, the perfumes make it seem almost a celebration: all America, "from east and west," is invited. The most "delicious" scenes of nature (section 11), the most exhilarating aspects of America (section 12) come to the poet's mind, transforming the sadness and pain, enveloping everything in the hymn to this affection and joy.

At this point, in a passage of great effect (section 13), Whitman cuts from the public scene and returns to the theme of the "thrush" who, singly, singing from the "recesses" renews the fullness and the Calamus-nature of the joy. This solo suspends our attention for a moment in such a way that the great section 14 gushes forth truly as the *"climax"* of the ode, its summation and entire significance. Its three pages, in fact, restate all the themes of the visible America—her seas, fields, labors and richness—and of the "secluded recess," meditative and solitary, and culminate finally in the concluding hymn to death. The great value of this hymn, greater even than that of Whitman's other ecstatic works, lies perhaps in his creation of the figure of death as a universal presence, a feminine essence, a wife, a veiled mother with passionately enwinding arms.

What follows then in the poem are only the necessary closing measures, the assuaging of the ecstasy and lyrical tempest that culminated in this hymn; the vision of death and the war that brings peace and nirvana (section 15), the pensive return to the Calamus-like recesses (section 16), and finally the intimate allusions and the farewell to the "sweetest wisest soul of all my days and lands."

Such is the hymn to Lincoln's death. In it the "martyr" disappears into the background of the larger hymn to the universe. And yet, this figure of Lincoln, because it could transform itself through death into a hymn of love, remains truly the "dear comrade," indeed the most dear comrade of America's prophet.[71]

No one reading these paragraphs of the thesis could foretell with certainty that the young scholar who wrote them would go on to become, among other things, a fine critic and editor; learning that he did, though, it would come as no surprise. Pavese's attention to Whitman's structure, language, images, transitions, tone, and movement indicates a mind attuned to the components of literary creation, independent of any specific critical theory, and interested in how a master practitioner put all the pieces together. One could say of Pavese as Eliot did of Whitman, in one of the pieces of criticism Pavese never read, "When [he] speaks of lilacs or of the mockingbird, his theories and beliefs drop away like a needless pretext."[72]

While Pavese never published his thesis, it was not for lack of trying. He did an extensive markup of the original thesis in 1931, based, it would appear, on direct input from no one less than Benedetto Croce. In May 1931 he wrote to Chiuminatto, "But that's more news. A desperado-publisher will perhaps undertake my old study about your older Whitman and so make me a world-famous scholar about American literature. Should it turn out good, I'll be . . . hanged . . . no, I'll be sure to find a new place somewhere in scholarly America and so, after my damned term in the army, hug and kiss at last my unique friend, over there."[73]

Though "desperado-publisher" scarcely characterizes the venerable Bari-based Laterza firm (Giuseppe Laterza & Figli S.p.A.), it seems likely that was the house to which Pavese was referring. Laterza published virtually all Croce's works as well as his journal, *La Critica*; Croce worked as an editorial consultant for the house and had enormous influence there. By 1931, Croce was dealing with Leone

Ginzburg on a basis of mutual respect, and Ginzburg, generous friend to Pavese that he was, asked Croce in the spring of that year to comment on Pavese's original work. Croce did so in writing. In August of the same year Ginzburg then asked Croce to propose to the head of Laterza the publication of Pavese's revised work. Croce, as usual, was spending his summer holidays in the Piedmontese mountain town of Meana, as was Giovanni Laterza. Ginzburg wrote to Croce, "My friend Cesare Pavese has given me the manuscript of his monograph on Whitman, which he has revised following the suggestions you so kindly put in writing last spring. Now permit me to ask you if you could speak to Laterza in Meana about it and if at some point we should send the manuscript there."[74]

Laterza himself wrote the rejection letter back to Ginzburg in November 1931:

> Senator Croce has very much recommended the publication of Cesare Pavese's critical essay on Walt Whitman in which you have taken an interest. Both from what Croce has told me and as a result of the written summary, I am convinced that it is a genuinely worthwhile piece of work. We are, however, passing through a period in which this kind of work is generally ignored and if one succeeded in selling a couple of hundred copies, it would be a miracle. Thus, at least for the moment, there would be no commercial basis for publishing it and I think we have to wait until we see some interest again in these types of studies.[75]

As characterized him all his life when he believed in something, Ginzburg did not give up easily. He immediately wrote back to Laterza:

> I cannot help but express my regret that not even with the authoritative help of Senator Croce was I able to convince you to accept Dr. Pavese's monograph on Whitman for your [series,] The Library of Modern Culture. While it is true that in these last few years scholarly interest in modern literatures in general has been waning, American along with Russian literature enjoys such a vogue in Europe, and not just with the general public, that I had hoped you would find the book publishable. Furthermore, the outpouring of studies, especially in France, on American literature in general and Walt Whitman in particular, indicates that it is not advisable to wait for what you called more propitious times since in a few years Pavese's monograph will have lost a large part of its polemical interest,

while conserving its intrinsic value. Therefore, buttressed with Croce's gratifying judgment of the work, I will submit the work to another publisher, with the regret that I was not able to obtain for my friend the public support of a house with the glorious reputation in Italian studies that yours has.[76]

No record exists of any further submissions either by Ginzburg on Pavese's behalf or by Pavese himself. As to Croce's written comments on Pavese's thesis, the best we can say is that perhaps they have survived. One file in the Pavese archives contains four undated, unsigned, typewritten pages with the title *Introduzione a Walt Whitman*. Whoever wrote them suggested an outline for a work on Whitman that would have had a much simpler structure than Pavese's original thesis. It would have had four major sections (Walt Whitman's Culture, Walt Whitman's Language, The Thought of Walt Whitman, and The Poetry of Walt Whitman) each with several subdivisions. The author had evidently read Pavese's thesis: toward the end of the outline the author wrote that "it will be necessary to discuss the superiority that Pavese claims for the great songs in relation to the shorter poems and especially those of old age" because "it seems to me that often the celebratory emphasis in the great songs obscures the simple expression of that immediate and loving contact with reality, which is the great value of Walt Whitman's best pages."[77]

I think one can reasonably speculate that Benedetto Croce wrote these four pages because we know he did send something to Pavese about the thesis and Pavese kept this particular typescript all his life. Confirmation of the provenance will come only with further research. We do know, however, how Pavese revised the thesis when he was hoping for publication.

He based his revisions on an exact duplicate of the original he turned in to the university archives in 1930. Given the technology of the time, that meant a carbon copy, the only other copy of the thesis known to exist outside the archives.[78] In preparing the work for publication, he first went through it and interlineally translated into Italian all the considerable amount of English it contained. (When it came to Whitman's poetry he thus produced his own translations, rather than using Gamberale's published versions.) He then went through the work again, page by page, and made grammatical corrections, some slight word changes, and many cuts, some several pages long. He reworked entirely only a few passages and added no new ideas or interpretations. Had the revised version ever seen print, general Italian readers would have read a tighter, less verbose version than the thesis Neri approved, but with the same principal themes of the poetry of making poetry and the figure of the pioneer.

In all, while keeping the chapter titles, he cut from the original almost ten thousand words, about 20 percent of the text, and added less than one thousand, making the revision about 42,000 words compared to the 51,000 of the thesis. Yet in the process he lost none of the thrust of his arguments. He cut almost nothing from his fine reading of "When Lilacs Last in the Dooryard Bloom'd," one of the high points of both works. He removed references to himself, dropped most of the jejune attacks on previous critics, and downplayed his knowledge of American slang. With these cuts, Pavese was also revising his own literary persona: he was making himself sound more grown-up. In only a few cases did Pavese cut and rewrite paragraphs; mostly he cut and generated appropriate transitions for the remaining text. When he did cut and rewrite, he did so with an eye to the realities of Italian national and literary politics, in the hopes of publication. For example, on page 184 of the thesis, in a discussion related to America and World War I, Pavese had referred unfavorably to journalist/critic G. G. Napolitano and also commented on the Italian (Fascist-censored) press's reaction to Erich Maria Remarque's novel *All Quiet on the Western Front*. In the 1931 reworking, he cut the references to Napolitano, an influential literary figure at the time, along with all comments pro or con about Americans or Italians in World War I and all references to the Italian press's reaction to Remarque's book and the film based on it. The revised version of the thesis shows that already by 1931 Pavese had improved as an editor. More's the pity, then, that he did not do this kind of self-editing in 1930, because it would have produced a much tighter and more forceful work, making all the same points with much greater economy.

While this revised version of the thesis never saw light, Pavese did publish a shorter essay, "Interpretation of Walt Whitman, Poet," in 1933. A comparison of the 1930 thesis, the 1931 revision, and this essay shows a consistent aim in all three, with greatest success in the last.[79] As Roger Asselineau said of this "fine essay," it is indeed "lucid and passionately sincere."[80] The slight change in title from that of the thesis ("Interpretation of the Poetry of Walt Whitman") reflects Pavese's broader concerns in the essay. It also signals that Pavese is still operating within a Crocean context, since he intends to treat Whitman as artist, as opposed to, say, Whitman as democrat, polemicist, or example of change in America. Yet while Pavese could still be classified as Crocean in 1933, he was by then no longer, as one critic put it, "a 'pure' Crocean in that he did not completely exclude sociological analyses, the links between a literary work and the historical-social context in which it came to life."[81]

The essay, which runs to about 7,500 words, carried forward several of Pavese's points from the thesis, sometimes in the exact same words. Still, the many borrowings from the thesis notwithstanding, the essay is a different piece of work and shows how much Pavese had matured as a critic and essayist in those three years. Calvino, editing Pavese's essays in 1962, gave this one the subtitle "The Poetry of Making Poetry," and that did remain one of Pavese's main contentions. Yet while the essay discusses the myth of discovery, the figure of the pioneer, so prominent in the thesis, merits only a passing reference. Most importantly, gone are the sophomoric posing and sloppy prose, replaced by a well-expressed, self-assured evenhandedness that inspires confidence in Pavese's assertions and conclusions. (Pavese still could not resist taking a few digs at earlier critics, but only in the one long paragraph devoted to them does he revert to the supercilious sarcasm of the thesis.)[82]

In the thesis, Pavese wanted to impress his professors with the extent of his research and the validity of his approach. In the essay, he wanted to persuade a wider literary audience of Whitman's genius, and with his appreciative enthusiasm provide them with ways to approach the poet. He now named only eight poems, quoted five others without naming them, and dealt with only one, "Song of Myself," at any length. He did not drive home one or two specific points but rather provided readers with a set of critical observations that they could test themselves.

Pavese opens with several pages putting Whitman into an American cultural context, a most un-Crocean maneuver designed to delineate "the external culture of Walt Whitman." He begins his actual critical commentary by stressing that Whitman was not a "great primitive." Rather, "what is really important is to hammer home the fact that Walt Whitman knew what he was doing, and that, in brief, like every artist who achieves anything, Walt Whitman pondered his achievement, labored it, lived it, *intended it*."[83] This intention leads to the success of Whitman's poetry, as interpreted by Pavese in a passage virtually unchanged from the thesis:

> Walt Whitman lived so intensely the idea of this mission that, while not saving himself from the obvious failure of such an intention, through it his work was saved from failure. He did not make the primitive poem he dreamed, but the poem of this dream. He did not succeed in the absurdity of creating a poetry appropriate to the democratic and republican world and to the principles of the newly discovered land—because poetry is, after all, one and only one thing—but spending his life repeating in various ways this intention, he made of the intention poetry, the poetry of the discovery of a new world in history and of the singing of it. In brief, to spell out the apparent paradox, he made poetry out of making poetry.[84]

He goes on to assert that Whitman created the "miracle of *Leaves of Grass*" not by putting into poetry any of the many programmatic ideas expressed in his prose but rather by making it embody "a Person, a sensibility, who moves in the real world." To back up this important point he quotes Whitman himself: "*Leaves of Grass* indeed (I cannot too often reiterate) has mainly been the outcropping of my own emotional and personal nature—an attempt, from first to last, to put a *Person*, a human being (myself in the latter half of the Nineteenth Century, in America,) freely, fully and truly on record."[85] Pavese then adds here a point not made in the thesis, one that reflects his wider concerns with America after graduation. "That idea, quite apart from its critical application to the works of Walt Whitman, possesses a singular historical importance, because it constitutes the first time anyone in America defined the problem that in the twentieth century every artist in the States once more began to propose for himself."[86]

Pavese thought the organization of *Leaves of Grass* fairly unimportant for an appreciation of Whitman; he writes that he does not "believe that the architecture of the volume as a whole has any great efficacy, despite the constant desire of Walt and his disciples that it should." He contends that the "very great poem, the most difficult piece in the *Leaves*, 'Song of Myself,'" which "is something like a quintessence of *Leaves of Grass* . . . has no value as construction; this poem would manage to sustain without damage huge cuts or huge additions or rearrangements, and besides its author did do this and would still be doing it, were it not for the completely accidental chance of old age and death." Meter, too, is unimportant in approaching Whitman: "It is a waste of time." Furthermore, "Whitman never desired to achieve musicality in sound effects," nor, though he occasionally used it, did the poet care much about rhyme.[87] Where, then, lay the essence of Whitman? Pavese points to it in the heart of the essay, with observations that had figured nowhere in the thesis:

> Walt Whitman obeys what we might call an imaginative law. He expresses a thought, a click of thought, an image, and then he is off again. He sings through waves of imagination—when the thought within him becomes imaginative—and the harmony spreads from one unit to another unit, clothing and furnishing a voice to the very labor of releasing these visions or thoughts, which are all valuable for themselves and which can burst out in an instant, or over twenty pages, that, except for the weariness or the mental encumbrances of the poet, never reciprocally confuse or cancel each other out. This is the rhythm, created and expressed by the verse, of all the best of the *Leaves*.[88]

The form Whitman used to express those clicks of thought was not the stanza or section but the line: "The line, the phrase shouted or whispered, the oratorical period—always measured in lines—these are the real form of 'Song of Myself' and thus of the *Leaves* as a whole."[89] Pavese argues that "Walt Whitman thinks in lines, that is to say, that with him every thought, every flash of inspiration, creates for itself a definitive form in which it consists, and does not lapse into a rhythm preexistent or subject to other laws . . . and therefore they are not fragments [but rather] a poetry that simplifies itself to the point of revealing itself founded and created by the line, by the end-stop of every metrical unit."[90] Pavese had first mentioned this idea in a slightly earlier essay on Dos Passos, when, in linking him and Carl Sandburg to Whitman, he wrote, "The Americans after Walt Whitman separate their lines according to the logical law of the succession of their thoughts rather than according to any musical law of phonic harmony. This is their originality, derived at a distance from the Bible."[91]

Though Pavese does not credit him here, Basil de Selincourt had developed the idea of the importance of the line in Whitman nineteen years earlier, and did so in the book Pavese read and quoted from extensively in his thesis. The English critic, in a chapter titled "Constructive Principles," wrote that "Each true line of Whitman's comes to us, as I have said, floated separately on an independent breath. Like the sea-waves to which he himself so often compared them, his lines are not less recognizably units because of their variable shapes and sizes." To emphasize his point, de Selincourt ended this chapter by stating that "Whitman makes an original contribution to poetic craft in that he discovers and exhibits a new standard, a new basis for variation. The freedom of his lines is pleasurable to us and conveys an intelligible impression only in so far as we instinctively recognize the common principle they exemplify, and measure them by tacit reference to it."[92]

In the thesis Pavese did not address the issue of the line in Whitman's poems, not even in his close readings of several of the longer ones; rather, he looked in each for its "lyricism," the quality that, in a Crocean sense, made it art. By the time of the 1933 essay, however, Pavese had clearly outgrown the necessity of a Crocean vocabulary. He was now concerning himself much more with the components of Whitman's creation, combining and linking those components to Whitman's overriding poetic persona: "All Whitman's great pages, all the poems of the prime of life, always take the same pattern: the strong, thoughtful 'receptive' man who passes among the phenomena of the world and absorbs them all, enraptured just by their simplicity, their normality, their reality, and who responds to them with an affection, a perpetual ecstasy, born from the imaginative identification of the man with men and things."[93]

Pavese then goes on at some length to demonstrate Whitman's unity of approach by quoting from several poems, for the most part identifying them not by name but rather by what section of *Leaves of Grass* they appeared in. Pavese uses these citations to support his view that at all times Whitman "is the poet of this discovery, whether it be the discovery of a blade of grass, or of President Lincoln, or, in the moments of a vein less pure, less ours, of the American Union."[94] Going on to deal with another aspect of Whitman's "form," Pavese defends Whitman's use of "catalogs," stating that "Except in some cases where a political statement intrudes, whether practical or bravura, all Whitman's catalog poems belong among his best." This is especially true of "the conclusion of 'Song of Myself,' where there is no longer a catalog of experiences with which the 'myself' identified itself, but a tremulous atmosphere of miracle come to pass is spread before the vision-laden eyes of the reader."[95] After quoting in full the concluding sections (50–52) of "Song of Myself," Pavese comes to his own conclusions:

> Anyone can now see how Walt Whitman's poetry works: it consists of successive thoughts, all exploding from the plenitude that the identification with all things experienced begets in the "myself." It is the joy of the successive discovery of these thoughts, and thus their dynamic importance, not their logical value that matters . . . Every thought is really thought on the instant, the verse made of the daring and diversity of the mind in action, which beholds itself in the act of thinking the thought, and expresses its consciousness of it. Walt Whitman sings the joy of discovering thoughts . . .
>
> The true nature of Walt Whitman is precisely in his not being satisfied with a little scene, a perfected vignette, for its own sake, but with the expression—and in his weak moments with the invocation—of the desire and the yearning and the ever-resurgent pleasure of feeling the whole surrounding universe as a presence brotherly and real.[96]

In the thesis, Pavese examined a large number of Whitman's poems individually and asked of each, "Is it art?" In the essay, he looks at *Leaves of Grass* more as a whole and attempts to explain how Whitman achieved his poetic mastery and what the reader should look for in approaching the book. In both thesis and essay, Pavese's enthusiasm for Whitman shines through, but in the thesis he failed to control it sufficiently. Not so in the essay: there Pavese channels his passion for Whitman into well-crafted, intriguing, valid observations, economically and effectively expressed. In 1930 the student was struggling with his identity as a critic; by 1933 he had won that particular battle.

When all is analyzed, it is Pavese's attachment to Whitman that gives the thesis and the essay their momentum. The thesis was more a work of aesthetic appreciation than scholarly criticism, and if Pavese had not become the famous writer he did, it would certainly interest us less. Yet, Pavese's thesis, purely as criticism, illuminates and entertains. We will never know how much weight his examining committee gave to its enthusiasm, but its fervor and energy cannot be ignored, nor can its frequent insights and sense of purpose. Anyone reading the thesis knows that its young author cared deeply about his subject and had immersed himself in Whitman's poetry. (And an English-speaking reader knows with certainty that this Italian student understood perfectly Whitman's original English.) While one might disagree with Pavese's "thesis" as the one true explanation of Whitman, one would have to admit that the concept of "the poetry of making poetry" is an idea worth considering.

The thesis shows how a gifted embryonic writer/critic like Pavese can use and at the same time go beyond established critical theory; in his case, Croce's. The essay presents Pavese, only three years later, as no longer an embryonic critic. Both also give witness to the now perhaps bygone ability of America to provide imaginative alternatives to those abroad who feel constrained by government-imposed limits on their own cultures. Walt Whitman proved crucial for the artistic, intellectual, and even emotional development of Cesare Pavese. The American truly was, for the young Italian, "good health," and did "filter and fibre" his blood, just as Whitman promised to all in the next-to-last stanza of "Song of Myself." Whitman drew Pavese into American literature. He also showed Pavese the importance of developing a personal, individualistic artistic persona. As artist and as man, Whitman stood in stark and appealing contrast to Fascism's sanctioned models. Pavese learned through Whitman that "making poetry" not only creates art but defines and authenticates the person who creates the art.

In his own poetry Pavese never aspired to Whitman's breadth and sweep, but he did consciously use colloquial, idiomatic, almost spoken Italian to carry forward his rhythmic but unrhymed lines. He credited his poetic style in part specifically to "the discovery of the American vulgate during my studies."[97] In the end it is this vivifying encounter of a fine twentieth-century writer with a great nineteenth-century poet that makes Pavese's pieces on Whitman works that will endure, that reminds us of the ability of literature to speak so passionately across time and borders.

SEVEN
"The peach of the world"

After finishing his thesis, Pavese published between 1930 and 1934 ten essays on American writers, wrote four reviews of books relating to America, translated four American novels, including *Moby-Dick*, and added prefaces to two of these and an *avvertenza* (notice to readers) to a third.[1] (In 1934 he also translated James Joyce's *Portrait of the Artist as a Young Man*.) While he continued to translate American fiction after his return from confino in 1936, these earlier years constitute his most productive period of the 1930s, a decade Pavese later called, referring not only to his own work, the "decade of translations."[2] These first five years of the 1930s represent a continuation and eventual culmination of his enthusiastic love for American literature that began around 1925 during his liceo years.

Before looking at Pavese's contributions to the Italian literary discourse on America in these years, we do well to place them in context. To do that we must consider two phenomena: first, the extraordinary impact of American popular culture on Italy in the interwar period, and, second, the prevailing opinions about America held by Italian intellectuals in the 1920s and early 1930s. Doing so will make it clear that, despite assertions to the contrary, Cesare Pavese did not single-handedly invent the Italian "myth of America" when he published his Sinclair Lewis essay in 1930.[3] Nor, even though their names are often the only two mentioned and invariably linked in this respect, was it Pavese and Elio Vittorini alone "who together discovered and launched the American novel into the Italian culture of the thirties."[4]

As Valerio Ferme has reminded us, not only Pavese but all Italians involved in "literary americanism" "depended on the much larger phenomenon of cultural americanism that swept across the Italian peninsula in the first years of Mussolini's dictatorship."[5] American popular culture began its invasion of Europe in the second decade of the twentieth century as the doughboys of World War I returned home. While it spread rapidly throughout all of Western Europe, it found Italy particularly receptive, in part because the hopeful, though often idealized, vision of the millions of Italians who had emigrated to America predisposed Italians as a whole to accept as reality America's various portrayals of itself, particularly in films. Between 1910 and 1920 alone, and despite the interruption of the war years, some two million Italians emigrated to the United States, accounting for approximately 35 percent of all immigrants entering America in that period.[6] During the one hundred years from 1820 to 1920 Italy trailed only Germany and Ireland in the total number of emigrants to America.[7] Up until 1900 the majority of Italian emigrants came from the north of Italy, with the northeast and Piedmont accounting for 45 percent of the departures. By 1910, southern Italians made up 70 percent of those leaving for America.[8] Thus, a vision of America as "the modern paradise and guide" had already taken root in large swaths of Italy.[9]

American literature did not lead the cultural invasion of Europe; that distinction goes to American movies.[10] Italy, before World War I, had developed a sizeable motion picture industry of its own, centered in fact in Turin. In 1914, twelve different production companies were operating in that city, producing a total of two hundred and fifty films viewable in the city's seventy-three movie theaters.[11] *Cabiria* (1914), written in significant part by Gabriele D'Annunzio and directed by Giovanni Pastrone, the first internationally successful blockbuster movie and one of the greatest successes of the silent film era, was filmed in Turin. World War I and the recession that followed, however, devastated the Italian film industry and it recovered its early luster only after World War II, by which time it had migrated south to Rome. Despite entrepreneurial efforts and Fascist subsidies for national productions, American films came to dominate Italian screens during the interwar period, so much so that when in 1938 the regime tried to limit the number of American films, it found strong resistance among distributors because by then American imports accounted for two-thirds of all films projected and 75 percent of all ticket sales.[12]

American films in the 1920s and '30s framed the way the rest of the world saw America and had an enormous impact on European ideas about America. They certainly affected Pavese. He loved movies and frequently sent his fictional characters to them, generally in small, smoke-filled theaters in Turin's working-class neighborhoods, the kind he himself frequented.[13] Finally, American movies could lead Pavese to specific American books or authors. He reported, for instance, that it was seeing King Vidor's 1928 silent masterwork *The Crowd* that led him to John Dos Passos, because he had read that Vidor based the film on *Manhattan Transfer*.[14] It was fitting, therefore, that the first book he translated, Sinclair Lewis's *Our Mr. Wrenn*, should begin in front of a movie theater on 14th Street in New York City.

Since American films arrived in Italy well before most twentieth-century American fiction, the mostly anonymous writers who translated into Italian the caption cards for American silent films could be called the first *americanisti*. According to his good friend Massimo Mila, Pavese can be counted among them, for at least one film.[15] There is even credible evidence to support the attribution to him of two 1933 translations of Mickey Mouse comic books into Italian, the first to appear in Italy.[16]

Furthermore, a good case can be made, as Ferme has already done, that the success of American movies in Italy paved the way for the first translations of contemporary American writers.[17] No direct link can be established between American films and the success of particular American authors in Italy. When one considers, though, that the two most popular American writers of interwar Italy were not Sinclair Lewis or Sherwood Anderson, whom Pavese translated, nor John Steinbeck or Erskine Caldwell, whom Vittorini translated, but Jack London and Zane Grey, then Ferme's hypothesis that American westerns and adventure films predisposed the Italian public toward London and Grey's kind of fiction seems entirely plausible.[18] Pavese himself thought that certain types of American adventure films created a favorable climate for Melville translations. In the spring of 1932 Pavese received a letter from Alessandra Scalero, whose translation of Dos Passos's *Manhattan Transfer* appeared that year.[19] A publisher had asked her to translate *Moby-Dick* and she wrote Pavese because she had heard he was working on a translation of the same book. Pavese responded that in fact he had already submitted his translation, and he hoped that she had not put too much work into her version. He then went on to say, "In any case, a great deal of Melville remains to be done, for sure *Typee* and *Omoo* and *White Jacket*—the publisher Formica of Turin last year announced a translation of the first, which, however has not yet been seen.[20] Italy nowadays is so swept up in the mania for seagoing and Polynesian stories—inspired I believe by movies—that Melville is all *up to date* [English in original]. I remember your very fine version of *Back to Harlem* and I can think of no one better than you to give us a good *Typee* or *Omoo*."[21]

A look at the American writers published in translation in Italy before and during the time Pavese, Vittorini, and, to a lesser extent, Eugenio Montale were translating shows that American "genre fiction" (e.g., mysteries, westerns, adventure stories, romances) found a much wider reading audience than did serious American "literary fiction."[22] Since that was true of Italian literature also and of literature in America (then and now), this observation certainly should cause no surprise. Its relevance lies in the context it provides for Pavese's essays and translations and later for Vittorini's anthology, *Americana*. An appreciation of the impact of American films on Italy and of the wide acceptance of America's popular writers helps make it clearer that, while Pavese did not invent the myth of America, he did, through his essays and translations, reimagine that myth and in doing so created an energetic, highly personal, and compelling vision. That vision differed significantly from those shown in movies or presented by the few Italian scholars, journalists, and critics who were writing about America when Pavese began his work, the most important of whom were Emilio Cecchi, Carlo Linati, and Giuseppe Prezzolini.

The Florentine Emilio Cecchi (1884–1966) had a long and productive career as poet, literary and art critic, essayist, and screenwriter. In addition to an abiding interest in Italian literature, he became interested in the early years of the twentieth century in English and then American literature. In 1910 he wrote a monograph on

Rudyard Kipling and in 1915 published a history of nineteenth-century English literature; in 1935 he published a collection of essays on English and American writers.[23] His preferred American writers were Poe and Melville.[24] Almost all his writings fall into the category of *prosa d'arte*, a genre one scholar has described as "short, elegantly crafted prose pieces, noticeable for the complexity of their syntactical and phonetic constructions."[25] In addition to literature he had strong interests in art. He was much influenced in his approach by Bernard Berenson and in 1936 translated into Italian Berenson's 1930 *Italian Painters of the Renaissance*. In 1939 he and his daughter co-wrote the first monograph on Emily Dickinson published in Europe, and in that same year he published the book that has ever since linked his name with a certain strain of Italian *americanismo*: *America amara* (America the Bitter).[26] In 1940, when the Fascist minister of popular culture rejected Vittorini's introduction and notes to *Americana*, the publisher Bemporad asked Cecchi to write a replacement piece because Cecchi was by then, as Jane Dunnett puts it, "a figure of some prestige, having been appointed to the Italian Academy, and hence could act as a sort of guarantor, ensuring that this new edition of the book met with the approval of the Ministry."[27]

Pavese's opinion of Cecchi's introduction was so unflattering that the editors of Pavese's diary excised it from the published text until after Cecchi's death: "Knavish, politically and critically," he called it (*canagliesca—politicamente e criticamente*).[28] Cecchi never saw Pavese's comment and the two men maintained cordial relations during the rest of Pavese's life. Cecchi wrote several favorable reviews of Pavese's novels and a generous overall appreciation of Pavese immediately after his death.

Carlo Linati (1878–1949), unlike Cecchi, wrote no book specifically on America, but concerned himself mainly with English and Irish literature. Indeed, Linati holds a place of interest in Joyce studies because Joyce, in a letter of September 21, 1920, to Linati, enclosed a "scheme" to explain his *Ulysses* that has become known as the "Linati scheme," to distinguish it from the one he drew up for Stuart Gilbert.[29] In 1916 Linati translated some of Lady Gregory's comedies and in 1944 both Sean O'Casey's *The Shadow of a Gunman* and J. M. Synge's *Deirdre of the Sorrows*. His 1932 book, *Scrittori anglo-americani d'oggi*, established him, almost by default, as a leading *americanista*. In 1934 he translated Henry James's *The American*.[30] Pavese reviewed *Scrittori anglo-americani d'oggi* for *La Cultura*, and we will soon consider what Pavese thought of it. Linati traveled avidly, by bicycle, train, car, and, later, airplane. He appeared extensively in the cultural pages of Italy's leading newspapers and wrote travel books, including several about his native Lombardy.[31]

Giuseppe Prezzolini (1882–1982), though he had no university degree, spent over thirty years as a professor at Columbia University in New York City, and as head of that university's Casa Italiana. This establishment, founded in 1927, housed the university's Italian department and served for decades as the most important institute for Italian studies in the United States. While Columbia paid the professorial staff, New York's Italian-American community funded most of the institute's programs, as it did the construction of the notable McKim, Mead, and White neo-Renaissance building that houses the institute. Prezzolini served, voluntarily, as an officer in the Italian army during World War I. He was a personal friend of Mussolini and in 1924, just two years after the march on Rome, wrote a favorable biography.[32] He never hid his nationalistic tendencies, but denied the accusations of Fascism that dogged him throughout most of his long life (and which would beyond). A 1934 article in the *Nation*, for example, called the Casa Italiana "an official adjunct of the Italian Consul-General's office in New York and one of the most important sources of fascist propaganda in the U.S."[33] The unquestionably anti-Fascist expatriate Gaetano Salvemini considered Prezzolini a covert Fascist apologist and apparently included his name on a list submitted to the FBI during World War II.[34] Twenty years after Prezzolini died at the age of one hundred, the distinguished American Italianist William Weaver could still refer to him as "pro-Fascist."[35] The left-leaning Mario Soldati, whom Prezzolini brought to Columbia in 1929, and who lived to be 92, is reported to have said in his later years of Prezzolini that "the only thing we have in common is our longevity."

Regardless of his politics, Prezzolini played a significant literary role in Italy, especially in the early years of the 1900s when he founded, with Giovanni Papini, *La Voce*, one of the most influential of the young century's literary journals. Prezzolini taught himself English and in 1910 translated Hume's *Philosophical Essays Concerning Human Understanding*. In 1924 he showed a prescient respect for the most popular American author in Italy when he translated Jack London's *The Sea-Wolf.* Nine years later he titled the first work he wrote after his arrival at Columbia *Come gli Americani scoprirono L'Italia, 1750–1850* (How the Americans Discovered Italy, 1750–1850). Even though the book was published in Italy, in Italian, the *New York Times Book Review* reviewed it in 1934 under the title "American Visitors to Italy" and described it as "an extremely amusing little volume."[36] Pavese also reviewed this book in 1934; he did not find it so amusing, as we will see in a moment.

These men, and others, such as the established academic Mario Praz, described in elegant language a vibrant, dynamic, practical America that, however, crucially lacked culture and soul. Pavese derided this prevalent view of America in his thesis:

> For many Italians, even those "au courant," the United States is a country with, well yes, a great future . . . however . . . the Latin genius . . . but . . . and in any case absolutely without a past. Millionaires as happy to marry a dancer as a duchess. Unimpressive nouveau riche on the make, disguised provincials. Every once in a while, almost miraculously, a writer distinguishes himself over there but in the end he is not as good as people say. In sum, an obscene democracy.
>
> These ideas, and others like them, have become so tritely common that it is difficult to quote anyone specific. They are embedded in the assumptions and emerge in the tone of all writing and discourse and thus no one is responsible.[37]

Actually, one could quote specific "responsible" people, as Pavese did in his polite but caustic comments on Prezzolini's *Come gli Americani scoprirono L'Italia*:

> I was sorry, however, to find the well-known contrast between the so-called practicality-efficiency of America and the so-called indolence-appreciation of life in Italy resolved with the stale ethnic generalization, "it is necessary to have behind one a civilization in order to be able to enjoy things, inasmuch as pleasure arises from a mental activity that consists in the associations of ideas and in memories; and how could these exist in a people who act solely for practical purposes and immediately forget what they have done and move on to that which remains to be done?"[38]

That Prezzolini had turned Pavese down for a graduate scholarship in 1931 could well have predisposed Pavese against him, as

Prezzolini himself later suggested.[39] That link aside, however, the views Pavese expressed here he expressed consistently in his letters and in print up to 1934. He felt he had to do so. Not only were nationalistic-leaning critics like Prezzolini denying America a true culture, but so were more independent-minded writers such as Linati (who would, even so, join Pavese, Montale, and others as a contributing translator to Vittorini's *Americana* in 1941). After all, Linati wrote, in 1932, in an almost Jamesean mode:

> In my opinion, a true and deep transformation in the life of a people, of a race, cannot take place today if not in the sense of a true and deep transformation of its culture. But America, for the time being, is far indeed from being able to give us a culture . . .
>
> European civilization has behind it thousands of years of history, innumerable political and moral transformations, revolutions, national struggles, the fall and rebirth of empires, immense religious exertions, customs, ideologies, and an entire past of marvelous aesthetic creations; has reached, at the cost of much effort, its own psychology, [and] I cannot imagine how it could abdicate with all these precious goods in its hands in favor of Babbitt. The European soul aspires to something deeper than just the ability to build machines or enjoy one's self without worries. It aspires to the grace of culture, to the sweetness of emotion. It lives by thoughts, by passions; it not only glories in its musical and poetic artistic genius but finds nourishment there; tradition is its second nature . . .
>
> Europe, in sum, only wants to remain Europe . . . because she feels that it is fine to live in richness and prosperity, but in the end an honest indigence is preferable to the degradation of its own nature and soul.[40]

Despite Linati's prominence as an Italian critic of literature in English, Pavese, in his 1932 review of the book, called it "at best, mostly only average journalism." He complimented the author for his knowledge and taste, while pointing to Linati's book as another example of what he considered wrong about most Italian criticism of American writers.

> I'd rather for the moment now say something about what appears to me to be an organic defect of the criticism of American literature presently being offered by our experts.
>
> At most it's only a half-dozen years that living American writers have been spoken of and argued about in Italy, and what

is happening in this field runs parallel to that which happened with film. Having discovered that movies are an art, a great number of people—letterati—hurried to discuss them with great confidence and no preparation. Having discovered that the United States produces not only industrial goods but also books of some interest, a certain number of Italian letterati have undertaken the enterprise of keeping us informed. Let us be clear. Things have gone worse for film because as regards literary criticism of America all that has happened is that established critics nurtured on English literature have come to believe that they have to include now these newcomers in their commentaries.

All things considered, that's not all that bad for America so long as someone with Linati's taste is doing the talking, but when you get down to the level of the herd, things degenerate.[41]

One can find confirmation of Pavese's take on the then-predominant Italian and European intellectual's view of American culture among American observers. Writing in 1932, the indefatigably prolific, popular, and now forgotten Ludwig Lewisohn came independently to many of the same conclusions:

Translations of the works of the more eminent American contemporaries abound in Germany, in France, in Holland and the Scandinavian countries. Spanish and even Italian publishers are beginning to follow this example. But these books are rarely read by Europeans and more rarely criticized by them as works of art, comparable to European works of the creative imagination. They are regarded most often as documents which the European mind uses to fortify its waning sense of superiority by feeding upon American criticism of America, or else it uses them as a warning for Europe, in the sense of Georges Duhamel, against that Americanization, that standardization and mechanization of life which the cultivated European regards, whether rightly or wrongly, as due to the example and influence of the United States. Hence, the more non-polemical an American work is, the smaller—except within restricted circles—is its European success likely to be. For Europe consciously or unconsciously regards America, upon the whole, as a young barbarian.[42]

In 1929, at the zenith of Mussolini's reputation, *L'Enciclopedia Italiana*, Italy's equivalent of the *Encyclopaedia Britannica*, offered, as a definition of *americanismo*, "The admiration, whether naïve or reasoned, but mostly excessive, for American ideas or things; an admiration which at times even becomes a fashion, in contrast to European cultural traditions." Writing in 1993, Emilio Gentile summarized the "polemic against Americanism" during the Fascist era: "All the anti-American images were based on the antithesis between 'quality' and 'quantity,' 'spirit' and 'matter,' 'man' and 'machine.' The myth of the primacy of European classical civilization (which for the Fascists coincided with the primacy of Italian civilization), and the contrast between the 'civilization of the spirit' and the 'civilization of the machine' provided the various versions of anti-Americanism with the basic judgement categories for defining American civilization as a degenerate derivation of European civilization."[43]

Neither the "polemic against Americanism" nor the spirited responses of Pavese, Vittorini, and others in their essays and reviews constituted central issues for the Italian literary world in the interwar years. Italy's own literature, followed by that of France and Germany, received much more critical attention; indeed, for a time, Russian literature interested the younger generation as much as America's did. Examination of the main vehicle for Pavese's American essays, the journal *La Cultura*, illustrates these points, and also shows Pavese's crucial importance in creating a different "myth of America."

Pavese published thirteen essays and book reviews in the five years from 1930 through 1934, and all except one of them (on O. Henry) appeared in *La Cultura*. Never robust financially, the journal almost closed in 1933, but managed to carry on in reduced form when Giulio Einaudi's newly formed publishing house took it over beginning with the first issue (March) of 1934. At that time, it had fewer than five hundred subscribers, and little cash to spare.[44] Pavese's Turin-based friends read the journal, as did Vittorini, and Pavese sent copies to Chiuminatto whenever one of his own essays appeared; otherwise, we simply do not know who read *La Cultura*. The editors divided each issue into three categories: articles, book reviews, and notes. Each year they also provided several indexes listing the title and author of every piece published, along with a list of every book mentioned in the journal during the year in any of the three editorial categories. Those annual indexes reveal how marginal American literature and culture were, even to a journal one can categorize as liberally non-Fascist and tending toward outright anti-Fascist. (The regime would in fact close it down in 1935.) The 1930 issues, for example, contained a total of sixty-nine articles. As was true for this whole period, the majority dealt with Italian writers and culture, but four articles appeared on Russian, four on English, and, in yet another example of their cultural ascendancy at the time, ten on French writers. One—Pavese's on Sinclair Lewis—dealt with an American writer, which put American on a par with Danish literature. None of the year's thirty-four notes dealt with an American writer. During that same year, a total of 233 books were reviewed or mentioned in the journal. Other than the eleven by Sinclair Lewis that Pavese mentioned in his essay, one by Poe was the only other American book discussed, in a review of selected tales translated by Emilio Severado.

From an Americanist's viewpoint, 1931 looked a little better. Two of that year's sixty-four articles dealt with American writers, and Pavese wrote both of them, one each on Sherwood Anderson and Edgar Lee Masters. Two of the 182 books mentioned during the year involved American writers: a review of a translation of Hawthorne's *The Scarlet Letter* and Pavese's short note/review of a French anthology of Whitman. (I do not include in these figures the few reviews of books by American authors each year dealing with non-American subjects; for instance, a 1932 review of Frank Tenney's *Life and Literature in the Roman Republic*.)

Of the forty-three articles to appear in 1932, one, Pavese's on Melville, dealt with an American author. Only one of the 149 books reviewed or mentioned concerned Americans, a French anthology of American novelists on which Pavese commented in a short note.

The year 1933, the high point of Pavese's enthusiasm for American literature, saw fifty-one articles appear in *La Cultura*, of which three, all by Pavese, dealt with American writers (Dos Passos, Dreiser, and Whitman). Out of a total of 113 books either mentioned or reviewed, there were two reviews of American-related authors, one of the Italian translation of de Tocqueville's *Democracy in America*, the other an interesting review of Pavese's translation of *Moby-Dick* by Alberto Rossi.

In 1934 the journal went to a new format. While larger in page size, almost tabloid format, each issue contained fewer pages and shorter articles. Ten monthly issues appeared this year, beginning in March, with Einaudi as the publisher and, as of May, Pavese as the managing editor (*direttore responsabile*). The new editors published fifty articles this year, three of which related to American authors. For the first time, someone other than Pavese wrote one of them—an article on Artemus Ward by Aldo Camerino. Pavese wrote the other two: his only essay on William Faulkner and his second on Sinclair Lewis. Another article also dealt with American politics: Mario Einaudi's (Giulio's brother) "Dopo un anno di governo di Roosevelt" (After a Year of Roosevelt's Government).[45] Of the 153 books reviewed or mentioned in this year, two concerned America. The first, Prezzolini's book on the American discovery of Italy, received Pavese's short review mentioned above. Arrigo Cajumi gave negative notices to the second, Sinclair Lewis's *Work of Art*, in a review of four new works by different authors.

The journal managed only four issues in 1935, before being shut down at the time of the same May 1935 round-up that saw Pavese arrested and eventually sent to confino. Even though Pavese remained listed as the managing editor, none of the seventeen last articles to appear in *La Cultura* involved American writers or themes, nor did any of the forty-eight books reviewed or mentioned.

To sum up, in one of the most lively literary journals of the time, edited by acquaintances and friends of Pavese and then by Pavese himself, there appeared in the five and one-third years between January 1930 and April 1935 some 294 articles dealing with various topics of literature and culture. Of those, a total of ten (3.4 percent) had to do with America, and Pavese wrote nine of them. In that same period, approximately 875 different books were mentioned or reviewed in the journal, of which only nineteen (2.2 percent) were by American authors; eleven of them, all by Lewis, were mentioned only in Pavese's first 1930 essay. The quantitative data helps us remember that, in the Fascist years, though *americanismo* deeply affected a number of important artists and intellectuals, especially Cesare Pavese, it did not run wide in Italian culture, even among intellectuals.

A phrase Pavese used in an April 1930 letter to Chiuminatto (who was then living in Green Bay, Wisconsin) indicates how deeply America affected Pavese, as well as the vast difference that separated him from critics like Linati or Prezzolini. Chiuminatto, fulfilling an agreement with Pavese, had sent him a packet of recent American novels, checked out from the Green Bay Public Library. In his response, Pavese described the United States as "the peach of the world," not a phrase Linati, Prezzolini, and certainly not Cecchi, would ever have used. This letter, written in Pavese's characteristically just-slightly-off-key English, demonstrates better than anything else now available how Pavese's feelings about America had already developed before he graduated from the university.

> Now ... I hurry on to the library's ones which I got safely and be sure, I'll leisurely wade through. I began with [Glenway Wescott's] The Grandmothers and want once more to proclamate there is no other living country in the world which be able to boast such a contemporary literature.
> You are the peach of the world! Not only in wealth and material life but really in liveliness and strength of art which means thought and politics and religion and everything. You've got to predominate in this century all over the civilized world as before did Greece and Italy and France. I'm sure of it. What in their little sphere have American Movies done in old Europe—- and I've always abused those who maintained it was their financial organization and advertisements which brought them up; I say it is, not even their artistic value, but their surpassing strength of vital energy don't mind whether pessimistic or joyful—what, I say, have done Movies will do the whole of your art and thought. Each of your worthy writers finds out a new field of existence, a new world, and writes about it with such a downrightness and immediateness of spirit it's useless for us to match. Don't think I'm here coaxing you for some hidden purpose, or for the bad taste of a rhapsodical style: I'm in my earnestest when stating that a good modern European book is, generally speaking, only interesting and vital for the nation which produced it, whereas a good American one speaks to a larger crowd springing, as it does, from deeper wants and really saying new things not only queer ones, as we at our best are to-day doing.
> I beg your pardon for this lot of spiel but you know, I'm so stuffed with American readings, I must sometimes give a little vent. Otherwise I'll be choking.
> I see *The Grandmothers* is another book about your history, one of your national books, which demonstrate a thing not yet generally known here in Europe: that you, as a nation, have already a tradition and a pride, a great thing which fills your last want. Now you can really go and conquer the earth.[46]

While not linked specifically in the letter, it is clear that Pavese sensed in Whitman what he saw in American movies, a "surpassing strength of vital energy." But while in the first flush of his infatuation with Whitman his enthusiasm often remained unfocused and uncritical, the same does not hold for the essays and prefaces written after the thesis. In these works Pavese created an integrated critical rationale, one having little to do with Croce, that both justified his interest in America and encouraged him further. The first principle of that rationale held that America had a culture worth studying.

To contend in Italy in the early 1930s that America had a culture worth studying was, while not outright subversive, slightly suspect, and not just from the narrow political viewpoint of the official and hyper-nationalistic *Italianità* of the Fascist regime. It also challenged the prevailing intellectual orthodoxy of the day as exemplified by the older critics mentioned above. The intellectual environment in which he was operating explains in part Pavese's aggressive energy in discussing American literature. He felt he had a biased, unappreciative school of thought to oppose, older critics to attack, and a vital culture righteously to defend. What more could a young intellectual ask for?

Pavese not only started from the position that America possessed a cultural tradition, he further suggested that it was equal to that of Europe and perhaps even its superior. "In general, we Europeans tend too much to see our own sources in American spiritual phenomena and as a result we reduce a literature to a maladroit playing out of our themes when in fact, in terms of art [*poesia*], it could now, if anything, be teaching us. It is simply a fact that America has long possessed its own rich tradition, which is, moreover, still new enough that even when unsought is capable of nourishing its young without those efforts of forced renovation that among us often give even the best intentioned works a merely literary tone."[47]

In the preface to his own translation of *Moby-Dick*, in an only partially veiled reference to the Fascist trumpeting of an Italian tradition that went from Mussolini back through Dante to the original Romans, Pavese said (in one of his more famous sentences, set off as a paragraph to itself), "For to have a tradition is less than nothing; it is only in searching for it that one can live it." [Poiché avere una tradizione è meno che nulla, è soltanto cercandola che si può viverla.][48]

But what was this American tradition and what did he find in his search for it? He found several things—and first of all a language, which he came to call "the American vulgate." That form of English particularly attracted Pavese, I would argue, because it coincided with and reinforced the ideas he was then developing about the poetic language most fit for what he wanted to accomplish with his own creative writing.

During these immediate post-university years Pavese not only occupied himself with translations, essays, and book reviews but also, crucially, with his own poetry and fiction. Pavese had been writing poetry since he was about fourteen; his earliest now-published poem dates to 1923, when he was fifteen. Before 1930, Pavese filled his poetic output with adolescent self-absorption and expressed himself in forced, brooding, melodramatic language. Poet and Pavese translator Geoffrey Brock describes that early work as what "one would expect from a precocious teenager: formal experiments, satires of established styles, self-indulgent expressions of teenage lust and angst."[49] Beginning in September 1930, however, three to four months after finishing the thesis on Whitman, Pavese's poetry changed dramatically. In that month he composed most of what would become one of his most famous poems, "I mari del Sud" ("South Seas"), and between then and 1934 composed the great bulk of the remaining poems that went into his first published book, the 1936 *Lavorare stanca*. A quick comparison of the first lines of "I mari del Sud" with a representative poem composed only a year earlier make clear the break and advance that had occured. The first stanza of an untitled poem composed in April 1929 reads:

> *Rondini lente*
> *vòlano sul crepuscolo incolore.*
> *Piú tetro non sarò piú: soltanto*
> *un po' piú stanco, all'ultima agonia.*
> *[Slow swallows*
> *fly in the colorless dusk.*
> *More dismal I will never be: just*
> *a little more tired, at the last agony.]*[50]

"I mari del Sud" of 1930 begins:

> *Camminiamo una sera sul fianco di un colle,*
> *in silenzio. Nell'ombra del tardo crepuscolo*
> *mio cugino è un gigante vestito di bianco,*

che si muove pacato, abbronzato nel volto,
taciturno. Tacere è la nostra virtú.
Qualche nostro antenato dev'esse stato ben solo
—un grand'uomo tra idioti o un povero folle—
per insegnare ai suoi tanto silenzio.
[We're walking one evening on the flank of a hill
in silence. In the shadows of dusk
my cousin's a giant dressed all in white,
moving serenely, face bronzed by the sun,
not speaking. We have a talent for silence.
Some ancestor of ours must have been quite a loner—
A great man among fools or a crazy old bum—
to have taught his descendents such silence.][51]

The rhythm and meter he first used in "I mari del Sud" characterized all his poetry of the 1930s. As Brock puts it, "his standard line is thirteen syllables long and is composed of four anapestic feet."[52] This reverse-waltz rhythm carries forward the narrative elements of the poem with energy and elegance and Brock caught that rhythm well in his translation. Natalia Ginzburg remembers that Pavese's poems of this era "had a long, drawn-out, lazy rhythm, a sort of bitter sing-song quality."[53]

In an essay written in 1934 (though published only in 1943) Pavese said of *Lavorare stanca*, "The composition of this collection lasted three years. Three years of youth and discovery, during which my own ideas about poetry and my intuitive capacities naturally became deeper . . . Simply, I have here a body of work that concerns me, not so much because it was composed by me but rather because for a time I believed it to be the best that was being written in Italy." Pavese went on to say that while he was writing the poetry of this collection he was also engaged in three other activities: "the study and translation of American literature . . . short stories half in dialect [published posthumously as *Ciau Masino*], and, in collaboration with a painter friend [Mario Sturani], an amateur compilation of pornography, about which I don't think there's much more I can appropriately say." All these activities affected his poetry: "In each of the three cases I entered variously into contact with the development of a linguistic creation based on dialect or at least on the spoken word. I mean, by this, the discovery during my studies of the American vulgate [*il volgare nordamericano*] and the use of Turinese or Piedmontese slang in my attempts at naturalistic prose dialogue. Both were enthusiastic, youthful adventures, serving as a basis for more than one thought that quickly evaporated and became integrated through the identifying theory of poetry and language." Pavese added that, as a result of these developing ideas (all emphases are his), "I insisted at that time on stylistic *straightforwardness* [*sobrietà stilistica*] as a fundamental polemical position: it was a question of acquiring imaginative evidence outside *all the other* expressive attitudes that seemed to me corrupted by rhetoric. It was a question of proving to myself that straightforward energy in conception carried within itself closely associated, immediate, and essential expression."[54]

His personal style of poetry, according to Pavese, turned out to be narrative, objective, and at the same time highly imaginative. He coined the phrase "story-poem" [*poesia-racconto*] to describe "I mari del Sud" and most of the other poems in the collection. "I had gone back (or so I thought) to the source of all poetic activity, which I have defined as follows: the power to render as a self-sufficient whole a complex of imaginative relationships in which is embodied the true perception of a reality." Then, after describing some of the dangers of his own approach and what he considered lapses from it in some poems in the collection, he wrote in the last paragraph of this essay, "I became [during the composition of the poems] ever more capable of allusions, of half tints, of extravagant composition, and ever less convinced of the honesty, of the *necessity* of my work. In comparison, the naked and almost prosaic verse of 'I mari del Sud' seemed to me ever more justified and I remained faithful to the clearly defined principle: the straightforward and direct expression of a clearly perceived imaginative relationship. I dearly wanted to tell a story and so I could not let myself get lost in unnecessary frills."[55]

This piece of artistic self-analysis, written before confino, is important because it shows Pavese looking back at the beginning of his poetic efforts while they were still fresh in his memory. The essay is not free of self-serving stratagems, but, placed against the poems of *Lavorare stanca* and the stories of *Ciau Masino*, it rings mostly true. Furthermore, one finds implicit in this essay the links between Pavese's own early ideas about poetics and his reasons for being attracted to American literature, just as one finds them explicitly in the openly "American" works of this period. "Linguistic creation based on dialect or at least on the spoken word," "straightforward style," "straightforward energy in the conception," and "true perception of reality" not only describe the aims for his own poetry of this period but also appear as continuing themes in his American essays. If any of these concerns dominates in the essays, it is "linguistic creation." Indeed, a concern with the freshness and directness of language represents the leitmotif of Pavese's American writings through 1934.

In his first essay, for instance, Pavese praised Sinclair Lewis for many qualities, but chief among them Lewis's language. In the summer of 1930, when he wrote this piece, Pavese felt that Lewis deserved more credit than any other twentieth-century writer for the creation of a new type of American language. Lewis "understands and loves slang so much that the end result is the creation of a language—the American vulgate; something of which we have no examples since the times in which the neo-Latin people forged their virgin languages in art and life. Before Lewis, American *slang* [English in original] was local color or journalistic improvisation. Perhaps only O. Henry, that happy, mad genius, made it at times into a literary language. But in the others—M. Twain, W. D. Howells being the best—the American vulgate remained too much as it was in the speech of the negro Jupiter in Edgar Poe's *The Gold Bug*."[56]

Before committing this essay to paper, Pavese already knew he was going to emphasize Lewis's use of language. The day after defending his thesis and receiving his laurea he wrote Chiuminatto, "You'll read a corking essay on Lewis, it will beat everything. You wait and see. *Va sans dire*, you'll receive the review. I've something to say about slang, also, it will be grand and glorious. I'll teach a few fellers here that are now overflowing Italy with vacuum-gabble about America what people must say and how they must say it."[57]

Even earlier, at least by January 1930, Pavese had conceived but not yet named the new language he had discovered in America. In that month he wrote Chiuminatto:

> You speak always of slang as of a special language or dialect, which exists by itself and is spoken only on certain occasions or places and so on. Now, I think, slang is not a diversified language from English as, for instance, Piedmontese is from

Tuscan, so that a word, or a phrase, can be told to belong to a class or another . . .

I mean there is not a line to be drawn between English and the slang words, as two different languages usually spoken by different people and only in certain cases used together.

That book you know, *Dark Laughter*, for instance, is written in English, but there are numberless slang-expressions in it and they are not as French words in an Italian book, but they are a natural part of that language. And I said always English, but I should have said American for I think there is not a slang and a classic language, but there are two diversified languages, the English and the American ones. As slang is the living part of all languages, English has become American by it, that is the two languages have developed themselves separately by means of their respective slangs.

My conclusion is then that there are not a slang and a classic language but there is an American language formed by a perfectly fused mixture of both.[58]

Pavese made Sherwood Anderson the topic of his second American essay, written toward the end of 1930, and in Anderson he found also a fresh and important use of language. "Anderson's style! Not the crude, still too localized dialect—the kind our dialect specialists use, even the most notable examples of which always seem a bit shabby—but a new structure of English, made up entirely of American idioms, of a style that is no longer *dialect* but *language*, rethought, recreated, *art*. In a tale written by Anderson there is always the echo of the American speaker, *the living man* who narrates as he feels, with balance and vitality."[59]

In a 2004 interview, Fernanda Pivano recalled the pleasure Anderson gave Pavese in the 1930s. In response to the question, "And why did he like Anderson?" Pivano said, "Because Anderson was the first one in America who wrote with this everyday 'low,' as opposed to 'high' language, and he wrote of an everyday world. At that time in Italy one wrote with the high style, for example, 'the youth arrived at his dwelling.' Instead of that Anderson would write, 'the boy came home' and this was the basis of the new language."[60]

Pavese also found O. Henry's use of language both appealing and impressive. In 1931, while still involved with his *Moby-Dick* translation, Pavese composed a four-thousand-word essay on the short story writer, making clear how much he admired O. Henry because of his ability to tell a good story in a language that Pavese considered one of the high points of the American vulgate tradition.

> His is a dialect literature. It is a curious dialect literature because we imagine dialect as something localistic and we would have expected a dialect literature rather from New England. But in America dialect is the common language spoken by everyone, in contrast to the courtly English taught in the schools.
>
> The dialect quality of *short-stories* [English in original] from Mark Twain to O. Henry came out of the need to speak to a predominantly democratic audience (miners, sometimes), and, in any case, always to a striving middle class that wanted to understand and recognize itself in its newspapers. Because, naturally, from Mark Twain to O. Henry all the literature that was alive was journalism.[61]

O. Henry, in Pavese's eyes, brought to a close one phase in the development of the American language and provided the basis for the next generation of writers to take it to a higher level. Pavese saw a tradition that started with Twain and Bret Harte ("the pioneers of the new literature, no longer New Englandish but national") and included Artemus Ward, Ambrose Bierce, and Jack London before culminating in O. Henry, whose language, Pavese stated in closing this essay, would outlive its author. In fact, "the generation that followed O. Henry—Dreiser, Lindsay, Lee Masters, Sandburg, Lewis, Anderson—has not forgotten his lesson and in its work of interpreting and recreating the U.S.A. is bringing to conclusion the great linguistic rebellion, which, in new hands, is becoming the conscious instrument of a completely spiritual search."[62]

Just as language could attract Pavese to a writer, it could also repel him. In his expressively titled 1934 essay, "Faulkner, a Bad Pupil of Anderson," he gave the already highly respected writer what Calvino called a "maiming" because, among other important reasons, Pavese thought Faulkner used language badly. Pavese found the interior monologues of *As I Lay Dying* "flat and tiring" and the style of *Sanctuary* "asthmatic."[63]

While their use of direct language always remained important for Pavese, he often admired American writers for other reasons. As his warm love of Melville shows, Pavese's strong preference for what he called the American vulgate didn't necessarily apply in all cases; rather, he reserved it as a first test for twentieth-century writers.

Pavese's preference for the vulgate in American literature did not come from a polemical desire to attack the predominately older rulers of Italian literary taste, nor from simplistic ideas about plain style, but from deeper impulses. He felt that the use of a "straightforward," "virile" style had important, indeed crucial, implications for all literature because it represented the most effective way to penetrate to the deepest levels of reality and to communicate truthfully what one found there.

Reality, of course, defies definition, especially when one seeks to explain it as seen though another's eyes. In one sense, all Pavese's mature writing served as exercises in his own myth-infused definition of reality, and the early American essays show that the problem concerned him even at the beginning of his career. Just as in his own fiction and poetry in the early 1930s he wanted to arrive at "the true perception of reality," at "immediate and essential expression," so, too, he looked for this type of perception in American writers. Interestingly enough, the reality he discovered was *not* the same as his own understanding of the real in later years.

Pavese saw the American search for a new kind of reality as beginning with Whitman. In his 1933 essay on Whitman he wrote, "For the first time the problem was formulated that in the twentieth century every artist has begun again to pose. However expressed, the problem is always freshly relevant because while a European artist, an ancient, will maintain that the secret of art is to construct a more or less imaginative world, to deny reality in order to substitute for it another, perhaps more important world, an American of the recent generations will tell you that his aspirations lie completely in reaching the true nature of things, to see with virgin eyes, to arrive at that 'ultimate grip of reality' [English in original] that alone is worth knowing."[64]

As this passage implies, in the early 1930s Pavese believed that to evade reality, even if to create a "perhaps more important world," was an abdication by the artist of his responsibilities. Thus the straightforward vulgate language was helpful in approaching reality in the twentieth century because frills, or prose for the sake of prose, increased the danger of distractions and distortions, when the aim should be maximum clarity and immediateness. Yet for all his claims that the Americans were aiming at reality and the Europeans not, Pavese never gives us in these essays any clear statement of his own definition of reality. To say that an artist must not evade reality but rather must perceive it freshly and grasp it is not to say what reality is.

A sense of the meaning of realism for Pavese does emerge from these essays, but by inference, not in any direct statement. Geno Pampaloni characterizes Pavese's realism mostly in terms of mimetic language: "not in the sense of realistic documentation [*documentazione veristica*] but more in the sense of a search for a language that *becomes one with the things described.*"[65] Yet, though Pavese's realism is certainly linked to language, it is even more essentially a question of the relationship of the artist with the external world and with the characters he creates. I would hazard a definition of realism in literature, for Pavese in the 1930s, as what results from the fresh, sane, balanced, hopeful, immediate yet moral perception of the world, made possible by sympathy and compassion and expressed in direct and therefore honest language. This conception of realism differs in crucial ways from his ideas in the last seven years of his life. In these mature years, while Pavese would still insist on the need for compassion, sympathy, and a straightforward style, the hope and promise that he had once seen as inherent in perception itself had given way to a stoical acceptance of life as destiny (or fate, or one's own set of personal symbols, personal myths: terms which came to be almost interchangeable for the older Pavese). Until roughly 1935, though, the world *was* promising for Pavese, and during that period none of the American writers he admired created protagonists who accepted fate passively. Quite the opposite: from Captain Ahab and Whitman's pioneer to Lewis's Babbitt and Dodsworth, these were characters or personae who, while not always overcoming fate, never surrendered stoically to it.

Sympathy and compassion remained always for Pavese key characteristics of a good writer. He demanded not a generic compassion going out to humanity as a whole, but one centered on the characters brought to life by the writer. At times, such compassion could even make up for poor language. For instance, Dreiser, whom Pavese thought wrote badly, "without affection for words," still had worth because of his compassion:

> He does not have the temper of a thinker as his essays make clear ... He wants to limit himself to "representing"—and

this is an unconscious negation of himself as a thinker—but his representations reach the depth of many human gestures and express their essential tragedy and therefore essential pity ... And, I repeat, this tragedy [*An American Tragedy*] has no moral conclusion, it has none and can have none because such was not in the author's mind, but the miracle of human pity revealed in the complex and unending "equation of emotions" is enough to make of it one of the greatest books of recent time.[66]

Many of the twentieth-century writers Pavese admired combined direct language and compassion: most notably, Sinclair Lewis, Sherwood Anderson, and John Dos Passos. Of the last, Pavese wrote in 1933, "The narrative pages [of *1919*] cleared of theories and avant-gardisms remain the true Dos Passos, composed of human comprehension and immediateness and of a judicious morality that goes beyond every polemic and every stylistic experiment."[67]

Sinclair Lewis attracted Pavese, too, for reasons that went beyond Lewis's use of language. Pavese described Lewis as a "sane, balanced provincial," and provincialism had positive connotations for Pavese. He considered *Babbitt* Lewis's best work: "Babbitt is his masterpiece; in him, better than in any other character, Lewis fuses the ridiculous puppet with the human brother we should all cry with."[68]

The few times that Pavese recorded seeing in a writer both a lack of compassion and deficient language, he predictably attacked with particular severity. The first negative article he ever wrote about an American writer came in 1934 and dealt with William Faulkner. We have already seen that he considered Faulkner's style "asthmatic." On the issue of compassion he is even more damning. In a riff on Arnold Bennett's blurb that appeared on some of Faulkner's original dust jackets ("An American who writes like an angel"), Pavese wrote, "William Faulkner sees things from on high, so much so that between Popeye's bloody corncob and Benbow's pipe there is no difference of perspective. It is not a man who is writing, it is an angel; an angel, I mean, who does not care for souls."[69] For Pavese, nothing could so surely exclude an author from the line of great American writers as not caring for souls.

The compassionate search for reality coupled with direct language did not, however, close the Pavesian ideal critical circle. These had to be accompanied by a "sane" and "balanced" approach to life and art. In view of Pavese's intense and amply documented feelings of loneliness beginning in 1935, in view of his later willed withdrawal from life, it seems sadly ironic, but not surprising, that in his earliest critical pieces he put so much emphasis on sanity (*sanità*) and balance (*equilibrio*). This emphasis in the early 1930s arose from Pavese's own inner cravings and also from the ideas Augusto Monti propounded at the Liceo D'Azeglio. I would argue that the Monti impulse in these essays can be seen in Pavese's comments on style, sanity, the positive value of provincialism, the democratic basis of art, and the relationship of an artist's life to his work. The statement and treatment of these themes showed that Pavese had absorbed and accepted a great many of his ex-teacher's critical premises.

Nowhere does Monti's influence show itself more clearly—and, paradoxically, nowhere does Pavese seem more himself—than in Pavese's celebrated first essay on Melville (1932). One should read it not only as a competent piece of Melville criticism but as a statement on a writer's ideal life. Melville's strength and vital energy attracted Pavese just as Whitman's had, but Melville came to his art by a different path: Melville had first lived intensely a life unrelated to art, and then brought his experiences to bear in art. That Pavese considered this sequencing important goes back to Monti's ideas about the necessity of the writer having a vigorous life outside art before attempting to create art. "Herman Melville," Pavese wrote, "first lived through real adventures, through the primitive state. He was first a barbarian and then later he entered the world of culture and thought, bringing with him the sanity and balance he had acquired in the life he had been leading."[70] Pavese did not see Melville as an isolated case but as representative of American writers as a whole. "It is not an accident that Herman Melville is an American. These newcomers in the field of culture are held responsible by their defenders for the re-barbarization [*rimbarbarimento*] of our ideals, and, bias aside, justly so, for they have much to teach us in this regard. It is they who have discovered how to reinvigorate culture, sieving it through primitive and actual experience, not like us who substitute one term for another, but by enriching, modifying, and strengthening literature through what is called life."[71]

Melville, to Pavese in 1932, appeared as truly a man in all senses, whole and balanced, just as Whitman did to the younger Pavese in 1926. Indeed, Pavese's admiration for Melville the man almost outstripped his praise of Melville's works. Interestingly, the terms Pavese used to describe Melville in 1932 call to mind those Pavese had used two years earlier to characterize the cousin in "I mari del Sud," another self-possessed masculine figure, the "giant dressed all in white, moving serenely." Toward the end of that poem he wrote:

> *Only one dream*
> *has stayed in his blood: once, when he worked*
> *as a stoker on a Dutch fishing boat, the Cetacean,*
> *he saw the heavy harpoons sail in the sun,*
> *and saw the whales as they fled in a frothing of blood*
> *and the chase and the flukes lifting, fighting the launches.*
> *Sometimes he mentions it.*
> *But whenever I tell him*
> *that he's one of the lucky ones to have seen the sun rise*
> *over the loveliest islands in the world,*
> *he smiles at the memory, then says that the sun*
> *didn't rise till the day for them was already old.*[72]

Pavese wrote that "Herman Melville entered life sickly and alienated. It seems that by nineteen he was already scribbling. Then, suddenly, the sea. Four years of wanderings and companions, whaling, the Marquesas, a woman, Tahiti, Japan, sperm whales, some reading, a lot of imagining, Callao, Cape Horn and in October 1844 there disembarked in Boston a complete man [*un uomo quadrato*], sunburnt and experienced in the vices and value of men."[73]

The cousin in white, who recalls both Whitman and Melville, and this perfectly whole Melville who turns up in Boston in 1844 represented magnetizing ideals for the young Pavese. His emotional commitment to the type emerges in almost every paragraph of the Melville essay—for, after all, did not Pavese begin life "sickly and alienated" and was not Pavese scribbling at age nineteen? But Pavese's attachment to this ideal also arose from a deep belief that only in a full integration of work and art could the artist find salvation, and only thus produce truly regenerative, life-giving art.

Because the creators of the best in American literature seemed to understand the necessity of integrating work and art, mind and body, emotions and intellect, in essence the necessity of *sanità* and *equilibrio*, Pavese though it a more vital, virile, and creative literature than anything contemporary Europe had to offer, just as earlier he had found American films more vital than those being produced in Italy.[74] To find a valid comparison for American culture, said Pavese, one had to turn to the best of ancient Greece.

> That "A thought signifies nothing unless it is thought with the whole body" is clearly an American sentence, and the whole literature of the United States, from Thoreau to Sherwood Anderson, has consciously or unconsciously tended toward this ideal, resulting in the production of powerful individuals who spend a good number of years barbarously, living and absorbing, who then dedicate themselves to culture, reworking the reality they experienced in thoughts and images which for their dignity and serene and open virility have something of that balance we normally associate with the Greeks.[75]

The parallel with ancient Greece struck Pavese as particularly illuminating in Melville's case. To Pavese, Greek literature enlarged mankind, helped in its re-creation, and Melville did the same, while modern European literature most definitely did not.

> Melville was truly a Greek. Read the European evasions of literature and you feel more literary than ever; you feel teeny, cerebral, effeminate. Read Melville—who was not afraid to begin *Moby-Dick*, that poem of the barbarous life, with eight pages of quotations and to go even further, arguing, bringing more quotations to bear, and being a letterato—and you feel your lungs expand, your brain growing; you feel more alive and more a man. And as with the Greeks, the tragedy (*Moby-Dick*) may be dark, but so strong is the serenity and clarity of the chorus (Ishmael) that we always leave the theater exalted in our own capacity for life.[76]

Revitalizing barbarism was not enough for a culture, but neither was art by itself. American literature, especially its seminal figures like Whitman and Melville, managed to fuse both: "Herman Melville is therefore above all a letterato and a thinker who began as a whaler, a Robinson Crusoe, a vagabond."[77] Melville could talk with a seaman, hunt a whale, quote the bible and Shakespeare, and felt equally at home in a library or a forecastle. For Pavese, in short, Melville and the American literature he represented were healthy and balanced, just as Pavese wanted to be himself.

Neither "barbarism" (read vitality, experience, work, energy, and, in part, sex) nor "art" (read classicism, tradition, discipline, style) could stand alone, for that would mean a lack of *equilibrio*. Pavese insisted—and here he differed from most of the older Italians, who looked favorably on American literature only for its vitality—that America had both barbarism *and* art. Again, Melville combined them at the highest level. He demonstrated it best in *Moby-Dick*, which for Pavese was not just a barbaric hymn—though it was that also—but a magnificently constructed work of art, "a miraculous balance of minute, realistic technical details that describe the customs of the sea and of whaling and the wild supernatural sections of signs and prophesies, emanating like a halo from the ferocious and biblical Ahab."[78] Referring to his plot synopsis and commentary earlier in the essay, Pavese added that, with all that said,

> how much the reader has still to learn from its austere, legendary tone, from that style which, above and beyond its wealth of fantasy, is pregnant with strict moral thought. Or from the tense and solemn pace, accompanied at times by a mischievous smile, with which the chapters of realistic description, information, and discussion proceed. But above all it is the constant sense of the enormous, of the superhuman, toward which the whole book converges in a miracle of construction by which, little by little, the gay and puritanical atmosphere of the beginning and the learned atmosphere of the long explanations of the central passages are finally blended in a spirit of conscious and daring action which is almost mythical, as the name and fame of the White Whale, which only appears toward the end of the book, grow until they seem gigantic and occupy all places, all actions, and all thoughts.[79]

American literature, then, and Whitman and Melville in particular, essentially served Pavese in the period 1926–33 as a means to better define his own ideals as a man and artist. It was this still vital literary tradition that best showed how his own forming values could be realized in life and art, how a fusion of "barbarism" and "art" could give life to culture and culture's participants. While it oversimplifies matters to say that Pavese found in American literature only what he was looking for, he certainly overlooked what he did not want to see. How writers like Edgar Allen Poe, Henry James, Henry Adams, Edith Wharton, Willa Cather, F. Scott Fitzgerald, William Faulkner, Thomas Wolfe, or the great American poets other than Whitman would fit into Pavese's scheme is hard to say. (Except for the pieces on Whitman and Edgar Lee Masters, none of Pavese's essays dealt with

American poets, nor did he ever publish translations of American poetry other than as excerpts in the essays on Whitman and Masters.) As any serious critic must, he created his own great tradition for the literature he was dealing with. That tradition started with Whitman, culminated in Lewis and Anderson, and included Twain, O. Henry, Dreiser, Masters, and, supremely, Melville—a tradition for which Thomas Hart Benton might serve as the ideal illustrator. It was based on Pavese's concept of the "American vulgate," that mixture of formal English and slang he thought so defining.

That Pavese constructed his own tradition of American literature did not mean that he tried to fit all the authors he wrote about into one lineage. His treatment of Melville, an almost baroque, decorative, image-rich stylist whom he considered representative of much of the best in American literature, offers a clear illustration. A reading of his essays shows, too, that Pavese took each writer on that writer's own terms and sought to discern what was life-giving in each work. He was no longer giving out Crocean Pass-Fail grades but trying rather to convey to the educated Italians for whom he was writing what made each of these Americans worth reading. As Sergio Pautasso has said of these essays and prefaces of the 1930s, "Pavese adopted a tone and style of expression outside those of any scheme. He demonstrates in these works not a successful but derivative exercise based on a master—even one as great as Croce—but rather his desire to meet head-on with the reality of each text he was studying."[80] In trying to meet head-on with each writer, Pavese always sought to identify what exactly it was that brought their works to life, to point out to the reader where lay the "poesia." Often, he found one overriding quality that defined each writer. For O. Henry, for example, "there's no need to be afraid to declare that O. Henry's poetry consists specifically and exclusively in the ironic and slightly painful sense of these paradoxical contrasts."[81] For Dreiser it was his capacity for pity, "the simple need to see at the bottom of every tragedy the comfortless and enraging discovery that justice is not of this world . . . his representations arrive at the heart of many human gestures and express their essential tragedy and therefore their essential pity."[82]

In addition to their use of the vulgate language, their search for "the ultimate grip of reality," their *sanità* and *equilibrio*, and their compassion, most of the American writers who attracted Pavese shared another characteristic. They were, to use Pavese's own word, "provincials." Pavese found fascinating that the writers who were doing the most to revitalize American literature generally had not grown up in New York, Chicago, or any other big city, but in the provinces, particularly in the Middle West. He believed that America had figured out how to turn provincial themes into national literature, something Italy was still struggling with. He first dealt with the topic in the conclusion of his first essay, that on Lewis:

> Taken as a whole, one thing is especially conspicuous in these novels by Lewis. The characters, and with them the author, are great provincial types. In every sense of the word, great. They begin as innocents. Those from the prairies go to be provincials in New York and those from New York go to be provincials in Europe. They end in dignity, but—charlatans or distinguished scientists or industrialists as they are—a room full of people in evening dress will always make them uneasy.
>
> Still, it was such people—with whom the Middle West, the American heartland, perpetuates itself in art—that the national literature needed.[83]

He drew an unfavorable comparison of America's success in making provincialism national and the situation in Italy in his 1931 essay on Sherwood Anderson (whose title Calvino changed in his 1962 edition from Pavese's simple "Sherwood Anderson" to "Middle West and Piedmont"). Writing of "the three innovators Theodore Dreiser, Sinclair Lewis, and Sherwood Anderson," Pavese said there was an historical parallel with Italy:

> And the parallel exists, clear and exact. We might think of the significance, for Italian literature, of the discovery of regions, which went hand in hand with the quest for national unity, a discovery that belongs to the last part of the eighteenth and to the entire nineteenth century. From Alfieri on down, all the Italian writers try, sometimes and indeed often unconsciously, to achieve a more profound national unity through penetrating always further the character of their own region, as it exists in them, their *true* nature, thus to achieve the creation of a human awareness and language rich with all the blood of the province and with all the dignity of life renewed. And especially my countrymen from Piedmont might think about these things, for it is in Piedmont that the urgency of this aspiration is still felt most powerfully and is furthest from realization, lost as we now are behind too much specialization of dialect . . . We

have never had that man and that work which, in addition to being most dear to us, would truly achieve that universality and originality which would make him comprehensible to all men and not only to his countrymen. This is our still unsatisfied need. Meanwhile, the American novelists of whom I speak have in fact met the corresponding need of their nation and regions. We must therefore learn from them.[84]

Pavese believed that America's "provincials" transcended dialect and regionalism and that their works spoke to the entire American nation. As the translator of his American essays put it, "What excited Pavese about the American Midwest was not so much its actualities, about which he can be scathing, as its imaginative 'centrality.'"[85] In Italy, on the other hand, the use of dialect resulted mostly in a localistic literature that had little interest for readers outside the region involved. Pavese thought this a pity because, as he said in a famous sentence from the first essay on Lewis (a sentence Calvino used as the title for the essay when it was published in book form after Pavese's death), "Without provincials a literature has no verve."[86]

In expounding such ideas Pavese used an Italian that differed not only from that used by an earlier generation of critics, but from the orotund language that characterized almost all Italian literary discourse of the time, the Futurists excepted. Pavese expressed his ideas with an informality that disguised his intensity. For example, he did not waste time with elaborate introductions but rather drew the reader right into the subject matter along with him. He had a particular knack for engaging first sentences. The first sentence of his first essay to appear in print (on Sinclair Lewis, 1930) reads, "These Americans have invented a new way of drinking."[87] Other representative opening sentences from essays and prefaces spanning seventeen years:

> To translate *Moby-Dick* is to put yourself in touch with the times.[88]
>
> The excellent translation that Giacomo Prampolini's has recently published of a well selected group of O. Henry's stories brings again to our attention one of America's most embarrassing figures.[89]
>
> Toward the end of the last century the author of this work [Sherwood Anderson] was a young worker who passed his evenings sprawled on a narrow bed in a badly furnished room reading absent-mindedly anything at hand.[90]

The Americans are really mad at Dreiser.[91]

I don't think I'm the only one in Italy to go looking for my first book by Dos Passos because of the impact of [the film] *The Crowd*.[92]

Fernanda Pivano has translated *The Spoon River Anthology* . . . and introduced it with a preface that implies more than it states.[93]

Edgar Lee Masters, who died recently in his eighties after a full and productive life, is now himself a voice from Spoon River.[94]

The times are over in which we discovered America.[95]

Pavese did not use in these essays and prefaces the overly informal, almost colloquial style that characterized his Whitman thesis, but he did use, as he used for the rest of his life, a direct, compact, sparse but dense Italian that makes him seem to be conversing with the reader rather than lecturing to an audience. He mixed long with short sentences and used fragments rather than sentences when he wanted to emphasize something quickly. He often put the verb phrase at the end of a sentence, a placement grammatically permitted in Italian but uncommon because, like English, it is primarily a subject-verb-object language. He liked to emphasize points by setting them off with dashes. He managed simultaneously to engage and keep the reader slightly off balance. His prose—essays and fiction—requires close attention; a lot can happen in a few sentences. Here is one example from the 1931 essay on Anderson, which I quote in the original Italian with a translation that follows Pavese's sentence structures:

> Tutta la vita dell'America di Roosevelt, Sherwood Anderson l'ha vista. C'è piombato in giovinezza, l'ha vissuta e l'ha sofferta—l'ha amata—ha cercato in ogni modo di sfuggirne ed un giorno s'è accorto che lui, fin dagli anni dell'infanzia, fin dal padre, fannullone fantasioso, dalla nonna, l'italiana risoluta, terra e sangue, bevitrice e centenaria, ne era sempre stato un evaso, un sognatore, un facitore di racconti.[96]
>
> [All the life of (Theodore) Roosevelt's America, Anderson saw. He threw himself into it in his youth, he lived it and he suffered it—and he loved it—and he tried in every way to get away from it and one day he realized that he, from the years of his infancy, from his father, a daydreaming good-for-nothing, from his grandmother, a strong-minded Italian, earth and blood, drinker and centenarian, had always been an escapist, a dreamer, someone who made up stories.]

Here is a full paragraph from the 1933 essay on Whitman in which he is discussing Whitman's treatment of soldiers:

> Cosí i soldati whitmaniani. Non sono né gli eroi epici di un canzone di gesta né i riluttani doughboys della grande Guerra; sono i comrades che nei momenti piú programmatici lavorando a salvare l'unione democratica e nei momenti di poesia a condividere con Walt Whitman le esperienze, le tenerezze, la scoperata risoluta di alrri esseri umani.[97]
>
> [Thus the Whitmanian soldiers. They are neither the epic heroes of a *chanson de geste* nor the hesitant doughboys of the Great War; they are the comrades who in programmed moments work to save the democratic union and in poetic moments share with Walt Whitman the experiences, the tendernesses, the resolute discovery of other human beings.]

Or this from one of his post–World War II newspaper pieces:

> Parlare. Le parole sono il nostro mestiere. Lo diciamo senza ombra di timidezza o di ironia. Le parole sono tenere cose, intrattabili e vive, ma fatte per l'uomo e non l'uomo per loro.[98]
>
> [To speak. Words are my trade. I say that without any shadow of timidity or of irony. Words are tender things, irreducible and alive, but made for man and not man for them.]

Valerio Ferme sees the Italian Pavese used in his translations as a deliberate attack on the then current literary Italian, so much so that in his book on the subject he entitled the relevant chapter "Translation as Literary Subversion: Cesare Pavese's Attack on the Dominant Literary Language."[99] Ferme contends that, at least between 1931 and 1935, Pavese was not translating mainly for the money, though he welcomed it, but because he wanted to get into Italian certain authors he considered important. He would choose whom to translate and then work to get a publisher to agree. Ferme believes Pavese deliberately chose books with certain themes, and in translating them consciously used the Italian he did as a protest against and an attack on the Italian "establishment." After discussing Pavese's correspondence with his editor at Mondadori regarding one of his Dos Passos translations, Ferme goes on to say:

> Here, the agreement between the translator and the publisher to maintain the polemical integrity of the text as much as possible in spite of the authorities is evident, and demonstrates that

Pavese was learning how to cope with the censors, conceding them some modifications but maintaining for the most part the subversive tone and the symbolism of the original text, as demonstrated also by his subsequent translations, almost all of which show the same desire to confront the *establishment*—political or literary—both on the symbolic level of the contents (the thematic representation of the common man who fights against great adversity, the struggle against evil, the calm life of the country as opposed to progress) and on that of linguistic innovation and subversion (linguistic research as a method of transforming language and for recreating a new mythical world of significances).[100]

Ferme sees Pavese's stylistic habit of adhering to the structure and even the syntax of the American authors he translated as the key evidence for Pavese's deliberate linguistic subversion. Pavese did not believe in making his American authors sound as though they were Italian writers of the 1930s. In translation theory terms, that means that Pavese respected the language of origin more than that of arrival, and in doing so went against the practice of most Italian translators of the time.[101] I think Pavese's own prose, though as "subversive" in the 1930s as that of his translations, did not have the same kind of conscious motivation. I do think his ten-year deep engagement with the English language, beginning when it did in his life, affected his prose style just as it did his poetry. Beginning around 1924 Pavese was, as Fussell so well puts it, "elbow deep in a word-for-word scramble with actual texts in a foreign language."[102] His Italian does not read like English, but neither does it read like the Italian of any other Italian author or critic, certainly not like that of any of the established literary figures of the 1930s.[103]

Pavese was not the only young Italian to set himself apart from the older established critics by expressing appreciative views of America and its literature. Three deserve special mention: Mario Soldati, Giaime Pintor, and, most importantly, Elio Vittorini. Generational factors play a role here. In 1930, when Pavese published his first essay, Carlo Linati was fifty-two, Prezzolini forty-eight, and Cecchi forty six. Pavese had recently turned twenty-two and Elio Vittorini was the same age; Mario Soldati was twenty-four and Giaime Pintor was only eleven. The three established critics were adults during World War I and the troubled times that followed it; they belonged to a generation that had fully matured by the time Mussolini became prime minister in 1922. Pavese, Vittorini, and Soldati were too young to have fought in the war, and were fourteen to sixteen when Mussolini came to power. Pintor was born in 1919, and though not as many years separate him from Pavese and Vittorini as separates those two from the older critics, Pintor belongs to the literary generation that followed Pavese, the same one that included Fernanda Pivano (b. 1917) and Italo Calvino (b. 1923). Pintor thought these age differences significant. In his 1943 review-essay of Vittorini's *Americana*, in trying to explain the difference between Cecchi's view of America and those of the newer generations, Pintor wrote that one reason "we cannot argue about, but which decides every controversy definitely—the years which separate us—can explain the conflict in our understanding of the name America."[104] Pintor was twenty-four in 1943, Cecchi fifty-nine.

Of this younger group, Mario Soldati, though he had some of the best credentials as an americanista, concerned himself with America only briefly, if famously. Born 1906 in Turin, Soldati was educated from elementary school straight through the liceo by the Jesuits at the Istituto Sociale, the prominent comprehensive school whose ginnasio inferiore Pavese attended for three years, 1918 to 1921, at which point Soldati would have already moved on to the school's ginnasio superiore and liceo. Soldati also preceded Pavese by three years at the University of Turin, and thus Soldati's last year there was Pavese's first. Soldati studied in the same department Pavese did, Letters and Philosophy, and had many of the same teachers as Pavese, but the two students do not seem to have been friends. Not only did Soldati have three years on him, but Soldati's main interest was art; his tesi di laurea in 1927 dealt with the early Renaissance artist Boccaccio Boccaccino. Visual art did not much interest Pavese then or ever. No correspondence between Pavese and Soldati has come to light, but they certainly knew each other as adults and occasionally spent time together.[105]

Unlike any of the younger americanisti, Soldati actually emigrated to America, or at least intended to when he embarked from Genoa in November 1929 to take up a one-year teaching fellowship at Columbia University, the very kind Pavese unsuccessfully applied for in 1931.[106] Soldati's stay in America lasted only two years, however, because he did not manage to obtain U.S. citizenship. He returned to Italy in 1931 and several months later married Marion Rickelman, an American ex-student of his at Columbia. He returned to America for shorter stays in 1932 and 1933 and based on those experiences he published, in 1935, *America, primo amore* (America, First Love), a book that has achieved the same kind of iconic status as Cecchi's *America amara*.[107] Soldati went on to write successful fiction, books and articles on wine and gastronomy, and, like Linati, travel books. He also had a credible career as a screenwriter and then as a film and TV director. While he did set one of his late novels, *La sposa americana (The American Bride)*[108], in America, he never really dealt at length with American topics after *America, primo amore*, though he wrote occasional pieces related to America and always retained his fondness for the United States. However, he expressed that fondness in *America, primo amore* in a most ambiguous way, perhaps because, as he said, "I have started to love America less and understand her more."[109]

America, primo amore has none of the strident harshness of Cecchi's book, yet it does portray in clear, relaxed, and readable prose a generally sad and bland America filled with unhappy people who often do not realize their unhappiness. Other than the New York City subways and American movies, Soldati found little to like wholeheartedly and much to dislike or to damn with faint praise. He adopted, though less overtly, the same stance that Cecchi later did, that of the cultured European who sees things about America that Americans do not because his European culture gives him a perspective Americans do not have. He criticized America in muted tones but with considerable bitterness, despite the nostalgia for America expressed several times in the book. Soldati's America was not, as the blurb on the jacket of its latest edition suggests, "halfway between Cecchi's 'bitter' America and the willed enthusiasm of Pavese and Vittorini."[110] Even though Soldati's tone differs, his views and his book are much closer to those of Cecchi. It is therefore not surprising that in discussions of the americanismo of the 1930s Soldati, despite being only two years older than Pavese and Vittorini, is rarely linked with them and almost always with Cecchi.

Giaime Pintor's view of America definitely links him with Pavese and Vittorini. If anything, he went beyond them in the idealistic warmth of his enthusiasm. Like Pavese, he never visited America, and despite his attachment to the idea of America he wrote only one piece about it, a 1943 review-essay of Vittorini's *Americana*.[111] Like Leone Ginzburg's, Pintor's is a voice manqué of post–World War II Italian literature because he, too, died during and because of the war. A lieutenant in the Italian army, Pintor found himself in Rome when the king arrested Mussolini in July 1943 and installed Marshall Badoglio as head of government. He stayed there through the forty-five days between Mussolini's arrest and Italy's armistice with the allied powers in September 1943; he commanded some of the Italian troops in the futile resistance against the Germans who invaded the city as soon as Hitler learned of the armistice. Pintor then left Rome, crossed German lines, and went south, first to Brindisi where Badoglio had set up a feeble government center and then to Naples where the English and American armies had their headquarters. He found little support there for his idea of forming regular Italian army units to fight the Germans and decided to cross the lines back north to join the Partisans who had already begun to fight in German-occupied Italy. He had English support for this move and with a small unit of Italians set out to cross the lines north again. On December 1, 1943, he stepped on a mine, one of the thousands the Germans had laid on the banks of the Garigliano River in anticipation of a British army thrust. He was twenty-four years old.

In the one essay he wrote about America, Pintor left us the best description we have of the power the idea of America possessed for Italians of his generation. He moved in his review-essay between praise for America and the book *Americana* and condemnation of Cecchi, who, of course, wrote the introduction to the edition Pintor was reviewing.

> [The book] is valuable as the straightforward message of a people to the ones who have not touched their shores, and the proud response of America to the problems of the world of the future . . . *Americana*—the brevity of its name suggests the richness of its intentions—evokes the visions of travelers rather than the study of philologists . . .
> Where Cecchi has scrupulously collected a museum of horrors, where he has isolated sickness and decadence and described a world which it is impossible for us to believe in, we have heard a voice, deep and very close, the voice of our true friends and first contemporaries.
> The presence of this America has filled up the emptiness and shadowy places of our souls.

Pintor ended his essay with a moving passage that neither Cecchi nor Soldati could ever have written:

> In our words dedicated to America, much may be naïve and inexact, much may apply to ideas that are extraneous to the historical development of the United States and its present reality. But it doesn't matter very much because, even if the continent did not exist, our words would not lose their significance. This America does not need a Columbus; it is discovered within us. It is the land we are striving to reach with the same hope and trust of the first immigrants and of whoever decides to defend, at the price of pain and error, the dignity of the human condition.[112]

One wonders if America will ever again be perceived in such a warmly favorable light.

Elio Vittorini wrote much more than just one essay on America. He began working in the field later than Pavese but in their lifetimes became equally prominent as an americanista. His anthology, *Americana*, with his introductory notes, was more influential than any individual piece Pavese wrote. Though linked by their common interest in American literature and, after the war, by their near-equal status at the Einaudi publishing house, they had enormously different personalities, literary styles, editorial interests, and even approaches to translations. Though never overtly hostile, Pavese did not much like Vittorini, who in fact had just the kind of *sanità* and *equilibrio* that Pavese had admired in Melville and wanted for himself but could never achieve. In an oft-quoted journal entry of late 1949 Pavese presented himself as calmly confident about his ultimate worth compared to Vittorini's. Unlike Pavese, Vittorini was translated into English in his lifetime and his most important novel, *Conversazione in Sicilia*, appeared in the United States that year as *Conversations in Sicily* with a preface by Ernest Hemingway. Pavese wrote, "Does Vittorini's American fame make you envious? No. I am not in a hurry. I will beat him in the long run."[113] At least as regards the early twenty-first century, Pavese was right in his prediction. More than anything, Vittorini just annoyed Pavese. Part of that came from their clash of personalities. As Ernesto Ferrero, who followed them at Einaudi, put it, "Pavese was a perfectionist in perennial torment. Vittorini was an intuitive for whom feeling, emotion, the rush of a project were more important than any philological scruple . . . Pavese felt like an ant and thought Vittorini a grasshopper and because of this he could not bear him."[114]

The reorganization of Einaudi after the war also contributed to Pavese's annoyance with Vittorini. Giulio Einaudi, as we have seen, set up three co-equal branches, Turin, Rome, and Milan. For a while Pavese headed the Rome office before returning to Turin. Vittorini was in charge of Milan and never moved permanently from there. Pavese and Vittorini often disagreed on the advisability of publishing particular books, but, more importantly, they had different visions for the publishing house: Vittorini wanted more emphasis on current politics, technology, and the hard sciences, while Pavese thought the firm should concentrate, as it had in the past, almost exclusively on the humanities and social sciences. Giulio Einaudi liked the competition between them and happily acted as the final decision-maker when a yea or nay was needed to decide the fate of a book or an editorial project such as a new series. Pavese did translate one piece for Vittorini's *Americana*, but not what Vittorini had hoped he would (Dos Passos) or what Pavese wanted (Melville's *Billy Budd*, which Vittorini had already given to Montale). Pavese contributed Gertrude Stein's "Melanctha." This caused him no effort at all since he had already translated it as part of *Three Lives*: all Pavese had to do was get Giulio Einaudi's permission to let Vittorini's publisher, Bompiani, include it in the anthology. Despite Vittorini's repeated requests after the war, Pavese resisted contributing to the cultural weekly, *Politecnico*, published by Einaudi but created and edited by Vittorini in Milan.

Vittorini was born in Sicily just two months before Pavese's birth in Piedmont. Like Prezzolini, he had no university degree; like Pavese and Prezzolini, he taught himself English. He attended, apparently with little interest, an accounting institute, and left Sicily for good in 1924. He worked various jobs in the north, married Salvatore Quasimodo's sister in 1927, and in 1930 moved to Florence where he got a job as a copy reader of the local daily, *La Nazione*. He was an early and enthusiastic Fascist at a time when Fascism had not fully defined itself. He left the party, as did many others, when Italy supported Franco in the Spanish Civil War with men and arms. He began learning English when he settled in Florence and by 1933 was writing journal articles and reviews on American topics and doing translations. His first translation, of D. H. Lawrence's short novel, *St. Mawr*, came out in 1933. His first translation of an American author, Edgar Allen Poe, appeared in 1937. Between then and the beginning of the war for Italy he translated several English authors (Defoe, Dickens, Galsworthy, Maugham, and more of Lawrence) as well as Faulkner's *Light in August*, Steinbeck's *Tortilla Flat* and *Pastures of Heaven*, Erskine Caldwell's *God's Little Acre*, Kenneth Roberts's *Northwest Passage*, and William Saroyan's *The Daring Young Man on the Flying Trapeze and Other Stories*. Much more so than Pavese, Vittorini translated multiple books by the same author: ten different selections by Poe, for example, six books each by D. H. Lawrence and Somerset Maugham, and five by John Galsworthy. Pavese, on the other hand, translated two works each by Melville, Dos Passos, and Gertrude Stein, but only one each of eleven other authors. Thus, while they translated roughly the same number of different authors—Vittorini eighteen, Pavese fourteen—Vittorini produced a total of forty-five translations to Pavese's seventeen.[115] Vittorini's translation output outstripped that of Pavese not because Vittorini lived longer (in fact, only eight of Vittorini's translations appeared after Pavese's death) but because he employed a method Pavese would have found abhorrent. We do not know if for all, but for his first and for most of his translations from English Vittorini used the paid services of Lucia Rodocanachi to produce something between a literal crib and a literary first draft. Eugenio Montale, who used her in the same fashion and referred to her as the *"négresse inconnue,"* introduced her to Vittorini. Both of them seem to have paid her between one-third and one-half of the translation fees they received from their publishers. Neither ever acknowledged her contribution; in fact, they required her secrecy as part of the terms of using her.[116]

Regardless of his grasp of English or his translation methodology, Vittorini did conceive and produce *Americana*. That work, rather than his translations, forms the rightful basis of the parity he shares with Pavese in any discussion of the impact of America on Fascist-era Italy. The anthology is, as Lorenzo Mondo has described it, "the memorable monument" of americanismo, and as Sergio Pautasso puts it, "the *summa* and the exemplary document of the Italian literary discovery of America."[117] For reasons that go beyond its contents, upon its publication the book took on an almost mythic quality, even though—and in part because—the first version the Italian public saw in 1942 did *not* contain Vittorini's commentary. When Bompiani republished the book after World War II, with those comments, it became also a culturally historic document.

Vittorini and Valentino Bompiani, his publisher, planned in the late thirties to produce a series of anthologies of foreign literatures, beginning with the United States. By the summer of 1940 Vittorini had already chosen the authors he was going to include in this first anthology. He had accepted Bompiani's condition that he limit them to "narrators," a category that included novelists, short story writers, and dramatists, but not "essayists, poets, etc."[118] He chose thirty-three American writers beginning with Washington Irving and ending with John Fante. Vittorini translated about one-quarter of the book and enlisted nine other translators, including assigning Eugenio Montale another quarter of the work, which means that Lucia Rodocanachi probably deserves a co-credit for about half the total text translated.

Vittorini did not write a general introduction to the anthology; instead, he provided three-to-seven-page introductions to each of the nine sections into which he divided the anthology. While distributed throughout the book, they served as the work's connective tissue and highlighted Vittorini's interpretation of American literature as one that "roars," its literary tradition as a continual search for "purity" (*purezza*), and its appeal as universal ("a type of universal literature in just one language"). Unfortunately, the censors in the Ministry of Popular Culture (called by the Italians, not altogether affectionately, "Minculpop") rejected Vittorini's commentary, though not the anthologized pieces, and the first edition of the book (April 1941) was sequestered before being distributed to bookstores. In late 1941 Bompiani suggested that Emilio Cecchi write an introduction. Cecchi's preface met with ministerial approval, but, to Vittorini's disappointment, the ministry also ruled in March 1942 that for the book to go forward Vittorini needed to remove all his own introductions to the various sections. Bompiani and Vittorini reluctantly agreed and the book was finally published in December 1942 with Cecchi's preface. As introductions to the various sections Cecchi provided short comments about individual authors by different critics, both Italian and foreign, including himself. Cecchi quoted most prominently—in seven of the nine chapter introductions—from Ludwig Lewisohn's

The Story of American Literature (1932). In each section introduction he also included some of Vittorini's comments on particular authors. *Americana* sold well and Bompiani ordered a second printing in 1943, only to see a new minister of popular culture order all available copies sequestered in June of that year.[119] Thus, copies of both the 1942 and 1943 editions became scarce; those of 1941 were already rare.

Even with Cecchi's introduction, however, and without Vittorini's notes, the book had great impact. Coming as it did three years after Cecchi's *America amara*, some of the initial commentary contrasted the largeness of spirit Vittorini saw in America with the meanness and narrowness that Cecchi saw there. For example, Pavese, who had a copy of the book with Vittorini's introductory notes, wrote Vittorini a letter that has itself become an important document of americanismo:

Turin, 27 May 1942

Dear Vittorini,

I think it will please you to hear that we are all in solidarity with you against Cecchi. His introduction is knavish—politically and critically—and the entire value and sense of Americana lies in your notes. In the ten years that I've been browsing in that literature I have never yet found such a sound and illuminating synthesis. I want to tell you this because I'm sure that when your notes reach the world in a Short History of American Poetic Culture they will be seen as, yes, whimsical but also marvelous. Now it must be shouted that they are illuminating precisely because they constitute a story, a novel if you will, an invention. Let me leave aside the accuracy of your judgments of single pieces, which come out of so many equally well-informed mini-monographs, because I want to speak of the thematic play of your presentation, of the drama of corruption, ferocious purity and innocence that you have set up in that history. It is not by chance, nor something arbitrary that you begin it with abstract furies inasmuch as its ending is, though not stated, Conversazione in Sicilia [Vittorini's 1941 novel]. In this sense it is something great: you have brought to it the tension and cries of discovery of your own artistic history, and because this history has not been one of chasing clouds but rather a struggle with world literature (that world literature which is implicit in the universality of American literature—did I get you right?) the result is that the American century and a half is there reduced to the essential evidence of a myth that we all have lived and which you have recounted.

There are naturally some nits I could pick with you on small points (*The Scarlet Letter* greater than *The Brothers Karamazov*; the New Legend [the last section of the anthology] that's too similar to the earlier one [the third section, entitled "Birth of the Legend"]; some generalities about Whitman and Anderson, etc.), but they don't matter. The fact remains that in 50 pages you have written a great book. You should not get your head full but it has for you the meaning and worth that De Vulgari must have had for Dante: a literary history seen by an artist as the history of his own art.

I have not had time to read the translations because I've already sent the book to the binder. I liked the illustrations.

Till soon, dear Vittorini[120]

Fascist-linked reviewers generally ignored *Americana* or reviewed it favorably, finding little to object to in it. One strongly pro-Fascist reviewer, Ezra Pound, reviewed it, in Italian, on the front page of the weekly *Meridiano di Roma* on May 2, 1943.[121] He never mentioned the Cecchi introduction and declined to comment on the quality of the Italian translations, saying that he would leave those judgments to "those who know better than I all the shadings of the Italian language." He limited himself to comments on Vittorini's choices, added observations of his own, and included for good measure anti-Semitic remarks typical of the Pound of this period when he was acting, willingly, as a paid propagandist for the Fascist regime. While praising Vittorini for his conscientiousness several times, Pound essentially trashed him for his editorial choices. He thought Vittorini misguided for following the conventional opinion of "miscreated professors of American literature, idiots" who think that "the origin of polished American prose goes back to that runt of a man who was Washington Irving." No, according to Pound, "American thought does not arise from this sub-species of a literary man. Rather, one finds a graceful and mature style in the correspondence between John Adams and Thomas Jefferson and whoever wants to understand the legacy of that unfortunate country should first learn how they wrote." As regarded recent writers, Pound thought Vittorini erred seriously in omitting anything by Robert McAlmon—a now largely unread American expatriate writer of Pound's Paris years—because "a half-dozen of the authors represented in *Americana* are indebted to McAlmon, perhaps without all of them knowing it," and in leaving out any of the short stories of William Carlos Williams, whom Pound had first met around 1902 when both attended the University of Pennsylvania. "With some constructive and historic effort one could give true authority to a second edition of the anthology by adding twenty or so pages of Williams and McAlmon, giving more importance to Stephen Crane and recognizing the strength of the Jewish influence in the writing and especially in the distribution of literature in America."

But most of all Pound berated Vittorini for not sharing his own valuation of certain writers. "Vittorini," Pound wrote, "mentions some important writers, but his opinions, his assessments differ greatly from those of the undersigned. It is useless to argue *de gustibus*. I would say nonetheless that he likes third-rank works, some truly dreadful, rather than true writing, and naturally he would respond to me in kind, putting works that for me are off-putting or rotten in the place of [e. e. cummings's] *EIMI*, [William Carlos Williams's] *Passaic River* or [Robert McAlmon's] *Miss Knight*. And he would have the entire support of the current New York newspaper scene. This results naturally from his having taken Ludwig Lewisohn as his guide and adviser (this Jew is cited often by Vittorini and his comrades)."

Looked at from the twenty-first century, the choices Vittorini made, whether Pound agreed with them or not, seem more conventional than controversial; most of them would not have seemed out of place in an anthology for American high schools or colleges in the 1930s. No glaring omissions appear among the thirty-three different "narrators" he includes.[122] One can argue, of course, as almost all who have commented on the book have, about his individual choices, especially about the then contemporary writers.[123] The book's enduring value lies, as Pavese predicted, in Vittorini's notes, which do indeed constitute a short history of American poetic culture. As Umberto Eco said in 2001:

> From today's point of view the collection was fairly complete, perhaps overly ambitious, and certainly unbalanced—Fitzgerald undervalued, Saroyan overvalued, and authors like John Fante given places of prominence that in the future they would not occupy in literary annals. But this anthology did not try so much to relate the history of American literature as to construct an allegory, a sort of *Divine Comedy* where paradise and hell

coincide.... The America that Vittorini describes in those pages is a prehistoric land where, instead of dinosaurs and mammoths, giants rule. Jonathan Edwards wakes up Rip van Winkle and invites him for an epic duel with Edgar Allan Poe, who rides atop Moby Dick like a jockey.[124]

Vittorini's short introduction to the first section of the anthology, "The Origins" set the tone for the rest of his commentary. Eco had it right, as these excerpts from Vittorini's commentaries show:

> It seems that the Pilgrim Fathers came from Europe tired and full of disappointment; they came to finish, not start, something. Disappointed with the world, they no longer wanted the world; abstract furies wracked them, the ideas of grace and sin, the ferocious preconceptions of Calvinistic dualism . . . They found in America the necessary ferocity to live out those ferocious preconceptions [and] writing to either sustain or attack them they found a new voice . . . Cotton Mather . . . Roger Williams . . . the famous preacher, Jonathan Edwards . . . We hear how the voice is different from that used and which was still being used to express the same concepts in Europe. Here there is the continual roar of hyperbole. And it will be this way always, a roaring voice will signal the interior development of man in America.[125]

With his introduction to the second section, "The Classics," Vittorini developed in full his vision of America's literary tradition.

> The struggle will always be the same . . . it is purity [*purezza*] they seek; to convince man of the purity that is in the hot blood of his heart all his life. Thus also a fight against Puritanism, which limits life. The ways of purity are similar to those of corruption. *Similar* to those of corruption, I say, because he who has never seemed corrupt has never been pure.
> This, I think, is the significance of the American literature from Poe, Hawthorne, and Melville forward, especially today. With Melville, the third bloody father, the ways of purity and those of corruption overlay each other almost impressionistically through his stylistic élan. He is the most modern of the three . . . He does not believe that purity will emerge victorious; he doubts but believes, however, in the struggle. And he is stubborn; skepticism makes him stubborn. He wants a fight to the death for the purity that he does not know how to believe in. Thus he completes Poe and Hawthorne with an adjective. Melville is the adjective of Poe and Hawthorne's nouns. It is he who says that purity is ferocious. Purity is a tiger. No one who is pure can have mercy. Without being conscious of shouting essentially

just these things, Herman Melville shouted and shouted and created apotheoses of purity in images of self-destruction, such as that of the hanged Billy Budd. But it is precisely these images that make clear his proclamation of ferocity that explains all the earlier and later roars of the American voice.[126]

Vittorini continued in the same vein throughout the book. In introducing his third section, "Birth of the Legend," he mentioned a number of writers he considered mediocre and then added, "But the American voice continued to roar. Hawthorne was not yet dead, Melville had not yet written *Billy Budd* when Walt Whitman published his first poems."[127] In his introduction to the next-to-last section, "Contemporary History," he wrote, referring to the works of Faulkner, Hemingway, Wilder, Cain, Steinbeck, and Wolfe, "New classics that bring with them new sealed discoveries and in which we find now realized the value of 'purity' and that of 'ferocity,' and the significance of the ferocious fight for purity."[128] He ended his extended though fragmented essay with a thought he had expressed before: "American literature, now infused with the instincts of every race, is a universal literature in one language only."[129]

Pavese was right that Vittorini in creating his American tradition had written a story, perhaps even a novel—but then, any attempt to create one "tradition" out of the works of disparate authors over two centuries must perforce end as a story. What matters is the internal coherence and vitality of the story, and Vittorini's provides both. His story also provides an interesting contrast to Pavese's while at the same time demonstrating a common origin for both.

Pavese never wrote a history of American literature as a whole, as Vittorini did in his *Americana* notes, but he nonetheless created his own American tradition. Pavese's tradition emphasized the search for reality conducted in direct language, the vitalizing role of provincials, the importance of sanity and balance. Pavese never contended that Sinclair Lewis, Sherwood Anderson, or even Herman Melville roared, or that Edgar Lee Masters or O. Henry was ferocious, though in a stretch he might have agreed that the efforts he saw in Americans to arrive at the "ultimate grip of reality" resembled Vittorini's fight for "purity." Vittorini's America comes across as much more bloody and passionate than Pavese's, a continual, ferocious struggle against sin and corruption to achieve and maintain purity. Yet their different views share a common origin, one found not in America but in Italy. They described different Americas, but, importantly, neither of those Americas resembled in the least Fascist-dominated contemporary Italy. Indeed, one can argue that without Fascism and the cultural environment it created in Italy, Pavese and Vittorini might never have discovered America, certainly not the particular mythic America they did. As Patrizia Lorenzi-Davitti puts it, "Without a Fascism, without the tragic and banal absurdity of that vague rhetoric with which the regime stifled the mass of Italians, and the official culture in particular—not to mention outright political persecution—perhaps there never would have been a myth of America; but without that myth, without that fideistic quality that characterized the unconditional adhesion of the intellectual progressives to American culture, neither would we have had two writers so representative and unmistakable as Pavese and Vittorini."[130]

The very last sentence of Vittorini's notes, for instance, with its praise of the multiracial characteristics of American literature, spoke directly against the Fascist (and Nazi) insistence on the superiority of one race. That America, not Italy with its two-thousand-year Latin-based tradition, produced a universal literature contradicted Fascist orthodoxy. Writers who roared with ferocity to preserve purity and writers who spoke directly to better approach reality offered not just models different from, but models antithetical to the *prosa d'arte* authors then ascendant in Italy.

Pavese, Vittorini, and many other young Italians saw their country as awash in artificiality, corruption, hypocrisy, megalomania, cronyism; they found the cultural environment stultifying and the political situation repressive when not outright deadly. In sum, Italy was life-denying while America was life-affirming, life-giving. Thus, while these two grand figures of americanismo described different Americas, they both started from the same impulse. From the cultural poverty and political repression of Italy they emigrated intellectually to America, just as millions of their compatriots actually did because of real poverty. Both the americanisti and the emigrants went in search of a mythic America, and in their different ways they all found it.

29. In Brancaleone, Pavese went almost every day to the Bar Roma, which looked seventy years later much as it did in 1935. Photograph by Mario Dondero.

30. Pavese at work. "For many years he did not want to submit to office hours or accept a definite job; but when he did agree to sit behind a desk in an office he became a meticulous employee and a tireless worker" (Natalia Ginzburg, *The Little Virtues*, trans. Dick Davis [New York: Arcade, 1989], 15).

31. Sketch of Pavese made by Tina Pizzardo, c.1934.

32. Tina Pizzardo in a studio portrait, c. 1930.
Photograph by Giovanni Navarini.

33. Fernanda Pivano in July 1945, the month she turned down Pavese's second marriage proposal.

34. Bianca Garufi.

35. Elio Vittorini and Pavese during a 1950 publicity tour for Einaudi. They appear to be on the top deck of a ferry or excursion boat.

36. Italo Calvino.

37. Carnival-time booths and tents in Turin, Piazza Vittorio, 1940s. In *Among Women Only*, Pavese's narrator writes of a scene like this: "I remembered it was carnival time . . . stands with *torrone*, horns, masks, and colored streamers filled the arcades. It was early morning but the people were swarming toward the square at the end of the street where the booths were" (*Selected Works of Cesare Pavese*, trans. R. W. Flint [New York: New York Review of Books, 2001], 193).

38. Pavese smoked his entire adult life, characteristically a pipe but sometimes cigarettes as here, c. 1949–50.

39. Pavese in a picture taken by Giulio Einaudi, c. 1949–50.

40. Pavese, June 1950, in Rome at the time of the Strega Prize award. Photograph by Ghitta Carell.

41. Constance Dowling in a publicity photo.

42. Constance Dowling visiting her sister Doris (in costume) on location for the 1949 neo-realist film *Bitter Rice*, in which Doris starred.

43. Pavese and Constance Dowling, Cervinia, March 1950.

44. Pavese at the Strega Prize ceremony, Rome, June 24, 1950.

45. Strega Prize ceremony. Constance Dowling had by then left for America and Doris accompanied him. Three weeks after the event, he wrote in his diary, "The last sweetness I had from Doris, not from her."

46. View from the room in the Hotel Roma, Turin, in which Pavese killed himself.

47. Bust of Pavese by the sculptor Nino Ferreri in Santo Stefano Belbo. It stands in the courtyard of the town's middle school, now named Scuola Media Statale Cesare Pavese.

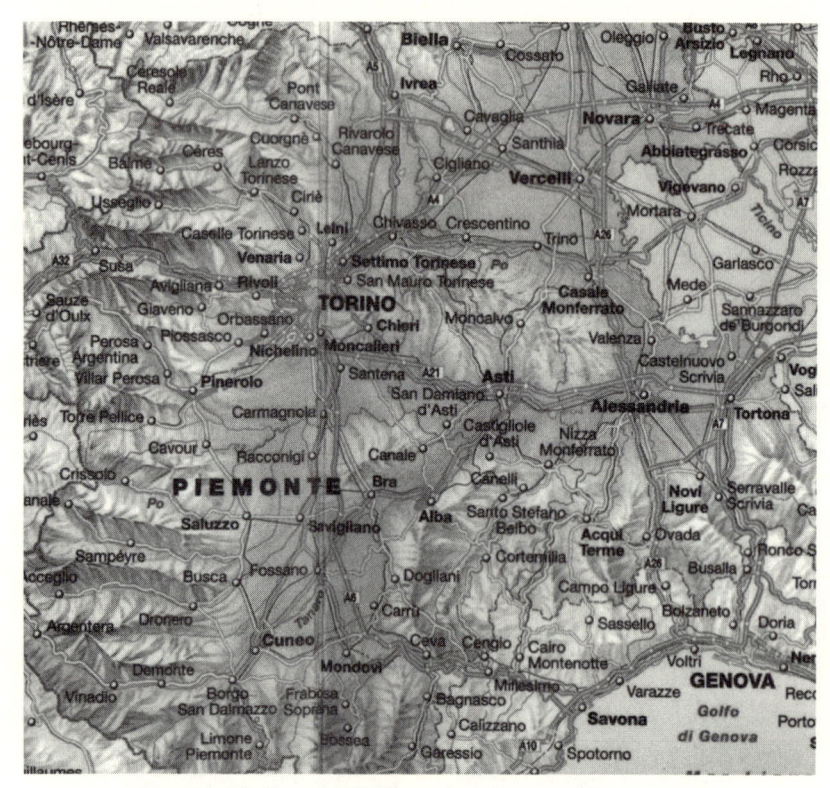

48. Regional map of Piedmont and surrounding areas.

EIGHT
"Storia passata"

In the July–August 1933 issue of *La Cultura* Pavese published his essay on Whitman; his next for the journal would be the one on Faulkner in April 1934. The Whitman essay carried forward the same enthusiastic, warm appreciation of Whitman and of American culture that characterized all of Pavese's writings about America beginning a decade earlier in the liceo. One has to search hard and generally in vain to find *anything* negative about America in all Pavese's writing up to and including the Whitman essay of 1933. Not so in 1934. Things changed that year.

In the short (one-thousand-word) piece on Faulkner, Pavese panned *Sanctuary* for, among other reasons, its violence, its constricting language, and what Pavese considered its moral indifference.[1] He ended by calling the book "an overly ambitious crime novel." In and of itself, this article does not demonstrate any wholesale change in Pavese's view of American literature. That he did not like Faulkner, especially *Sanctuary*, could well mean simply that he did not like Faulkner. (Certainly, many American reviewers did not like *Sanctuary* when it came out in 1931.)[2] In an April 1932 letter Pavese wrote that he found what he had read of *As I Lay Dying* "a tremendous bore."[3] Still, the essay represents the first negative opinion Pavese ever published about an American writer and foreshadows a larger shift in his attitude.

The real evidence of the change I refer to appears in his second essay on Sinclair Lewis, another approximately one-thousand-word piece, written around March 1934 and published in the May issue of *La Cultura*.[4] It represents a striking and dramatic change in approach and tone from all his earlier American essays. Here Pavese rejected virtually every claim Lewis might have to artistic worth, and did so in a truly sour way. Furthermore, he suggested a poverty in *all* of twentieth-century American literature that contradicted much of what he wrote—and thought—earlier. Since this essay contradicts so much that went before while characterizing most of what came after it, the work truly does signal the turning point in Pavese's relationship with American literature and culture. Furthermore, not only is what he wrote here remarkable in context, so is the whole tone of the piece: unlike the excited and generous approach of his earlier pieces, one finds here a bad-tempered and almost strident negativity.

Pavese started the essay by pointing out that the two novels Lewis had published since winning the 1930 Nobel Prize (*Ann Vickers* and *Work of Art*) made clearer "the documentary nature of his work." He admitted to his past fondness for Lewis, that he read "lovingly" many of his works, but he was now "more than ever convinced that this writer's interest lay rather in the 'matter' of his books than in that artistic workmanship which some people would like to impute to them." He did not accuse Lewis of the soullessness that he attributed to Faulkner; indeed he said that in "*Ann Vickers* especially the compassionate and youthfully enthusiastic soul of the author is completely—and indeed too much—revealed." But, although Lewis "actually goes beyond satire, he lacks that power of transfiguration, of restoring the virginal freshness of reality, which can make something definitive even of a pun." Pavese now believed that "there is something mechanical—virtuoso and amateurish at once—in all this. Lewis decides on a background, a profession, and out it comes. By those who want to be malicious these gadget novels could be called biographies à la [Emil] Ludwig." He went on to say that "it is not worth the trouble to insist on the scheme that reveals the intimately mechanical nature of the invention. It is evident that Lewis's heroes all live the same adventure of suffocation, restlessness and return to themselves: an ironic alternation of flights and imprisonments. That much established, it is useless to comment on the inventive poverty of the author." So as not to be totally malicious, however, Pavese ended the piece with faint praise: "It is more profitable, instead, to settle for, and to search out, that which in him, after all, deserves to be enjoyed: the spectacle of a mutable and man-colored reality, full of evidence of a life lived with much, even with too much, enthusiasm." This Sinclair Lewis does not sound like the one Pavese described in a 1930 letter to Chiuminatto after finishing his first essay, nor does this Pavese sound like the man who wrote that letter. He described Lewis then as a "corker": "He's a genius, your Sinclair. I had a lot to say about him and yet I've only expressed a bit of what I found and admired in him."[5]

He also dismissed Lewis's language, and not just that of these later novels. It was now no longer a prime example of the American vulgate, nor—and this is crucial—had it ever been. It was, rather, a "philological document," that is, good reporting, not good art. Indeed, it had become necessary to renounce "the attractive notion that Lewis marks a step forward in the creation of an autochthonous linguistic medium [and admit] that slang and the vernacular remain in him local color, not yet stripped of their corporeality . . . and that his linguistic fireworks are limited to dialogue, and that the style of the narrative proper doesn't escape from the slightly flat generality of journalistic jargon." No, Pavese added, "To write the true story of the native American language [*il volgare nordamericano*] you would have to linger over such names as Walt Whitman, Mark Twain, O. Henry, Sherwood Anderson, and John Dos Passos."

While these assertions reflect the critical consensus on Lewis that has developed since they were made, they are quite astonishing when one considers that three and a half years earlier, in the very same journal, Pavese had credited Lewis almost single-handedly with the *creation* of the American vulgate, that mixture of high and low, national and regional English that Pavese saw as the new American tongue.[6] But Pavese did much more in this essay than deny Lewis his former status as a linguistic innovator: he renounced his own oft-stated claims for the vitality and abundance of modern American literature itself. In countering an assertion made by a contemporary Italian commentator that, of the literary generation that came to maturity between 1910 and 1915, only Lewis represented the human vision that America sought, Pavese wrote, "It is, at the very least, cruel to make Lewis assume by himself the responsibility for what little the industrious

American twentieth century has created in the way of art."[7] The last phrase of that sentence is truly remarkable, given that for the previous four years Pavese had been insisting on the parity, if not the superiority, of modern American literature in comparison with that of Europe. It sounds even nastier in Italian: "quel poco che di buono il laborioso '900 nordamericano avrebbe prodotto in fatto di poesia."

What caused Pavese to change his attitude toward Lewis and America so drastically, suddenly, and permanently? No one knows for sure, but I believe the evidence points most convincingly and consistently to Tina Pizzardo's first rejection of him as a lover. I come to this conclusion because it fits best with what little evidence we have and because no one has put forward a better explanation; in fact, no one has put forward any explanation at all. The critical literature simply notes that Pavese had an important role in introducing nineteenth- and twentieth-century American writers to Italy and then at some point lost interest in and later rejected contemporary American literature. No one has sought to explain why that change came so suddenly and so early in his career. Here is one attempt.

Let us look more closely at the chronology relating to Pavese and America during the period involved. Pavese wrote what turned out to be his last letter to Antonio Chiuminatto in January 1933. He never responded to Chiuminatto's reply of March eighth.[8] He composed his essay on Walt Whitman, the last essay before those on Faulkner and Lewis, in the spring of 1933, and it appeared that year in the July–September edition of *La Cultura*. In February 1933 he willingly agreed to translate for Mondadori John Dos Passos's *The 42nd Parallel* and he mailed in the typescript on July twelfth.[9] Just before turning that in he begged off writing an essay on Dos Passos for a Mondadori magazine, saying that he had nothing to add to his Dos Passos essay that appeared earlier that year in *La Cultura*.[10]

The written record then goes silent as regards anything American from the summer of 1933 until the end of March 1934. In fact, it pretty much goes silent regarding anything at all; there are no letters extant between August 30, 1933, and March 30, 1934, and Pavese did not begin his diary until 1935.[11]

In late 1933 or January 1934 he did compose the review of Giuseppe Prezzolini's book, *Come gli Americani scoprirono l'Italia, 1750–1850*, which appeared in the March 1934 issue of *La Cultura*, and then in successive months came the Faulkner and Lewis articles. That is all the documentation there is of Pavese's ideas and feelings on American subjects, from the publication of the Whitman essay of 1933 to the second Lewis piece in 1934. We do know that he composed in 1933 and 1934 a good many of the poems that went into *Lavorare stanca*, though for only a few did he indicate the exact dates. Nothing in this material hints at the reversal of opinion expressed in the Lewis essay, though the Faulkner review can be seen in retrospect as a portent. The review of the Prezzolini book, in fact, reads more like what I would call, in this context, the old pro-American Pavese. Thus, we have no evidence of any slowly maturing new aesthetic preference that would make American literature less appealing to him than before. Rather, we have the enthusiastic Whitman essay published in July 1933, the moderate review of Prezzolini's book in March 1934, the negative review of Faulkner in April, and then the savage attack on Lewis and the disparagement of twentieth-century American literature in May. If we assume Pavese finished his *La Cultura* pieces roughly two months before their publication dates, it makes sense to look closely at the months of February and March 1934 for some clue to Pavese's abrupt change of heart regarding America.

In chapter 3 I described the on-again-off-again nature of the relationship between Pavese and Tina Pizzardo in the years before Pavese's arrest, jailing, and confino. In light of Pavese's change of heart concerning America in 1934, I would like to revisit certain events in that relationship in more detail. As recounted, Pavese went silent on Pizzardo in the summer of 1933 after their five outings on the Po; they then met again in January 1934 and began seeing each other regularly in February. Tina was also seeing comrade Henek, and while she had a growing, seemingly unreciprocated, affection for him, she felt that Pavese, at least at this point, compared quite favorably to the Pole. With Henek, she listened to monologues; with Pavese real dialogue occurred. Her feelings for Pavese, however, were far from simple. Her own words describe best what I believe led up to one of the key events in Pavese's life, and I quote here at some length from her memoirs.

> The 25th of February [1934] was a Sunday but I had not gone skiing nor had I gone to break off with Henek. That afternoon my sister and Nina [the three shared an apartment] were out, and Pavese and I found ourselves alone.

We are in my bedroom/studio where I receive students and friends, I reclining on the sofa-bed, he at my feet on a footstool. Our conversation is running smooth and fast like other times.

Something that I said pleases him greatly and, smiling, he looks at me, enthralled, and suddenly he kneels down and hides his face in my hands. He stays still and I have to take him by a tuft of his hair to pull him up. Still smiling he says, "I'm afraid I'm falling in love with you."

And I in the same tone: "I thought you already had. Last August it almost happened to me."

I told him that during the excursion to the mountains then I had thought of him continually as . . . as a god.

"As a god" (that came to me just like that, as a joke) gives rise to a tender and mischievous dialogue between two people too sharp to give in to the trite language of the usual lovers' skirmishes. A happy, spirited dialogue punctuated—jokingly—by a few quick light kisses.

When, around seven, he left and we had agreed to meet again at nine, I felt myself reborn: a strong, decisive man, sure of himself, who will never ask for my comforting, my guidance, my energy as did all the others, boys and girls alike, in love with me. After the canine adoration of my usual flirtations I had found, I thought, my equal. An exchange of kisses, but also of sincere, pitiless confidences, good for analyzing and for destroying my strange and melancholy link with Henek.

That evening we chatter in the dark streets (where he tries to kiss me, and this seems to me infantile not to mention inappropriate), then in a café where we stay till late. Because of the things he is saying all evening I begin to feel a little less sure about all of this and I ask him, "How old are you?"

He is twenty-six; he knew I was thirty-one and says, "In true love, age differences do not count."

True love? I had been thinking of a delicious fling. But if I had said no to him then, I would have looked like a fool; "true love" meant about as much as that "with passion" that he had written when giving me a book a few days earlier.

I was not, however, so sure of myself as to tell him, "You've already understood, if it's a mess for us to stay apart, then I'll jump in headfirst, but the ending is going to be painful." Or to tell him (without mentioning Henek's name) that "I'm grabbing on to you to save me and I assure you it will be a rescue that we both will enjoy."

And help he did give me just the same, I reflected, because of his lively interest in me, because I am attracted to him, because he is my equal and I can stay with him as long as I want and never be bored and without thinking of the other. I'll figure a way out of all of this just as I have always done.[12]

February twenty-fifth, the twenty-fifth in general, became a talismanic date for Pavese, just as did April 9, 1936, and August 13, 1937. In 1938, for example, he thought that year's February twenty-fifth might be the last he would record, since he had reached a "pause" in his "passionate turmoil."[13] Pizzardo goes on to recount how on February 26, 1934, she went to see Henek to break off her relationship with him, but did not succeed, and that in the following days she was seeing both of them again in cafes and in her home. Pavese made her feel better, but Henek, the committed Communist and therefore committed anti-Fascist, made her feel serious: "With Pavese, who considered me experienced in life and thought that important—'your knowledge of life,' he called it—I felt young, extroverted, brilliant and extremely cheerful. And also irresponsibly thoughtless as though a little drunk. With the other, who called me 'foolish baby,' I felt truly foolish and a little sad, even when joking, and always alert, conscious of myself and of the struggle in which we were both engaged."[14]

And then came March 5, 1934, the date of the encounter I think crucial:

> On the fifth of March, exactly eight days after February 25 (the date of the beginning), at a table of the café that is still there on the corner of Piazza Statuto and Via Cibrario, I say to Pavese that our love, as he calls it, is craziness, and that it's up to me, five years the older, to think for both of us: we are made to be friends and I hope it's not too late for that. Either friends or nothing. Either friends, or we stop seeing each other.
>
> And now observe the strong man who one week earlier I thought would help me, the bantering man who ought to ask, "Who's the other man?" Observe Cesare Pavese who begins to cry like a baby. I remember my disillusionment, my annoyance and embarrassment at those tears that fell like rain and rolled down the lapels of his overcoat.
>
> "Better friends than nothing," he said submissively and tearfully. He'd put his hope in my pity. He still had hopes. If he didn't have hope he would kill himself.
>
> He would kill himself, he was capable of doing it, of being the comedian who acts his part to the very end. Here was yet another who was putting his life in my hands. Well, I thought, I asked for it and now I have to watch over and help him until this passes.
>
> Friendship pact, then? We see each other once a week. Not even a kiss? No, not even one.[15]

The story of Tina and "Cesarino," as she would come to call him, did not end on March 5, 1934, but it took a decisive turn. It's worth stopping a moment here to see why Pavese and Pizzardo might be linked to Pavese and Sinclair Lewis and indirectly to Pavese and America writ large.

I believe that in mid-1933 Pavese began losing interest in America and American writers without at first realizing it. His enthusiasm for America having begun with Whitman, perhaps composing the essay on Whitman that spring provided a symbolic and psychologically necessary closure that in some sense, albeit unbeknownst to Pavese, cleared the way for that enthusiasm to wane over the coming months. This was, too, the year he read Sir James Frazer's *The Golden Bough*, the book that catalyzed the interest in myth that intellectually characterized his later years.[16] Furthermore, he began this year to concentrate on his own poetry, so critical essays about any subject meant less to him than before. Other signs of growing disinterest include the fact that Pavese stopped corresponding with Chiuminatto in 1933, stopped asking for books from America, and wrote no long American pieces for *La Cultura*, even though he was the managing editor and the journal still accepted long pieces. I would call this kind of loss of interest and change in emphasis a natural falling away, something that happens gradually, until at some point the realization hits that one is no longer much interested in a topic that earlier one found fascinating.

Then in early 1934 come the intense six weeks with Tina leading up to the scene on March 5, 1934, that she so deftly and dramatically describes, and which we have thus approached from her point of view. But let us reconsider that encounter from the point of view of Pavese, beginning with "those tears that came down like rain and rolled down the lapels of his overcoat."

This incident, so far as I can tell, is the *only* documented time in his adult life that Pavese cried in front of a woman. He cried for Constance Dowling in 1950, but only in the privacy of his hotel room. Pavese prided himself on his Piedmontese, especially Langhe-derived, stoicism, which required an almost misogynistic bravura:

> *But there's one shame we won't ever suffer:*
> *we'll never be women, never anyone's slaves. . . .*
> *We are all of us born to wander these hills,*
> *without women, clasping our hands at our backs.*[17]

For Pavese to cry in public, and in front of and because of a woman, means something overpowering was happening. Crying, unlike anger, is generally an unfocused response to an overwhelming emotional stimulus. Conflicting feelings fight with each other, none can clearly predominate, and all come tumbling out in tears. Tina's sudden rejection after six weeks of seemingly increasing closeness must have been a sharp blow. He'd had such high hopes: the woman really seemed to love him, willingly spent time with him, and genuinely seemed to promise both emotional and sexual fulfillment. And then in an instant everything changed: "Friends or nothing"! After spending time with him alone and in company, after kissing him and saying she thought of him often, Tina had suddenly changed the rules of the game. There went the sex (he was twenty-six, remember), and he did not need friends, for he had plenty (he always did, his whole life). It was too much for Pavese: with neither anger nor indignation seemingly available to him, he welled up and cried "like a baby." When he stopped, he meekly accepted her terms out of fear, resignation, and whatever remained of his hopes. From that moment on, Pizzardo dominated their relationship, set its ground rules, and eventually decided when it would end. Not for the last time, Pavese thus found himself in an asymmetrical relationship with a woman—and the story of this one, like the others to come, unfolded for him in the passive voice.

And how does this incident relate to Pavese's feelings about American literature? I would argue that if Pavese composed the second Lewis essay in March 1934, as seems likely, his whole mentality at the time would have been affected by Tina's rejection of him as a lover. If, as I also propose, he had already been gradually losing interest in American literature, I think it entirely possible that the dark mood the March fifth incident put him in led to the sour tone of the second Lewis essay. One might even derive an emotional analogy to his history with Tina up to that moment in terms of the essay's content. Recall Pavese's conclusions in it: Lewis's later works disappoint, he had never been the genuinely innovative writer Pavese believed him to be, he had not invented the American vulgate after all. It is not unreasonable to imagine that his immediate conclusions regarding Tina were much the same: she had never been what he'd imagined her to be, never been what she'd made herself out to be.

I do not think one can draw a straight line from Pizzardo's rejection of Pavese to his rejection of Lewis, but I do think it probable that the former set the stage for the latter. I say "probable" because, while we know the date of Pizzardo's rejection, we do not have definite dates for the composition of the second Lewis essay, just its publication date (May 1934).[18] There is no proof, then, that Pavese wrote part or all of the second Lewis essay after March 5, 1934. The internal evidence seems coherent, however. The Pavese-Pizzardo relationship began with him in the ascendancy. The jaunty Pavese of the Po had allowed Pizzardo in his punt in 1933, and had decided when they should stop their river outings. When they started seeing each other again he assumed the role of teacher, she that of student. But Pizzardo soon reversed their roles. Pavese had tried to create for himself a bravura persona, based in part, and consciously so, on Whitman and Melville. Recalling that, for Pavese, Whitman and Melville served as much more than models of craft—they were ultimately, as we have seen, models of the poet as such, and models of manliness, inextricably bound up with the idealized America Pavese had constructed—we can only imagine how much he may have invested in it. I mean invested psychologically and perhaps even intellectually, in this period when he felt his powers as a poet growing. Pizzardo essentially crushed that persona, and I think her rejection accelerated his already changing feelings about America.

In making this argument I am not setting up a simple correspondence between America as a literary interest and Pizzardo as a love interest, so that as long as Pizzardo loved him, he loved America, and when she made it clear she did not, he stopped loving America. The association of these two realms in Pavese's interior life was surely more subtle than that, and the intersection between them that I have posited was in any case temporary. Despite the March fifth friends-only pact, Pizzardo and Pavese's relationship developed into something significantly deeper as 1934 progressed, even as Pavese was becoming more and more confirmed in his new attitudes toward America. They eventually did have sex and, from her account, they passed a fine summer together, so much so that, in an obvious reference to the book that later won Pavese the Strega prize, she entitled the chapter of her memoirs dealing with 1934 "Pavese e la bella estate" (Pavese and the Beautiful Summer).[19] No, Tina Pizzardo was not the cause of Pavese's disenchantment with America, but her rejection of

Pavese—temporary though it was—was a triggering event, just as in an even more serious and final way Constance Dowling's rejection of Pavese in 1950 triggered his suicide.

Whether one event triggered the change or not, in 1934 Pavese's whole attitude toward America demonstrably and permanently changed. From then on he felt no enthusiasm for contemporary American literature or culture; a decade later he would publicly reject it. By 1935 he knew his "American" period had ended, that americanismo was part of his past. As early as the fifth entry in the diary he began in 1935 he noted, on October 11 of that year, "Now, American culture just doesn't interest me at all any more."[20]

All of which is *not* to say that he had no further involvement with American literature, only that he had changed the terms of engagement. Between 1937 and 1943 he translated six American novels plus "Benito Cereno," added prefaces to three of these, and revised his introduction to *Moby-Dick*.[21] He did all this mainly to make a living. Despite the publication of *Lavorare stanca* in 1936, his professional reputation rested on his knowledge of American writers and his skill as a translator. That's what publishers valued in him. That he wrote no stand-alone essays on American writers during this period, except one on Edgar Lee Masters in connection with the publication of Fernanda Pivano's translation of *Spoon River Anthology*, demonstrates the falling away of his critical interest in American literature.

When, in 1938, he composed the seven-hundred-word preface to his own translation of Gertrude Stein's *The Autobiography of Alice B. Toklas*, he had not published a word on American writers in four years. In it he returned to one of his "American" themes—the effort of American writers to locate and reveal reality through language—and mentioned Whitman's seminal importance in this regard. He said that those who study Stein can "retrace her precursors in the figures of Walt Whitman or Henry James—of Walt Whitman especially, to whom she is the perhaps unconfessed debtor for that wholly American idea of a mystic reality incarnated and imprisoned in the word, that disturbing realism of the subconscious life which is still, down to the present moment, the most vital contribution of America to culture."[22] Pavese wrote nothing in this preface unfavorable about Stein or American literature. He liked Stein's light and ironic tone. Yet his own rather matter-of-fact tone lacked noticeably the warmth of his pre-1934 essays and prefaces, as did his next American piece, also a preface to a translation of a Stein book, *Three Lives*.[23] For Pavese this work was "preeminently the discovery of a language, of an imaginative rhythm which tends to become itself the argument of the tale, the spiritual boundary of a magic and motionless daily reality." *Three Lives*, originally published in 1909, was "a perfect early example of what will be the constant goal of American fiction in the new century: an imaginary world which is reality itself, caught in the process of becoming expressive." Still, he had his doubts about Stein's work as a whole: he believed that in her later works one "sometimes feels the human material tremble and become pure form which contemplates and transcends itself. Later there will come the pure inhuman style where life, here miraculously suspended, will evaporate, leaving a residue of dead cadences and psychological flashes."[24] As he said in a 1938 letter to Stein herself, he was "skeptical as to the possibility of succeeding in translating and publishing your subtle works."[25]

Both Stein prefaces were competent, workmanlike short pieces and show that in the years before World War II Pavese had keyed down his approach to American literature but had not yet reversed himself about what he saw as its basic values. Of course, he might have been more critical had he not been writing prefaces for books he himself had translated and which his own firm was publishing. Einaudi also published Pavese's next American work, a translation with preface of Melville's "Benito Cereno."[26] Pavese had not changed his opinion about Melville's greatness but in this preface we find none of the brio of the earlier Melville essay or the introduction to *Moby-Dick*. In 1940 Pavese no longer gives us a Melville as true Greek, healthy and balanced, revitalizing and enlarging the reader; instead he provides a slightly academic introduction, fitting the novella into the overall scheme of Melville's life and works. His preface to *Moby-Dick* begins, "To translate *Moby-Dick* is to put yourself in touch with the times. The book, hitherto unknown in Italy, has through half of the past century inspired the greatest books of the sea. And for several decades English-speaking readers have been returning to Melville as to a spiritual father, discovering in him, enormous and vital, the many themes an exoticising literature had later reduced, over half a century, to vulgarity." The preface to "Benito Cereno" is decidedly less enthusiastic: "This novella, which appeared for the first time in 1855, and was included the year after in *The Piazza Tales*, is one of the last creative flashes attempted by the imagination of Herman Melville." Pavese had not needed any critical support to declare *Moby-Dick* an "original sacred poem, in which neither heaven nor earth has failed to lend a helping hand." Now he wrote, "'Benito Cereno' belongs, by a now common consensus, to Melville's best vein."[27] The divergence in approach and tone from the earlier, almost ecstatic Melville pieces shows the emotional distance Pavese had traveled between 1932 and 1940. Description is one thing, intensity another.

Because he had lost interest in America by now, it seems ironic that his first real taste of literary fame came from the popular and critical reception of the novel most influenced by his American studies, *Paesi tuoi*. When it came out in 1941, *Paesi tuoi* caused more of a stir than either Pavese or Giulio Einaudi had expected. As Laura Nay and Giuseppe Zaccaria say in their comprehensive yet compact historical survey of the critical reception of Pavese's novels, *Paesi tuoi* was "the literary event of 1941."[28] The book sold well, so well that Einaudi published a second edition of five thousand that same year. The title comes from an Italian proverb, *Moglie e buoi dei paesi tuoi*, which translates literally as "Wives and oxen from your own villages"—meaning, broadly, that in important matters, especially those involving women, men are safest with their own kind.[29] Much of the critical commentary on the book centered on what were perceived as American influences on Pavese's characters and setting. Most critics also praised his language, without—one important critic excepted—attributing any specifically American derivation to it.

The plot of *Paesi tuoi* involves two men just released from the Turin jail: Berto, a Turinese mechanic, and Talino, a farm worker from a small Langhe village. Talino convinces Berto to accompany him to the village where, he assures him, Berto can find good work repairing farm machinery. Once there, Berto becomes involved with Talino's sister, Gisella, who "smelled like apples." In the climactic scene, Talino, who we learn had previously had an incestuous relationship with Gisella, stabs her with a pitchfork in a sudden jealous rage. After the loss of an enormous amount of blood, she dies.

The critics who saw the strong influence of American writers in the book most often mentioned Caldwell, Steinbeck, and Faulkner as Pavese's models. For example, Salvatore Rosati wrote that "Even if it is not an imitation . . . it is necessary to recognize that in large part it is influenced by Anglo-Saxon literature . . . Its similarities to Caldwell's *God's Little Acre* are not limited to the nature of some of the characters but continue with analogous settings. The principal orientation is that of neorealism, which brings us to Faulkner, not only because the events of *Paesi tuoi* are recounted in the first person, as seen, lived and remembered by Berto, but also and most importantly because the physical and psychic facts—the action and the feelings—are developed on the same plane."[30] The americanista Emilio Cecchi also saw Steinbeck in the background: "Assiduous student and translator of American literature, Pavese does not know how to forget his experiences in that cultural field. Those experiences, in some aspects of the story, make themselves visible even more than necessary. To give one example, the presence of Steinbeck's *Of Mice and Men* [which Pavese had translated in 1938] is visible not only in the construction of the characters but also in the setting and minor episodes."[31] Later, Leslie Fiedler wrote that "The novel smacks of Erskine Caldwell in its gratuitous brutality, its pretended realism, which is really an exoticism of the sordid."[32]

Pavese did not think of himself as a neorealist, and if critics could have read the manuscript of *Il carcere*, written before *Paesi tuoi*, they might have thought otherwise as well. Yet those critics were not mistaken regarding the American influences in the book, nor did Pavese ever deny them. Seven years after composing the novel he even identified an American writer the critics had missed in 1941: "The American who for his 'tempo' and his narrative rhythm most influenced me at the time of *Paesi tuoi* was James Cain, whom none of the critics even mentioned."[33] Some of Pavese's (conscious or unconscious) borrowings seem easy to identify. Incest in the deep country is certainly a Faulknerian theme. The opening plot device of two men going into the country to work a harvest probably comes from *Of Mice and Men*, George and Lennie for Steinbeck, Berto and Talino for Pavese. The city boy, Berto, is a mechanic who has been jailed several times, as is Frank the drifter in Cain's *The Postman Always Rings Twice*, and the continued narrative drive, as Tibor Wlassics suggests, may well indeed derive from Cain.[34] One should not concentrate on plot, narration, and characterization, though, to find what Pavese's immersion in American literature really brought to this novel. One should look rather to the language that he used.

Many critics noted the inventive importance of Pavese's language; almost all praised it. Even the critic for the Fascist-sponsored bi-weekly magazine *Primato*, Eugenio Galvano, liked it, and he characterized it correctly when he wrote that "the work was conceived in Piedmontese with a result that is nonetheless *italianissimo*, to be considered in its linguistic aspect a notable and admirable contribution for its effects and the imaginative possibilities it provides. There is virtually no separation between the material of this story and its style."[35] Galvano implicitly assumed what Italian readers, but not readers of an English translation, would know: the characters, the narrator included, would all be speaking Piedmontese dialect, yet Pavese wrote the book, dialogue included, in Italian. Pavese explained what he wanted to achieve linguistically in a letter he wrote shortly after finishing the novel in 1939. He had sent a copy of the manuscript to his friend Tullio Pinelli, and Pinelli had raised questions about the language.

> As to the language, I admit that at times some of the language is offensive—the flesh is weak—but note well that it is something entirely different from naturalistic impressionism. I did not write the way Berto—the only one who speaks to the reader—would really talk but translated his thoughts, the shocks he felt, his taunts, etc. as he would have said them *if he spoke Italian* . . . I did not want people to know how Berto would sound if forced to speak Italian (which would be dialect impressionism) but how he would speak if his words were to become—through a Pentecost—Italian. In sum, how he thinks.[36]

This approach bears a striking resemblance to what Pavese had seen years ago in Sinclair Lewis and Sherwood Anderson. Indeed, it mirrors almost exactly what he said about Anderson's style; in his essay on Anderson, Pavese called it "a new structure of English, made up entirely of American idioms, of a style that is no longer *dialect* but *language*, rethought, recreated, *art*."[37] Similarly, Pavese conceived *Paesi tuoi* in Piedmontese dialect, but "rethought it" into a dialect-infused Italian, just as he believed Sinclair Lewis fused slang and standard English to create the American vulgate.

Critics of the time took note that with the language in *Paesi tuoi* Pavese was attempting something unusual. Salvatore Rosati commented favorably that Pavese wrote in an Italian whose "syntactical violations and dialectal modulations permit a rapidity that contributes to the immediacy of expression."³⁸ Luigi Vigliani called it "a truly vernacular language largely intertwined with dialect-type voices, with no few concessions to slang, that contrasts with the voices of the more elite literary tradition."³⁹ Aided by his knowledge of American literature and of Pavese's career, Emilio Cecchi picked up immediately the American influence on Pavese's language. He also compared Pavese's linguistic approach to that of Giovanni Verga, the founder of Italian Realism (*verismo*), who often wrote in Italian what his Sicilian characters would be saying in their dialect.

> The example of American literature has pushed, or at least encouraged, Pavese to consider the problem of a language that, in the first place, would not be formal and conceptual, nor fall into dialect, but rather would be capable of adhering to lived reality and rendering its deepest shadings . . .
> In the attempt to create for himself a more immediate and biting language, Pavese has not used, or at least only scarcely, regionalisms, and that is to his credit. He has instead fallen back on the syntax of the language spoken in his province; most of the time this results in wonderful effects, but at times also undeniable harshness and obscurity. But is this not something very similar to the old process used by Verga at the time of his work of renewal? Pavese has received the impulse from America and has made America his trampoline . . . He has in fact, figuratively, gone round the world to return to his own home. What is important is that the journey was not useless. The distance was more than anything else illusory, but it served to increase in him the sense of risk and commitment to the adventure.⁴⁰

Not every critic considered Pavese's linguistic experiment successful. Alberto Moravia, never a great admirer of Pavese, said that in *Paesi tuoi* Pavese had attempted "the impossible task of having common people, with common language, say things about psychology and decadent experiences that mattered to him, a cultured man."⁴¹ Someone for whom Italian is a second language treads lightly here, but I think Moravia got it wrong. Pavese achieved what he intended; the task was possible. An analogy in American literature, one which Pavese knew well, would be the voice Mark Twain established for Huck Finn in *The Adventures of Huckleberry Finn*. Twain had Huck say things in "common language" about weighty matters that concerned Samuel Clemens, a quite cultured man, just as Pavese had Berto say things that concerned Pavese. Pavese and Twain differed, however, in the treatment of the next most important character in each of their books. Twain uses what Pavese would call "dialect impression" for Jim's speech. Two examples, from chapter 12: "I doan' want to go fool'n' 'long er no wrack. We's doin' blame' well, en we better let blame' well alone, as de good book says. Like as not dey's a watchman on dat wrack." "Oh, my lordy, lordy! *Raf?* Dey ain' no raf' no mo'; she don' broke loose en gone!—en here we is!" Twain provided no Pentecost for Jim; Pavese did for Talino and for everyone in Talino's family in the deep country.

Pavese dealt in *Paesi tuoi* with both personal and essentially Italian themes, creating an artful work of Italian literature. Yet, to echo Leslie Fiedler's comments, he could not have written it without American literature, especially without the concentrated attention he paid to the Americans he wrote about and translated. Though its composition came five years after his last essay on an American author, *Paesi tuoi* shows how much Pavese had absorbed from his years of American immersion.

An essay/review that Pavese wrote in 1943 shows his ability still to respond to an American author while expressing at the same time his emotional distance from America. Einaudi published that year Fernanda Pivano's translation of Edgar Lee Masters's *Spoon River Anthology* and Pavese reviewed it for *Il Saggiatore*.[42] Since he had always liked Masters, since he had encouraged Pivano to do the translation, since his own firm was publishing it and he editing it, and since, finally, he was in love with the translator, one would expect a favorable review, and he gave one. For Pavese the translation was "all suffused with an innocent joy of discovery, it fascinates and persuades. If this is, as it seems, Pivano's first literary labor [which he knew perfectly well it was], I may say that seldom has a young writer been so well able to contain her enthusiasms and to chasten her pleasure with so much awareness. It looks like the labor of an expert authority, whom long and loving acquaintance with the text has taught to select and transfigure, in calmness of memory, the places of the soul." While Pivano had in fact produced a fine translation, the first of many in her distinguished career, it took love to bring out that kind of Pavesian praise. But neither Masters's original nor Pivano's translation could recreate for Pavese the feelings he'd once had about American literature: "To speak of this book is thus to return to the source of some of the most vivid poetic experiences of our adolescence, to the heroic period when for the first time we cast a glance at a marvelous world which seemed to us something more than a culture: a promise of life, a call of destiny. Past history [*storia passata*]. Still, we are grateful to the young translator for having, with her frank and measured discourse, put us once again face to face with this lost image of ourselves."[43]

In their personal relationship Pivano had also put Pavese face to face with a lost image of himself, but his remarks here hold more interest for the way they encapsulate so well Pavese's mature feelings about America. One finds no bitterness but rather an elegiac sadness about a lost ideal, nostalgia for a time when he felt heroic and saw in America "a promise of life." In 1943, sitting out World War II, he no longer felt heroic. Furthermore, he had come to the intellectual and personal conclusion that destiny called in mythic, repetitive ways and that the promise of life was increasingly restricted.

One month after the essay-review of *Spoon River* appeared, Italy signed a formal armistice with the Allies and her twenty-month civil war began. Pavese wrote nothing about America during these months, which he spent in Serralunga di Crea and Casale, and when he returned to Turin in the late spring of 1945 America was definitely *storia passata*. He had other concerns then, above all his struggles to come to terms with himself, which he was trying to do through his self-willed, public, political commitment, through the exploration of myth, and in his own fiction. The years immediately after the war saw him join the Communist Party, write his *L'Unità* articles, and declare in a radio broadcast that "The times are over in which we discovered America."[44] How surprising, then, that the first piece he wrote after the war about an American author showed as much deeply felt admiration, kinship, and excitement as did any of his early American essays. Pavese titled this 1946 essay "American Maturity"; it was a discourse on F. O. Matthiessen's *American Renaissance*.[45]

For Pavese, reading Matthiessen turned into a second discovery comparable only to his first encounter with Melville. Calvino has called this 3,500-word review/essay a "key document" for understanding Pavese. In his preface to Pavese's collected essays, Calvino wrote:

> There is an evident congruence between the interests of the Piedmont writer and the American critic: several of their favorite authors were the same, the desire for that "organic union

between labor and culture," attention to the regeneration of language, and also—I would say—a certain tremulous respect for the mystery of art and reality. The similarities between the two figures do not stop at those evident in this volume but carry over into the personal sphere: the epigraph, "Ripeness is all," passed from Shakespeare to Melville to Matthiessen, to arrive at Pavese via this exceptional chain, and Pavese's suicide followed that of the American (April 1950) by four months.[46]

Leslie Fiedler even thought that Matthiessen was one of three Americans "who presided over [Pavese's] death."[47] Certainly Pavese felt strongly about Matthiessen, felt a sense of cultural kinship that in 1946 was exhilarating and liberating. It seemed to him that they shared the same literary and social concerns, that both were interested in artistic expression as it related to the larger context of human communication—that is, expression growing out of the personal involvement of an individual with his own chosen material and his community of fellow men. Both men valued the same artists, especially Whitman and Melville, and, more profoundly, they both instinctively considered the same values to be important. Matthiessen's phrase (which, as Pavese rightly stated, expressed Matthiessen's own drives as well as those of his "five writers" treated in *American Renaissance*) concerning the desire "that there should be no split between art and the other functions of the community, that there should be an organic union between labor and culture," struck Pavese in 1946 as a virtual summing up of all he then wanted to achieve in his own life and see realized in postwar Italy.[48]

Matthiessen had also written during the war in a different work that "the only healthy state for the critic and scholar is to keep breaking down all the barriers of segregation and false privilege that shut him away from the fullest participation in the life of the community."[49] Pavese almost certainly never read that particular sentence, but had he, he would have recognized in it a great many of his own feelings. Matthiessen crystallized Pavese's belief that only in community participation lay salvation. In 1946 Pavese was acutely aware of his nonparticipation in Italy's civil war and was doing his best now to participate in Italian civil society. As he said in a 1947 diary entry, "By yourself you are not enough and you know it."[50]

Matthiessen's insights came to Pavese as Melville's symbols did to Matthiessen, "with the freshness of a new resource."[51] Pavese thought

Matthiessen's approach right, exquisitely right. He found his critical technique remarkably valuable, even surpassing that of Pavese's early model, Benedetto Croce. "The importance of this work goes beyond the particular American cultural problems it treats, despite its success at making them new and passionate, to become a model of approach and method even for us, who until very recently could only be forced with difficulty to recognize critical mastery in anyone not a follower of our idealistic humanism."[52] Pavese's sense of kinship arose from the Italian's recognition that Matthiessen went to the quick of art and that his definition of the central concerns of literature was nearly the same as Pavese's. Pavese had been attracted first to Whitman and then to the other American authors he valued because of what he considered their new language and heightened sense of reality. In 1946 Pavese saw Matthiessen drawn to his five American writers for the same reasons, and saw him developing implications about the use of language that confirmed Pavese's belief in his own insights.[53] He saw Matthiessen documenting more fully how language and symbols, when used by masters like Melville, could act as knife-cuts into reality. In rephrasing what he saw as one of Matthiessen's central points, Pavese wrote:

> The numberless partial analyses, the play of comparison and references, the use of the most ingenious sources (the originals of Hawthorne's diary that had been cut and edited by prudish publishers, or Melville's underlinings and febrile marginal annotations of books he read)—all this tends to confirm and reassert that which was the obsession of the creative life of the five: to arrive at a language which would identify itself so closely with things as to break down every barrier between the ordinary reader and the most dizzying mythic and symbolic reality.[54]

Pavese began the conclusion of the essay by quoting, in English, the Shakespearian lines:

> *Men must endure*
> *their going hence even as their coming hither:*
> *ripeness is all.*

He added, in finishing the essay, "It is the sentence that Melville underlined in his copy of *King Lear* and it seems to us a worthy epigraph and conclusion to this long disquisition on the first truly 'mature' pleiad of the young America."[55]

This essay on Matthiessen and his first on Melville stand out from the rest of Pavese's American works for their combination of intellectual drive and emotional energy. They are certainly the most important of his American expository pieces for understanding what attracted him to certain American writers and in revealing his own approach to language, symbol, and reality. Both the nineteenth-century writer and the twentieth-century critic attracted Pavese because he saw in them the kind of fusion of work and life, of "labor and culture," in Matthiessen's phrase, that he thought essential for civil existence. More's the pity, then, that neither Matthiessen nor Pavese managed to realize in their own tormented maturities the balanced harmony they so dearly sought.

The Whitman thesis, the 1930–33 essays, especially that on Melville, the 1943 review of Pivano's *Spoon River* translation, and, finally, the 1946 Matthiessen essay demonstrate that Pavese needed personal emotional involvement to bring out his enthusiasm for American subjects. They also show that such enthusiasm for individual American writers appeared before, during, and after World War II, although never after 1934 for America as a cultural whole. The general progression of his American works moved from almost unbounded fervor for everything American (1930–33) to disinterest (1934–43) to outright hostility (1945–50). The 1946 Matthiessen essay acts as a counterpoint to Pavese's late hostility, demonstrating as it does his ability still to react warmly to individual American artists when they touched something deep in him.

His early attraction to America predated his first essays and went back to the mid-1920s with his enthusiasm for Whitman and American movies. One way to approach the change from enthusiasm to hostility is simply to ask, "Between the mid-1920s and the late 1940s did America change or did Cesare Pavese?" The answer of course is that both did. I contend, though, that Pavese changed more, and, in any case, objective shifts within American culture did not interest Pavese, for his America was always a country of the mind. Pavese realized and stated publicly after World War II that he had moved far from his earlier positions on America. In August 1947, writing on this great alteration in attitude since the early 1930s, he, too, wondered how much he had changed and how much America had changed:

> Now the times are changed and everything can be said, and in a certain sense everything has been said. So it happens

that the years go by and more books come to us from America than ever before, but today we open and read them without excitement. There was a time when even a minor book from over there, even a mediocre film, stirred up and posed living questions. Is it we who grow old? Or is this little liberty we have enough to distract us? The creative and narrative triumphs of the American twentieth century remain—Edgar Lee Masters, Anderson, Hemingway and Faulkner have taken their places among the classics—but for us not even the long fast of the war years is enough to make us genuinely love what comes to us nowadays from over there.[56]

Pavese did not deny that he and his generation had grown old (though he was only thirty-eight when he wrote the comments just quoted), but he did contend that the major changes had taken place in the United States, not in the Italians of his generation. Pavese believed that in the early twentieth century the good American writers represented the best part of an America struggling toward new ideals, social as well as literary. He also felt that the works he first loved did more than form a vulgate tradition: they had also played a part in the battle against oppressive tendencies in American life. Now, however, he thought that contemporary American writers, even the United States itself, had withdrawn from the struggle. As he put it in phrases that Matthiessen could just as easily have written, "Without a fascism to oppose, without a progressive historical idea to personify, even America—for all its skyscrapers and automobiles and soldiers—will no longer be in the vanguard of anybody's culture. Without an ideal and without a progressive struggle, it even runs the risk of surrendering itself to its own form of fascism, though it be in the name of its best traditions."[57]

In the 1920s and 1930s, skyscrapers, especially the New York City skyline as depicted in countless movies, had represented for Pavese and his generation life-enhancing urban vitality. Automobiles, so much more common in America than in Italy, had promised an especially modern kind of personal freedom. Now, in 1947, Pavese used them as stock clichés along with soldiers to represent American materialism and power. His own critical theory would define such mindless imagery as tired rather than vital symbols, and therefore as imperfect perceptions of reality. This one example, furthermore, does not represent an isolated case, for in reading the postwar articles on

America, the Matthiessen essay excepted, one is struck continually by the stereotyped nature of their ideas and the bland quality of the prose, characteristics foreign to Pavese's younger works on America and foreign to most of his other prose writing after World War II. One comes to sense something less spontaneous in his public reaction against America than in either his first enthusiasm for America or his mature interest in other subjects. He had now made up his mind about America, which, he decided, had nothing more to offer him; therefore he saw no need to treat the subject in any vital way. A synthetic quality seems to pervade the short but crucial anti-American articles of 1947. For example, in his review of the Italian translation of Sherwood Anderson's *A Storyteller's Story* he wrote that in "words, sentences, literary modes" are reflected "a whole economic, ideological, and social situation. Anyone who has class consciousness realizes this. But he must also realize that it is inconsistent to strive to renew the structure and ideologies of a given society, if he then continues to be happy with a style of painting, a way of making music, or of writing, clearly determined by an environment in my opinion already condemned."[58] That is *not* the way Pavese wrote about subjects that really engaged him.

Still, regardless of how he expressed himself, Pavese definitely did feel that America had changed in basic ways and that as a result its writers had lost the qualities that first attracted him to that country's literature. "It seems to us," he wrote, again in 1947, "that today, after the war and Occupation, after having walked among us and spoken with us, the young Americans have undergone an interior process of Europeanization and have lost a large part of that exotic and tragic openness that was their destiny."[59] While he did think America had changed, Pavese did not—in the 1947 articles or in any other of his writings—deny the importance that America once had for him and his generation, nor did he change his mind as to why America once seemed so appealing. In a 1947 passage, often quoted because so central to all discussion about Pavese and America, he said, speaking about the 1930s:

> Anyone who goes beyond merely leafing through the dozen or so of the most striking books that arrived from overseas in those years—anyone who shakes the tree to make the hidden fruit fall, anyone who digs down to discover the tree's

roots—soon becomes aware that the rich expressiveness of this people was born not so much out of its splendid quest for new social forms, which was after all banal, but out of a dogged determination, already a century old, to convert the experience of daily life completely into verbal form. This is the source of their continual striving to adjust their language to the new reality of the world—to create in substance a new language, material and symbolic, whose only justification is in itself rather than in some passive traditionalism. And this style, even though in some books it became hackneyed, still mostly surprised us, and was easy to trace back to its inventors and pioneers in the nineteenth century: Walt Whitman the poet and Mark Twain the narrator.

At that point American culture became for us something very serious and precious, a sort of great laboratory where others were working, under different conditions of liberty and with different means, on the same task of creating a taste, a style, a modern world, as the best of our writers were, perhaps with less immediacy but with the same stubborn will. And so this culture seemed to us an ideal place for work and experiment, strenuous and embattled experiment, rather than a mere Babel of clamorous efficiency, of crude neon-lit optimism that stunned and blinded the naïve and which if it could have been seasoned with a little Roman hypocrisy would have pleased even our own Fascist bureaucrats. After several years of study we understood that America was not *another* country, *another* historical beginning but merely the gigantic theater where, with more openness than was possible anywhere else, a universal drama was being enacted. And if at the time it seemed worthwhile to repudiate ourselves and our past to throw ourselves body and soul into that free world, it was because of the absurd and tragicomic condition of civil death that history had for the moment trapped us in.[60]

In the end, though, Pavese's postwar indictment of America represented much less a change of opinion than the recognition that his attraction to America formed part of a closed chapter of his earlier life. Pavese never accused America of betraying his youthful hopes, just of growing old, as he, too, had done. Pavese's own words reinforce this interpretation. He referred to his American period twice as *storia passata*, once in the 1947 article already cited and then again in 1950 in the last American piece he ever wrote, a short article on Edgar Lee Masters occasioned by the poet's death.[61] That phrase—and the variant, "But now it is finished"[62]—imply that Pavese considered his

American phase as a datable period in his life, and other remarks confirm that this period coincided with his equally datable youth, which ended in 1936: "Now America, the great American culture, has been discovered and recognized and one can predict that for some decades to come nothing will arrive from that people similar to the names and revelations that excited us in our prewar youth."[63] The chapter had finished and Pavese went on to other things.

One must remember that America did not represent a major concern for Pavese after the war and that his "rejection" of American culture has become more important for those who study Pavese than it was for him. Collected in book form, all of Pavese's postwar writings about America amount to only twenty-five pages (ten of which comprise the Matthiessen essay). Put against his own fiction in these years, the dialogues, his editorial work at Einaudi, his diary—or even against his thesis and the 1930–33 essays—this indicates how unimportant he had come to consider the whole issue of America.

America did appear, however, in his last novel, *The Moon and the Bonfires*, and his fictional treatment of the theme is consistent with his postwar essays and journalism. The novel contains thirty-two chapters, almost all four and a half pages long; their regularity and Pavese's tactic of ending each with one or two crisp declaratory sentences, almost like the ending beat of a measure of music, contribute to the rhythmic momentum of the book. The novel brings together almost all the themes associated with Pavese: the mythic, erotic sanctity of the Langhe hills, the pull of the city, America, the paradox of childhood, the symbolic and ritual repetition of violence—particularly against women—the ambiguous value of the Resistance, and the unchanging world of the peasants. The first-person narrator, Anguilla ("Eel"; we are never told Anguilla's/Eel's real given name and no one in the book addresses him by name), a bastard brought up by foster parents in an unnamed village that has the exact topography of Santo Stefano, leaves the village for Genoa to do his obligatory military service. He stays there after his discharge and emigrates to America, because of some potential political problems with the Fascists. Though not spelled out, Eel probably shipped out in 1926 when the Fascists stepped up their attacks against all opponents. He spends twenty years in America, where he makes and loses a small fortune. He is interned by the U.S. government, just as some ten thousand

Italian-born Americans really were during World War II. Pavese provides no details of life in an internment camp but has Eel return to Genoa after the war, presumably in early 1946. His business skills allow Eel to remake his fortune, apparently in wholesaling of some kind. Before the novel begins he had already returned to the village for a short stay; it opens with him there about a year later for a two-week vacation in August. The thin Eel has grown "big and fat" and no one recognizes him. He spends a lot of time with his boyhood friend Nuto—a clarinet-playing carpenter based on Pinolo Scaglione—who gradually reveals to him what happened in the village during the war. Pavese moves the novel back and forth in time.

Pavese shifts throughout the book between the time when Eel was a boy and worked in a grand house, La Mora, for a family that included three attractive and, to his country eye, sophisticated daughters, and the present, when he befriends a boy with one crippled leg, Cinto, who reminds him of himself when young. Indeed, Cinto lives in the same poor farmhouse where Eel began, on the hillside named Gaminella. Cinto's father, Valino, now works the property as a sharecropper along with his own mother. Valino, a widower, has taken into his house and bed his dead wife's sister.

As in *La casa in collina,* Pavese waits until toward the end of the novel to introduce the defining violent incidents. One takes place in the present, one in the past; each results in a symbolic bonfire. In a frustrated rage Valino kills his mother and his consort, tries to kill Cinto, sets fire to his cottage and stable, and then hangs himself. Only some rabbits and Cinto manage to escape. In the last chapter of the book Eel finally learns what happened to Santa, the youngest, most desirable, and most provocative of the three daughters of La Mora. During the civil war she took up with Fascists in the nearby town of Canelli, slept with several of them, and began spying on the Partisans for them. In a scene recounted by Nuto, the Partisan group leader, Baracca, has her brought to a farmhouse on Gaminella hill, calls her to account, reads out her crimes, lists the damage she has caused, including killed Partisans, and sentences her to death. Santa is led outside, wearing the white dress she had on when she left Canelli. She is to be executed by a firing squad but instead is machine-gunned when she tries to escape. The novel ends immediately after Nuto tells Eel this story, with the two of them sitting on the low wall of the courtyard where Santa was killed. Eel looks around, asks a question, which Nuto answers in the book's final paragraph:

> I looked at the broken, black walls of the farmhouse, I looked all around and asked him if Santa was buried here.
> "Isn't there a chance they might find her one day? They found those other two . . ."
> Nuto was sitting on a low wall and watching me with his stubborn eyes. He shook his head. "No, not Santa," he said. "They won't find her. You can't cover a woman like that with dirt and just leave her. Too many men still drooled at the thought of her. Baracca took care. He had us cut all the dry branches we could find in the vineyard and cover her over. Then we poured gasoline on her and lit it. By noon it was all ash. The mark was still there last year, like the bed of a bonfire."[64]

Pavese makes this second burning of a just-murdered woman the finale of the story in a totally believable way, coherent with the rest of the plot. Yet he wants to make sure we understand the symbolic nature of Santa's death. On the surface she appears to be an innocent: her name means holy and she was burned in a white dress she just happened to be wearing when she left Canelli. She was not innocent, however, and her sin was her sexuality as much as her politics: she had such great power over men that even dead she could tempt them to sex. Her death and burning bring back some balance between women and men—for now. In Pavese's world, another Santa will appear to tempt men, and, in one form or another, meet the same fate.

The symbolic significance of Valino's beating his consort and his mother senseless and then burning them, possibly while still alive, remains uncertain. As with Santa, their bodies become unrecognizable ashes mixed with the earth, and perhaps Pavese is saying all three women went to fertilize the earth, that the earth requires this kind of blood. Even Nuto, generally the voice of peasant wisdom in the book, has no explanation. All he can do is look at Eel "with swollen eyes, seeming half asleep." Valino had gone berserk before beating the women because the owner of Gaminella, a stereotypically avaricious landowner—except a woman—had been hounding him for more crops and more work. Pavese implies that all sharecropping peasants in Valino's situation feel profoundly both despair and rage, "the madness of that life without relief," and that some from time to time rise up to challenge fate.[65] Valino, however, did not have the nature of an insurrectionary; his destiny was to be truly powerless and so instead of killing the owner he killed his weak consort, sick mother, and himself.

America appears in this novel both as theme and setting. The three scenes set in California, in chapters 3, 11, and 21, are the only ones Pavese ever set in America. In the first, a truck driver from the Langhe stops at a diner in the hills above Oakland, where Eel works alongside a woman he is sleeping with but for whom he has lost respect and no longer cares about, a setting surely derived from Cain's *Postman*. When the driver and Eel strike up a conversation, Eel offers him a glass of bootleg whiskey, which the driver accepts, lamenting that in America they don't have good wine. "They don't have anything," Eel snaps back, "It's like the moon."[66] As the title of the book indicates, the moon carries high symbolic value. Here, Pavese reverses its usual meaning: shining over the Piedmont countryside it means fertility, renewal, and ritual; in America the moon becomes a symbol of barrenness. The talk with the truck driver makes Eel homesick. After work he ignores his woman, sits on the grass of an embankment, and with the croaking of tree frogs in the background wonders why he ever came to this scary, lonely, country.

> Now I knew why every so often a girl was found strangled in a car on the highway, or in a room at the end of an alley . . . Well, it was a big country, there was some of it for everyone. There were women, there was land, there was money. But nobody had enough, nobody stopped no matter how much he had, and the fields, even the vineyards, looked like public gardens, fake flower beds like those at railway stations, or else wilderness, burned-over land, mountains of slag . . . That was the frightening part. Even among themselves they didn't know each other . . . So they beat up drunks, threw them in jail, left them for dead. And it wasn't only liquor that made them ugly, it was also bad-tempered women. A day would come when just to touch something, to make himself known, a man would strangle a woman, shoot her in her sleep, crack her head open with a monkey wrench.[67]

Eel's contempt for his unnamed women, and his inclusion of "soulless and narcissistic"[68] women as one of the reasons Americans were greedy, artificial, alienated, and murderous represent the first two of the three times Pavese uses women in the novel to express his feelings about America. The third occurs in chapter 21, in which Eel says of a different live-in girlfriend, Rosanne, "the legs she stretched out on my bed were all the power she had."

She had come west to get, in some unspecified way, "noticed." "She was ready to be photographed even in the nude, even with her big legs on a fireman's ladder, anything to make herself known." Pavese presents her as more pathetic than gallant in her struggle. At the end of the chapter she says she is going back to her home in the Midwest. "But she didn't go home, she went to the coast instead. She never appeared in the color magazines. Months later she wrote me a card from Santa Monica asking for money. I sent her some and she didn't answer. I've never heard from her since."[69]

The most effective of the three American scenes, chapter 11, takes place in the Yuma desert close to the Mexican border. As night approaches, Eel's pickup truck breaks down on a little-traveled road that parallels the railroad tracks. The American night scares him: "I knew that poisonous lizards and centipedes ran around in the hollows of that plain; this was the kingdom of the snake. Wild dogs began howling. They weren't the danger, but they made me think that here I was at the bottom of America, in the middle of a desert, three hours by car from the nearest gas station." He drinks some of the whiskey he has with him. "Many old stories I'd heard ran through my mind, stories of people who started out on these roads when there were still no roads and later were found sprawled in a gully, bones and clothes, nothing else." Pavese continues with this melodramatic setup to the main part of the scene: "The plain was dim, blotched with vague shadows . . . The wind kept up its cold whistling over the sand."

> Then the train came. At first it was like a horse, a horse rattling a cart over stones, and you could already make out the headlight. At first I'd hoped it was a car or that wagonload of Mexicans. Then it filled the whole plain with its noise and shot out sparks. What must the snakes and scorpions think, I wondered. It plunged down on me, throwing light from its narrow windows on my truck, on the cactus, on a scared little animal that hopped to safety; and it snaked by, banging, sucking up air, cuffing me with its backwash. I'd waited for it so long, but when the darkness came back and the only sound was the whistle of wind over sand, I said to myself that not even in a desert do these people leave you in peace. What if I had to light out tomorrow and hide to escape internment? Already I could

feel the cop's hand on my back, like the shock of the train. This was America.

The scene seems like one from a movie. The train coming out of and disappearing into the night is indeed a stock cinematic image. Here, it has no role in relation to the intricate play of the past and present in Santo Stefano that occupies most of the book. Its inconsistencies make one wonder what Pavese wanted to do with this scene. Trains run on tracks and, since his truck stopped by a railroad track, it makes no sense that Eel should consider a passing train a deliberate attempt to ruin his peace. Pavese ends this chapter with another cinematic image, and once again he gives the moon a symbolic value opposite to that it has in Santo Stefano: "Later that night . . . a slip of moon had broken out of the low clouds and looked like a knife wound bloodying the plain. I stood watching a long time. It gave me a good scare."[70]

These episodes, spaced as they are toward the beginning, middle, and end of the book, serve almost as intermissions for the drama developing in the main plot. Had Pavese omitted them, the events of the time-shifted central story would play out the same way and with the same effect. At most, the American chapters flesh out Eel's misogynistic characteristics. Most likely, Pavese, having decided for plot purposes to absent Eel for twenty years, decided to send him to America as a way of imagining what it would have been like if he had gone to America himself. I would have made my way, Pavese implies, but I would have been lonely, scared, and alienated among an alienated people. I would have found only pitiful women who meant nothing to me, and to top it off, the American government would have put me in an internment camp, just as the Italian government sent me to confino. I would have had to return to Italy to remake my fortune and to find out what happened in my real home.

That imaginary journey would have turned out much differently if Pavese had tried to describe it at almost any point between 1926 and 1933. That younger Pavese could not have imagined such disappointments in America; he would have imagined teaching in New York City, seeing movies and plays, listening to jazz, meeting interesting women, for as Pavese wrote to Tullio Pinelli back in liceo days, "life, the real modern life that I dream of and am afraid of, is a great city, full of noise, of factories, of enormous buildings, of crowds and beautiful women."[71] Life for him had changed a great deal by the time Pavese wrote *The Moon and the Bonfires* in 1949—so, consistent with what he was writing in his newspaper pieces, he described a barren, deadening, dangerous America, an America one does not go to, but rather leaves.

Donald Heiney reads the chapters set in America much the same way. He dates the present time of the novel as 1948 and observes, "The narrator therefore emigrated about the time that Pavese himself 'discovered America,' that is around 1928–1930 . . . The return of the emigrant twenty years later coincides approximately with the writing of the novel itself . . . The disillusionment of the returned emigrant is therefore not only that of a physical disappointment in America; in a deeper sense it is an expression of Pavese's own relation to the myth of America and his pessimism when the events of the postwar period made him see things in a different light."[72] I disagree with Heiney only in a subsidiary point: he implies that the events of the postwar period caused Pavese's pessimistic change of mind about America. I would argue that Pavese's pessimism itself, generated by personal events of 1935–45, caused that change of mind, and also determined his view of postwar Italy.

Pavese dampened his misogyny, at least as expressed in his fiction, in the books that led up to *The Moon and the Bonfires*. He described Cate in *The House on the Hill*, Gabriella in *The Devil in the Hills*, and especially Clelia in *Among Women Only* as attractive, strong women, fully capable of dealing as equals with the men in the books. The Fascists arrest Cate and we do not know what happened to her, but neither Gabriella nor Clelia are harmed (though a separate female character does commit suicide in *Among Women Only*). Thus Pavese's use of attractive but incompetent, indeed contemptible, women as central symbols of America in his last book deserves some attention. I believe the link goes back once again to Tina Pizzardo. He met her at the height of his enthusiasm for America, 1932–33. The intense period of their relationship started with Pavese giving her English lessons and their reading American novels together. Once she gained control of the relationship and, after toying with him in 1937 and 1938, broke with him for good, I believe Pavese thereafter was simply incapable of thinking about America without relating it to Pizzardo. When he undertook his imaginary journey there in 1949 he populated America with women he could control, whom he could leave, as Eel did all the American women he met. One cannot conceive of

Pavese's meeting these kinds of women if he had made his imaginary journey in 1932. Thus, in fiction as well as in his journalism and critical prose, America served Pavese in the postwar years as a symbol of lost youth and disappointment. He projected onto it his negativity, just as he had earlier given it his enthusiasm. Like Pavese's train, America roared into his life and then departed, leaving behind a slip of moon like a knife.

As the biographical section of this book tries to make clear, the Cesare Pavese of 1949 differed decisively from the Pavese of 1930. In the years from 1926 to 1933, the high point of his enthusiasm for America, he was young, chronologically and spiritually. America had come to him, in Lorenzo Mondo's words, as a "liberating shock."[73] All his studies had gone well, he had good friends, Tina Pizzardo was not a bitter memory, he was being published regularly, and he could realistically expect a permanent teaching job. The time in which he discovered America, also, had not yet seen Hitler come to power nor had it seen Mussolini embark on any of the dangerous and disillusioning conquests or alliances that brought Italy to disaster. Pavese found America "an ideal place for work and experiment" at the same time he found time for, in addition to his essays, his own poetry, the *Ciau Masino* stories, his joint effort at pornography. In short, when Pavese thought America the hope of the world, the whole world for him was filled with hope. He could see in front of him that kind of balanced fusion of work and art that Monti had emphasized and that Pavese so admired in Melville and later found stressed by Matthiessen. He would teach or perhaps support himself in some other way, and he would write—oh, how he would write! And he would be happy and loved. In later years, America perforce had to be one link in the whole chain of associations that was his youth, that period he himself described as "the time when I was translating *Moby-Dick* and everything was still to come."[74]

How different, how ironically different, things seemed after World War II. Ironic because in fact he did write, even became a famous writer, and he supported himself as a writer and respected editor. In terms of his own art he never abandoned his belief in the value of straightforward language or the necessity of immediateness in literature. In his maturity he infused his economical prose line with a quickening symbolism that both portrayed and transformed reality. His late novels, especially *The House on the Hill* and *The Moon and the Bonfires*, testify to his success in blending realism and symbolism in a timelessly classic and yet distinctly modern way. Furthermore, he knew he had achieved in his art the goals he had set out to reach. The irony lies in Pavese's recognition that it all did not seem to matter, because he himself had never managed to connect in a life-giving way with reality. The more Pavese's sense of personal alienation grew after the war, the more remote did his youth seem. The times in which he discovered America had ended. After confino, after Pizzardo threw him over, after Pintor's and especially Ginzburg's deaths in the war, after his withdrawal during the Resistance, after Fernanda Pivano turned him down, after all the disappointments that measured out his life, the times were over in which he could believe in America—any America.

Pavese never really rejected America; he simply grew out of it. His love for American culture had been, in the best sense of the words, young, even adolescent, full of emotion, energy, openness, and strong attachment. Perhaps if he had discovered America under different conditions his interest might have lasted longer, but surely it might also have produced duller and less lively appreciations.

In the end it seems fitting that America should have appeared as such a symbol of hope in Pavese's hopeful youth. It seems equally sad that in his mature years he lost hope in America, because for him this loss signified the loss of belief in hope itself, a loss that for Cesare Pavese led directly to suicide.

Notes

"Introducing Cesare Pavese"

1. Editors' introduction to *"Sotto il gelo dell'acqua c'è l'erba": Omaggio a Cesare Pavese*, ed. Mariarosa Masoero et al. (Alessandria: Edizioni dell'Orso, 2001), v. See Leslie A. Fiedler, "Introducing Cesare Pavese," in *No! In Thunder: Essays on Myth and Literature* (Boston: Beacon Press, 1960), 135–49; originally published in *Kenyon Review* 16, no. 4 (Autumn 1954): 536–53.

2. Fiedler, "Introducing Cesare Pavese," 135n.

3. Donald Heiney, *America in Modern Italian Literature* (New Brunswick, N.J.: Rutgers University Press, 1964).

4. The two works which bracket this period are Áine O'Healy, *Cesare Pavese* (Boston: Twayne, 1988), and *Cesare Pavese and Anthony Chiuminatto: Their Correspondence*, ed. Mark Pietralunga (Toronto: University of Toronto Press, 2007).

5. The Centro di Studi di Letteratura Italiana in Piemonte "Guido Gozzano–Cesare Pavese" is based at the Università degli Studi di Torino (see http://www.gozzanopavese.it). The index is available at http://www.ad900.it/homesito.asp?IDSezione=33&IDSito=1 (accessed September 9, 2007).

6. Italo Calvino, "Pavese: Essere e fare," in *Una pietra sopra: Discorsi di lettertura e società* (Turin: Einaudi, 1980), 63.

7. *The Selected Works of Cesare Pavese*, trans. R. W. Flint (New York: New York Review of Books, 2001), 88–91.

8. Geno Pampaloni, *Trent'anni con Cesare Pavese: Diario contro diario* (Milan: Rusconi, 1981), 114. Pampaloni uses as an example the same long passage in full that I have chosen to excerpt and gloss.

9. See Roberto Gigliucci, *Cesare Pavese* (Milan: Bruno Mondadori, 2001), 157–58.

10. Pavese, *Lett. am.*, 294.

11. *Selected Works of Cesare Pavese*, 5.

12. Pavese himself categorized his last four novels as "symbolic reality" in his diary entry of November 26, 1949; *Il mestiere*, 378. Now, literature courses in Italian universities are devoted to this aspect of Pavese. For example, Pietro Luxardo Franchi teaches a three-credit course at the University of Padua on "Il realismo mitico e simbolico di Cesare Pavese."

13. *Il mestiere*, 166 (entry for December 14, 1939).

14. William Arrowsmith, introduction to *Hard Labor: Poems by Cesare Pavese* (Baltimore: Johns Hopkins University Press, 1979), xxix; Pampaloni, *Trent'anni con Cesare Pavese*, 137, 46, and 182; Fiedler, "Introducing Cesare Pavese," 147; John Simon, "Return to the Scenes of Childhood," *The New York Times Book Review*, March 24, 1968, 5.

15. William Arrowsmith, "Boom Fiction," *New York Review of Books*, July 30, 1964. Available online at http://www.nybooks.com/articles/13266.

16. Pampaloni, *Trent'anni con Cesare Pavese*, 115.

17. Pavese, *Romanzi*, 803.

18. Anco Marzio Mutterle, *I fioretti del diavolo: Nuovi studi su Cesare Pavese* (Alessandria: Edizioni dell'Orso, 2003), 81.

19. *Selected Works of Cesare Pavese*, 169.

20. Ibid., 174.

21. "Tenting Tonight on the Old Camp Ground," words and music by Walter C. Kittredge (1863). The full lyrics of the main chorus are:

> Many are the hearts that are weary tonight
> Wishing for the war to cease;
> Many are the hearts looking for the right
> To see the dawn of peace.
> Tenting tonight, tenting tonight,
> Tenting on the old camp ground.

In the final chorus, the last two lines change to:

> Dying tonight, dying tonight,
> Dying on the old camp ground.

22. Susan Sontag, "The Artist as Exemplary Sufferer," first published 1962; included in her first collection of essays, *Against Interpretation* (New York: Farrar, Straus & Giroux, 1966).

23. Calvino, *Una pietra sopra*, 59–60.

24. Italo Calvino, Preface to *Lett. am.*, xi.

25. *Sigma* (Genoa), nos. 3 and 4, December 1964. The authors of the various pieces in the issue included, among others, Lorenzo Mondo, Marziano Guglielminetti, Claudio Gorlier, Furio Jesi, Sergio Pautasso, Giorgio Barberi Squarotti, and Johannes Hösle.

26. Fiedler, "Introducing Cesare Pavese," 139.

27. Patrizia Lorenzi-Davitti, *Pavese e la cultura americana: Fra mito e razionalità* (Messina-Florence: G. D'Anna, 1975), 179.

28. The bibliography of writings about Umberto Eco rivals that of writings by him. A good English-language introduction is Peter Bondanella, *Umberto Eco and the Open Text: Semiotics, Fiction, Popular Culture* (Cambridge: Cambridge University Press, 1997). For Celati, see the full-length study by Rebecca J. West, *Gianni Celati: The Craft of Everyday Storytelling* (Toronto: University of Toronto Press, 2000).

29. *Il mestiere*, 392 (entry for March 6, 1950).

1. The End Game

1. Pavese, *Il mestiere*, 387 (entry for January 14, 1950).

2. Bosley Crowther, review of *Bitter Rice*, *New York Times*, September 19, 1950, available online at http://movies2.nytimes.com/mem/movies/review.html?title1=Bitter%20Rice&title2=&reviewer=BOSLEY%20CROWTHER&pdate=19500919&v_id=5775 (accessed September 19, 2007).

3. For further information on Constance Dowling's Italian films and on how she and Pavese met, see Lorenzo Ventavoli, "Ricordo di Constance," in *Cesare Pavese: Atti del Convegno internazionale di studi, Torino–Santo Stefano Belbo, 24–27 Ottobre 2001*, 131–36 (Florence: Leo S. Olschki, 2005).

4. *Il mestiere*, 392 (entry for March 9, 1950). "Friday the thirteenth" refers not to the general superstition but to August 13, 1937, when, as we will see later, Tina Pizzardo confronted Pavese about his sexual inadequacy.

5. "To C. from C." *Le poesie*, 133.

6. *Il mestiere*, 392 (entry for March 16, 1950).

7. Ibid. (entry for March 6, 1950).

8. Pavese to Constance Dowling, Turin, March 17, 1950, *Lettere II*, 493.

9. Pavese to Constance Dowling, Turin, March 19, 1950, *Lettere II*, 494.

10. The original of the postcard can be found in the files at the Centro Gozzano-Pavese; Mariarosa Masoero provides the background for it in "Mon coeur reste encore à toi: Cesare Pavese e Constance Dowling," *Sincronie*, no. 5 (January–June 2001): 77–81.

11. *Il mestiere*, 392 (entry for March 20, 1950).

12. Ibid., 393 (entry for March 22, 1950).

13. Augusto Monti, *I miei conti con la scuola: Cronaca scolastica italiana del secolo XX* (Turin: Einaudi, 1965), 261.

14. Cesare Pavese, *Disaffections: Complete Poems, 1930–1950*, trans. Geoffrey Brock (Port Townsend, Wash.: Copper Canyon, 2002), 347; original in *Le poesie*, 136.

15. *Il mestiere*, 394 (entry for March 25, 1950).

16. All entries can be found in *Il mestiere*, 394–400.

17. Mario Motta, quoted in Bona Alterocca, *Cesare Pavese: Vita e opere di un grande scrittore sempre attuale* (Quart, Aosta: Musumeci Editore, 1985), 145.

18. Pavese to Constance Dowling, Turin, April 1950, *Lettere II*, 505.

19. While Dowling landed several small television roles after returning to the United States, she in fact did not make another film until 1954: the low-budget science-fiction *Gog*, which turned out to be her last movie.

20. *Le poesie*, 143.
21. Pavese to Constance Dowling, Turin, April 17, 1950, *Lettere II*, 506–7.
22. Constance Dowling to Pavese, New York City, May 15, 1950, *Lettere II*, 527.
23. Pavese to Constance Dowling, Turin, May 19, 1950, *Lettere II*, 525.
24. Constance did send Pavese one more picture postcard, of and from Tucumcari, New Mexico. She was obviously driving cross-country to California; Route 66 ran through the middle of the town, the first of any size west of the Texas border. It is postmarked June 27, 1950, and reads, "Ciao caro! The trip is endless—will write shortly, Come stai? Connie." See *Lettere II*, 543n.
25. Elia Kazan, *A Life* (New York: Da Capo Press, 1997), 166–67.
26. Ibid., 194.
27. Ibid., 195–96.
28. Ibid., 248.
29. Ibid., 229.
30. Bosley Crowther, review of *Up in Arms*, *New York Times*, March 3, 1944. Available online at http://movies2.nytimes.com/mem/movies/review.html?ti tle1=Up%20in%20Arms&title2=&reviewer=BOSLEY%20CROWTHER&pda te=19440303&v_id=51959 (accessed September 23, 2007).
31. Kazan, *A Life*, 229.
32. Tim Parks, "The Outsider's Art," *The New York Review of Books*, November 6, 2003.
33. *Il mestiere*, 395 (entry for April 26, 1950).
34. See, for example, the publisher's blurb on the first inside page of the most recent English translation of *La luna e i falò*, that of R. W. Flint: *The Moon and the Bonfires* (New York: New York Review of Books, 2002).
35. Pavese to Doris Dowling, Turin, July 6, 1950, *Lettere II*, 543.
36. *Il mestiere*, 397–98 (entry for July 14, 1950).
37. Ibid., 398 (entry for July 20, 1950).
38. Ibid., 398–99 (entry for August 16, 1950).
39. "Sea Foam," *Dialogues with Leucò*, trans. William Arrowsmith and D. S. Carne-Ross (Ann Arbor: University of Michigan Press, 1965), 45.
40. *Il mestiere*, 399–400 (entry for August 17, 1950).
41. The phrase in Italian is "Scrivo: o Tu, abbi pietà. E poi?" He wrote almost the exact same thing on November 25, 1937, in the midst of the breakup with Tina Pizzardo: "Scrivo: T., abbi pietà. E poi?" The capitalization of "Tu" in the 1950 entry has led most commentators to assume Pavese is addressing God. He might, however, have been addressing Constance, or Tina, or the goddess from the sea, the "tormented restless one."
42. *Il mestiere*, 400 (entry for August 18, 1950).
43. Pavese to Romilda Bollati, Turin, August 17, 1950, *Lettere II*, 563.
44. Pavese to his sister Maria, Turin, August 17, 1950, *Lettere II*, 562.
45. Alterocca, *Cesare Pavese*, 157.
46. Davide Lajolo, *An Absurd Vice: A Biography of Cesare Pavese*, ed. and trans. Mario Pietralunga and Mark Pietralunga (New York: New Directions, 1983), 240.
47. Pavese to Giuseppe Vaudagna, Turin, August 25, 1950, *Lettere II*, 569.
48. Pavese to Franca Violani Cancogni, Turin, August 25, 1950, *Lettere II*, 567.

49. Pavese to Mario Motta, Turin, August 26, 1950, *Lettere II*, 571.

50. Rosabianca Cernuschi, daughter of Teodoro; interview with the author, Hotel Roma, Turin, April 23, 2004. The quote attributed to her father, Teodoro, is in the handwriting of her husband on notepaper of the Hotel Roma in the author's possession.

51. Natalia Ginzburg, *Lessico famigliare* (Turin: Einaudi, 1999), 199.

2. Family and Friends

1. A copy of his birth certificate with the three middle names he never used is lodged in his folder at the archives of the University of Turin. A copy of the original entry in the civil registry of Santo Stefano can be found on the web at http://www.internetculturale.it/upload/immagini/atto%20grande.jpg (accessed September 24, 2007).

2. Bona Alterocca, *Cesare Pavese: Vita e opera di un grande scrittore sempre attuale* (Quart, Italy: Musumeci, 1985), 12.

3. Davide Lajolo, *An Absurd Vice: A Biography of Cesare Pavese*, ed. and trans. Mario Pietralunga and Mark Pietralunga (New York: New Directions, 1983), 4.

4. Alterocca, *Cesare Pavese*, 13.

5. Lorenzo Mondo, *Quell'antico ragazzo* (Milan: Rizzoli, 2006), 12. The story fragment referred to, "Il signor Pietro," is found in *Racconti*, 767.

6. Augusto Monti to Pavese, Turin, November 5, 1930, as quoted in Attilo Dughera, *Tra Le Carte di Pavese* (Rome: Bulzoni, 1992), 71.

7. *Il mestiere*, 201 (entry for September 21, 1940).

8. Lajolo, *Absurd Vice*, 8.

9. Natalia Ginzburg, "Portrait of a Friend," in *The Little Virtues*, trans. Dick Davis (New York: Arcade Publishing, 1989), 17.

10. Beginning in 1924, the Ministry of Education increased the number of elementary school grades to five, and since then Italian students have needed thirteen years of schooling before university. *Liceo*, the last three years of schooling before university, has several possible translations, such as secondary school, high school, senior high school, prep school, or lyceum.

11. Monti's most famous novel was *I Sanssossì* (Milan: Ceschina, 1929), which he situated in rural Piedmont.

12. English has no good translation for the Italian word "letterato," and especially not for its plural, "letterati." While the French have "litterateur," which means the same as its Italian equivalent, no one has followed Whitman in his use of "literatus" and "literatuses." "Man [or men] of letters" is the most common translation but that is not only wordy but inadequate, since "letterati" can, and often does, mean both men and women. For these reasons I use "letterato" and "letterati."

13. Augusto Monti, *I miei conti con la scuola: Cronaca scolastica italiana del secolo XX* (Turin: Einaudi, 1965), 252.

14. Ibid.

15. Norberto Bobbio, *A Political Life*, ed. Alberto Papuzzi, trans. Allan Cameron (Cambridge, England: Polity Press, 2002), 18–19, emphasis in original.

16. Monti, *I miei conti*, 221.
17. See Alterocca, *Cesare Pavese*, 27; and Mondo, *Quell'antico ragazzo*, 20.
18. Monti, *I miei conti*, 251.
19. Pavese to Monti, Reaglie, August 1926, *Lettere I*, 26.
20. Pavese to Monti, Turin, May 18, 1928, *Lettere I*, 93–94.
21. Monti, *I miei conti*, 263, emphasis in original.
22. Pavese to Tullio Pinelli, Turin, in class at liceo, winter 1925–26, *Lettere I*, 17.
23. Pavese to Monti, Reaglie, August 1926, *Lettere I*, 27.
24. Pavese to Pinelli, Turin, August 1, 1926, *Lettere I*, 29.
25. Pavese to Pinelli, Reaglie, in response to Pinelli's letter of September 19, 1926, *Lettere I*, 35.
26. Pavese to Pinelli, Reaglie, October 12, 1926, *Lettere I*, 40–41.
27. Shaun O'Connell, email message to author, February 21, 2007.
28. Pavese to Pinelli, Reaglie, August 18, 1927, *Lettere I*, 74.
29. "Spasmi d'ali" in *Racconti*, 246.
30. Cesare Pavese, *Lotte di giovani e altri racconti, 1925–1930* (Turin: Einaudi, 1993), xii.
31. Giacomo Matteotti, a prominent Socialist member of the Italian House of Deputies, was kidnapped and murdered in June 1924 after delivering a scathing attack on Mussolini. The discovery of his body two months later led to a crisis of the regime. In a speech on January 3, 1925, Mussolini, who probably never directly ordered the murder, took full "political, moral, and historical responsibility" for Matteotti's death. For more on the Matteoitti crisis see R. J. B. Bosworth, *Mussolini's Italy: Life Under the Fascist Dictatorship, 1915–1945* (New York: Penguin, 2006), 210–14.
32. A good definition of "classic" Italian liberalism is that given by Norberto Bobbio in describing the essence of Luigi Einaudi's thought: "The defense of all civil and political liberties, including specifically economic liberties, against the protectionist, interventionist, dirigiste, programmatic state, which instead of doing what it should—guaranteeing freedom and mediating social conflicts—had grown into a dispenser of benefits and favors for whoever had the most influence, to the point of becoming with Fascism the Leviathan in which every spark of individual or group freedom had been extinguished." *Trent'anni di storia della cultura a Torino, 1920–1950* (Turin: Einaudi, 2002), 36.
33. Leslie A. Fiedler, "Introducing Cesare Pavese," in *No! In Thunder: Essays on Myth and Literature* (Boston: Beacon Press, 1960), 141.
34. Monti, *I miei conti*, 259.
35. For the details of Ginzburg's parentage see the entry by G. Sofri in *Dizionario biografico degli Italiani* (Rome: Istituto della Enciclopedia Italiana, 2000), 55:53.
36. See, for example, the letter of July 28, 1924, quoted in full in *Da Odessa a Torino: Conversazioni con Marussia Ginzburg*, ed. M. Clara Avalle (Turin: Claudiana, 2002), 26–27.
37. Norberto Bobbio, introduction to *Leone Ginzburg: Scritti* (Turin: Einaudi: 2000), lii–liii.
38. Einaudi published Ginzburg's collected writings in 1964 and reissued them in 2000 as *Leone Ginzburg: Scritti*, ed. Domenico Zucàro, pref. Luisa

Mangoni, intro. Norberto Bobbio (Turin: Einaudi 2000). The letters he wrote from confino have been published as *Leone Ginzburg: Lettere dal confino, 1940–1943*, ed. Luisa Mangoni (Turin: Einaudi, 2004).

39. Bobbio, introduction to *Leone Ginzburg: Scritti*, lxv.

40. The original of Pavese's examination results can be found in his folder at the archives of the University of Turin. Passing the examination represented a considerable achievement; in his years, sometimes as many as 75 percent of the students sitting for the examination failed it the first time.

41. Pavese to Chiuminatto, Turin, July 20, 1930, *Chiuminatto Correspondence*, 89.

42. Pavese to Chiuminatto, Turin, July 31, 1930, ibid., 92.

43. Mark Pietralunga, "L'amico del *Middle West*: Lettere inedite di Antonio Chiuminatto e Cesare Pavese," *Levia Gravia* 5 (2003): 267.

44. Pietralunga has compiled all the explanations and Italian translations that Chiuminatto provided Pavese as an appendix to *Chiuminatto Correspondence*.

45. Valerio Ferme, *Tradurre è tradire: La traduzione come sovversione culturale sotto il Fascismo* (Ravenna: A. Longo Editore, 2002), 101.

46. Pavese to Frank D. Fackenthal, Turin, June 13, 1930, *Lettere I*, 204.

47. Pavese to Giuseppe Prezzolini, Turin, July 9, 1930, *Lettere I*, 210.

48. Prezzolini to Pavese, New York, December 18, 1930, *Lettere I*, 255.

49. Pavese to Prezzolini, Turin, April 19, 1931, *Lettere I*, 292; Prezzolini to Pavese, New York, May 2, 1931, ibid., 292n.

50. Pavese to Chiuminatto, Turin, May 1931, *Chiuminatto Correspondence*, 133.

3. Tina

1. Davide Lajolo, *Il vizio assurdo: Storia di Cesare Pavese* (Milan: Il Saggiatore, 1960); available as *An Absurd Vice: A Biography of Cesare Pavese*, trans. Mario Pietralunga and Mark Pietralunga (New York: New Directions, 1983).

2. Almost all the information about Pizzardo, other than that which Pavese recorded in his diary, comes from two related sources: her own memoirs, *Senza pensarci due volte* [Without Thinking Twice About It] (Bologna: Il Mulino, 1996), and the chapter titled "Tina Pizzardo" in Giovanni De Luna, *Donne in oggetto: L'antifascismo nella società italiana, 1922–1939* [The Women in Question: Antifascism in Italian Society, 1922–1939], 273–306 (Turin: Bollati Boringhieri, 1995). De Luna published his book a year before Pizzardo's memoirs came out; he based his comments on the typescript of the memoirs. Dating on that typescript, then in the possession of Pizzardo's son, shows that Tina composed the bulk of it in 1962, not long after she read Lajolo's biography of Pavese.

3. De Luna, *Donne in oggetto*, 276.

4. While Spinelli started his political life as a communist, he was expelled from the Italian party in 1937. After World War II he became one of the principal proponents of democratic European federalism—indeed, the Italian equivalent of Jean Monnet or Robert Schumann.

5. Pizzardo, *Senza pensarci*, 135.

6. Ibid., 153.
7. Ibid., 155.
8. Ibid., 156.
9. Ibid., 157.
10. Ibid., 166.
11. They need not have worried; Leone Ginzburg called him "Cesarito." See *Lettere I*, 370.
12. Pizzardo, *Senza pensarci*, 166–67, ellipsis in original.
13. Ibid., 168–69.
14. Others, including Giulio Einaudi, mention Pavese's dislike of the mountains. See, for example, Giulio Einaudi, *Frammenti di memoria* (Milan: Rizzoli, 1988), 44.
15. Pizzardo, *Senza pensarci*, 171–72.
16. Lorenzo Mondo, *Quell'antico ragazzo* (Milan: Rizzoli, 2006), 62.
17. Guido Modena, "Introduzione storico-giuridica: dal domicilio coatto al confino di polizia," conference presentation at "Festa della Liberazione: Antifascismo e Confino," Turin, Centro Sociale Comunità Ebraica, April 27, 2006.
18. This figure comes from the presentation of Carlo Capogreco, "Tempi, luoghi e soggetti colpiti," made at the same conference mentioned immediately above. It is confirmed in many standard histories of Fascism; see, for example, R. J. B. Bosworth, *Mussolini's Italy: Life under the Fascist Dictatorship, 1915–1945* (New York: Penguin, 2006), 242.
19. The original of the telegram is found at the Centro Gozzano-Pavese in AP X, 58.
20. Pavese to his sister Maria, Brancaleone, August 9, 1935, *Lettere I*, 423.
21. Tina often went up in the mountains, even in the summer, as did many other of Pavese's friends.
22. Pavese to his sister Maria, Brancaleone, August 19, 1935, *Lettere I*, 425–26.
23. Pavese to Tina Pizzardo, Brancaleone, September 17, 1935, *Lettere I*, 441.
24. Pizzardo, *Senza pencarci*, 183.
25. Einaudi first published *Il mestiere di vivere* in 1952, only two years after Pavese's death, in an annotated but excised version. The edition edited by Guglielminetti and Ney, which I cite, restored the excisions and included new annotation.
26. Sergio Pautasso, *Cesare Pavese, L'Uomo Libro: Il mestiere di scrivere come mestiere di vivere* (Milan: Arcipelago, 1991), 10.
27. Richard M. Koffler, "The Job of Living (Diary 1935–1950); An Annotated Translation of Cesare Pavese's *Il mestiere di vivere*" (PhD diss., Rutgers University, 1973); Cesare Pavese, *This Business of Living: A Diary, 1935–1950*, trans. A. E. Murch (London: Peter Owen, 1961), also published as *The Burning Brand: Diaries 1935–1950* (New York: Walker, 1961).
28. "Terra d'esilio" is found in *Racconti*, 447–59. Though composed in late 1938 and early 1939, *Il carcere* was first published only in 1948 as one of two novels that made up *Primo che il gallo canti* [Before the Cock Crows] (Turin: Einaudi). The only English translation is *The Political Prisoner*, trans. W. J. Strachan (London: Peter Owen, 1955).
29. Ettore De Giorgis, "A Trent'anni dalla morte di Cesare Pavese," in *"Sotto*

il gelo del' acqua c'è l'erba": *Omaggio a Cesare Pavese*, ed. Mariarosa Masoero et al. (Alessandria: Edizione dell'Orso, 2001), 315.

30. Pavese to Mario Sturani, Brancaleone, November 27, 1935, *Lettere I*, 470.
31. Pavese to Augusto Monti, Brancaleone, December 12, 1935, *Lettere I*, 475.
32. *Il mestiere*, 24 (entry for December 20, 1935).
33. Ibid. (entry for December 29, 1935). Pavese often used the verb *studiare* (study, investigate) interchangeably with *leggere* (read).
34. Cesare Pavese, *Hard Labor: Poems by Cesare Pavese*, trans. William Arrowsmith (Baltimore: Johns Hopkins University Press, 1979); *Work's Tiring* in Pavese, *Disaffections: Complete Poems, 1930–1950*, trans. Geoffrey Brock (Port Townsend, Wash.: Copper Canyon Press, 2002); Pavese, *A Mania for Solitude: Selected Poems, 1930–1950*, trans. Margaret Crosland (London: Peter Owen, 1969).
35. Pavese to his sister Maria, Brancaleone, March 2, 1936, *Lettere I*, 513.
36. Pavese to Nina Perini, Brancaleone, August 27, 1935, *Lettere I*, 433.
37. Pizzaro, *Senza pensarci*, 184.
38. Pavese to his sister Maria, Rome, Regina Coeli Prison, July 12, 1935, *Lettere I*, 402.
39. Pavese to his sister Maria, Brancaleone, February 23, 1936, *Lettere I*, 507.
40. Pavese to his sister Maria, Brancaleone, February 24, 1936, *Lettere I*, 509.
41. Pavese to his sister Maria, Brancaleone, February 29, 1936, *Lettere I*, 512.
42. Pavese to his sister Maria, Brancaleone, March 3, 1936, *Lettere I*, 515.
43. Pavese to his sister Maria, Brancaleone, March 5, 1936, *Lettere I*, 516.
44. Pavese to his sister Maria, Brancaleone, March 12, 1936, *Lettere I*, 517.
45. Pavese to his sister Maria, Brancaleone, March 13, 1936, *Lettere I*, 518.
46. Pizzardo, *Senza pensarci*, 182.
47. Ibid., 184.
48. Ibid., 184–85.
49. Ibid., 185, mentions April 19 parenthetically as the date of the wedding. I use the ninth for several reasons. Giovanni De Luna had access to the typescript of Pizzardo's manuscript, and in his book *Donne in oggetto*, composed and published before Pizzardo's memoirs appeared, says the date was April 9. Pavese's diary entry of April 10, 1936 (*Il mestiere*, 31), clearly implies that Tina was already married. Furthermore, his entry of December 25, 1937 (ibid., 69), refers to April 9 as the day that "annihilated" his dreams. I believe that the "19" that appears in Pizzardo's book is a typo rather than evidence of a faulty memory; Pizzardo was not alive to check the book, as it was published seven years after her death. Finally, since Henek was a non-naturalized foreign citizen living in Italy, it is possible he and Tina had two wedding ceremonies, one at the Turinese registry office and one at the Polish consulate; if so, one may have taken place on the ninth and the other on the nineteenth.
50. Ibid., 186.
51. Ibid.
52. Ibid., 187.
53. Natalia Ginzburg, *Lessico famigliare* (Turin: Einaudi, 1999), 125.
54. Pizzardo, *Senza pensarci*, 188.
55. Ibid., 189–90, ellipsis in original.
56. *Il mestiere*, 50 (entry for July 4, 1937).

57. Pizzardo, *Senza pensarci*, 190.
58. Ibid., 191.
59. De Luna, *Donne in oggetto*, 273.
60. *Il mestiere*, 50 (entry for August 3, 1937).
61. Pizzardo, *Senza pensarci*, 191.
62. *Il mestiere*, 70 (entry for December 30, 1937).
63. Ibid., 72 (entry for December 31, 1937).
64. Ibid., 98 (entry for March 27, 1938).
65. Bona Alterocca, *Cesare Pavese: Vita e opere di un grande scrittore sempre attuale* (Quart, Aosta: Musumeci Editore, 1985), 120.
66. Indeed he did confide in friends. In a January 1938 letter to Enzo Monferini he states, "The fact is this: I come too quickly and *there's nothing to be done about it*." *Lettere I*, 533; emphasis in original.
67. Alterocca, *Cesare Pavese*, 109.
68. Pizzardo, *Senza pensarci*, 192.
69. *Il mestiere*, 51 (entry for October 12, 1937).
70. Pizzardo, *Senza pensarci*, 192.
71. *Il mestiere*, 52 (entry for November 13, 1937).
72. Pizzardo, *Senza pensarci*, 192.
73. All cited entries appear in *Il mestiere* between pages 53 and 70. See also the following entries (70–118): December 30, 1937; December 31, 1937; January 1, 1938; January 5, 1938; January 17, 1938; January 19, 1938; January 26, 1938; February 2, 1938; February 3, 1938; February 15, 1938; February 21, 1938; February 23, 1938; February 25, 1938; March 16, 1938; March 23, 1938; March 26, 1938; March 27, 1938; April 25, 1938; May 6, 1938; May 13, 1938; June 11, 1938; June 16, 1938; July 8, 1938; August 2, 1938; September 21, 1938.
74. Pizzardo, *Senza pensarci*, 196.
75. *Il mestiere*, 111 (entry for July 7, 1938).
76. Ibid., 37 (entry for April 25, 1936).
77. Ibid., 304 (entry for December 7, 1945).
78. "Terra d'esilio," in *Racconti*, 447–59.
79. *Racconti*, 544–55.
80. Ibid., 555.
81. Thomas Stauder, among others, makes the link to Pavese's misogyny in this period. See "La svolta verso il mito nella prosa pavesiana della seconda metà degli anni Trenta," in Masoero et al., *Sotto il gelo dell'acqua c'è l'erba*, 63.
82. For a discussion of the origin of *Senza pensarci*, see Ugo Berti Arnoaldi's introduction to it, i–v.
83. Alterocca, *Cesare Pavese*, 61.
84. Pizzardo, *Senza pensarci*, 201.
85. Pavese to Enzo Monferrini, Turin, January 1938, *Lettere I*, 533, emphasis in original.
86. "Ritorno di Deola," *Le Poesie*, 324.
87. *Il mestiere*, 32 (entry for April 10, 1936).

4. Einaudi, Fernanda, and World War II

1. In his year-end summation for 1937, Pavese noted, "Gave many private lessons and found a steady stream of students." *Il mestiere*, 70 (entry for December 30, 1937).

2. Pavese to Amministrazione dei telefoni, Torino, Turin, February 19, 1937, *Lettere I*, 525.

3. The three named poems can be found in *Le poesie* at 330, 326, and 86, respectively.

4. Augusto Monti, *I miei conti con la scuola: Cronaca scolastica italiana del secolo XX* (Turin: Einaudi, 1965), 253.

5. Giulio Einaudi to Cesare Pavese, Turin, April 27, 1938, *Lettere I*, 537.

6. From the same year-end summary mentioned above; *Il mestiere*, 70 (entry for December 30, 1937). The average exchange rate for the lire in both 1937 and 1938 was approximately 19 lire to one U.S. dollar. Thus, in dollar terms, he went from an annual income of between $368 and $473 in 1937 to $631 in 1938. Before thinking this meant impoverishment, one should remember that in 1938 a pound of beef in Italy cost the equivalent of thirty cents, a liter of milk three cents, and a pound of pasta six cents. Pavese's 1938 salary from Einaudi of 12,000 lire was twice the Italian per capita income that year (5,800 lire). Historical exchange statistics available at http://www.bancaditalia.it/statistiche/storic/collanastorica/tavII/tavII.pdf (accessed October 7, 2007). For the cost of goods in 1938, see William D. Grampp, "The Italian Lira, 1938–45," *Journal of Political Economy* 54, no. 4 (August 1946): 318. For Italian per capita income in 1938, see Henry S. Miller, review of *Italy in International Cooperation* by Karel Holbik, *American Economic Review* 50, no. 4 (September 1960): 753.

7. By far the best source for the history of Einaudi from its beginnings to the mid-1960s is Luisa Mangoni, *Pensare i libri: La casa editrice Einaudi dagli anni trenta agli anni sessanta* (Turin: Bollati Boringhieri, 1999).

8. Natalia Ginzburg, *Lessico famigliare* (Turin: Einaudi, 1999), 126.

9. Interview with Giulio Einaudi in *Giulio Einaudi: Tutti i nostri mercoledì*, ed. Paolo Di Stefano (Bellinzona, Switzerland: Casagrande, 2001), 47.

10. See Ernesto Ferrero, *I migliori anni della nostra vita* (Milan: Feltrinelli, 2005), 60.

11. Quoted in Mangoni, *Pensare i libri*, 234.

12. Ferrero, *I migliori anni*, 60.

13. *Il mestiere*, 147 (entry for January 1, 1939), emphasis in original. The entry for December 30, 1937, he refers to is found at page 70.

14. *Romanzi*, 285–368.

15. Ibid., 91–146 and 149–281.

16. Ibid., *Casa in collina*, 369–485; *La luna e il falò*, 781–896.

17. *Il mestiere*, 169 (entry for January 1, 1940).

18. Pavese composed *La bella estate* between March 2 and May 6, 1940, but published it only in 1949. He wrote *La spiaggia* between November 1940 and January 1941; his only novel not to be published first by Einaudi, it appeared in 1942 under the imprint of the Roman publisher, Edizioni Lettere D'oggi.

19. Gianni Venturi, "Pavese," *Il Castoro* 25 (January 1969): 68.

20. *Il mestiere*, 215 (entry for January 14, 1941).

21. "Sulle orme della Beat Generation: Incontro con Fernanda Pivano," interview by two students of the Liceo "G. Parini," Milan, published in the student newspaper, *L'urlo*, November 2000; available online at http://www.liceoparini.it/pariniweb/reprint/pivano.htm (accessed October 10, 2007).

22. Interview conducted February 14, 2004, by Laura Vitali and Pierluigi Vaccaneo, *Sincronie* 5, no. 15 (January–June 2004): 18.

23. *Il mestiere*, 196 (entry for July 26, 1940).

24. Ibid. (entry for July 28, 1940).

25. Pavese to Pivano, all in *Lettere I*, Turin, August 22, 1940, 563; Turin, October 20, 1940, 568; Turin, November 5, 1940, 572; and Turin, March 15, 1941, 583.

26. From the poems "Mattino" and "Notturno," *Le poesie*, 80 and 82, respectively.

27. Pavese to Pivano, Turin, August 22, 1940, *Lettere I*, 563–65.

28. Ibid., 565n.

29. *Il mestiere*, 202 (entries for September 25 and 29, 1940). Unlike most entries, which just carry a date, the latter states specifically, "evening of 29 September."

30. Richard M. Koffler, "The Job of Living (Diary 1935–1950); An Annotated Translation of Cesare Pavese's *Il mestiere di vivere*" (PhD diss., Rutgers University, 1973), 322n64.

31. See *Il mestiere*, 303.

32. "Le paure di F." (The Fears of F.), informal essay included by Pavese in letter to Pivano, Turin, March 15, 1941, *Lettere I*, 586.

33. *Il mestiere*, 202 (entry for September 30, 1940).

34. Ibid., 203 (entry for October 5, 1940).

35. Ibid., 206 (entry for October 17, 1940).

36. Ibid., 205 (entry for October 15, 1940); trans. Koffler, "The Job of Living," 303.

37. Lorenzo Mondo, *Quell'antico ragazzo* (Milan: Rizzoli, 2006), 92.

38. Edgar Lee Masters, *Antologia di Spoon River*, trans. Fernanda Pivano (Turin: Einaudi, 1943).

39. Pavese to Pivano, Turin, October 20, 1940, *Lettere I*, 568.

40. Pavese to Pivano, Rome, February 2, 1946, *Lettere II*, 56.

41. *Il mestiere*, 322 (entry for October 26, 1946).

42. Aldo Cazzullo, "'Con Hemingway neanche un bacio. Il mio vero amore è stato De André': Fernanda Pivano; io, la letteratura e le delusioni sentimentale," *Corriere della Sera*, July 11, 2004; available at http://archivio.corriere.it/archiveDocumentServlet.jsp?url=/documenti_globnet/corsera/2004/07/co_9_040711047.xml (accessed October 13, 2007).

43. Ibid. Pivano's web site is at http://www.fernandapivano.it/.

44. He did translate one more book after the war, the English novelist Robert Henriques's tumid, experimental 1943 novel, *Captain Smith and Company* (published in the United States as *The Voice of the Trumpet*). He regretted doing so, calling it "prose that would kill an ox."

45. Pavese to Giambattista Vicari, Turin, June 22, 1941, *Lettere I*, 596.

46. See letter of October 18, 1941, *Lettere I*, 611.

47. Pavese to Pivano, Turin, July 26, 1943, *Lettere I*, 718.

48. Pier Luigi Bassignana, *Torino sotto le bombe: nei rapporti inediti dell'aviazione alleata* (Turin: Edizioni del Capricorno, 2003), 77.

49. *Il mestiere*, 257 (entry for September 11, 1943).

50. Davide Lajolo, *Il vizio assurdo: Storia di Cesare Pavese* (Milan: Il Saggiatore, 1960), 281.

51. For a vivid description of the experience of someone who made a different choice, see Pavese's close friend Massimo Mila's recounting of his leaving Turin, at the same time Pavese did, to join the Partisans. Massimo Mila, *Scritti civili* (Turin: Einaudi, 1995), 45–54.

52. *Il mestiere*, 272 (entry for January 29, 1944), trailing ellipsis in original; trans. Koffler, "The Job of Living," 418.

53. Giovanni Baravalle, in *Il Secolo XIX*, Genoa, August 27, 1970; trans. Koffler, "The Job of Living," 452n2.

54. *Il mestiere*, 272–73 (entry for February 1, 1944), ellipsis in original; trans. Koffler, "The Job of Living," 419.

55. Ibid., 296 (entry for January 9, 1945). "Notable creative work" probably refers to the four short stories he wrote during the year, three of which he deemed publishable when he returned to Turin, plus the eight essays he included with the collection of stories.

56. Ibid., 276 (entry for March 3, 1944) (emphasis in original).

57. Ibid. (entry for March 8, 1944).

58. Pavese to Giuseppe Vaudagna, Serralunga di Crea, December 18, 1944, *Lettere I*, 740.

59. *Il mestiere*, 295 (entry for December 28, 1944).

60. Quotes otherwise unidentified in the immediately following passage are from "Del mito, del simbolo e d'altro," in *Feria d'agosto* (1945); repr. in *Racconti*, 126–31.

61. Pavese, *Fuoco grande*, 49.

62. "La selva," *Lett. am.*, 323.

63. *Il mestiere*, 287 (entry for August 19, 1944).

64. Ibid., 312 (entry for March 31, 1946).

65. "Il mito," *Lett. am.*, 345.

66. *Il mestiere*, 304 (entry for December 7, 1945).

67. "The Road," in *Dialogues with Leucò*, trans. William Arrowsmith and D. S. Carne-Ross (Ann Arbor: University of Michigan Press, 1965), 62.

68. Lorenzo Mondo, "Pavese: il taccuino segreto," *La Stampa*, August 8, 1990, "Società e Cultura" section.

69. Ibid., 16, emphasis and ellipses within paragraphs in original. The article includes photocopies of Pavese's notebooks from which Mondo transcribed the quotes.

70. *Il mestiere*, 273 (entry for February 2, 1944).

5. Liberation?

1. Lorenzo Mondo, *Quell'antico ragazzo* (Milan: Rizzoli, 2006), 130.

2. *Lett. am.*, 218–19. Fifteen years earlier (July 31, 1930), he had written to Anthony Chiuminatto, "I adore words"; *Chiuminatto Correspondence*, 92.

3. Natalia Ginzburg, *Lessico famigliare* (Turin: Einaudi, 1999), 198.
4. Pavese to Silvio Micheli, Turin, June 11, 1945, *Lettere II*, 15.
5. Pavese to Giulio Einaudi, Rome, August 18, 1945, *Lettere II*, 26.
6. Bona Alterocca, *Cesare Pavese: Vita e opere di un grande scrittore sempre attuale* (Quart, Aosta: Musumeci Editore, 1985), 113; Mondo, *Quell'antico ragazzo*, 133.
7. Phrases of Pavese in unpublished letters to Garufi, as quoted by Mariarosa Masoero, introduction to Cesare Pavese and Bianca Garufi, *Fuoco grande*, ed. Mariarosa Masoero (Turin: Einaudi, 2003), vi.
8. Pavese to Garufi, Turin, November 25, 1945, *Lettere II*, 38–40 (emphasis in original).
9. *Il mestiere*, 303 (entry for November 27, 1945).
10. Alterocca, *Cesare Pavese*, 109.
11. *Il mestiere*, 304 (entry for December 7, 1945) (emphasis in original).
12. Italo Calvino, editor's note, Cesare Pavese, *Poesie edite e inedite*, ed. Italo Calvino (Turin: Einaudi, 1962), 222.
13. Cesare Pavese, *Disaffections: Complete Poems, 1930–1950*, trans. Geoffrey Brock (Port Townsend, Wash.: Copper Canyon, 2002), 309; original, "Terra rossa terra nera," in *Poesie*, 120.
14. Brock translation in Pavese, *Disaffections*, 329; original, "Sei la terra e la morte," in *Poesie*, 130.
15. Cesare Pavese and Bianca Garufi, *Fuoco grande* (Turin: Einaudi, 1959).
16. Augusto Monti to Pavese, Turin, December 12, 1947, in Attilo Dughera, *Tra Le Carte di Pavese* (Rome: Bulzoni, 1992), 91–92.
17. *Il mestiere*, 306 (entry for January 1, 1946).
18. Ibid., 314 (entry for April 25, 1946), emphasized words are in English in original.
19. "Le piante del lago" and "Anche tu sei l'amore," *Le poesie*, 337 and 338, respectively.
20. "The Bonfires," *Dialogues with Leucò*, trans. William Arrowsmith and D. S. Carne-Ross (Ann Arbor: University of Michigan Press, 1965), 92–93.
21. *Il mestiere*, 354 (entry for October 8, 1948).
22. The best summary of the history of this series is Cesare Pavese and Ernesto de Martino, *La collana viola: Lettere 1945–1950*, ed. Pietro Angelini (Turin: Bollati Boringhieri, 1991).
23. *Il mestiere*, 331 (entry for April 12, 1947).
24. Ibid. (entry for April 5, 1947). By "clandestine period," Pavese may have meant either the whole Fascist era after 1925, when all opposition had to go underground, or the twenty months he spent hiding at Serralunga and Casale. The thrust of the remark remains the same either way.
25. Ibid., 333 (entry for June 4, 1947).
26. Ibid., 338 (entry for November 7, 1947).
27. Mondo, *Quell'antico ragazzo*, 157.
28. *Il mestiere*, 342 (entry for January 1, 1948).
29. Cesare Pavese, "The House on the Hill," in *The Selected Works of Cesare Pavese*, trans. R. W. Flint (New York: New York Review of Books: 2001), 166–67. I have made one change to Flint's translation. He has Giorgi say, "For my sins I've

taken an oath," implying that in repentance for his Fascist past he has sworn an oath to the Partisans. The Italian reads "Per mia disgrazia avevo fatto un giuramento." He means that it was his misfortune to have taken the Fascist oath.

30. Ibid., 169–70.
31. Ibid., 175.
32. Ibid., 175–76.
33. Ginzburg, *Lessico famigliare*, 151–52.
34. Primo Levi, *Se questo è un uomo*, Biblioteca Leone Ginzburg 3 (Turin: De Silva, 1947). In commercial terms, Pavese and Ginzburg's judgment seemed justified at the time: De Silva printed only two thousand copies and not all of those sold. Einaudi, however, did play a direct role in bringing Levi the recognition he still holds, when it acquired the rights from De Silva and republished *Se questo è un uomo* in 1958. That was the edition, in Italy and in translation abroad, that propelled Levi's book to worldwide consciousness. Einaudi also published the first edition of Levi's *La tregua* (*The Truce*) in 1963 and remained Levi's primary publisher thereafter. http://www.bncf.firenze.sbn.it/cgi-opac/schedbib/schedbib.cgi?BID=RAV0114122&TIPO=B&Lingua=ITA&unicode=F.
35. *Il mestiere*, 360 (entry for December 31, 1948).
36. Ibid., 367 (entry for April 10, 1949).
37. Ibid., 370 (entry for June 22, 1949).
38. Ibid., 371–72 (entry for July 1, 1949).
39. Pavese, "L'arte di maturare," *Lett. am.*, 360–61. The lines from Shakespeare are in English in the original.
40. *Il mestiere*, 374 (entry for September 30, 1949).
41. Ibid., 375 (entry for November 17, 1949); emphasis in original.
42. Ibid.
43. Ibid., 377–78 (entry for November 26, 1945).
44. Ibid., 376 (entry for November 24, 1949).
45. Ibid., 380 (entry for December 15, 1949).
46. Ibid., 380 (entry for December 5, 1949).
47. Ibid., 349 (entry for March 28, 1948).
48. Ibid., 382 (entry for December 29, 1949).
49. Ginzburg, *Lessico famigliare*, 200.
50. "La tragica morte di Cesare Pavese," *Corriere della Sera* (Milan), August 29, 1950. A copy of the article can be found in *Cesare Pavese: biografia per immagini, la vita, i libri, le carte, i luoghi*, ed. Franco Vaccaneo (Cavallermaggione: Gribaudo, 1989), 136.
51. Pavese, *The Moon and the Bonfires*, trans. R. W. Flint (New York: New York Review of Books, 2002), 6.

6. "Viva Walt Whitman"

1. Pavese's attempts to gather materials for his thesis are documented in various letters. See, for example, all in *Lettere I*: to Massimo Mila, September 4, 1929, 143; to "a professor," October 1929, 148; to Chiuminatto, November 29, 1929, 156; to "a librarian," November 29, 1929, 161.

2. Centro Gozzano-Pavese, AP.X. 25; AP.X. 26; AP.X. 27.

3. Biblioteca scolastica multimediale del Liceo Massimo D'Azeglio, Turin. Photocopies of some of the annotations can be found in the exhibition catalog *Cesare Pavese e la "sua" Torino* (Turin: Lindau, 2007), 69.

4. Pavese to Chiuminatto, Turin, November 29, 1929, *Chiuminatto Correspondence*, 25.

5. Pavese to Chiuminatto, Turin, February 22, 1930, *Chiuminatto Correspondence*, 48.

6. Pavese to Enzo Monferini, Turin, February 20, 1930, *Lettere I*, 177.

7. Cesare Pavese, "Interpretation of the Poetry of Walt Whitman" (undergraduate thesis, University of Turin, 1930), 97.

8. For Christmas 2006, Einaudi published the thesis in a special gift edition of one thousand copies, edited and introduced by Valerio Magrelli. The book carries no ISBN number and did not enter commercial channels.

9. Edgar Allan Poe, *Le poesie*, trans. Federico Olivero (Bari: Laterza, 1912); Federico Olivero, *Edgar Allan Poe* (Turin: L'Erma, 1932); Olivero, *Francis Thompson* (Rome: Tip. Unione, 1912); Olivero, *Lirica religiosa inglese* (Turin: Soc. Ed. Internazionale, 1941 and 1942); Olivero, *Saggi di letteratura inglese* (Bari: Laterza, 1913); *Beowulf*, trans. Camille Monnet, intro. Federico Olivero (Turin: S Lattes, 1937).

10. See Minute Book of the Faculty of Letters and Philosophy, University of Turin, 1930, University Archives.

11. Lionello Sozzi, "Le letterature straniere," in *Storia della Facoltà di Lettere e Filosofia dell'Università di Torino*, ed. Italo Lana (Florence: Leo S. Oslchki, 2000), 441; Angelo D'Orsi, *Allievi e maestri: L'Università di Torino nell'Otto-Novecento* (Turin: Celid, 2002), 52; Norberto Bobbio, *Trent'anni di storia della cultura a Torino, 1920–1950* (Turin: Einaudi, 2002), 74.

12. See Angelo d'Orsi, *La cultura a Torino tra le due guerre* (Turin: Einaudi, 2000), 20. According to Monti, "Pavese's degree thesis was a Crocean thing presented to Olivero, who had maintained himself virginally closed to that kind of culture. Smelling those pages, he—with horror—rejected them." In Domenico Zucaro, "Gli Anni dell'università di Cesare Pavese," *Avanti!* (Milan), November 29, 1963, 3.

13. Davide Lajolo, *An Absurd Vice: A Biography of Cesare Pavese*, ed. and trans. Mario Pietralunga and Mark Pietralunga (New York: New Directions, 1983), 61. Lajolo, also characteristically, gets his facts slightly wrong in Pavese's favor. The paragraph in which this citation appears ends, "Pavese graduated with the highest honors." Pavese graduated but not with the highest honors.

14. Angelo d'Orsi, "'L'ago calamitato': Pavese, 'La Cultura,' il Fascismo e l'Antifascismo," in *Cesare Pavese: Atti del Convegno internazionale di studi, Torino–Santo Stefano Belbo, 24–27 ottobre 2001* (Florence: Leo S. Olschki, 2005), 154.

15. H. Stuart Hughes, *The United States and Italy*, rev. ed. (Cambridge: Harvard University Press, 1965), 242.

16. Pavese, "Interpretation of the Poetry of Walt Whitman," 130.

17. The chapter titles were: (1) The Myth of Discovery, (2) The Pioneer, (3) Manly Love, (4) The Great "Songs" ["Songs" in English in original], (5) The National Epic, (6) The Meditations, and (7) The Passage of the Soul and Old Age.

18. Pavese, "Interpretation of the Poetry of Walt Whitman," 19.

19. Ibid., 35.
20. Ibid., 37–38.
21. Richard Chase, *Walt Whitman Reconsidered* (New York: William Sloane, 1955), 170, emphasis in original.
22. Pavese, "Interpretation of the Poetry of Walt Whitman," 153, 107, 111.
23. Ibid., 239.
24. Ibid., 265.
25. Edwin Miller, *A Century of Whitman Criticism* (Bloomington: Indiana University Press, 1969), xi.
26. Willard Thorp, "Walt Whitman," in *Eight American Authors: A Review of Research and Criticism*, ed. Floyd Stovall (New York: Norton, 1963), 300.
27. Pavese, "Interpretation of the Poetry of Walt Whitman," 296.
28. T. S. Eliot, Introduction to Ezra Pound, *Selected Poems* (London: Faber & Gwyer, 1928); Eliot, review of Emory Holloway's *Whitman: An Interpretation in Narrative*, in *The Nation & The Athenaeum* 40 (December 18, 1926); D. H. Lawrence, "Whitman," in *Studies in Classic American Literature* (New York: T. Seltzer, 1923); Stuart P. Sherman, "Walt Whitman," in *Americans* (New York: Scribner, 1922); Paul E. More, "Walt Whitman," in *Shelbourne Essays*, 4th ser. (New York: Putnam, 1906); William James, "The Religion of Healthy-Mindedness," Lecture 4 in *The Varieties of Religious Experience* (New York: Longman Greens, 1902); William James, *Le varie forme della coscienza religiosa: Studio sulla natura umana*, trans. G. C. Ferrari and M. Calderoni (Turin: Fratelli Bocca, 1904); Barrett Wendell, "Walt Whitman," in *A Literary History of America* (New York: C. Scribner's Sons, 1900); William Dean Howells, "On Walt Whitman's *November Boughs*," *Harper's New Monthly* 77 (February 1889); John Jay Chapman, "Walt Whitman," in *Emerson, and Other Essays* (New York: C. Scribner's Sons, 1898).
29. See Rea McCain, "Walt Whitman in Italy," *Italica* 20, no. 2 (1943): 4–16. As far as I can tell, this 1943 article contains the first published reference in English to Pavese. In commenting on more recent Italian articles on Whitman, McCain notes that Pavese's was "a thoughtful approach." See also Mariolina Meliadò, "La fortuna di Walt Whitman in Italia," *Studi americani* 7 (1961): 43–76; and Roger Asselineau, "Whitman in Italy," in *Whitman and the World*, ed. Gay Wilson and Ed Folsom (Iowa City: University of Iowa Press, 1995), 268–74.
30. Walt Whitman, *Canti scelti*, trans. Luigi Gamberale (Milan: Edoardo Sonzogno, 1887); Pasquale Jannaccone, *La poesia di Walt Whitman e l'evoluzione delle forme ritmiche* (Turin: Frassati, 1898).
31. Gamberale's translation was published as *Walt Whitman, Foglie di erba: Con le due aggiunte e gli echi della vecchiaia, dell'edizione del 1900* (Palermo: Sandron, 1907).
32. Meliadò counts some twenty-six individual pieces of Whitman criticism prior to Pavese's thesis, Asselineau about the same number. Pavese cited ten Italian articles plus Jannaccone's book.
33. Pavese, "Interpretation of the Poetry of Walt Whitman," 23–25, emphasis in original.
34. Ibid., 102.

35. Basil de Selincourt, *Walt Whitman: A Critical Study* (London: Martin & Secker, 1914); John Bailey, *Walt Whitman* (London: Macmillan, 1926).

36. Pavese, "Interpretation of the Poetry of Walt Whitman," 41, 42, 190.

37. Ibid., 234.

38. For Pavese on de Selincourt and these three specific points, see ibid., 39, 105, 24.

39. Ibid., 17.

40. Ibid., 157.

41. Ibid., 163.

42. Ibid., 132–33.

43. Bailey's book was published in both New York and London. Pavese's bibliography indicates he read the New York edition, and that probably led to the error.

44. Pavese, "Interpretation of the Poetry of Walt Whitman," 246, 192.

45. "Camerado, this is no book; / Who touches this, touches a man."

46. Pavese to Chiuminatto, Turin, 21 June 1930, *Chiuminatto Correspondence*, 81.

47. H. Stuart Hughes, *Consciousness and Society* (New Brunswick, N.J.: Transactions Publishers, 2002 [1958]), 19, 201.

48. Giulio Einaudi, *Frammenti di memoria* (Milan: Rizzoli, 1988), 81.

49. M. Clara Avalle, ed., *Da Odessa a Torino: Conversazioni con Marussia Ginzburg* (Turin: Claudiana, 2002), 70.

50. Augusto Monti, *I miei conti con la scuola: Cronaca scolastica italiana del secolo XX* (Turin: Einaudi, 1965), 206, 216.

51. Norberto Bobbio, *Trent'anni di storia della cultura a Torino, 1920–1950* (Turin: Einaudi, 1977), 44, 45, 42.

52. Ibid., 40.

53. For various interpretations of Croce as neo-idealist see Hughes, *Consciousness and Society*, 200–229; Cecil Sprigge, *Benedetto Croce: Man and Thinker* (Cambridge: Bowes & Bowes, 1952), 38; Ernesto G. Caserta, "Croce, Benedetto," in *Dictionary of Italian Literature*, rev. exp. ed., ed. Peter Bondanella and Julia Conaway Bondanella (Westport, Conn.: Greenwood Press, 1996), 143; Antonio Gramsci, *Letters from Prison*, trans. Lynne Lawner (New York: Noonday, 1989), 243.

54. Translated by D. Ainslie (London: Macmillan, 1909); second edition, 1922.

55. *Encyclopaedia Britannica*, 14th ed., 1929, vol. 1, s.v. "Aesthetics," 263–72.

56. To be fair to Croce, he did include at the end of the entry a section entitled "History of Aesthetics," but he included no references to any then-contemporary theory of aesthetics other than his own.

57. All citations of Croce are to the *Britannica* entry unless otherwise indicated.

58. Antonio Catalfamo, "La tesi di laurea su Whitman e la letterature americana: l''io,' la realtà storico-sociale e il simbolo," in *Cesare Pavese: La dialettica vitale delle contraddizioni* (Rome: Aracne, 2005), 19.

59. Gian-Paolo Biasin, *The Smile of the Gods: A Thematic Study of Cesare Pavese's Works*, trans. Yvonne Freccero (Ithaca: Cornell University Press, 1968), 2.

60. Michele Tondo, "L'Incontro di Pavese con Whitman: La Tesi di Laurea," *Il Ponte* 25 (1969): 708–17.

61. Augusto Monti, as quoted by Domenico Zucaro, "Gli Anni dell'università di Cesare Pavese," *Avanti!* (Milan), November 29, 1963, 3.

62. Lajolo, *An Absurd Vice*, 61.

63. Valerio Ferme, *Tradurre è tradire: La traduzione come sovversione culturale sotto il Fascismo* (Ravenna: A. Longo Editore, 2002), 92–93.

64. Pavese, "Interpretation of the Poetry of Walt Whitman," 19.

65. Ibid., 229, 236.

66. Ibid., 192.

67. M. E. Moss, introduction to *Benedetto Croce: Essays on Literature and Literary Criticism* (Albany: State University of New York Press, 1990), 21.'

68. Benedetto Croce, "Critica e storia letteraria," in *Problemi d'estetica*, as quoted by Giovanni Gullace in translator's introduction to *Benedetto Croce's Poetry and Literature: An Introduction to Its Criticism and History* (Carbondale: Southern Illinois University Press, 1981), xli.

69. Pavese, "Interpretation of the Poetry of Walt Whitman," 39, 194.

70. Tondo, "L'Incontro di Pavese con Whitman," 710.

71. Pavese, "Interpretation of the Poetry of Walt Whitman," 223–28.

72. T. S. Eliot, review of Emory Holloway's *Whitman: An Interpretation in Narrative* (New York: Knopf, 1926), in *The Nation & The Athenaeum* 40 (December 18, 1926): 426.

73. Pavese to Chiuminatto, Turin, May 1931, *Chiuminatto Correspondence*, 134.

74. Leone Ginzburg to Benedetto Croce, Turin, August 9, 1931, in appendix to *Leone Ginzburg: Lettere dal confino, 1940–1943*, ed. Luisa Mangoni (Turin: Einaudi, 2004), 278.

75. Giovanni Laterza to Leone Ginzburg, November 7, 1931, ibid., 281n.

76. Leone Ginzburg to Giovanni Laterza, November 14, 1931, ibid., 282.

77. Unknown author, *Introduzione a Walt Whitman*, Centro Gozzano-Pavese, AP X. 82, 1–4.

78. The Centro Gozzano-Pavese's copy of the thesis is found in FE. 30. This revised version is in all probability the one Pavese's sister let Michele Tondo examine in 1969.

79. Pavese, "Interpretazione di Walt Whitman poeta," *La Cultura* 12, no. 3 (July–September 1933): 584–604. First published in book form in *Lett. am.*, 141–65. In English as "Interpretation of Walt Whitman, Poet," in Cesare Pavese, *American Literature: Essays and Opinions*, trans. and intro. Edwin Fussell (Berkeley: University of California Press, 1962), 117–41.

80. Asselineau, "Whitman in Italy," 271.

81. Catalfamo, "La tesi di laurea su Whitman," 19.

82. For example, in discussing previous criticism of the "Calamus" section of *Leaves of Grass*, Pavese wrote, "All of this confusion excites indignations and defenses and biographical disquisitions turning on the suspicion of homosexuality, which among other things, because of the restraints and unsubtle innuendoes of the heavy-handed literati of Puritan descent, becomes a damn nuisance to penetrate and follow." ("Interpretation of Walt Whitman, Poet," 133.)

83. Pavese, "Interpretation of Walt Whitman, Poet," 121, 120.
84. Ibid., 122.
85. The excerpt is from Walt Whitman, "A Backward Glance o'er Travel'd Roads," preface to *November Boughs* (1888), in *Complete Poetry and Collected Prose*, ed. Justin Kaplan (New York: Library of America, 1982), 671.
86. Pavese, "Interpretation of Walt Whitman, Poet," 124.
87. Ibid., 125, 126, 128.
88. Ibid., 128–29.
89. Ibid., 129.
90. Ibid., 130.
91. Pavese, *Lett. am.*, 128.
92. De Selincourt, *Walt Whitman*, 96, 117–18.
93. Pavese, "Interpretation of Walt Whitman, Poet," 132.
94. Ibid., 137.
95. Ibid., 138.
96. Ibid., 140–41.
97. Pavese, *Le poesie*, 108, repr. of appendix to *Lavorare Stanca* (Turin: Einaudi, 1943).

7. "The peach of the world"

1. Prefaces were to *Moby-Dick* and Sherwood Anderson's *Dark Laughter*, the *avvertenza* to Sinclair Lewis's *Our Mr. Wrenn*.
2. "L'influsso degli eventi," in *Lett. am.*, 247.
3. For the most influential statement of the argument that Pavese invented "the myth of America," see Dominique Fernandez, *Il mito dell'America negli intellettuali italiani dal 1930 al 1950* (Caltanisetta: Sciascia, 1969). Fernandez writes on the first page (11) of the first chapter ("The Birth of the Myth") that, though American literature did generate some serious commentary in the 1920s, "the myth, properly considered, did not begin until November 1930 with Pavese's essay on Sinclair Lewis."
4. Lorenzo Mondo, *Cesare Pavese*, 5th rev. ed. (Milan: Mursia, 1984), 53.
5. Valerio Ferme, *Tradurre è tradire: La Traduzione come sovversione culturale sotto il fascismo* (Ravenna: A. Longo, 2002), 22.
6. Harvard University Library, Open Collections Program, "Immigration to the United States, 1789–1930"; available at http://ocp.hul.harvard.edu/immigration/dates.html (accessed November 2, 2007).
7. Spartacus Educational, "USA History: Immigration"; available at http://www.spartacus.schoolnet.co.uk/USAES1920S.htm (accessed November 2, 2007).
8. Associazione Internet degli Emigrati Italiani, "L'Emigrazione Italiana negli Stati Uniti d'America"; available at http://www.emigrati.it/Emigrazione/Emiamerica.asp (accessed November 2, 2007).
9. R. J. B. Bosworth, *Mussolini's Italy: Life under the Fascist Dictatorship, 1915–1945* (New York: Penguin, 2006), 409.
10. My emphasis on American movies and fiction in this chapter does not mean

to imply that they constituted the entirety of the American "cultural invasion" of Europe. I have not discussed the third important channel, American popular music, including jazz, because it has little to do with literary *americanismo*, while film does.

11. G. Rondolino, *Torino come Hollywood* (Bologna: Capelli, 1980), as cited in Valerio Ferme, "Il giovane Pavese e la cinema americana," in *"Sotto il gelo dell'acqua c'è l'erba": Omaggio a Cesare Pavese*, ed. Mariarosa Masoero et al. (Alessandria: Edizioni dell'Orso, 2001), 19.

12. Ferme, *Tradurre è tradire*, 38; Bosworth, *Mussolini's Italy*, 410; Giovanni Belardelli, *Il Ventennio degli intellettuali: Cultura, politica, ideologia nell'Italia fascista* (Rome: Laterza, 2005), 80.

13. For a good treatment of Pavese and American movies, see Ferme, "Il giovane Pavese e la cinema americana."

14. Cesare Pavese, "John Dos Passos e il romanzo americano," *La Cultura* 12, no. 1 (January–March 1933).

15. Massimo Mila, *Scritti civili* (Turin: Einaudi, 1995), 64.

16. *Pavese e la "sua" Torino*, ed. Mariarosa Masoero and Giuseppe Zaccaria (Turin: Università degli Studi di Torino, Centro Interuniversitario "Guido Gozzano-Cesare Pavese," in association with Lindau, 2007). Catalog published in conjunction with the exhibition of the same name shown at the Turin branch of the Italian State Archives, May–June 2007. See pages 93 and 108.

17. In my discussion of American writers translated into Italian I have relied for bibliographic data mainly on two sources, one print and one electronic, both related to the Italian equivalent of the Library of Congress, the Biblioteca Nazionale Centrale di Firenze. The print source is the forty-one volume *Catalogo cumulativo 1886–1957 del Bollettino delle pubblicazioni italiane ricevute per diritto di stampa dalla Biblioteca nazionale centrale di Firenze* (Nendeln, Liechtenstein: Kraus Reprint, 1968–1969). The electronic source is the online public access catalog (OPAC) function of the *Biblioteca nazionale*, which can be accessed via that library's home page, http://www.bncf.firenze.sbn.it.

18. Valerio Ferme, *Tradurre è tradire*, 46.

19. John Dos Passos, *Nuova York*, trans. Alessandra Scalero (Milan: Corbaccio, 1932).

20. This would have been Bice Pareto Magliano's translation, *Typee: Un'avventura nelle isole Marchesi* (Turin: Formica, 1931).

21. Pavese to Alessandra Scalero, Turin, May 22, 1932, *Lettere I*, 336. The book Pavese refers to as *Back to Harlem* was in fact Claude McKay's *Home to Harlem* (New York: Harper, 1928); Scalero's translation appeared in 1930 as *Ritorno ad Harlem* (Milan: Modernissima).

22. For example, between 1931 and 1934 Pavese translated four American novels. In the same period seventeen novels by Zane Grey were published and no fewer than forty-one separate editions of Jack London's works appeared, including multiple translations of his most popular books such as *The Sea-Wolf* and *The Call of the Wild*.

23. Emilio Cecchi, *Rudyard Kipling* (Florence: Casa Editrice Italiana, 1910); Cecchi, *Storia della letteratura inglese nel secolo 19* (Milan: Treves, 1915); Cecchi, *Scrittori inglesi e americani* (Milan: Carabba, 1935).

24. See Cecchi's article in *Corriere della Sera*, November 27, 1931, as quoted by Elio Vittorini in his review/article on *Moby-Dick*, *Pègaso* 5, no. 2 (February 1933): 126.

25. Charles Burdett, "Visions of the United States: A Note on the Different Styles of Emilio Cecchi and the Americanisti," *MLN* III, no. 1 (January 1996): 164–70.

26. Bernard Berenson, *I pittori italiani del Rinascimento*, trans. Emilio Cecchi (Milan: Hoepli, 1936); Emilio and Giuditta Cecchi, *Emily Dickinson* (Brescia: Morcellina, 1939); Emilio Cecchi, *America amara* (Florence: Sansoni, 1939).

27. Jane Dunnett, "Foreign Literature in Fascist Italy: Circulation and Censorship," *TTR: Traduction, Terminologie, Rédaction: Études sur le texte et ses transformations* 15, no. 2 (2002): 97–123 (quote at 117); available online at http://www.erudit.org/revue/ttr/2002/v15/n2/007480ar.html.

28. *Il mestiere* (entry for May 27, 1942), 238.

29. A copy of the Linati scheme can be found at http://en.wikipedia.org/wiki/Linati_schema_for_Ulysses (accessed November 3, 2007).

30. Isabella Augusta Persse, Lady Gregory, *Commedie irlandesi*, trans. and intro. Carlo Linati (Milan: Ommbardo, 1916); Sean O'Casey, *Il falso repubblicano*, trans. Carlo Linati (Milan: Rosa e Ballo, 1944); John Millington Synge, *Deirdre l'Addolorata*, trans. Carlo Linati (Milan: Rosa e Ballo, 1944); Carlo Linati, *Scrittori anglo-americani d'oggi* (Milan: Corticelli, 1932); Henry James, *L'americano*, trans. Carlo Linati (Milan: Mondadori, 1934).

31. See, for example, Carlo Linati, *A vento e sole: Pagine di vagabondaggio* (Turin: Subalpina, 1939); *Aprilante: Soste e cammini* (Rome: Tumminelli, 1942); *Memorie a zig-zag* (Turin: Buratti, 1929); and *Passeggiate lariane* (Milan: Garzanti, 1939).

32. Giuseppe Prezzolini, *Benito Mussolini* (Rome: Formiggini, 1924).

33. "Fascism at Columbia University," *Nation*, November 7, 1934.

34. See Philip V. Cannistraro, "The Duce and the Prominenti: Fascism and the Crisis of Italian American Leadership," paper presented at the Conference on Fascism, Anti-Fascism, and the Italian American Community, John D. Calandra Italian American Institute, City University of New York, February 19, 2001, available in *Altreitalie* (Fondazione Giovanni Agnelli, Turin) 31 (July–December 2005): 76–86, and online at http://www.altreitalie.it/UPLOAD/ALL/84099.pdf (accessed November 3, 2007); and Gennaro Sangiuliano, "Che calcioni, anche con le pantofole," *Libero* (Milan), May 8, 2002.

35. William Weaver, response to a letter to the editor concerning a book Weaver reviewed in an earlier issue, *New York Review of Books*, October 10, 2002.

36. David Hume, *Ricerche sull'intelletto umano e sui principii della morale*, trans. Giuseppe Prezzolini (Bari: Laterza, 1910); Jack London, *Il lupo di mare*, trans. Giuseppe Prezzolini (Milan: Morreale, 1924); Giuseppe Prezzolini, *Come gli Americani scoprirono L'Italia: 1750–1850* (Milan: Treves, 1933); "American Visitors to Italy," *New York Times Book Review*, April 1, 1934, available online at http://www.hull.ac.uk/italian/American_Visitors_to_Italy.htm (accessed November 3, 2007).

37. Cesare Pavese, "Interpretation of the Poetry of Walt Whitman" (undergraduate thesis, University of Turin, 1930), 184 (ellipses in original). The term "obscene democracy," which Pavese uses ironically here, was a common Fascist trope for America.

38. Cesare Pavese, review of *Come gli Americani scoprirono L'Italia* by Giuseppe Prezzolini, in Masoero et al., *Sotto il gelo dell'acqua c'è l'erba*, 345; originally published in *La Cultura* 13, no. 1 (March 1934): 14.

39. Prezzolini brought this up in his introduction to a reprint of *Come gli Americani scoprirono L'Italia: 1750–1850* (Bologna: Boni, 1971).

40. Linati, *Scrittori anglo-americani d'oggi*, 64–66.

41. Cesare Pavese, review of *Scrittori anglo-americani d'oggi* by Carlo Linati, in Masoero et al., *Sotto il gelo dell'acqua c'è l'erba*, 342; originally published in *La Cultura* 11, no. 4 (October–December 1932): 867–68.

42. Ludwig Lewisohn, *Expression in America* (New York: Harper & Brothers, 1932), 503–4.

43. Emilio Gentile, "Impending Modernity: Fascism and the Ambivalent Image of the United States," *Journal of Contemporary History* 28, no. 1 (January 1993): 9.

44. See Leone Ginzburg's letter to his mother of January 30, 1934, in *Da Odessa a Torino: Conversazioni con Marussia Ginzburg*, ed. M. Clara Avalle (Turin: Claudiana, 2002), 68–69. Ginzburg proudly tells his mother that Giulio Einaudi has promised him that, as soon as the review reaches five hundred subscribers, Ginzburg will receive a salary equal to four percent of the annual profits.

45. Mario Einaudi, Giulio Einaudi's brother, emigrated to the United States in 1933 in protest against Fascism, and had a long and distinguished career as professor of government at Cornell.

46. Pavese to Chiuminatto, Turin, April 5, 1930, *Chiuminatto Correspondence*, 61–62.

47. Pavese, *Lett. am.*, 126.

48. Ibid., 91.

49. Geoffrey Brock, introduction to Cesare Pavese, *Disaffections: Complete Poems, 1930–1950*, trans. Geoffrey Brock (Port Townsend, Wash.: Copper Canyon, 2002), 5.

50. Untitled poem, dated April 21, 1929, in *Le poesie*, 267; my translation.

51. "South Seas," Brock translation, in Pavese, *Disaffections*, 17.

52. Geoffrey Brock, "Il ritmo del mio fantasticare: Pavese's Meter in Translation," *Yale Italian Poetry* 4 (2000): 77–82; available at http://comp.uark.edu/~gbrock/pavese_yip.html.

53. Natalia Ginzburg, *Lessico famigliare* (Turin: Einaudi, 1999), 126.

54. Pavese, "Il mestiere di poeta (a proposito di *Lavorare stanca*)," in *Poesie edite e inedite*, ed. Italo Calvino (Turin: Einaudi, 1962), 193, 196. *Sobrio* and *sobrietà* have in Italian the same connotations as "sober" and "sobriety" in English, when not used in connection with alcohol consumption. However, to describe a writing style in English as "sober" carries connotations of gravity and solemnity that "un stile sobrio" in Italian does not. One could translate *sobrio* as "restrained," "moderated," or "controlled"; I have chosen "straightforward" because it seems to catch best the

meaning Pavese was driving at: an unadorned style that presents itself without frills or decoration and asks to be taken only for what it is.

55. Ibid., 200, 201–2.
56. Pavese, *Lett. am.*, 28.
57. Pavese to Chiuminatto, Turin, June 21, 1930, *Chiuminatto Correspondence*, 82.
58. Pavese to Chiuminatto, Turin, January 12, 1930, *Chiuminatto Correspondence*, 33.
59. Pavese, *Lett. am.*, 42 (emphases in original).
60. Interview of Fernanda Pivano, conducted February 14, 2004, by Laura Vitali and Pierluigi Vaccaneo, in *Sincronie* 8, no. 15 (January–June 2004): 17–22.
61. Pavese, "Del trucco letterario," *Lett. am.*, 107; reprint of "O. Henry o del trucco letterario," *La Nuova Italia* 3, no. 3 (March 20, 1932): 88–93.
62. Pavese, *Lett. am.*, 113.
63. Pavese, "Un angelo senza cura d'anime," *Lett. am.*, 167–70; reprint of "Faulkner, cattivo allievo di Anderson," *La Cultura* 13, no. 2 (April 1934): 27–28.
64. Pavese, *Lett. am.*, 148.
65. Geno Pampaloni, *Trent'anni con Cesare Pavese: Diario contro diario* (Milan: Rusconi, 1981), 48, emphasis in original.
66. Pavese, "Dal naturalismo alla tragedia," *Lett. am.*, 139; reprint of "Dreiser e la sua battaglia sociale," *La Cultura* 12, no. 2 (April–June 1933).
67. Pavese, *Lett. am.*, 126.
68. Ibid., 8.
69. Ibid., 168.
70. Ibid., 77.
71. Ibid., 78.
72. Brock translation in Pavese, *Disaffections*, 21–23.
73. Pavese, *Lett. am.*, 78.
74. See, for instance, Valerio C. Ferme, "Il giovane Pavese e il cinema Americano," in Masoero et al., *Sotto il gelo dell'acqua c'è l'erba*, 15–40.
75. Pavese, *Lett. am.*, 78.
76. Ibid., 79.
77. Ibid.
78. Ibid., 82.
79. The translation of this passage is that of Barbara Melchiori Arnett in "The Literary Whaler," *Sewanee Review* 68 (Summer 1960): 414–15.
80. Sergio Pautasso, *Cesare Pavese, L'Uomo Libro: Il mestiere di scrivere come mestiere di vivere* (Milan: Arcipelago, 1991), 52.
81. Pavese, *Lett. am.*, 112.
82. Ibid., 138–39.
83. Cesare Pavese, *American Literature: Essays and Opinions*, trans. Edwin Fussell (Berkeley: University of California Press, 1962), 27; original in *Lett. am.*, 27.
84. Pavese, *American Literature*, 31; original in *Lett. am.*, 89.
85. Edwin Fussell, foreword to Pavese, *American Literature*, xi.
86. Pavese, "Senza provinciali una letteratura non ha nerbo," *Lett. am.*, 5.
87. Ibid.

88. Pavese, "Preface to Moby-Dick," *American Literature*, 69.
89. Pavese, "O. Henry o del trucco letterario," *Lett. am.*, 103.
90. Pavese, "Prefazione al *Riso Nero*," *Lett. am.*, 43.
91. Pavese, "Dreiser e la sua battaglia sociale," *Lett. am.*, 131.
92. Pavese, "John Dos Passos e il romanzo americano," *Lett. am.*, 115.
93. Pavese, "I morti di Spoon River," *Lett. am.*, 64.
94. Pavese, "La grande angoscia americana," *Lett. am.*, 73.
95. Pavese, "Un negro ci parla," *Lett. am.*, 189.
96. *Lett. am.*, 37.
97. Ibid., 159.
98. Ibid., 219. I have translated Pavese's editorial "we" with the first person singular.
99. Ferme, *Tradurre è tradire*, 85.
100. Ibid., 141.
101. See ibid., 112–13.
102. Edwin Fussell, foreword to Pavese, *American Literature*, vii. While still in the liceo Pavese made a translation of Shelley's lyric drama *Prometheus Unbound*, which was finally published in 1997; Percy Bysshe Shelley, *Prometeo slegato*, trans. Cesare Pavese, ed. Mark Pietralunga (Turin: Einaudi, 1997). In 1949–50 he did about half the translation of Arnold Toynbee's *A Study of History, Abridged*, published as Arnold J. Toynbee, *Le civiltà nella storia, compendio di D. C. Somervell*, trans. Cesare Pavese and Charis de Bosis (Turin: Einaudi, 1950).
103. For a good, concise discussion of the language Pavese used in his fiction, see Elisabetta Soletti, "Nota linguistica: Appunti sulla sintassi di Pavese," *Romanzi*, 1147–57.
104. Giaime Pintor, "La lotta contro gli idoli (*Americana*)," in *Il sangue d'Europa* (Turin: Einaudi, 1950), 208–19. The translation is that found in "The Struggle against Idols," in *New World Journeys: Contemporary Italian Writers and the Experience of America*, ed. and trans. Angela M. Jeannet and Louise K. Barnett (Westport, Conn.: Greenwood, 1977), 162–70.
105. Pavese mentions having spent time with Soldati in Rome during the winter of 1942–43; Pavese to Enzo Giachino, Turin, March 17, 1943, *Lettere I*, 686.
106. See his remarks on intending to settle permanently in America in *America primo amore*, ed. Salvatore Silvano Nigro (Palermo: Sellerio, 2003), 305. Unless otherwise specified, all my citations are to this edition.
107. First published as Mario Soldati, *America, primo amore* (Florence: Bemporad, 1935). Soldati used the comma in the title for the book's first two editions, 1935 and 1945, but left it out in all succeeding editions.
108. Mario Soldati, *The American Bride*, trans. William Weaver (London: Hodder and Stoughton, 1979).
109. Soldati, *America primo amore*, 76.
110. Ibid., front jacket text, attributed to an unnamed article by Lorenzo Mondo in *La Stampa* (Turin), October 26, 1977.
111. Pintor, "La lotta contro gli idoli (*Americana*)."
112. Pintor, "The Struggle against Idols," 162–170.

113. *Il mestiere*, 382 (entry for December 29, 1949).

114. Ernesto Ferrero, *I migliori anni della nostra vita* (Milan: Feltrinelli, 2005), 68.

115. Vittorini translated twenty books by eight American authors, twenty-three books by eight English authors, one from Spanish (García Lorca), and one from French (Philippe Hériat), for a total of forty-five books by eighteen different authors. Pavese published seventeen translations representing fourteen different authors, not counting his contribution to the translation of Toynbee's *A Study of History, Abridged*.

116. Rodocanachi published around ten translations under her own name, including one of Dylan Thomas's *Portrait of the Artist as a Young Dog* which Vittorini accepted for publication by Einaudi in the "Gettoni" series that he edited. Dylan Thomas, *Ritratto di giovane artista*, trans. Lucia Rodocanachi (Turin: Einaudi, 1955). Because Vittorini and Montale destroyed her letters to them, what we know of her role comes mainly from their letters to her, which are available at http://www.ad900.it/homesito.asp?IDSezione=34&IDSito=2# (accessed November 4, 2007). For a discussion of her contribution to Vittorini and Montale's translations see Jane Dunnett, "Translation and Concealment: The Lost Voice of Lucia Rodocanachi," *Journal of Romance Studies* 4, no. 2 (2004): 37–53; and Valerio Ferme, "Che ve ne sembra dell'America?: Notes on Elio Vittorini's Translation Work and William Saroyan," in *Italica* 75, no. 3 (Autumn 1998): 377–98.

117. Lorenzo Mondo, *Quell'antico ragazzo* (Milan: Rizzoli, 2006), 45; Sergio Pautasso, "Appendice," *Americana: Raccolta di narratori*, ed. Elio Vittorini (Milan: Bompiani, 1968), 1054.

118. Vittorini to Pavese, Milan, August 21, 1940, *Lettere I*, 555–56.

119. I have taken most of the pre-publication details and printing history from Dunnett, "Foreign Literature in Fascist Italy."

120. Pavese to Vittorini, Turin, May 27, 1942, *Lettere I*, 634.

121. Titled, in a reference to the book's heft, "Scrittori e Zavorra" [Writers and Ballast] in *Meridiano di Roma*, Rome, May 2, 1943, 1.

122. They were, in order, Irving, Poe, Hawthorne, Melville, Twain, Harte, Bierce, Howells, Henry James, Crane, O. Henry, Norris, London, Dreiser, Cather, Cabell, Stein, Anderson, O'Neill, Lardner, Evelyn Scott, F. Scott Fitzgerald, Kay Boyle, Morey Callaghan, Faulkner, Hemingway, Wilder, Cain, Steinbeck, Wolfe, Caldwell, Saroyan, and Fante.

123. Alberto Moravia, for example, thought that "to include Hemingway and Cain in the same grouping for the bad reason that they were both Americans was, all things considered, culturally damaging." See "Mito e province," in *Corriere della Sera* (Milan), June 25, 1970, 11.

124. Umberto Eco, "Il cuore rosso del sogno americano," *L'Unità* (Milan), November 10, 2001, available online at http://www.ilportoritrovato.net/html/edicolaeco3.html (accessed November 29, 2007).

125. Vittorini, *Americana*, 2–3.

126. Ibid., 45–46.

127. Ibid., 242.

128. Ibid., 743.

129. Ibid., 964.

130. Patrizia Lorenzi-Davitti, *Pavese e la cultura americana: Fra mito e razionalità* (Messina-Florence: G. D'Anna, 1975), 186.

8. "Storia passata"

1. Reprinted as "William Faulkner: Un angelo senza cura d'anime," *Lett. am.*, 167–70. Because of financial difficulties the editors of *La Cultura* drastically reduced the size of the review in 1934. Through 1933 issues ran 120 to 160 pages, but beginning in 1934 they rarely amounted to more than twenty, including the cover and back page. Thus, Pavese had to reduce the length of his essays.

2. See *William Faulkner: The Contemporary Reviews*, ed. M. Thomas Inge (Cambridge: Cambridge University Press, 1995), xiii, 53.

3. Pavese to Chiuminatto, Turin, April 2, 1932, *Chiuminatto Correspondence*, 158.

4. "Le biografie romanzate di Sinclair Lewis," *La Cultura* 13, no. 3 (May 1934): 44–45; in English as "The Fictionalized Biographies of Sinclair Lewis," in Cesare Pavese, *American Literature: Essays and Opinions*, trans. Edwin Fussell (Berkeley: University of California Press, 1970), 146–49. Unless otherwise indicated all English quotes from this essay are from Fussell's translation.

5. Pavese to Chiuminatto, Turin, July 31, 1930, *Chiuminatto Correspondence*, 90.

6. In editing Pavese's American essays (*La letteratura americana e altri saggi*, cited here as *Lett. am.*), Calvino chose to group them not chronologically but by subject. These radically different views of Lewis and his language lie only three pages apart, and the contrast is made even more stark.

7. My translation of original at Pavese, *Lett. am.*, 30. Pavese was responding to, and cited, Benjamino De Ritis, "Mente puritana in corpo pagano" [A Puritan mind in a pagan body], *Nuova Antologia*, February 16, 1934.

8. Pavese to Chiuminatto, Turin, January 24, 1933, *Chiuminatto Correspondence*, 167; Chiuminatto to Pavese, Chicago, March 8, 1933, ibid., 168.

9. See *Lettere I*, 361 and 366.

10. Pavese to Luigi Rusca, Turin, late June/early July 1933, *Lettere I*, 365.

11. See *Lettere I*, 369–72.

12. Tina Pizzardo, *Senza pensarci due volte* [Without Thinking Twice About It] (Bologna: Il Mulino, 1996), 163–64.

13. *Il mestiere*, 93 (entry for February 25, 1938).

14. Pizzardo, *Senza pensarci*, 164–65.

15. Ibid., 165.

16. In his journal entry of July 21, 1946, Pavese noted that he was rereading Frazer and asked himself, "In 1933 what did you find in this book?" (*Il Mestiere*, 319). In a June 29, 1949, letter to Ernesto de Martino he described the book as the one that "converted him to ethnology" (*Lettere II*, 406).

17. "Ancestors," in Cesare Pavese, *Disaffections: Complete Poems, 1930–1950*, trans. Geoffrey Brock (Port Townsend, Wash.: Copper Canyon Press, 2002), 27.

18. No manuscripts have yet been discovered for the 1934 essays on Faulkner and Lewis.

19. Pizzardo, *Senza pensarci*, 161–70.

20. *Il mestiere*, 12 (entry for October 11, 1935).

21. The prefaces were to translations of Gertrude Stein's *The Autobiography of Alice B. Toklas* (1938) and *Three Lives* (1940) and to Melville's "Benito Cereno" (1940). In addition, at his publisher's request, he wrote a two-page "Notice to Readers" (*Avvertenza*) to his 1941 translation of Christopher Morley's *The Trojan Horse*.

22. Einaudi published the translation in 1938 as *Autobiografia di Alice Toklas*; the preface is reprinted in *Lett. am.*, 171–73, and an English translation appears in Pavese, *American Literature*, 153–55.

23. Einaudi published the translation in 1940 as *Tre esistenze*; the preface is reprinted in *Lett. am.*, 173–76, and an English translation appears in Pavese, *American Literature*, 161–65.

24. Pavese, *American Literature*, 163, 162.

25. Pavese to Gertrude Stein, Turin, April 11, 1938, in "Lettere di Cesare Pavese e di Alberto Moravia," *Sincronie* 15 (January–June 2004): 12.

26. The novella was published in a stand-alone volume as Herman Melville, *Benito Cereno* (Turin: Einaudi, 1940). Pavese's preface is reprinted in *Lett. am.*, 97–101, and Fussell's English translation in Pavese, *American Literature*, 156–60.

27. All quotes are from Fussell's translations of the two prefaces. The preface to *Moby-Dick* is found at Pavese, *American Literature*, 69–74.

28. Laura Nay and Giuseppe Zaccaria, "La ricezione critica," in *Romanzi*, 1115. Einaudi's 2001 edition of *Paesi tuoi* includes a compilation of the critical reception of just this novel, also by Nay and Zaccaria; it expands on that included in *Romanzi*.

29. Understandably enough, the only English translation of the novel does not attempt to capture the sense of the original title: Pavese, *The Harvesters*, trans. A. E. Murch (London: Peter Owen, 1961).

30. Salvatore Rosati, review of *Paesi tuoi*, in "Antologia della critica," in Cesare Pavese, *Paesi tuoi* (Turin: Einaudi, 2001), 115; originally published in *L'Italia che scrive* 19, no. 7–8 (1941): 216–18.

31. Emilio Cecchi, review of *Paesi tuoi*, in ibid., 118–19; originally published in *Nuova Antologia* 1679 (1942): 66–67.

32. Leslie A. Fiedler, "Introducing Cesare Pavese," in *No! In Thunder: Essays on Myth and Literature* (Boston: Beacon Press, 1960), 147.

33. "L'influsso degli eventi," *Lett. am.*, 247.

34. Tibor Wlassics, "Il primo Pavese 'americano': *Paesi Tuoi*," in *Pavese falso e vero: Vita, poetica, narrativa* (Turin: Centro Studi Piemontesi, 1987), 107.

35. Eugenio Galvano, review of *Paesi tuoi*, in Pavese, *Paesi Tuoi* (2001 ed.), 114; originally published in *Primato*, July 15, 1941.

36. Pavese to Pinelli, Turin, December 4, 1939, *Lettere I*, 548–49 (emphasis in original).

37. Pavese, *Lett. am.*, 42; originally published as "Sherwood Anderson," *La Cultura* 10, no. 5 (May 1931).

38. Rosati, review of *Paesi tuoi*, 116.

39. Luigi Vigliani, review of *Paesi tuoi*, in Pavese, *Paesi Tuoi* (2001 ed.), 117; originally published in *Leonardo* 12 (1941): 216–18.

40. Cecchi, review of *Paesi tuoi*, 119.
41. Alberto Moravia, "Pavese decadente," in *L'uomo come fine e altri saggi* (Milan: Bompiani, 1964), 187–91.
42. "I morti di Spoon River," reprinted as "Il poeta dei destini" in *Lett. am.*, 64–72, and in English as "The Dead at Spoon River," in Pavese, *American Literature*, 168–76.
43. Pavese, *American Literature*, 168, 169.
44. "Un negro ci parla," radio broadcast, May 1947; transcript reprinted as "Sono finiti i tempi in cui scoprivamo l'America," in *Lett. am.*, 189–92. Fussell's translation appears as "A Negro Speaks to Us," in Pavese, *American Literature*, 192–95.
45. "Maturità americana," *La Rassegna d'Italia*, December 1946. Reprinted as "Maturità americana," in *Lett. am.*, 177–87. Fussell's translation appears as "American Ripeness," in Pavese, *American Literature*, 177–88.
46. Italo Calvino, introduction to *Lett. am.*, xxi.
47. Fiedler, *No! In Thunder*, 143. The other two he named were Herman Melville and Constance Dowling.
48. F. O. Matthiessen, *American Renaissance* (New York: Oxford University Press, 1941), xiv.
49. F. O. Matthiessen, letter to editors in *Twentieth Century Authors: A Biographical Dictionary of Modern Literature*, ed. Stanley J. Kunitz and Howard Haycraft (New York: H. W. Wilson, 1942), 993.
50. *Il mestiere*, 331 (entry for April 12, 1947).
51. Matthiessen, *American Renaissance*, 286.
52. Pavese, *Lett. am.*, 178.
53. See ibid., 181. Pavese refers back to his own 1933 essay on Whitman to show how he agreed with Matthiessen even before reading him.
54. Ibid., 180.
55. Ibid., 187.
56. Pavese, "Yesterday and Today," in Pavese, *American Literature*, 198; originally published as "Ieri e oggi," *L'Unità*, Turin edition, August 3, 1947; reprinted with same title in *Lett. am.*, 193–96.
57. Pavese, *Lett. am.*, 196.
58. Pavese, "A Useful Book," in Pavese, *American Literature*, 191; originally published as "Un libro utile," *L'Unità*, Turin edition, March 9, 1947; reprinted as "L'arte: non natura ma storia" in *Lett. am.*, 47–49.
59. Pavese, *Lett. am.*, 190.
60. Ibid., 194.
61. Pavese, "La grande angoscia americana," *L'Unità*, Turin edition, March 12, 1950. Reprinted with the same title in *Lett. am.*, 73–75. In English as "The Great American Anguish," in Pavese, *American Literature*, 200–202.
62. Pavese, *Lett. am.*, 189.
63. Ibid.
64. Pavese, *The Moon and the Bonfires*, trans. R. W. Flint (New York: New York Review of Books, 2002), 154.
65. Ibid., 48.
66. Ibid., 14.

67. Ibid., 16.

68. Donald Heiney, "The Geography of the Moon," *Contemporary Literature* 9, no. 4 (Autumn 1968): 533.

69. Pavese, *The Moon and the Bonfires*, trans. R. W. Flint, 98–102.

70. Ibid., 52–54.

71. Pavese to Tullio Pinelli, Reaglie, September 1926, *Lettere I*, 35.

72. Donald Heiney, *America in Modern Italian Literature* (New Brunswick: Rutgers University Press, 1964), 173.

73. Lorenzo Mondo, *Quell'antico ragazzo* (Milan: Rizzoli, 2006), 44.

74. Pavese to his sister Maria, Brancaleone, March 2, 1936, *Lettere I*, 513.

Suggested Reading

In 2007 Luisella Mesiano published her annotated bibliography, *Cesare Pavese di carta e di parole: Bibliografia ragionata e analitica* (Alessandria: Edizioni dell'Orso, 2007). This wonderfully comprehensive and intelligently organized work not only includes bibliographic data on all works by Pavese but lists virtually everything written about him in Italian through the end of 2006. Her many summaries and annotations make the book invaluable and essential for research on all aspects of Pavese.

With such a resource already available, I include here only those sources in Italian that proved to have particular relevance to my topic. As for English-language material, I concentrate on works that can provide both general and specific background information.

PAVESE AND AMERICA, INCLUDING PAVESE AS TRANSLATOR

Bellesia, Giovanna T. "The Translation Work of Elio Vittorini, Cesare Pavese and Eugenio Montale with a Brief Introduction to Translation Theory in Italy." PhD diss., University of North Carolina, 1985.

Ferme, Valerio. "Cesare Pavese and Elio Vittorini's Translations from American Literature: The Americanization of Aesthetics and the Subversion of Culture Under the Fascist Regime." PhD diss., University of California, Berkeley, 1998.

———. *Tradurre è tradire: La traduzione come sovversione culturale sotto il fascismo*. Ravenna: A. Longo Editore, 2002.

Fernandez, Dominique. *Il mito dell'America negli intellettuali italiani dal 1930 al 1950*. Trans. Alfonso Zaccaria. Caltanissetta: Salvatore Sciascia Editore, 1969.
Heiney, Donald. *America in Modern Italian Literature*. New Brunswick, N.J.: Rutgers University Press, 1964.
Jeannet, Angela M., and Louise K. Barnett, ed. and trans. *New World Journeys: Contemporary Italian Writers and the Experience of America*. Westport, Conn.: Greenwood Press, 1977.
Lorenzi-Davitti, Patrizia. *Pavese e la cultura americana: Fra mito e razionalità*. Florence: G. D'Anna, 1975.
Noble, Cinzia D. *Cesare Pavese e la letteratura americana: Saggi e ricerche*. Pescara: Editrice Italica, 1983.
Pietralunga, Mark, ed. *Cesare Pavese and Anthony Chiuminatto: Their Correspondence*. Toronto: University of Toronto Press, 2007.
Stella, Maria. *Cesare Pavese: Traduttore*. Rome: Bulzoni, 1977.
Tondo, Michele. "L'incontro di Pavese con Whitman: La tesi di laurea." *Il Ponte* 25, no. 5 (1969): 708–17.

GENERAL COMMENTARIES ON PAVESE

Biasin, Gian-Paolo. "Cesare Pavese." In *Dictionary of Italian Literature*. Edited by Peter Bondanella and Julia Conaway Bondanella. Westport, Conn.: Greenwood Press, 1996.
———. *Italian Literary Icons*. Princeton Essays in Literature. Princeton: Princeton University Press, 1985.
———. *The Smile of the Gods: A Thematic Study of Cesare Pavese's Works*. Translated by Yvonne Freccero. Ithaca: Cornell University Press, 1968.
Fiedler, Leslie A. "Introducing Cesare Pavese." In *No! In Thunder: Essays on Myth and Literature*. Boston: Beacon Press, 1960.
Flint, R. W. Introduction to *The Selected Works of Cesare Pavese*. New York: New York Review of Books, 2001.
Fussell, Edwin. Introduction to *American Literature, Essays and Opinions*, by Cesare Pavese. Berkeley: University of California Press, 1970.
Heiney, Donald. *Three Italian Novelists: Moravia, Pavese, Vittorini*. Ann Arbor: University of Michigan Press, 1968.
O'Healy, Áine. *Cesare Pavese*. Boston: Twayne, 1988.
Pacifici, Sergio. *A Guide to Contemporary Italian Literature: From Futurism to Neorealism*. Cleveland: World Publishing, 1962.
Riccobono, Rossella, and Doug Thompson, eds. *'Onde di questo mare': Reconsidering Pavese*. Market Harborough, U.K.: Troubador, 2003.
Sontag, Susan. "The Artist as Exemplary Sufferer." In *Against Interpretation, and Other Essays*. New York: Farrar, Straus and Giroux, 1966.

Thompson, Doug. *Cesare Pavese: A Study of the Major Novels and Poems*. Cambridge: Cambridge University Press, 1982.

BIOGRAPHIES

Alterocca, Bona. *Cesare Pavese: Vita e opere di un grande scrittore sempre attuale*. Quart (Aosta): Musumeci Editore, 1985.
Lajolo, Davide. *An Absurd Vice: A Biography of Cesare Pavese*. Edited and translated by Mario Pietralunga and Mark Pietralunga. New York: New Directions, 1983.
Mondo, Lorenzo. *Cesare Pavese*. 5th rev. ed. Milan: Mursia, 1984.
———. *Quell'antico ragazzo*. Milan: Rizzoli, 2006.

LEONE GINZBURG AND THE CONFRATERNITY

Avalle, M. Clara, ed. *Da Odessa a Torino: Conversazioni con Marussia Ginzburg*. Turin: Claudiana, 2002.
Bobbio, Norberto. *A Political Life*. Edited by Alberto Papuzzi, translated by Allan Cameron. Cambridge, England: Polity Press, 2002.
Ginzburg, Leone. *Lettere dal confino, 1940–1943*. Turin: Einaudi, 2004.
———. *Scritti*. Turin: Einaudi, 2000.
Ginzburg, Natalia. *Lessico Famigliare*. Turin: Einaudi, 1999.
———. *Le piccole virtú*. Turin: Einaudi, 1966.
Mila, Massimo. *Scritti civili*. Turin: Einaudi, 1995.
Monti, Augusto. *I miei conti con la scuola: Cronaca scolastica italiana del secolo XX*. Turin: Einaudi, 1965.
Tranfaglia, Nicola, ed. *L'itinerario di Leone Ginzburg*. Turin: Bollati Boringhieri, 1996.

TURIN AND THE UNIVERSITY OF TURIN DURING PAVESE'S LIFETIME

Bobbio, Norberto. *Trent'anni di storia della cultura a Torino, 1920–1950*. Turin: Einaudi, 2002.
D'Orsi, Angelo. *Allievi e maestri: L'Università di Torino nell'otto-novecento*. Turin: Celid, 2002.
———. *La Cultura a Torino tra le due guerre*. Turin: Einaudi, 2000.
Lana, Italo, ed. *Storia Della Facoltà di Lettere e Filosofia dell'Università di Torino*. Florence: Leo S. Olschi, 2000.

TINA PIZZARDO

De Luna, Giovanni. *Donne in oggetto: L'antifascismo nella società italiana, 1922–1939*. Turin: Bollati Boringhieri, 1995.
Pizzardo, Tina. *Senza pensarci due volte*. Bologna: Il Mulino, 1996.

CONSTANCE DOWLING

Kazan, Elia. *A Life*. New York: DaCapo, 1997.
Schickel, Richard. *Elia Kazan: A Biography*. New York: Harper Collins, 2005.
Ventavoli, Lorenzo. "Ricordo di Constance." In *Cesare Pavese: Atti del Convegno internazionale di studi, Torino–Santo Stefano Belbo, 24–27 Ottobre 2001*. Florence: Leo S. Olschki, 2005.

GIULIO EINAUDI AND HIS PUBLISHING HOUSE

Di Stefano, Paolo. *Giulo Einaudi: Tutti i nostri mercoledì*. Bellinzona, Switzerland: Casagrande, 2001.
Einaudi, Giulio. *Frammenti di memoria*. Milan: Rizzoli, 1988.
Ferrero, Ernesto. *I migliori anni della nostra vita*. Milan: Feltrinelli, 2005.
Mangoni, Luisa. *Pensare i libri: La casa editrice Einaudi dagli anni trenta agli anni sessanta*. Turin: Bollati Boringhieri, 1999.

GENERAL BACKGROUND ON ITALY UNDER FASCISM

Bosworth, R. J. B. *Mussolini's Italy: Life under the Fascist Dictatorship, 1915–1945*. New York: Penguin, 2005.
Hughes, H. Stuart. *The United States and Italy*. Rev. ed. Cambridge: Harvard University Press, 1965.
Landrum, Becky, and Mike Landrum. *Americanata: Three Sisters in Italy, 1938*. Philadelphia: Xlibris, 2001.
Marchionatti, Roberto, ed. *"From Our Italian Correspondent": Luigi Einaudi's Articles in* The Economist, *1908–1946*, vol. 2, *1925–1946*. Florence: Leo S. Olschki, 2000.

Illustration Source Credits

With few exceptions, the people who took the photographs included in this book can no longer be identified. Where they can be, they have been. Virtually all the pictures of Pavese, his family, and friends have been previously published in Italy, most more than once and often without attribution or credit, a tradition that goes back to the first Pavese biography in 1960. Davide Lajolo's *Il Vizio Assurdo* (Milan: Il Saggiatore) contains thirty-two photographs, none of them credited or identified by source even though Pavese's sister probably supplied most of the originals. In 1961, in a series of short illustrated biographies called *Chi l'ha visto: biblioteca illustrata dei personaggi,* Trevi editore of Milan published a volume on Pavese, with text by Giuseppe Trevisani. It contains more than sixty photographs, some duplicates of those in the Lajolo book and some new. No credits or sources are listed. Even Einaudi, publishing in 1983 a cumulative catalog for its fiftieth anniversary, *Cinquant'anni di un editore: Le edizioni Einaudi negli anni 1933–1983,* lists no credits or sources for the three pictures of Pavese or for any of the other dozens of photographs that precede the text. Franco Vaccaneo's pictorial biography, *Cesare Pavese, una biografia per immagini: la vita, i libri, le carte, i luoghi* (Cavallermaggiore, Gribaudi, 1989) does include a list of sources but does not link the sources to specific images. Thus, in reproducing here images that appear in this book, which Mr. Vaccaneo has courteously permitted, the original source is not always identified.

In 2007 the Centro Interuniversitario per gli Studi di Letteratura Italiana in Piemonte "Guido Gozzano–Cesare Pavese," in collaboration with other cultural and governmental entities, organized in Turin a major multimedia exhibition about Pavese. In the catalog of the show, *Cesare Pavese e la "sua" Torino*

(Turin: Lindau, 2007), the editors, Mariarosa Masoero and Giuseppe Zaccaria, give specific sources for each image in the catalog, images they selected from the hundreds projected as slides or as parts of filmstrips at the exhibition. I am particularly grateful to Professor Masoero for arranging to provide me with copies of many of the projected images. Those included here are listed together with their original source information.

Author. 4, 46, 47.
Author's collection. 41.
Casa editrice Il Mulino. 31.
Centro Interuniversitario per gli Studi di Letteratura Italiana in Piemonte "Guido Gozzano-Cesare Pavese." 30, 34, 39.
Cesare Pavese e la "sua" Torino
———. Archivio I.R.A., Insegne Reclames Artistiche. 23.
———. Archivio Storico della Città di Torino. 20, 21, 37.
———. Augusta Monferini. 17.
———. Casa editrice Il Mulino. 32.
———. Centro Studi Piero Gobetti, Archivio Fotografico. 10, 13, 14, 15, 35.
———. Cesarina Sini and Maria Luisa Sini Cossa (Fondo Sini). 6, 8, 9.
———. Fondazione Torino Musei, Archivio Fotografico, Fondo Gabinio. 18, 19, 22, 24.
———. Giulio Einaudi editore. 12, 27.
Fondazione Benetton Studi Ricerche: Biblioteca Riccardo e Fernanda Pivano. 33.
Fondazione Cesare Pavese, Santo Stefano Belbo. 1, 2, 3, 5, 11, 16, 26, 29, 38, 40, 42, 43, 44, 45.
Fondazione Franco Antonicelli. 7, 25.
Giulio Einaudi editore. 28, 36.

Index

Adams, Henry, 195
Adventures of Huckleberry Finn (Twain), 230–31
"Aesthetica in nuce" (Croce), 153
Aesthetics as Science of Expression and General Linguistics (*Estetica come scienza dell'espressione e linguistica generale*) (Croce), 153
Allason, Barbara, 59
All Quiet on the Western Front (Remarque), 162
Alterocca, Bona, 31–32, 36, 77, 83, 110, 112–13
America amara (Cecchi), 173, 203, 209
American, The (James), 174
Americana (Vittorini), 207–13; authors included in, 274n.122; Cecchi's introduction to, 173, 204, 208–10; Eco on selection of authors of, 211–12; influence of, 205; Linati as contributor to, 176; Pavese as contributor to, 172, 206; Pintor's review-essay of, 202, 204–5; Pound on selection of authors of, 210–11; Vittorini's introductions to, 173, 208, 212–13

American films. *See* films, American
americanismo: Cecchi and, 173; *L'Enciclopedia Italiana* on, 177–78; Linati as leading *americanista*, 173–74; as not running wide in Italian culture, 180; Pavese's letter to Vittorini as important document of, 209; Pavese's period ends, 225; Soldati and, 202, 203; Vittorini as *americanista*, 205; Vittorini's *Americana* as monument of, 207
American literature and culture: ancient Greek culture compared to, 194; Cecchi on, 172–73; in *La Cultura*, 178–80; Linati on, 173–74; Pavese's change in attitude toward, 215–27, 235–39; Pavese's degree thesis on Whitman, 135–68; Pavese's essays on, 169–201; Pintor on, 203–5; praising as challenge to Italian intellectual environment, 182; Prezzolini on, 174–76; Soldati on, 202–3; types published in translation in Italy, 172; Vittorini on, 205–14. *See also* Anderson, Sherwood; Dos Passos, John;

American literature and culture (*cont.*)
Dreiser, Theodore; Faulkner, William; Hemingway, Ernest; Henry, O.; Lewis, Sinclair; Masters, Edgar Lee; Melville, Herman; Twain, Mark; Whitman, Walt; *and others by name*
American Renaissance, The (Matthiessen), 13, 126, 232–35
American Tragedy, An (Dreiser), 191
America, primo amore (Soldati), 203, 273n.107
Among Women Only (Pavese). See *Tra donne solo* (*Among Women Only*)
Anderson, Sherwood: ancient Greeks compared to by Pavese, 194; Pavese article on, 179, 187, 198; Pavese on compassion of, 191; Pavese on language of, 187, 188, 217, 229; Pavese on provincialism of, 197; in Pavese's construction of tradition for American literature, 196, 213; and Pavese's narrative rapidity, 5; Pavese's style influenced by, 5; Pavese's style in writing about, 199–200; *A Story Teller's Story*, 91–92, 94, 237; in Vittorini's *Americana*, 274n.122
Ann Vickers (Lewis), 216
Antonicelli, Franco, Fig. 25
Arrowsmith, William, 6
"Artist as Exemplary Sufferer, The" (Sontag), 9
As I Lay Dying (Faulkner), 215
Asselineau, Roger, 162
Autobiography of Alice B. Toklas, The (Stein), 86, 225, 276n.22

Babbitt (Lewis), 190, 191
Badoglio, Pietro, 97, 204
Bailey, John, 146, 147–48, 149
Baraldi, Elico, 34
Baravalle, Giovanni, 101, 106, 107, 121, 126
Baretti, Il (journal), 48
Beach, The (Pavese). See *Spiaggia, La* (*The Beach*)

Beats, 95
Beautiful Summer, The (Pavese). See *Bella estate, La* (*The Beautiful Summer*)
Bella estate, La (*The Beautiful Summer*) (Pavese): composition of, 90, 259n.18; favorable reviews of, 128; and Pavese's relationship with Tina Pizzardo, 62, 224; published with *Il diavolo sulle colline* and *Tra donne sole*, 128; Strega Prize for, 29
"Benito Cereno" (Melville), 5, 96, 225, 226–27
Bennett, Arnold, 191
Benton, Thomas Hart, 196
Berenson, Bernard, 173
Biasin, Gian-Paolo, 154
Bierce, Ambrose, 188, 274n.122
Big Money, The (Dos Passos), 86
Billy Budd (Melville), 206, 213
Bitter Rice (*Riso amaro*) (film), 17
Bobbio, Norberto: in "confraternity" of Pavese, 47; on Croce, 152; on Ginzburg, 50–51; liberalism of, 48, 254n.32; on Monti, 41; photograph of, Fig. 14; political passion of, 140
Boccaccio, 45, 202
Boiardo, Matteo Maria, 45
Böll, Heinrich, 2
Bollati, Giulio, 29, 89
Bollati di Saint Pierre, Romilda, 29–30, 31
Bompiani, Valentino, 208, 209
Boringhieri, Paolo, 89
Boyer, Charles, 27
Boyle, Kay, 274n.122
Brancaleone Calabro, 66, 69, Fig. 29
Brock, Geoffrey, 22, 183, 184
Burning Brand, The (Pavese), 68
"By Blue Ontario's Shore" (Whitman), 156

Cabell, James Branch, 274n.122
Cabiria (film), 170
Cain, James M., 5, 213, 228, 242, 274n.122

Cajumi, Arrigo, 180
Caldwell, Erskine, 171, 207, 227, 228, 274n.122
Callaghan, Morey, 274n.122
Calvino, Italo: edits Pavese's essays, 10, 197, 198, 275n.6; as "hard worker in school of Pavese," 88; in literary generation that followed Pavese, 202; on more attention paid to Pavese's suicide than to his work, 9–10; Pavese gives advice to, 128; on Pavese's "American Maturity," 232–33; and Pavese's "Interpretation of Walt Whitman, Poet," 163; on Pavese's poetry turning to his love life, 113; photograph of, Fig. 36; as well-known in English-speaking world, 3; works as editor under Pavese, 89
Camerino, Aldo, 180
Capa, Robert, 26, 28
Captain Smith and Company (*The Voice of the Trumpet*) (Henriques), 260n.44
Carcere, Il (*The Political Prisoner*) (Pavese), 120; and attributions of neorealism to Pavese, 228; as biographical source, 69; delay in publication of, 90; in historical cycle of Pavese's times, 128; personal experience as basis of, 120; publication of, 120, 256n.28; sexual liaison of contrasted with Pavese's situation, 69–70
Carducci, Giosuè, 145
Carli, Dan, Fig. 11
Carroll, Paul Vincent, 26
Casa in collina, La (*The House on the Hill*) (Pavese), 120–25; centrality in Pavese's work, 119; characters and places as identifiable, 120–21; as classic, 2, 10, 118; *Il compagno* contrasted with, 118; cowardly betrayal as theme of, 124; dialogue in, 4–5; ending of, 9, 122, 123–24, 250n.21; on Fascist dead, 9, 106, 122; in historical cycle of Pavese's times, 128; length of, 90; Pavese's reputation solidified by, 125; personal experience as basis of, 120; plot of, 121–22; priest and rector as depicted in, 106; prose of, 6; publication of, 120; strong, attractive woman in, 245; as "symbolic reality," 128, 247; universalism of, 8–9
Casa Italiana (Columbia University), 54–55, 174
Catalfamo, Antonio, 154
Cather, Willa, 195, 274n.122
Cazzullo, Aldo, 95
Cecchi, Emilio, 172–73; *America amara*, 173, 203, 209; on American influence on Pavese's *Paesi tuoi*, 228, 230; introduction to Vittorini's *Americana*, 173, 204, 208–10; Pavese on introduction to Vittorini's *Americana*, 173, 209–10; Pavese's view of American contrasted with, 181; Pintor on, 202; in previous generation of critics, 201
Celati, Gianni, 12
Centro Gozzano-Pavese, 2
Cernuschi, Teodoro, 34
"Chanting the Square Deific" (Whitman), 157
Chapman, John Jay, 145
Chase, Richard, 142
childhood, Pavese on destiny as located in, 6, 103–5
Chiuminatto, Anthony, 53–54; *La Cultura* read by, 178; Pavese ceases corresponding with, 218, 222; and Pavese's lack of sources on Whitman, 145; Pavese writes about Columbia scholarship to, 55; Pavese writes about his degree thesis to, 136, 151, 159; Pavese writes about Lewis to, 217; Pavese writes about slang to, 186–87; sends Pavese library books from Green Bay, 180–81
Ciau Masino (Pavese), 82, 183, 185, 246

INDEX · 287

Collegio Trevisio (Casale Monferrato), 100
Collezione di studi religiosi, etnologici e psicologici, 119
Columbia University, 54–55, 174
Come gli Americani scoprirono L'Italia, 1750–1850 (Prezzolini), 175, 180, 218–19
Compagno, Il (Pavese): as expression of Pavese's political commitment, 117–18; as "the extremes: naturalism and detached symbols," 128; as helping assuage Pavese's guilt, 129; length of, 90; publication of, 119
Conversazione in Sicilia (*Conversations in Sicily*) (Vittorini), 205, 209
Crane, Stephen, 274n.122
Croce, Adele Rossi, 152
Croce, Benedetto: aesthetic theory in Pavese's thesis on Whitman, 138, 151–59; as anti-Fascist, 152; on art as lyrical intuition, 153–54, 155; contributes to Gobetti's *Il Baretti*, 48; on criticism as judgment, 156; daughter lives near Pavese in Turin, 55, 152; Fascists proscribe works from liceos and universities, 138–39; and Ginzburg, 50, 152, 159–60; Laterza as publisher of, 159; literary and intellectual influence of, 151–52; Matthiessen compared with, 234; Monti enlarges on idea of history of, 41; Pavese's approach to American literature and, 182, 196; and Pavese's "Interpretation of Walt Whitman, Poet," 163, 166; on Pavese's thesis on Whitman, 160, 161; philosophy of the spirit of, 152–53; on unity of art, 154, 155–56
"Crossing Brooklyn Ferry" (Whitman), 149, 156
Crowd, The (film), 171, 199
Crowther, Bosley, 17, 27

Cultura, La (journal), 56, 65, 178–80, 215, 275n.1

D'Annunzio, Gabriele, 145, 170
Dante: Croce on, 154; in Fascist view of Italian tradition, 182; Monti's teaching of, 41–42; in Pavese's early cultural milieu, 48
Dantine, Helmut, 27
"Death Will Come and Will Have Your Eyes" (Pavese), 22, 30
Defoe, Daniel, 86, 207
De Giorgis, Ettore, 69
De Luna, Giovanni, 57, 76, 83, 255n.2, 257n.49
De Martino, Ernesto, 119
De Santis, Giuseppe, 17
de Selincourt, Basil, 146, 147, 149, 165–66
destiny, Pavese on childhood and, 6, 103–5
Devil in the Hills, The (Pavese). See *Diavolo sulle colline, Il* (*The Devil in the Hills*)
Dialoghi con Leucò (*Dialogues with Leucò*) (Pavese): composition of, 116, 118; as "the extremes: naturalism and detached symbols," 128; Garufi as influence on, 115; Pavese's suicide note inscribed in, 33–34; publication of, 119; "tormented restless one" in, 30
Diavolo sulle colline, Il (*The Devil in the Hills*) (Pavese): characters not blamed for their actions in, 7; composition of, 118, 126; dialogue in, 4; morality in, 7; published with *La bella estate* and *Tra donne sole*, 128; as still rewarding, 10; strong, attractive woman in, 245
Dickinson, Emily, 173
Dodsworth (Lewis), 190
Dos Passos, John: *The Big Money*, 86; *The 42nd Parallel*, 218; *Manhattan Transfer*, 171, 172,

199; Pavese article on, 179; Pavese links Whitman to, 165; Pavese on American language and, 217; Pavese on compassion of, 191
Dowling, Constance, 25–28; acting career of, 27–28, 251n.19; affair with Robert Capa, 26, 28; affair with John Houseman, 26–27, 28; affair with Elia Kazan, 25–27, 28; affair with Pavese, 13–14, 17–28; as hoyden, 28; as incarnation of America to Pavese, 20, 28; as interrupting Pavese's creative process, 130; in Italy to revive her film career, 17; last letter to Pavese, 25; last postcard to Pavese, 252n.24; meets Pavese, 18; *The Moon and the Bonfires* dedicated to, 23; Pavese cries for, 222; with Pavese in Cervinia, 18, 28; Pavese's goodbye letter to, 24; Pavese's poems to, 18–19, 22, 23–24, 30; photograph with Pavese, Fig. 43; photograph with sister Doris, Fig. 42; possible return to Italy of, 33; publicity photo of, Fig. 41; returns to United States, 23; uses and is used by men, 28
Dowling, Doris, 17–18, 21, 28, 29, 32, Fig. 42, Fig. 45
"Draga, La" (Pavese), 82–83, 87
Dreiser, Theodore: American vulgate in, 188; Pavese on compassion of, 190–91; Pavese on provincialism of, 197; Pavese's article on, 179, 199; in Pavese's construction of tradition for American literature, 196; in Vittorini's *Americana*, 274n.122
Dubliners (Joyce), 33
Dunnett, Jane, 173

Eco, Umberto, 3, 12, 211–12, 251n.28
Einaudi, Giulio: Collezione di studi religiosi, etnologici e psicologici approved by, 119; on competition between Pavese and Vittorini, 206; in "confraternity" of Pavese, 47; on Croce, 152; family background of, 47; in founding of Einaudi publishing house, 51; on Pavese as hard worker, 88; Pavese hired by, 87; Pavese moves to same street as family of, 55; and Pavese's membership in National Fascist Party, 56; photograph of, Fig. 15; photograph of Pavese by, Fig. 39; returns to Turin in 1945, 106, 109; vacations at Bocca di Magra, 30
Einaudi, Luigi, 47, 152
Einaudi, Mario, 180, 271n.45
Einaudi publishing house: becomes Italy's most prestigious literary publisher, 125; becomes Levi's publisher, 263n.34; Collezione di studi religiosi, etnologici e psicologici published by, 119; *La Cultura* taken over by, 178, 179; Ginzburg and, 51, 87–88, 109; growth in influence and prestige of, 88; Pavese joins, 87–88; *Politecnico* published by, 206; reorganization of, 110, 206; three offices of, 88, 110; Vittorini at, 205, 206; after World War II, 109–10; during World War II, 96–97, 98
Eliot, T. S., 145, 159
emigration to America, 170
Enciclopedia Italiana, L', 177–78
Encyclopaedia Britannica, 153, 177
English language: literature translated into, 2–3; Pavese on American vulgate, 182–83, 185, 186–89, 217; translation of Pavese's work into, 1
"Estate" (Pavese), 87
Estetica come scienza dell'espressione e linguistica generale (*Aesthetics as Science of Expression and General Linguistics*) (Croce), 153
Excelsior (Longfellow), 142

"Faces" (Whitman), 157
Fackenthal, Frank D., 54
Fante, John, 208, 211, 274n.122
Farewell to Arms, A (Hemingway), 60, 91
Fascism: American literary freedom contrasted with, 47, 140; anti-Americanism of, 178; Croce as anti-Fascist, 152; Croce's works proscribed from liceos and universities under, 138–39; and discovery of American literature, 214; Ginzburg's opposition to, 50, 51; internal exile used by, 66; *Italianità* of, 182; on literature as propaganda, 154; Mussolini comes to power, 39; Pavese joins National Fascist Party, 56; Pavese's early cultural milieu as liberally anti-Fascist, 48; Pavese's thesis on Whitman affected by censorship of, 139–40; and Pound's review of Vittorini's *Americana*, 210; Prezzolini associated with, 174; Vittorini as party member, 206; Whitman contrasted with models of, 168; Whitman's stress on action compared with, 45. *See also* Mussolini, Benito
"Fast Anchor'd Eternal O love!" (Whitman), 157
Faulkner, William: *As I Lay Dying*, 215; *The Hamlet*, 96; *Light in August*, 207; Pavese article on, 180, 215, 219; Pavese on lack of compassion of, 191; Pavese on language of, 188; Pavese overlooks in his critical scheme, 195; Pivano translates works of, 95; *Sanctuary*, 215; seen as influence on Pavese's *Paesi tuoi*, 227, 228; in Vittorini's *Americana*, 213, 274n.122
"Faulkner, a Bad Pupil of Anderson" (Pavese), 188
Fenoglio, Beppe, 3
Feria d'agosto (Pavese), 110
Ferme, Valerio, 53–54, 155, 170, 171, 200
Ferrero, Ernesto, 89, 205

Fiedler, Leslie, 1, 6, 10, 49, 228, 231, 233
films, American: influence in Italy of, 170–72; Pavese on, 177, 181, 194; Pintor on, 203
Fitzgerald, F. Scott: Pavese overlooks in his critical scheme, 195; Pivano translates works of, 95; in Vittorini's *Americana*, 211, 274n.122
42nd Parallel, The (Dos Passos), 218
Franchi, Pietro Luxardo, 250n.12
Frank, Tenney, 179
Frassinelli, Carlo, Fig. 25
Frazer, Sir James, 222
Frumento, Luigi, 100, 121
Fuoco Grande (Pavese), 115
Fussell, Edwin, 201
Futurism, 45

Galsworthy, John, 207
Galvano, Eugenio, 229
Gamberale, Luigi, 145, 161
García Márquez, Gabriel, 3
Garufi, Bianca, 110–16; Pavese acts as mentor to, 115; Pavese composes poems for, 113–15; Pavese links with Pizzardo and Pivano, 113; Pavese offers to let her read his diary, 111, 113; Pavese proposes marriage to, 110; Pavese's *Dialogues with Leucò* as indirectly dedicated to, 115; photograph of, Fig. 34
"Gelosia" (Pavese), 87
genre fiction, 172
Gentile, Emilio, 178
Giacchero, Remo, Fig. 9, Fig. 11
Gigliucci, Roberto, 5
Ginnasio Liceo Massimo D'Azeglio, 39
Ginsberg, Allen, 95
Ginzburg, Fedor Nikolaevic, 49–50
Ginzburg, Leone, 49–51; and acceptance of Pavese's thesis on Whitman, 139; arrest of, 50, 65; in "confraternity" of Pavese, 47; and Croce, 50, 152, 159–60; and *La Cultura*, 271n.44; death of,

51, 102; at Einaudi publishing house, 51, 87–88, 109; liberalism of, 48; Pavese feels inadequate and guilty in relation to, 52; Pavese's guilt over death of, 116, 129; and Pavese's membership in National Fascist Party, 56; Pavese visits during special surveillance of, 74; photograph with Pavese, Antonicelli, and Frassinelli, Fig. 25; political passion of, 140; on publishing Pavese's thesis on Whitman, 160–61; refuses to sign Fascist loyalty oath, 51; returns to Rome after fall of Mussolini, 100–101; as writer, 50, 51, 254n.38

Ginzburg, Natalia: "adolescent" used to describe Pavese by, 21; on Einaudi publishing house in late 1940s, 125; on Pavese and his sister Maria, 38; on Pavese at Einaudi publishing house, 88; on Pavese's poetry, 184; on Pavese's reaction to Tina Pizzardo's marriage, 74; on Pavese's suicide, 130; photograph of, Fig. 12; on political commitment among writers, 108–9; in rejection of Levi's *Se questo è un uomo*, 125, 263n.34

Giustizia e Libertà (GL), 50, 59, 64–65

Gobetti, Piero, 48, 50

Gold Bug, The (Poe), 186

Golden Bough, The (Frazer), 222

Goldwyn, Samuel, 27–28

"Good-Bye My Fancy" (Whitman), 156

Grandmothers, The (Wescott), 181

Grass, Günter, 2

Gregory, Lady, 173

Grey, Zane, 171, 269n.22

Grillo, Count Carlo, 126

Grimaldi, Alda, 18

Guglielminetti, Marziano, 2

Hamlet, The (Faulkner), 96

Hard Labor (Pavese), 70

Harte, Bret, 188, 274n.122

Harvesters, The (Pavese). See *Paesi tuoi (The Harvesters)*

Hawthorne, Nathaniel, 179, 212, 213, 234, 274n.122

Heiney, Donald, 245

Hemingway, Ernest: *A Farewell to Arms*, 60, 91; and Pavese's narrative rapidity, 5; Pivano translates works of, 95; preface to Vittorini's *Conversations in Sicily*, 205; in Vittorini's *Americana*, 213, 274n.122

Henriques, Robert, 260n.44

Henry, O.: American vulgate in, 186, 188, 217; Pavese on Prampolini's translation of, 198; in Pavese's construction of tradition for American literature, 196, 213; Pavese's essay on, 187–88; in Vittorini's *Americana*, 274n.122

Houseman, John, 26–27, 28

House on the Hill, The (Pavese). See *Casa in collina, La (The House on the Hill)*

Howells, William Dean, 145, 186, 274n.122

Hughes, H. Stuart, 140, 151

Hugo, Victor, 45

"Interpretation of the Poetry of Walt Whitman" (Pavese), 135–68; acceptance of, 139; as appreciation more than scholarly criticism, 167–68; as calculated critical subversion with political subtext, 140; chapter titles of, 140–41, 264n.17; conversational tone of, 150–51; core contention of, 141; Croce on, 160, 161; Croce's aesthetic theory in, 138, 151–59; intended as revelation of Whitman to Italy, 136, 145; as intersection of Pavese's interest in Whitman with Italian critical theory, 136; number of pages of, 137; Olivero rejects, 138–39, 150; Pavese attempts to publish, 159–61; Pavese gathers

Interpr. of Whitman poetry (*cont.*)
material for, 135; as Pavese's first major work on American literature, 54; Pavese stresses in correspondence with Prezzolini, 55; on pioneer figure in Whitman, 141–43, 155; *relatore* for, 137–38; revisions for possible publication, 161–62; title page of, 137, 139; varied and contradictory nature of *Leaves of Grass* neglected by, 144; virtues and faults of, 137; on Whitman as the poet of making poetry, 146, 155, 168; Whitman criticism criticized by, 144–50; Whitman-like bravura prose in, 149; on Whitman's "myth of discovery," 141–43, 155

"Interpretation of Walt Whitman, Poet" (Pavese), 162–68

"Introducing Cesare Pavese" (Fiedler), 1

Irving, Washington, 208, 210, 274n.122

Istituto Privato Trombetta, 39

Istituto Sociale, 39, 202

Italian Painters of the Renaissance (Berenson), 173

James, Henry, 174, 195, 225, 274n.122
James, William, 144, 145
Jannaccone, Pasquale, 145
Job of Living, The (Pavese), 68
Joyce, James, 33, 55, 169, 173

Kaye, Danny, 27
Kazan, Elia, 25–27, 28
Kerouac, Jack, 95
Knickerbocker Holiday (film), 27
Koffler, Richard M., 68, 93
Korean War, 29

Lajolo, Davide, 32, 36, 38, 83, 99, 139, 155, 264n.13
Langhe region, 35, Fig. 4
Lardner, Ring, 274n.122
"Last Blues, to Be Read Some Day" (Pavese), 23–24

Laterza, Giovanni, 160
Laterza, Giuseppe, & Figli S.p.A., 159–61
Lavorare stanca (Pavese): "I mari del Sud" compared with, 183; Pavese asks Tina Pizzardo about poem selection for, 63; Pavese corrects proofs for, 70; Pavese sends copy to Tina, 72; Pavese's work as translator as more important to his professional reputation than, 225; and reversal of Pavese's opinion about American literature, 219; translation into English of, 70; as "words and sensations" to Pavese, 128; as written during years of discovery, 184–85

Lawrence, D. H., 145, 206, 207

Leaves of Grass (Whitman): Gamberale's translation of, 145, 161; Pavese gives Fernanda Pivano copy of, 92; Pavese makes capsule summaries of each poem, 135–36; Pavese reads in summer between liceo and university, 45; in Pavese's degree thesis, 141–49, 156–59; in Pavese's "Interpretation of Walt Whitman, Poet," 162–68; Pavese's marginal notes in liceo library copy of, 135

Levi, Primo, 125, 263n.34

Lewis, Sinclair: *Ann Vickers*, 216; *Babbitt*, 190, 191; *Dodsworth*, 190; *Our Mr. Wrenn*, 171; Pavese on compassion of, 191; Pavese on language of, 186–87, 188, 217, 223, 229, 275n.6; Pavese on provincialism of, 191, 197; in Pavese's construction of tradition for American literature, 196, 213; Pavese's first essay on, 55, 169, 179, 186–87; Pavese's second essay on, 55, 180, 216–18, 219, 223–24; Pavese's style influenced by, 5; Pavese turns against, 216–18; *Work of Art*, 180, 216

Lewisohn, Ludwig, 177, 208–9, 211

Liberation Day, 96

Liberty Jones (musical), 26–27
Life and Literature in the Roman Republic (Frank), 179
Light in August (Faulkner), 207
Linati, Carlo, 173–74; on America as lacking culture, 176; Pavese on view of America of, 177; Pavese's view of America contrasted with that of, 172, 181; in previous generation of critics, 201; *Scrittori anglo-americani d'oggi*, 173; travel books written by, 203
Lindsay, Vachel, 188
literature in translation, 2–3
"L. of G's Purport" (Whitman), 156
London, Jack, 171, 175, 188, 269n.22, 274n.122
Longfellow, Henry Wadsworth, 142
Lorenzi-Davitti, Patrizia, 10, 214
Lost Weekend, The (film), 17
Lotte di giovani (Pavese), 47
Ludwig, Emil, 216
Luna e i falò, La (*The Moon and the Bonfires*) (Pavese), 239–46; America in, 239–40, 242–45; brings together themes associated with Pavese, 239; characters not blamed for their actions in, 7; as classic, 2, 10, 118; composition of, 127; dedicated to Constance Dowling, 23; dialogue in, 4; in historical cycle of Pavese's times, 128; length of, 90; misogyny of, 244, 245; morality in, 7; Pavese as written out after, 129; Pavese's view of, 128; setting in Pavese's native town, 7–8; as "symbolic reality," 128, 247; symbolism in, 6; translation into other languages, 127–28; violence against women in, 82, 240–42

Maffi, Bruno, 65
Mangano, Silvana, 17
Manhattan Transfer (Dos Passos), 171, 172, 199
"Mari del Sud, I" (Pavese): as advance in Pavese's poetry, 183–84; beginning of, 183–84; cousin character recalls Whitman and Melville, 193; as story-poem, 185
Masoero, Mariarosa, 2, 47
Masters, Edgar Lee: Pavese article on, 179, 195; Pavese on death of, 199, 238–39; Pavese on language of, 188; in Pavese's construction of tradition for American literature, 196, 213; *Spoon River Anthology*, 60, 91, 94, 199, 225, 231–32, 235
Matteotti, Giacomo, 48, 254n.31
Matthiessen, F. O., 13, 23, 126, 232–35, 236, 246
Maugham, W. Somerset, 207
Mayo, Virginia, 27
McAlmon, Robert, 210, 211
McCain, Rea, 265n.29
Melville, Herman: adventure films create favorable climate for translation of, 171–72; ancient Greeks compared to by Pavese, 194, 226; barbarism and art combined in, 194–95; "Benito Cereno," 5, 96, 225, 226–27; *Billy Budd*, 206, 213; Cecchi writes on, 173; Celati as translator of, 12; as complete man to Pavese, 193; Matthiessen and, 233, 234; Pavese creates bravura personality based on, 224; Pavese essays on, 179, 235; Pavese on combination of scholarship and seamanship in, 12, 194; Pavese on sane and balanced approach to life and art in, 192–93, 246; in Pavese's construction of tradition for American literature, 196, 213; Pavese's style influenced by, 5; on "Ripeness is all" in *King Lear*, 126, 234; in Vittorini's *Americana*, 212–13, 274n.122. See also *Moby-Dick* (Melville)
Mestiere di vivere, Il (Pavese): editions of, 256n.25; entries after Constance Dowling's rejection, 23; entries while at Serralunga and Casale, 102–3; entry at end of 1938, 89–90; entry at end of 1939,

Mestiere di vivere, Il (*cont.*)
90; entry at end of 1945, 115–16; entry at end of 1948, 125–26; loneliness as theme of, 119, 192; meaning of title, 68–69; only entry touching on his upbringing, 37–38; Pavese makes first entry in, 68; Pavese offers manuscript to Tina Pizzardo, 80, 113; Pavese offers to let Bianca Garufi read, 111, 113; Tina Pizzardo's memoirs in understanding of, 83; publication makes Pavese more interesting to public, 9; as source of information about Pavese, 11; "We do not remember days, we remember moments," 92

Micheli, Silvio, 109

Mickey Mouse, 171

Mila, Massimo: arrest in May 1935, 65; in "confraternity" of Pavese, 47; liberalism of, 48; meets Anthony Chiuminatto, 53–54; as partisan, 100; on Pavese translating caption cards for silent film, 171; photograph of, Fig. 13; prison sentence of, 65–66

Miller, Edwin, 144

Moby-Dick (Melville): Ahab as never surrendering to fate, 190; barbarism and art combined in, 195; Greek tragedy compared to by Pavese, 194; Pavese as translator of, 5, 12, 55, 169, 172, 179, 182, 225, 226; Pavese's praise for, 227; Pivano writes thesis on, 92; Pizzardo reads Pavese's translation of, 59; Sturani does cover art for Pavese's translation of, 39

Moll Flanders (Defoe), 86

Mondo, Lorenzo: on America as "liberating shock" for Pavese, 246; on *La casa in collina*, 119; on Garufi, 110; on Pavese's courting of Pivano, 94; on Pavese's letter to Pizzardo from Brancaleone Calabro, 68; on Pavese's mother, 36–37; on Pavese's "The Return of Man," 107; "Pavese, The Secret Notebook," 105–6; on Vittorini's *Americana*, 207

Monferini, Enzo, 75, 84, Fig. 11, Fig. 17

Montale, Eugenio, 48, 172, 176, 207, 208

Monti, Augusto, 40; arrest in May 1935, 65; as Crocean, 152, 154–55; Dante as taught by, 41–42; on *Dialogues with Leucò*, 115; friendship with Pavese, 42–44; impact on Pavese of, 44; intellectual and psychological wholesomeness of, 42; on *letterati*, 40; letter of condolence on Pavese's mother's death, 37; as literature teacher of Pavese, 39–44; on Pavese as eternal adolescent, 21; on Pavese as workhorse of Einaudi firm, 87; Pavese becomes Pivano's, 96; on Pavese's friends, 49; on Pavese's thesis on Whitman, 155; Pavese writes from exile in Brancaleone Calabro, 69; photograph of, Fig. 10; photograph with members of confraternity, Fig. 11; prison sentence of, 66; on rejection of Pavese's thesis on Whitman, 138, 264n.12; on sane and balanced approach, 192, 246; as writer, 40

Moon and the Bonfires, The (Pavese). See *Luna e i falò, La* (*The Moon and the Bonfires*)

Moravia, Alberto, 230, 274n.123

More, Paul, 145

Morley, Christopher, 96

Motta, Mario, 33, 116

Motta, Teresa, 116–17

movies, American. See American films

Musil, Robert, 2

Mussolini, Benito: arrest of, 204; comes to power, 39; consolidates dictatorial regime, 48, 139; on Croce, 138, 152; cultural Americanism during regime

of, 170; as head of Republic of Salò, 97–98; Matteotti crisis, 48, 254n.31; Prezzolini biography of, 174; removed as prime minister, 95, 97. *See also* Fascism
Mutterle, Anco Marzio, 8
"Myself and Mine" (Whitman), 156
myth: Frazer's *The Golden Bough* catalyzes Pavese's interest in, 222; Bianca Garufi shares Pavese's interest in, 110; Pavese's *Dialogues with Leucò* on, 115; Pavese's World War II musings on, 101–5

Name of the Rose, The (Eco), 3
Napolitano, G. G., 162
Nay, Laura, 227, 276n.28
Nencioni, Enrico, 145
neorealism, 3, 228
Neri, Ferdinando, 139
Norris, Frank, 274n.122

O'Casey, Sean, 173
Of Mice and Men (Steinbeck), 86, 228
Olivero, Federico, 137–39, 150, 264n.12
Omoo (Melville), 172
O'Neill, Eugene, 274n.122
Ossi di sepia (Montale), 48
Our Mr. Wrenn (Lewis), 171

Paesi tuoi (*The Harvesters*) (Pavese), 227–31; American influences on, 227–28, 231; characters not blamed for their actions in, 7; composition of, 90; delayed publication of, 90; language of, 228–31; as literary event of 1941, 227; as most famous of Pavese's novels of the period, 91; plot of, 227; seen as neorealist, 3, 228; symbolism in, 6; violence against women in, 82
Pampaloni, Geno, 5, 6, 190
Papini, Giovanni, 174
Parks, Tim, 28
"Passage to India" (Whitman), 156
Pastrone, Giovanni, 170
Pautasso, Sergio, 68, 196, 207

Pavese, Cesare
on American literature and culture, 169–214; on America as model land of the imagination, 47; on America as "peach of a country," 181; on American authors as searching for a new reality, 189–90; American culture repudiated by, 11, 13; on American vulgate, 182–83, 185, 186–89, 217; on America seen as land without culture, 175; amount of postwar writings on, 239; articles in *La Cultura*, 178–80; on Cecchi's introduction to Vittorini's *Americana*, 173, 209–10; change in attitude toward, 215–27, 235–39; construction of tradition for, 196, 213–14; as contributor to Vittorini's *Americana*, 176, 206; discovers Whitman, 44–47; engaging first sentences of, 198–99; essays of early 1930s, 55–56, 178–80; Fascism and discovery of, 11–12, 214; first reference to Whitman, 44–45; general progression of works on, 235; gradually loses interest in, 223; as growing out of America, 247; high point of enthusiasm for, 179; informality of expression in essays of, 198; interest in Whitman while at University, 52–53; on Matthiessen's *The American Renaissance*, 13, 232–35; on "myth of America," 169, 172, 178, 214; Pivano's translation of *Spoon River Anthology* reviewed by, 225, 231–32, 235; Tina Pizzardo's rejection of and his changing attitude toward, 218–25, 245; poets overlooked by, 195–96; on Prezzolini's *Come gli Americani scoprirono L'Italia*,

Pavese, Cesare (*cont.*)
    175, 218–19; on provincialism of, 197–98; silent period on, 218–19; stereotyped nature of postwar writings on, 236–37; on tradition, 182; on Vittorini's *Americana*, 176–77; on Whitman as liberating ideal, 45
  characteristics of works of: Calvino on novels of, 3; as compact and efficient, 86–87, 199–200; connection between life and work of, 69; credible plots of, 8; fate as theme of, 85; Fiedler on, 1, 6, 10; as master of dialogue, 3–5; morality in, 7; narrative rhythm of, 5; of novels of, 3–5; short novel as preferred format of, 90; as straightforward, 185, 186, 189, 190, 246, 271n.54; subject matter treated at emotional distance, 38; symbolic realism of, 6–7, 128, 250n.12; villains lacking in, 7; violence against women in, 82–83
  as critic: on art as willed and perfectible profession, 43–44; on compassion and sympathy as characteristics of good writer, 190–91; integrated critical rationale of, 182; on sane (*sanità*) and balanced (*equilibrio*) approach to life and art, 191–95, 246
  diary. See *Mestiere di vivere, Il*
  early life of, 35–56; apartment building on Via Ponza, 39; applies for graduate teaching fellowship at Columbia University, 54–55; birth of, 35–36; cultural milieu of, 47–48; full name of, 36; general happiness of early years, 129; parents, 36–38; as teacher, 56, Fig. 26; transforming passion for reading of, 46; at villa in hills of Reaglie, 42

  education of, 38–50; elementary, 38–39; Esame di Maturità Classica passed by, 52; Monti as literature teacher of, 39–44; primary, 39; reading between liceo and university, 45; secondary, 39–44; teaches himself Greek, 39; at University of Turin, 52–54
  as Einaudi publishing house editor: Collezione di studi religiosi, etnologici e psicologici conceived by, 119; joins Einaudi, 87–88; as managing editor, 9; as managing editor of *La Cultura*, 56, 65, 179–80; rejection of Levi's *Se questo è un uomo*, 125, 263n.34; after World War II, 109–10; during World War II, 96–97, 98
  friendships of, 47–52; Anthony Chiuminatto, 53–54; "confraternity" of, 47; Leone Ginzburg, 52, 102; Augusto Monti, 42–44; Pinolo Scaglione, 36; Mario Sturani, 39
  in internal exile (confino) to Brancaleone Calabro, 65, 66–73; to Bar Roma, 67, Fig. 29; correspondence with Tina Pizzardo, 68; photograph with townspeople, Fig. 28; routine during, 67–68; tries to get news of Tina, 71–72
  literary career of: American academic work on, 1–2; American literature's influence on, 5–6, 10–14; first published reference in English to, 265n.29; on his literary maturity, 126–27; most fruitful and creative period of, 118; papers of, 2, 11; place in Italian literature, 3, 10; Il Premio Strega for, 9, 28–29; as public intellectual, 9; reputation in Italy of, 2; "state of transition"

of, 91; translation of work into English, 1; Vittorini compared with, 205–6; as written out after end of 1949, 129–30
personal characteristics of: asthma of, 69, 95, 97, 99; bravura personality based on Whitman and Melville created by, 224; dark hair of, 34; as eternal adolescent, 21–22, 30, 76; feels incomplete as man and human being, 84–85; films as interest of, 171; guilt about having sat out the war, 116, 129; lives with sister Maria, 36, 38, 55, 86; as man of great culture, 88; misogyny of, 82–83, 222, 244–45; money as of little concern to, 56; nasal turbinate dysfunction surgery of, 119–20; never sets foot out of Italy, 135; as obsessive about dates and memories, 68; Tina Pizzardo's description of, 61; self-identifying idealization of Whitman, 46; sexual dysfunction of, 18, 77–78, 84, 129; as smoker, 69, 74, Fig. 38; stoicism of, 190, 222–23; voice of, 91
photographs and images of: bust by Nino Ferreri, Fig. 47; during confino at Brancaleone Calabro, Fig. 28; with confraternity, Fig. 11; with Constance Dowling, Fig. 43; with female students, Fig. 26; in first communion outfit, Fig. 5; with Leone Ginzburg, Franco Antonicelli, and Carlo Frassinelli, Fig. 25; with Enzo Monferini, Fig. 17; with mother and sister, mid-1920s, Fig. 6; playing chess with friend, mid-1920s, Fig. 7; police pictures taken after arrest, Fig. 27; punting on the Po, Fig. 16; with secondary school class, Fig. 9; sketch made by Tina Pizzardo, Fig. 31; smoking a cigarette, Fig. 38; at Strega Prize ceremony, Fig. 44, Fig. 45; taken by Giulio Einaudi, Fig. 39; at time of Strega Prize, Fig. 40; with Pippo Traglio and Mario Sturani, Fig. 8; with Elio Vittorini, Fig. 35; at work, Fig. 30
poetry of: abandons as means of aesthetic expression, 90–91; continues to reward readers, 10; dramatic change in after September 1930, 183–86; earliest published poem of, 183; poems of late 1937, 87; reserves for writing about relationships with women, 91, 113; standard line of, 184; style of, 168
political involvement of: arrest in May 1935, 64–65; *Il compagno* as expression of political commitment of, 117–18; on constructing new socioeconomic order, 109; in Italian Communist Party, 13, 106, 107, 232; joins Fascist Party, 56; Mondo's "Pavese, The Secret Notebook," 105–6; as political out of instinct of self-preservation, 48–49; writes for *l'Unità*, 107, 119, 232
relationships with women of: adolescent crushes of, 49; as asymmetrical, 223; with Romilda Bollati di Saint Pierre, 29–30, 31; dates on which he received crushing blows from women, 93, 112, 221; first experience in a brothel, 43; how to achieve mature, loving, sexual relationship with a woman as mystery to, 95; with Teresa Motta, 116–17; rejection by women, 20, 21, 28, 30; women as sources of personal affirmation for, 38

Pavese, Cesare (*cont.*)
    relationship with Bianca Garufi, 110–16; composes poems for Bianca, 113–15; as mentor to Bianca, 115; proposes marriage, 110
    relationship with Constance Dowling, 13–14, 17–28; with Constance in Cervinia, 18, 28; falls in love with Constance, 18–20; film-script projects for Dowling sisters, 20–21, 28; goodbye letter to Constance, 24
    relationship with Fernanda Pivano, 91–95; as aware of Fernanda's unattainability, 94; dedicates *Feria d'agosto* to Fernanda, 110; ending of, 94; Fernanda disentangles herself without causing major damage, 93, 95; Fernanda rejects, 92–93; on Fernanda's marriage, 94; as Fernanda's Monti, 96; meets Fernanda, 91; on-again, off-again pattern of, 93; proposes marriage, 92, 94, 109; visits Fernanda during World War II, 98
    relationship with Tina Pizzardo, 57–85; on breakup with Tina, 252n.41; continues to see Tina after her marriage, 74–80; correspondence with Tina while in exile, 68; cries in front of Tina, 221–22; diary entries reveal torment and bitterness of, 79–80, 83; as faithful to Tina during exile, 73; falls in love with Tina, 60–61; February 25, 1934, meetings, 219–21; final conversation on the Po, 80; "friendship-only pacts," 60–61, 62, 64, 75, 78, 221, 223, 224; has sex with Tina after her marriage, 77, 84; hate letter to Tina, 78; loses touch with Tina after first five outings, 60; make love for first time, 61; March 5, 1934, encounter, 221–22; as marking turning point of personal and artistic life of, 85; meets Tina, 59; never escapes Tina's "bondage," 90; as overmatched by Tina, 84; reaction to Tina's marriage to Rieser, 72–74; scarred for life by Tina's rejection, 81–83, 84, 95, 129; Tina decides to break with for good, 77; Tina on nature of the relationship, 61–64; Tina on qualities of, 59–60; Tina's girlfriends watch over, 73–74; in Tina's memoirs, 83–84; Tina tells him he never satisfied her sexually, 77; treats Tina as an equal, 60; tries to get news of Tina while in exile, 71–72; trip to mountains for year-end holidays of 1934, 63–64; two stages of, 81
    suicide of, 33; becomes major news event, 131; Calvino on emphasis on, 9–10; death of hope as cause of, 130–31; discovery of body of, 34; Constance Dowling's rejection as immediate cause of, 14, 33, 130–31; funeral of, 131; Korean War depresses, 29; last letters of, 31, 33; Matthiessen's suicide as influence on, 23; Pavese on suicide as appropriate response to Dowling's rejection, 22–23; prepares to commit, 30–33; remains moved to Santo Stefano Belbo, 131; suicide note of, 33–34; thoughts of suicide after 1945, 116; Tina on capacity for suicide of, 221; view from hotel room of, Fig. 46
    as translator: of American literature from 1937 to 1943, 225, 276n.21; American poetry not translated by, 196; on

"decade of translation," 169; Dos Passos's *The 42nd Parallel* translated by, 218; Melville's "Benito Cereno" translated by, 5, 96, 225, 226–27; Melville's *Moby-Dick* translated by, 5, 12, 55, 169, 172, 179, 182, 225, 226; postwar translation of, 260n.44; respects language of original author, 201; translating career comes to end during World War II, 96; as translating to get important authors into Italian, 200–201; translation work to support himself, 86; Vittorini's translation compared with that of, 207

works of: "American Maturity," 232–35; *Ciau Masino*, 82, 183, 185, 246; "Death Will Come and Will Have Your Eyes," 22, 30; "La draga," 82–83, 87; "Estate," 87; *Feria d'agosto*, 110; *Fuoco Grande*, 115; "Gelosia," 87; "Last Blues, to Be Read Some Day," 23–24; *Lotte di giovani*, 47; *Primo che il gallo canti*, 120, 124, 256n.28; "La puttana contadina," 87; "The Return of Man," 107–9; "Il signor Pietro," 37, 253n.5; "Spasmi d'ali," 46–47; "Temporale d'estate," 82; "Terra d'esilio," 69; "To C. from C.," 19, 24. See also *Among Women Only*; *Bella estate, La* (*The Beautiful Summer*); *Carcere, Il* (*The Political Prisoner*); *Casa in collina, La* (*The House on the Hill*); *Compagno, Il*; *Dialoghi con Leucò* (*Dialogues with Leucò*); *Diavolo sulle colline, Il* (*The Devil in the Hills*); *Lavorare stanca*; *Luna e i falò, La* (*The Moon and the Bonfires*); *Mestiere di vivere, Il*; *Paesi tuoi* (*The Harvesters*)

during World War II, 95–106; called up for military service, 97; musings on religion, myth, and symbol, 101–5; reading while at Serralunga and Casale, 102; receives communion from Father Baravalle, 101, 106; returns to Turin in 1945, 106; in Serralunga and Casale Monferrato from September 1943 to April 1945, 99–103; teaches at Collegio Trevisio, 100

Pavese, Consolina Mesturini, 36–38, 42, 55, Fig. 2, Fig. 6

Pavese, Eugenio, 36, Fig. 1

Pavese, Maria: husband of, 55; letters from Pavese while in exile, 66–67, 70–72; Pavese as still dependent on in mid-1930s, 86; Pavese lives with, 38, 55; Pavese's funeral arranged by, 131; Pavese's relationship with, 38; photograph with Pavese and family, Fig. 6; in Serralunga di Crea during World War II, 98, 100; at time of Pavese's birth, 36

"Pavese, The Secret Notebook" (Mondo), 105–6

Pietralunga, Mark, 53

Pinelli, Carlo, Fig. 11

Pinelli, Tullio: in "confraternity" of Pavese, 47; family background of, 47; on language of Pavese's *Paesi tuoi*, 229; Pavese writes about life in great cities to, 244; Pavese writes about Whitman to, 44–45, 45–46; photograph with confraternity, Fig. 11; photograph with Pavese and secondary school class, Fig. 9

Pintor, Giaime, 203–5; appreciative view of America of, 201; death of, 102, 109, 116, 129, 204; joins the Allies, 101, 204; review-essay of Vittorini's *Americana*, 202, 204–5; in younger generation of critics, 202

Pivano, Fernanda, 91–95; and the Beats, 95; description of, 92; disentangles herself from Pavese

Pivano, Fernanda (*cont.*)
without causing major damage, 93, 95; ending of relationship with Pavese, 94; in literary generation that followed Pavese, 202; marriage of, 94; meets Pavese, 91; on-again, off-again pattern of relationship with Pavese, 93; Pavese as aware of unattainability of, 94; Pavese as Monti of, 96; Pavese dedicates *Feria d'agosto* to, 110; Pavese links Bianca Garufi with, 113; on Pavese on Anderson, 187; Pavese proposes marriage to, 92, 94, 109; Pavese visits during World War II, 98; photograph of, Fig. 33; Tina Pizzardo compared with, 95; rejects Pavese, 92–93; *Spoon River Anthology* translation of, 199, 225, 231–32, 235; as translator of American literature, 92, 94, 95

Pizzardo, Tina, 57–85; as always having at least two men on the string, 84; arrest in May 1935, 64–65; attempts to break off with Rieser, 221; background of, 57; as Cate in *La casa in collina*, 121; as communist, 58, 59, 60, 65; continues to see Pavese after her marriage, 74–80; decides to break with Pavese for good, 77; description of Pavese by, 61; does not attend Pavese's funeral, 80; enjoys Pavese's inability to stay away from her, 81; on February 25, 1934, meetings with Pavese, 219–21; final conversation on the Po, 80; "friendship-only pacts" with Pavese, 60–61, 62, 64, 75, 78, 221, 223, 224; has sex with Pavese after her marriage, 77, 84; hate letter from Pavese to, 78; jailed for communist activities, 58; loses touch with Pavese, 60; makes love with Pavese for first time, 61; on March 5, 1934, encounter with Pavese, 221–22; marries Rieser, 72, 257n.49; meets Pavese, 59; meets Rieser, 59; memoirs of, 83–84, 255n.2; on nature of relationship with Pavese, 61–64; on Pavese as eternal adolescent, 21, 76; Pavese corresponds with while in exile, 68; Pavese falls in love with, 60–61; Pavese links Bianca Garufi with, 113; Pavese never escapes "bondage" of, 90; Pavese offers diary manuscript to, 80, 113; Pavese on breakup with, 252n.41; Pavese overmatched by, 84; Pavese scarred for life by, 81–83, 84, 95, 129; Pavese's "La draga" and his relationship with, 82–83; on Pavese's qualities, 59–60; on Pavese's reaction to her marriage to Rieser, 73; Pavese treats her as an equal, 60; Pavese tries to get news of while in exile, 71–72; Fernanda Pivano compared with, 95; portrait photograph of, Fig. 32; pregnancy of, 80; rejection of Pavese and his changing attitude toward American literature, 218–25, 245; relationship with Spinelli, 58, 59–60, 72, 83–84; Rieser is romantically indifferent to, 60, 61, 63, 74–75, 76, 219; on Rieser's reaction to her seeing Pavese, 76; sketch of Pavese made by, Fig. 31; sources of information on, 255n.2; as teacher, 57–59; tells Pavese him he never satisfied her sexually, 77; on trip to mountains for year-end holidays of 1934, 63–64; two stages of relationship with Pavese, 81; at University of Turin, 57; as vivacious, active, and independent, 83

Poe, Edgar Allan, 173, 179, 186, 195, 207, 212, 274n.122
Politecnico (weekly), 206
Political Prisoner, The (Pavese). See *Carcere, Il* (*The Political Prisoner*)
Portrait of the Artist as a Young Man (Joyce), 55, 169

Postman Always Rings Twice, The (Cain), 228, 242
Pound, Ezra, 210–11
Prampolini, Giacomo, 198
Praz, Mario, 175
Predella, Carlo, Fig. 9
Premio Strega, Il, 9, 28–29
Prezzolini, Giuseppe: accusations of Fascism against, 174; *Come gli Americani scoprirono L'Italia, 1750–1850*, 175, 180, 218–19; Mussolini biography by, 174; Pavese applies to for scholarship to Columbia, 54, 55, 175–76; Pavese's view of America contrasted with that of, 181; in previous generation of critics, 201; writings on American literature of, 172, 174–76
Primo che il gallo canti (Pavese), 120, 124, 256n.28
Prometheus Unbound (Shelley), 273n.102
"Puttana contadina, La" (Pavese), 87

Quasimoto, Salvatore, 206

realism: neorealism attributed to Pavese, 3, 228; Pavese's symbolic realism, 6–7, 128, 250n.12; Pavese's understanding of in 1930s, 190
Remarque, Erich Maria, 162
Repubblica Sociale Italiana (RSI; Republic of Salò), 97–98, 105
Resistenza, La, 98, 106
"Return of Man, The" (Pavese), 107–9
Rieser, Henek: marries Tina Pizzardo, 72, 257n.49; reaction to Tina seeing Pavese, 76; as romantically indifferent to Tina, 60, 61, 63, 74–75, 76, 219; Tina attempts to break off with, 221; Tina meets, 59
Rieser, Vittorio, 83
rivoluzione liberale, La (review), 48, 50
Roberts, Kenneth, 207
Rodocanachi, Lucia, 207, 208, 274n.116

Rosati, Salvatore, 227–28, 229–30
Roselli, Carlo, 50
Rossi, Alberto, 179
Ruatta, Alfredo and Eugenia, 30
Rubino, Giovanni Francesco, 18, 77

"Sail Out for Good, Eidólon Yacht" (Whitman), 156
Salvemini, Gaetano, 174
Sanctuary (Faulkner), 215
Sandburg, Carl, 165, 188
Santo Stefano Belbo, 7–8, 35, 38, 66, 131, 239, Fig. 3
Saroyan, William, 207, 211, 274n.122
Scaglione, Pinolo: boyhood friendship with Pavese, 36; carpentry learned by, 68; Nuto of *La luna e i falò* based on, 240; Pavese tells him he expects call from Constance, 32
Scaglione, Vittoria, 36
Scalero, Alessandra, 172
"Scented Herbage of My Breast" (Whitman), 157
Sciascia, Leonardo, 3
Scott, Evelyn, 274n.122
Scrittori anglo-americani d'oggi (Linati), 173
Sea-Wolf, The (London), 175, 269n.22
Se questo è un uomo (*Survival in Auschwitz*) (Levi), 125, 263n.34
Severado, Emilio, 179
Shakespeare, William, 102, 126, 154, 234
Shelley, Percy Bysshe, 273n.102
Sherman, Stuart, 145
Sigma (journal), 10, 250n.25
"Signor Pietro, Il" (Pavese), 37, 253n.5
Simon, John, 6
Sini, Guglielmo, 55, 100, Fig. 6
Sini, Maria, 100
Sini, Maria Pavese. *See* Pavese, Maria
slang, 53, 55, 148, 151, 162, 186–87, 196
Soldati, Mario, 174, 201, 202–3
"Song of Myself" (Whitman), 156, 163, 164–65, 166–67, 168
"Song of the Answerer" (Whitman), 157

"Song of the Broad-Axe" (Whitman), 140, 149, 157
"Song of the Exposition" (Whitman), 157
"Song of the Open Road" (Whitman), 147
Sontag, Susan, 9
"Spasmi d'ali" (Pavese), 46–47
Spiaggia, La (*The Beach*) (Pavese): composition of, 90, 259n.18; dialogue in, 4; as end of preparatory period of Pavese's activity, 91; length of, 90; narrative rhythm of, 5; publication before World War II, 3; *Tra donne sole* compared with, 127
Spinelli, Altiero, 58, 59–60, 72, 83–84, 255n.4
Spoon River Anthology (Masters), 60, 91, 94, 199, 225, 231–32, 235
Sposa americana, La (Soldati), 203
Stein, Gertrude, 86, 96, 225–26, 274n.122
Steinbeck, John, 86, 171, 207, 213, 227, 228, 274n.122
Story of American Literature, The (Lewisohn), 209
Story Teller's Story, A (Anderson), 91–92, 94, 237
Strega Prize, 9, 28–29
Strings, My Lord, Are False, The (Carroll), 26
Sturani, Mario: becomes friend of Pavese, 39; does cover art for Pavese's books, 39; Pavese and Tina Pizzardo go punting with, 59; and Pavese collect pornography, 184; Pavese writes from exile in Brancaleone Calabro, 69; photograph with confraternity, Fig. 11; photograph with Pavese, Fig. 8
Survival in Auschwitz (*Se questo è un uomo*) (Levi), 125, 263n.34
Synge, J. M., 173

"Temporale d'estate" (Pavese), 82
"Terra d'esilio" (Pavese), 69
This Business of Living (Pavese), 68
Thoreau, Henry David, 194
Thorp, Willard, 144
Three Lives (Stein), 96, 226
"To C. from C." (Pavese), 19, 24
Tondo, Michele, 154
Tra donne solo (*Among Women Only*) (Pavese): composition of, 118, 126–27; dialogue in, 4; morality in, 7; photograph of carnival time in Turin, Fig. 37; published with *La bella estate* and *Il diavolo sulle colline*, 128; as still rewarding, 10; strong, attractive woman in, 245; symbolism in, 6
Traglio, Pippo, Fig. 8
Trojan Horse, The (Morley), 96
Twain, Mark: *Adventures of Huckleberry Finn* as influence of language of *Paesi tuoi*, 230–31; American vulgate in, 186, 188, 217, 238; in Pavese's construction of tradition for American literature, 196; in Vittorini's *Americana*, 274n.122
Typee (Melville), 172

Ulysses (Joyce), 173
Unità, l' (newspaper), 107, 119, 232
Up in Arms (film), 27

Vaudagna, Adele, 32
Vaudagna, Giuseppe, 32, 102, Fig. 11
Venturi, Gianni, 91
Verga, Giovanni, 230
Vidor, King, 171
Vigliani, Luigi, 230
Vittorini, Elio, 205–14; American authors translated by, 171; appreciative view of America of, 201; *Conversazione in Sicilia*, 205, 209; *La Cultura* read by, 178; at Einaudi publishing house, 205, 206; Fascism and discovery of American literature of, 214; as Fascist, 206; Pavese's attitude toward, 205–6; photograph with Pavese, Fig. 35; *Politecnico* edited

by, 206; seen as discovering
American novel for Italy, 170;
Soldati's views of America
compared with, 203; as translator,
172, 206–7, 274n.115; in younger
generation of critics, 202. See also
Americana (Vittorini)
Voce, La (journal), 174
Voice of the Trumpet, The
(*Captain Smith and Company*)
(Henriques), 260n.44

Walt Whitman (Bailey), 147
Walt Whitman: A Critical Study (de Selincourt), 147
"Walt Whitman in Italy" (McCain), 265n.29
Ward, Artemus, 180, 188
Weaver, William, 174
Wendell, Barrett, 145
Wescott, Glenway, 181
Wharton, Edith, 195
"When Lilacs Last in the Dooryard Bloom'd" (Whitman), 157–59, 162
White Jacket (Melville), 172
Whitman, Walt: barbarism and art combined in, 194; as barely read in Italy, 136; Fascist models contrasted with, 168; as incarnation of America to Pavese, 19, 20; Italian scholarship on, 145, 265n.32; as liberating ideal to Pavese, 45; Matthiessen and, 233; Pavese articles on, 179, 215, 217; Pavese creates bravura personality based on, 224; Pavese discovers, 44–47; Pavese on American language and, 217; Pavese on energy of, 181–82; Pavese on personal characteristics of, 12; Pavese on Stein and, 225; Pavese reviews French anthology of, 179; in Pavese's construction of tradition for American literature, 196, 238; Pavese's degree thesis "Interpretation of the Poetry of Walt Whitman," 54, 135–68; Pavese's first reference to, 44–45; Pavese's interest in at University, 52–53; Pavese's "Interpretation of Walt Whitman, Poet," 162–68; Pavese's self-identifying idealization of, 46; Pavese's style in writing about, 200; pioneer as never surrendering to fate, 190; as searching for a new reality to Pavese, 189; as wholly integrated artist and man to Pavese, 47. See also *Leaves of Grass* (Whitman)
Wilder, Thornton, 213, 274n.122
Williams, William Carlos, 211
Wlassics, Tibor, 228
Wolfe, Thomas, 195, 213, 274n.122
Work of Art (Lewis), 180, 216
Work's Tiring (Pavese), 70
World War II, 95–106

Zaccaria, Giuseppe, 227, 276n.28

LAWRENCE G. SMITH was born in Washington, DC, where he was educated through high school. He attended Harvard University, where he earned a BA, an MA, and a PhD, the last in the History of American Civilization. He also attended the University of Padua, Italy, as a Fulbright scholar. While a graduate student Smith taught two years at Harvard, but then left the university to pursue a career in banking and finance, living four years in Italy. He now resides in New York City with his wife, Marguerite.